China Candid

A

Philip E. Lilienthal

■   ■   ■

B O O K

The Philip E. Lilienthal imprint
honors special books
in commemoration of a man whose work
at the University of California Press from 1954 to 1979
was marked by dedication to young authors
and to high standards in the field of Asian Studies.
Friends, family, authors, and foundations have together
endowed the Lilienthal Fund, which enables the Press
to publish under this imprint selected books
in a way that reflects the taste and judgment
of a great and beloved editor.

China Candid

THE PEOPLE ON
THE PEOPLE'S REPUBLIC

Sang Ye

Edited by Geremie R. Barmé
with Miriam Lang

UNIVERSITY OF CALIFORNIA PRESS
BERKELEY   LOS ANGELES   LONDON

The publisher gratefully acknowledges the generous
contribution to this book provided by the Philip E.
Lilienthal Asian Studies Endowment Fund of the
University of California Press Foundation, which
is supported by a major gift from Sally Lilienthal.

University of California Press
Berkeley and Los Angeles, California

University of California Press, Ltd.
London, England

Library of Congress Cataloging-in-Publication Data

Sang Ye.
    China candid : the people on the People's Republic /
Sang Ye ; edited by Geremie R. Barmé with Miriam
Lang.
        p.   cm.
    ISBN 978-0-520-24514-3 (pbk. : alk. paper)
    1. China—Social conditions—1949–   2. China—
History—1949–   I. Title: People on the People's
Republic.   II. Barmé, Geremie.   III. Lang, Miriam
IV. Title.
HN733.5 Y415   2006
951.05'092'2—dc22   2005052871

Manufactured in the United States of America

15   14   13   12   11   10   09   08
10   9   8   7   6   5   4   3

Printed on Ecobook 50 containing a minimum 50%
post-consumer waste, processed chlorine free. The
balance contains virgin pulp, including 25% Forest
Stewardship Council Certified for no old-growth tree
cutting, processed either TCF or ECF. The sheet is acid-
free and meets the minimum requirements of ANSI/NISO
Z39.48-1992 (R 1997) (Permanence of Paper).

For Yang Xianyi
and
in memory of Gladys Yang

CONTENTS

SANG YE'S CONVERSATIONS
WITH CHINA

Geremie R. Barmé

"Tell a story!"

It was a simple request, as well as a frequently heard plea, during the waning years of the Cultural Revolution. It was also a common prompt for people anxious to exchange information, tales, rumors, and gossip in the declining years of Mao's rule and the painful years of recovery that followed.

Each request for the recounting of an individual story, for the surreptitious telling of a private tale, or for the sharing of an anecdote that would entertain or inform; every account that might elicit a sympathetic response resulting from shared experience; all of the reminiscences of sufferings (or lucky escapes) tinged with a bitter understanding of the absurdist tragedies that touched nearly every family; in fact, any description of life lived outside the realm of relentless public performance or away from collective surveillance, each was in breach of the greater story, the singular narrative of the nation's life as told by the Chinese Communist Party itself.

The reappearance of the individual and the endless variety of life was part of the unraveling of the story that the Communist Party told itself, one that, through its hold over the nation, it constantly reiterated to the people of China and indeed the world. It appeared first behind closed doors, through furtive exchanges of personal histories, and then in a more open and joyful atmosphere of celebration at the end of an era of totalitarian control, and finally, although always fitfully, in the mass media itself.

During the heyday of state socialism, the individual story was submerged by a collective tale of History writ large. In it, the complex skeins of personal lives were reduced to undifferentiated stereotypes and formulaic accounts. Living at the western extreme of the socialist world, the Czech writer and dissident Václav Havel observed how this singular story came to silence all others.

> It began with an interpretation of history from a single aspect of it; then it made that aspect absolute and finally it reduced all of history to it. The exciting multiplicity of history was replaced with an easily understood interaction of "historical laws," "social formations" and "relations of production," so pleasing to the order-loving eye of the scientist. This, however, gradually expelled from history precisely what gives human life, time and thus history itself a structure: the story. And banished from the kingdom of meaning, the story took with it its two essential ingredients: uniqueness and intrinsic ambiguity. Since the mystery in a story is merely the articulated mystery of man, history, having lost the story, began to lose its human content. The uniqueness of the human creature became a mere embellishment on the laws of history, and the tension and thrill inherent in real events were dismissed as accidental and so unworthy of the attention of scholarship. History became boredom.[1]

Biography has enjoyed a particular place within the tradition of China's socialist culture. When joining the ranks of revolutionaries or before being inducted into the party, each candidate was required to make a clean breast of their personal history by writing a detailed, confessional autobiography. Only after making such a confession and receiving official absolution could the aspirant be absorbed into the great collective enterprise. In each stage of the revolution and with each new political campaign or purge (and these occurred with increasing frequency from the early 1950s until the late 1970s), these autobiographical accounts were reexamined and used to determine the fates of the individuals as well as of their families and associates.

The party's own history projects, whether hagiographic renditions of revolutionary heroism or parables built up around the histories of villages and factories, were narratives in which individual tales of trial and tribulation were shaped to conform to the party's overarching story of victory over adversity and progress in the face of oppression. Even when a formerly dispossessed peasant or an exploited worker was interviewed for an official oral history, the uncomfortable details of individual lives that might threaten the coherence—and didactic value—of the account for others

---

1. Václav Havel, "Stories and Totalitarianism," *Index on Censorship*, 1988, no. 3, p. 16.

were glossed over. Everyone was allowed to be different, but in exactly the same way.

Sang Ye's *China Candid* is a unique collection of individual stories, powerful personal narratives that tell tales in the face of party rule as no other book from China has done. It shows little regard for the officially sanctioned version of modern Chinese history. That history, and the way it is told through the Chinese media, is influenced by the particular culture of communism, which defines the life of a society, and therefore of the individuals and groups that make up that society, in terms of party slogans and congresses, the speeches and meetings of leaders, and through the prism of its mass political (or, more recently, what are called "public information") campaigns. Sang Ye's history of China, in contrast, comprises the voices of the people who have lived that history under, but often despite, the Communist Party and its mechanisms of control. The interviews here were conducted over many years, and through them Sang Ye provides us with an alternative history of the People's Republic of China from its founding in 1949, and in particular since the collapse of Maoist high socialism and the rise of economic reform starting in the late 1970s.

The voices we hear through the pages of this book never offer a simplistic or categorical rejection of their history; neither do they offer a blanket condemnation of party policies or even of the baleful rule of Mao Zedong. The selective censorship of the reformist era, which began in 1978, inevitably colors individual memories of the past, especially when alternatives to the official version of history—both pre- and postrevolutionary history—find only scant purchase in the sphere of guided public discourse: the press, cinema, TV documentaries, mainstream publishing, even the Internet. When the past is actively manipulated by propagandists and commercial advertisers alike to legitimate the needs of the present, as well as constantly being used to bolster the image of the ever-victorious party, private and individual memory is all the more precious—and friable. To understand both the present and the past, it is vital to attend to the stories of individuals who, through their own lived experience and their articulation of it, recuperate for both themselves and others an understanding of a collective past that is all too often distorted by the media.

In a sense this book responds to the questions raised by the historian Michael Frisch when he wrote about Studs Terkel's *Hard Times: An Oral History of the Great Depression*—one of the works that first inspired Sang

Ye when he began writing in the early 1980s. Frisch emphasized that memory is at the center of the enterprise of oral history. He asks rhetorically: "What happens to experience on the way to becoming memory? What happens to experiences on the way to becoming history? As an era of intense collective experience recedes into the past, what is the relationship of memory to historical generalization?"[2] It is memory as history, and the way all history, collective or individual, is recast as memory, that, as the personal accounts in this book show, underpin the ways in which the past is invoked in the present. These narratives also bring to light the way people make sense of the world through telling themselves stories about their personal journeys.

Such truth-telling does not, however, exist in isolation, or merely at those moments when the individuals who speak to us here are in conversation with Sang Ye. Rather it is part of a broader story about the massive untruths that continue to obscure so much of modern Chinese history and life—untruths legislated by a system that, ultimately, holds the individual in contempt, a system in which socialist authoritarianism has now negotiated a strategic partnership with corporate capital. To an extent these narratives are possible only because of the rise of the "cult of the individual," the individuated subject and consumer-actor, that has been the most egregious feat of social engineering in reformist China. It is a time when cruising the mall has replaced party-organized street marches; an age in which the right to shop has unseated obligatory rituals of mass politics. The individuals who speak to us here are both in the embrace of China's particular brand of nationalistic consumer-socialism and at times wary of it.

The social production of memory—through individual stories, official histories, academic courses, and the mass media, along with the Internet—entails also a cultural production that includes volumes like this. Written originally for publication in China, *China Candid* has yet to appear on the mainland. Just as an entrepreneurial publisher in northeast China was planning a mainland edition, one of the regular publishing crackdowns—what

2. Michael Frisch, *A Shared Authority: Essays on the Craft and Meaning of Oral and Public History* (Albany: State University of New York Press, 1990), p. 188.

amounts to a biennale of censorship—was launched by the authorities in Beijing, resulting in bans on numerous book projects.[3]

Even if a mainland edition had been possible—and the frank nature of the material in this book made it unlikely—it would have been a truncated work. A number of the interview subjects, fearful that their candor would lead to reprisals from the local authorities, told Sang Ye that they did not want their conversations to appear in any form on the mainland. For example, the young athlete who speaks in "Unlevel Playing Field" (chapter 13) is aware of the highly sensitive nature of his revelations about drug use and China's international sporting aspirations, just as the eloquent executioner in "Parting Shot" (chapter 25) did not want his ruminations on the death penalty and firing squads to be read by his superiors or the families of executed criminals. A full version of the book did, however, eventually appear in Hong Kong, the southern extreme of the People's Republic. It was published under the title *1949, 1989, 1999*, and this edited and retitled English version is based on that edition. After translating the full text, I decided, for reasons of length and reader interest, to delete material that seemed too repetitious or obscure for an international audience.

Most of the interviews in this book, which could equally well be called conversation-narratives, superficially conform to the contours of the history of the People's Republic of China, but, more important, they reflect (and offer reflections on) the nation's tumultuous history from a personal level. Sang Ye investigates—and literally interrogates—this human dimension of China's history, giving us a perspective on both the past and the present that is as informative as it is unsettling. And this is not an account of communist rule or a record of the life of a country told by self-serving bureaucrats, ardent economic reformers, or frustrated dissenters. There is much bathos and humor among the characters in this book, people who have been and remain participants, victims, and in some cases persecutors enmeshed in modern Chinese life. Many of these interviews discuss in depth what could be called the mechanics and minutiae of the economic reform era initiated by Deng Xiaoping and the Communist Party in 1978. It is an era that has seen the country's economy transformed and the nation's aspirations and hopes realized and buoyed in an unprecedented fashion.

Some of those who speak in this book have been involved in the blatant

3. For details of the routinization of such "cultural correctives" in China, see my *In the Red: On Contemporary Chinese Culture* (New York: Columbia University Press, 1999), pp. 56–58.

or covert privatization and exploitation of state resources, collective wealth that in many cases was built up over decades through the labor and the sacrifice of countless people. For example, although since the late 1990s the People's Liberation Army has had to curtail its freewheeling business ventures, the man interviewed in "An Army on the March" (chapter 18) provides insights into the minds of men and women serving in the military who have discovered the profit motive; he shows how the PLA, a bastion of socialist values, learned to be money-grubbing. Then there is the old revolutionary who despises Deng Xiaoping for turning China capitalist (chapter 3, "The Nondissident"), although he continues to enjoy the perquisites of a retired, high-level party cadre living off the largesse offered by reformist prosperity. In contrast, we hear from the unemployed worker from the countryside (one of over two hundred million who have left the land to find work in the cities) who believes that another leader like Mao Zedong will one day appear in the midst of the "floating population" to champion the cause of the downtrodden against the exploiting party bureaucrats and new capitalists (chapter 2, "Chairman Mao's Ark").

Many of the interviewees also talk about the corrosive changes that have been wrought on the professional ethics and attitudes of men and women long nurtured by the socialist state and the public purse. The retired English professor in the northeast province of Jilin (in "Generating Income," chapter 19) has learned vital lessons about business scams from slick middlemen and market entrepreneurs who are now teaching the teachers how to make a quick buck. Her new acumen has helped her ex-colleagues and students increase their income at a time when public-funded education is sinking into ever-deeper crisis.

Others, like the self-styled "computer bug" *(diannao chong)* interviewed in chapter 12, belong to a brasher and more self-assured generation. This young man, working in Beijing's equivalent of Silicon Valley, is proud of both his commercial shrewdness and his nation's ancient civilization (while pointedly dismissive of his parents' generation, the former Red Guards, who once attacked it). He expresses an acute awareness of the humiliations his country has suffered as a result of technological backwardness, political upheavals, and imperialist avarice. His message is as unambiguous as it is unapologetic: We're here. We're mean. Get used to it.

Other conversations introduce us to people who have felt the frustrations produced by a rapacious market economy grafted onto a labyrinthine sociopolitical system; the resulting miscegenation is heir to all the shortcomings of senescent socialism and primitive capitalism. The man who starts a private orphanage is a portrait of patience and tenacity in the face of official obstruction (chapter 6, "Looking Ahead"), while a couple who have had their young son kidnapped by child traders offer heartrending insights into the failures of a state that once presumed to control every aspect of life for the collective good (chapter 7, "Getting Organized").

Undercurrents of violence run through the interviews, whether in the form of state-sanctioned punishment, acts of cruelty and unkindness perpetrated by the system, or individual acts both direct and covert. Many people in these pages recall chilling encounters with what are called "the organs of the people's democratic dictatorship" (the police, the law courts, jails, labor camps, or the army). Those who have survived the attentions of officialdom share a firm belief that living well is the best revenge. Some even try to live in ways that may change the nature of the system itself. Take, for example, the entrepreneurial farm manager (chapter 23, "Just One Party"), or the founder of the private orphanage mentioned earlier. In their conversations we find no hint of the bombast of public dissent, the grandstanding of the entrepreneur, the glib patter of the sanctimonious, or the rancor of the defeated. Even without systemic change and political reform, many of Sang Ye's interlocutors are creating individual futures far different from the somber collective realities of China's past.

Equally, some of the people in this book have profited immensely from the get-rich-quick opportunities provided by China's reform era (see, for example, chapter 1, "A Hero for the Times," and chapter 21, "Mastering New China"); others have used the wiles of their profession or their sex to trade their way up the socioeconomic ladder (see chapter 15, "Time as Money," and chapter 16, "Little Sweetie"). They are all people inured to China's capricious political and economic climate; they display a hard-won wisdom, one that is often thoughtful and always canny. Some celebrate their good fortune while wishing their fellows ill; some are satisfied with their lot and despise the new dispensation, one that has benefited many but also witnessed the growth of harrowing social inequities; others survive with tenacity, heedless of the grand plans of their rulers although always mindful of the precariousness of their own situation.

China Candid offers no simple entry point into China; no linear narrative emerges from these disparate and highly individual stories. It is a book that confronts and challenges many of the dominant views of China. Although they tell no single tale, these stories amount to something of a biography of the People's Republic of China. Of course, these life narratives can only ever constitute tiny parts of the story of the People's Republic; equally, they are "histories" that are narrated in the present, that is, in the era of economic weal (and concomitant political bane) of the 1980s, the 1990s, and the new millennium. Within these narratives there are elements of pure recall as well as of reflective summation. These voices speak to the past from the perspective of the present. Some narrate a tale of the here-and-now for an audience of one, Sang Ye, an interlocutor who is acting as an agent for all other audiences, including ourselves. Others speak only about the past; a few also address the future, such as the agricultural cooperative manager in "Just One Party" (chapter 23) who can envisage a time when the dominant Communist Party will give way to a pluralistic political environment, or the UFOlogist in "Beam Me Up" (chapter 24) who is ready to welcome extraterrestrials into China's midst.

Many of the stories are polished and are "performed" seemingly fluently. This is not merely a result of Sang Ye's editorial finesse, for China is a country where self-expression is an art form born of constant storytelling and honed by years of public political performance. These stories represent the efforts of individuals to make sense of their lives as they discuss with, debate, and at times refute Sang Ye. They seek a narrative cohesion for the multifaceted histories of their lives, a sense of self and biographical meaning, and readers are also invited to engage in this search. We are all involved in a similar enterprise, one enhanced by the entrée that Sang Ye provides to a world of particular diversity and richness.

These life-story interviews tell a history of a China that is itself a place created by individual histories. Of course, as Sang Ye tells us in his introduction, his choice of interview subjects is idiosyncratic and often the result of circumstance, even though his approach to each encounter is informed by his own history of writing and engaging in other conversations in China over several decades.

Sang Ye's search for the history of individuals who have lived through the People's Republic, and his often tenacious conversations with individuals from many walks of life, confronts readers with powerful and disquieting accounts that confound not only the public history of contemporary China, but even the versions of Chinese and Western memoirists, reporters, and scholars whose mass-market writings generally hold sway over popular impressions of that country around the world. In Sang Ye's telling, the party-imposed boredom of socialist history of which Václav Havel spoke dissolves; variety, ambiguity, and complexity take its place.

—

During the mid-1980s, as China's literary and publishing culture underwent a revival—a commercial boom born of new, market-oriented government policies that saw the gradual displacement of the party's monopoly over the media—Sang Ye and a Beijing woman novelist, Zhang Xinxin, joined forces. Together they interviewed dozens of Chinese people from all walks of life. These were people who until then had never had a voice in the mass media. Sang and Zhang's interviews were conducted outside the narrow confines of official, state-directed culture. Serialized in leading literary journals in 1985, the interviews created a publishing sensation, and the following year they resulted in a best-selling book titled *Beijing People: One Hundred Personal Accounts of Normal People (Beijingren,* literally "Peking Man"). An edited English version, published in the United States under the title *Chinese Lives,* featured a foreword by Studs Terkel.[4]

In writing *Chinese Lives,* Sang and Zhang were not only responding to new cultural opportunities, the growing appetite of a voracious reading public, and the enlivened publishing world of China. They were also extending a kind of popular social investigation that had come to enjoy considerable cachet following the Cultural Revolution. Writers of reportage— a style of Chinese "new journalism" or literary reporting—most notably the *People's Daily* journalist Liu Binyan, had for some years pursued stories about individuals who had fallen victim to the party's machinations, piquing the public's interest in tales of tragedy and woe from the Maoist era (spanning the 1950s to the late 1970s).[5] The two young oral historians were more catholic in their tastes and interests than veteran reporters like Liu, and, rather than rake over the details of recent political purges or use their writing to right perceived wrongs, they concentrated on reflecting the vibrant and unsettling realities of the present. Their work made them

4. Zhang Xinxin and Sang Ye, *Chinese Lives: An Oral History of Contemporary China,* ed. and trans. W. J. F. Jenner and Delia Davin (New York: Pantheon, 1987).
5. See, for example, Liu Binyan, *People or Monsters? And Other Stories and Reportage from China after Mao* (Bloomington: Indiana University Press, 1983).

famous: Zhang, already a well-known novelist, went on to become a TV personality before emigrating to the United States. But the accolades of urban readers did not satisfy Sang Ye, and he soon set out to travel China once more in search of new stories and other ways of engaging with the country of his birth and the culture that held him so powerfully in its thrall.

He moved permanently to Australia after 4 June 1989. Since then he has produced a number of new oral histories, one of which, *The Year the Dragon Came,* was published in 1996.[6] It was a controversial investigation of the state of recent, mostly mainland, Chinese immigrants to Australia, their abiding cultural values, the disturbing strain of xenophobia found among many of them, and much also that reflected badly on Australia and its treatment of new arrivals. Many had been lured to antipodean shores by the government's recently launched policy to sell education (in particular English-language courses) to a hungry Asia-Pacific market. They all had outspoken views about their adopted homeland and the fate of the new "overseas Chinese." Sang Ye's book revealed a less-than-comely face of immigrant experience in Australia that challenged the comfortable assumptions of multiculturalism.

After completing that book, Sang Ye began the search for interview subjects for the present volume back in China. By far his most ambitious project to date, *China Candid* is a portrait of China free from the censorship and editorial constraints that had marked *Chinese Lives.* For although *Chinese Lives* had an immediacy and honesty unique to China in the 1980s, setting a new standard for realistic journalism, the hand of the censor, as well as the more ineffable shadow of self-censorship, had wrought many changes in the text.

Born and raised in Beijing into a family of educators and cadres, Sang Ye (a nom de plume) studied at Tsinghua Middle School—an institution that gave birth to the Red Guard generation—and he came of age as one of the country's first freelance journalists. He is a tall and imposing figure who speaks the clipped and authoritative language of Beijing. He is a profoundly knowledgeable autodidact, an unaffiliated historian of modern China possessed of a sardonic wit. He also has a highly developed sense of the absurd that is informed by his years of obsessive research on the dialectical confusions and about-faces of the Maoist era and contemporary Chinese politics.

6. Sang Ye, *The Year the Dragon Came,* ed. Linda Jaivin (Brisbane: Queensland University Press, 1996).

He is also a noted writer of *causerie* or literary essays who, because of the elegance of his literary style, has often been mistaken for a septuagenarian.[7] As a chronicler of contemporary China, he is deeply suspicious of socialism and the state Marxism that for decades wrought havoc on the country, resulting in countless deaths in the past and continued suffering in the present. He is wary also of post-Deng economic nationalism and questions the long-term viability of a one-party state that has no sure footing in its own past or abiding confidence in the ideology that masquerades as the mainstay of Chinese civilization.

Sang Ye's family history—some of his relatives were functionaries in key state institutions—and his fascination with the organs of state control and the way that power is exercised in China, as well as his assiduous research into many aspects of the country's modern history, have provided him with a broad insider knowledge. As a result, he is a formidable interviewer who can both insinuate himself into the nuanced world of his interlocutors and turn an equitable exchange into an edgy interrogation: see, for example, chapter 21, "Mastering New China," where he provokes the speaker into revealing how some private enterprises flourish because of covert family and party connections.

But such insider knowledge is of a different order from that of his partners in discussion. Their understanding is the result of pressing daily reality; their insights are often born of trying circumstances. Much that was once hidden or secret in the lives of such individuals is now made public; many of the revelations of these people are also the product of agonized reflection on their own situations and the skein of Chinese social life. And Sang Ye's China is a voluble and often rancorous country. Although he is a member of the educated urban elite, he is acutely aware of the history of condescension and manipulation that has characterized interactions between the Chinese intellectuals (and here I include the communist intelligentsia, Mao Zedong being but primus inter pares)—men and women with a mandarin view of the world and their role as the voice and conscience of China—and the people. And the people Sang Ye speaks to are, for the most part, individuals whose actions, except in the intimate discourse of the private realm, have always been tempered by the need to explain themselves to the authorities—at school, in self-criticisms or polit-

7. These essays were published in the Beijing monthly *Dushu (Reading)* in the late 1990s, under the aegis of its then editor Shen Yuanshen.

ical study sessions, in written depositions about themselves, or in the coerced confessions about their actions during key political campaigns (as was the case after the 1989 mass protest movement and following the purge of adherents of the Falun Gong meditation sect, starting in 1999). They have all lived and worked in a sea of words, a morass through which each of them navigates a precarious individual course. And they are all talkers who confront assumptions about how China does and can "tell a story."

Sang Ye is also suspicious of contemporary intellectual agendas, be they neo-Marxist, neoliberal, or nationalist.[8] He is alert to and highly critical of the deracinated language of the elites as well as that of the commercial mass media; his ear is finely tuned to the rich variety of demotic voices. He is, above all, a skeptic, although not necessarily a cynic. For, as he shows both in his introduction to this book and throughout the interviews, his relationship with the People's Republic is both confrontational and codependent; he both respects and is repelled by what he encounters, and, while always engaged with the vastness of the country and its people, he searches too for his own worth as he plumbs both the humanity and the inhumanity of his fellows.

Sang Ye's interview style has evolved over many years. The majority of the conversations in this book are the result of extensive background research, followed by detailed discussion and familiarization with his interlocutors. The interviews themselves contain long digressions by Sang Ye to prompt his conversation partners to reflect on certain issues or to discuss matters that they might otherwise be unwilling to confront. When transcribing and editing his interviews, however, he omits his questions and interjections; he also effaces his own presence, a technique that is particularly (and tantalizingly) evident in his interview with the prostitute (chapter 15, "Time as Money") and the executioner (chapter 25, "Parting Shot"). If his own authorial voice remained, he argues, there would be probably just as much of him as there is of the interview subjects. To retain such material would leave us with a book perhaps twice as long.

Sang Ye's method of recording and transcribing his interviews entails a twofold transformation of the conversations. The transcript he creates on the basis of a recorded interview—deleting long pauses, rearranging mate-

8. Regarding such agendas, see my "Time's Arrows: Imaginative Pasts and Nostalgic Futures," in *Voicing Concerns: Contemporary Chinese Critical Inquiry,* ed. Gloria Davies (Boulder, CO: Rowman & Littlefield, 2001), pp. 226–57.

rial into a sequential and coherent narrative, cleaning up grammatical and syntactical lapses, and so on—effectively turns aural artifacts, that is, spoken conversational reflections, into visual objects, that is, final texts that fix the fluidity of exchange in a permanent printed form. As a result, the inflection of individual voices, the unique cadences of speech, the speed at which people talk, the dialectical peculiarities of the standard Chinese used by his interview partners—all their idiosyncratic verbal styles, quirks, and habits—are homogenized into text neatly divided into the sentences and paragraphs of publishable prose. Then, as noted, Sang Ye omits his questions (and his occasionally rather pointed interrogations), often creating the impression that these are fluent historical testimonies captured by some omniscient ear or, rather, scribe.

Of course, in these conversations Sang Ye has not necessarily elicited spontaneous narratives; neither is he sharing with the reader some sudden revelation. The interviews should not be seen as the product of a fortuitous recording of previously unthought-of or unsaid things about intimate lives. For many, these are articulated versions of stories that have been reconsidered and reformulated time and time again, though perhaps never so rigorously as here. That is to say, this is not a book that pretends to reveal an unsullied truth about "China" or "the Chinese." The attentions of a knowledgeable and gregarious reporter like Sang Ye, an ex–Chinese national who holds a foreign passport and who will publish their remarks in the international Chinese media, and in English, may well have encouraged some of his coauthors (and this is really what they are) to exaggerate or perhaps to color their stories. As he points out in his introductory essay, however, Sang Ye is fully aware of this possibility, and it is best to remember that rhetorical embellishment in these accounts is sometimes no more than that.

Another potentially misleading impression given by an immutable text like this is that Sang Ye's interlocutors would say the same things about themselves on all future occasions. This is because as soon as they are transcribed and edited, these interviews become as stable and unchanging as any other written document. I am not suggesting that these testimonies should in any way be discounted or undervalued. As with any other written document or recorded data, however, readers should be mindful of the contingencies surrounding the creation of the book and the state of tension in which the text inevitably exists.

The end result of this process is a collection of seamless narratives that, now edited and translated into a manageable English text, creates a double layer of disconnect between those original intimate conversations and you, the reader. Those who read Chinese, of course, may consult the published Chinese text to find some counterbalance to the often bland words that have been marshaled here to represent the many rich voices of this book's authors.

This translation has also had to take into account the fact that *China Candid* was written for a Chinese audience—to be more precise, a mainland-educated Chinese audience, one familiar with the history and sociopolitical context discussed by the interviewees. However, that original text makes few concessions even to Chinese readers, replete as it is not only with each speaker's verbal tics but also with local argot and what now sound like arcane political expressions, formulations familiar to people of earlier generations but foreign to many younger readers. I have added footnotes where necessary to guide the reader through the fog of political slogans, campaigns, and shifting party priorities that has suffused every aspect of Chinese life for over half a century and impinged on every life story told in this book.

It is inevitable, too, that the "treachery of translation" has meant that much of the flavor and verve of the original interviews has been lost. Sang Ye readily acknowledges that in transcribing the spoken word, the timbre of voices, regional differences, nuances and lilts were heavily discounted. In the passage of those texts into English, much more is diminished. The originals are fresh and powerful as only a language rarely seen in print in mainland China can be. The interview subjects do not speak the flat Newspeak of the official Chinese media, nor do they affect the faux-casual verbal posturing of urban hip-grunge, or chic-lit, that is often taken by the international media to represent the cutting edge of contemporary China. It is also far from the often stilted, pseudorealistic parole of the new wave of Chinese cinema that, more than any other cultural form, has come to represent the mien of China overseas.

The homogenizing effects of my own editorial hand have further flattened out much of the lively language used by the people in this book, although my collaborator in this enterprise, Miriam Lang, has done her best to maintain a scrupulous felicity while attaining a greater elegance in the final text than I could have hoped to achieve by myself. She meticulously compared the translations by various hands with the originals, correcting awkward expressions and editorial oversights with rigor, precision, and finesse. She offered so many apt suggestions that she must share the credit for producing the final work, although the clumsy turns of phrase that remain and the editorial selections made are solely my responsibility.

If it is impossible to replicate in English the colorful range of the original interviews, it is equally difficult to do more than intimate the effect of the wooden bureaucratese and formulaic expressions, tempered by decades of party propaganda, that appear in virtually every chapter of this book, sometimes spoken without irony by interview subjects but just as often used with a sardonic, if not satirical, edge by people both captive to yet dubious of China's officialese. Similarly, in creating this English version, to employ the colloquialisms of my native Australia would have made for a creole that non-Australian readers would find alienating, or even worse, comic; while to attempt an Americanization of expression would have produced for me a caricature of expression that I would find foreign. The result is a compromise in terms of both diction and voice, something that could perhaps be dubbed a pan-Pacific solution. Like Sang Ye, I have attempted to present the authors' voices using words without too much saliva.

ACKNOWLEDGMENTS

I thank Oanh Collins and Marion Weeks in the Division of Pacific and Asian History, Research School of Pacific and Asian Studies, at the Australian National University, for their help in preparing the final manuscript, and Sheila Levine at the University of California Press for her saintlike patience. Susan Brownell, who was one of the readers for the University of California Press, provided many constructive suggestions regarding the manuscript as a whole and my prefatory essay in particular.

I would also like to thank Mary Severance and Erika Büky for their careful editorial work, and Sandy Drooker for her cover design. Lois Connor, dear friend, colleague, and fellow traveler through the landscape of China, generously provided a picture she made on Tiananmen Square on the fiftieth anniversary of the People's Republic, 1 October 1999, for the cover illustration.

This book is dedicated to Yang Xianyi and to the memory of Gladys Yang, constant friends, drinking partners, and Beijing hosts. It was at their apartment in the Foreign Languages Press compound at Baiwanzhuang that Sang Ye and I first met in 1985.

Introduction

Words and Saliva

Sang Ye

I conducted the interviews that make up this book over a four-year period. In the process of searching out people to tell this history, their history, and, by default, a history of contemporary China, I visited over one hundred cities and villages in China and interviewed over a hundred citizens of the People's Republic.

The majority of people I chose to speak with have not had a public voice in this history; they are normal, everyday, and uncelebrated individuals. Their lives are unremarkable but compellingly real. As one of the people I spoke to remarked—and he's not such a common person really, he's one of China's new millionaires—he's only one of 1.3 billion Chinese, and "unless I suddenly murder someone, or am murdered, I'll never appear on TV." Even when they have spoken out, their voices have been weak.

The first person that I interviewed for this book was the pastor of an underground Christian church in Sayingpan, one of the poorest areas in the mountainous hinterlands of Yunnan Province, southwest China (see chapter 17, "Heaven's Narrow Gate"). This wiry old man confidently engaged with me and spoke about how he and his friends had survived the blood and tears of the past fifty years. He told me about the first work team sent into the village by the party after the Communist victory, and he related his story of those times, then spoke of the mass struggle meetings and denunciations of the Cultural Revolution and of the tortuous history since then. He concluded with the words, "If only this place had produced a gifted storyteller!" adding, with a hint of embarrassment that didn't detract from his insistence, "You tell everyone what happened here, but make sure you don't add your saliva to our words!"

It was a warning that I took to heart, and I have tried to give voice to all the words I heard without adding my own saliva.

Even though we might believe in vastly different things, and despite the fact that some of the people I spoke to were extremely annoying individuals, I still feel I developed a profound and caring relationship with every person in this book.

I don't believe in UFOs, nor do I subscribe to the popular premise of shows like *The X-Files* that would have us believe that aliens live among us, or that the truth is out there. But that didn't prevent me from engaging with the head of the Chinese UFO Research Organization (chapter 24, "Beam Me Up"). As Chairman Mao's Spanish interpreter, he had once been in close proximity to the star in China's firmament—the Red, Red Sun, as Mao was called in the Cultural Revolution. I was interested in how this UFOlogist had become so enamored of the stars of other galaxies and why he was so absorbed in the study of UFOs. But he is one of us; he lives among us and he expresses his fascination and concerns in a language that I could comprehend and that I hoped to share with others.

I dare say there were some who weren't always truthful, but they too have their place in my work. Their deceptions may have been unintentional, because what they were telling me was a story they had rehearsed in their own minds so many times that they now believed it was the truth. Others, perhaps, were more purposeful in their deceit, and they use their practiced lines to tell us or convince us of their story. Nonetheless, I respect their decision and their choices, and I respect their kind of self-representation. I leave it to you, the reader, to make of things what you will.

Although I am someone who has learned to listen carefully to the stories others tell me, and to become engaged in them, I am also able to distance myself from their world. Nonetheless, there are still some people and some stories that I have not been able to relate. That's why I also feel it is important to say something about what things are not in this book, and what has been lost from my earlier works.

People who work the land appear in the following pages, but there are many stories of people I spoke with in the far reaches of rural China—where the lifestyle and manner of farming are closer to the time of the first emperor Qin Shihuang, in the second century before the Christian era, than to the modern age—who are absent from my portrait of contemporary China. There are people I encountered—men and women, children, brothers and sisters, and wives from nearby villages—whose tales are as ancient as the Old Testament. They were powerful, too. Although I saw and listened, I left without putting them into my account, for I lack the art to translate those rich but uneventful lives into the pages of a book.

Then there are the highly specialized or unique dimensions of the oral histories that I have included that I have somehow missed, been too slow to pick up on, or lacked the wits to notice. Furthermore, there are all those subtle signs and hints—perhaps a tone of voice, a hand gesture, or the twitch of an eye—that I have not been able to express and that may have been telling their own important story. Surely there is something missing from the long interview I did with the police officer in charge of an execution squad (chapter 25, "Parting Shot"), or from my account of the agricultural manager who is undermining party control by creating a farmers' cooperative (chapter 23, "Just One Party"). But I let them talk to you as they wish, and I have not interfered.

The majority of people in *China Candid* are individuals I searched out on the basis of clues and leads, conversations with others, and my own curiosity. Before each trip I would sketch out a few rough ideas about the types of people and the places I wanted to visit, but the real work was a matter of constantly revising those notes, along with my preconceptions and my wish list. In some cases I found what I expected; in others I had to abandon my efforts.

Zhao Li is an exception (chapter 9, "Moonwalking"). I had come across her before I embarked on my first trip. She was one of a very few people I really wanted to see. I'd read about her in the *Beijing Evening News*. The article about her was on page 10 of that popular paper, directly underneath an advertisement for a venereal disease clinic run by the Tiananmen branch of the Armed Police at 35 Dongjiao Minxiang Alley. I clipped it out and stuck it in my notebook. It gave the name of Zhao Li's school in northeast China, and that's where I found her.

The paper said she was a student born without arms who had got into university, and now her life was "suffused with the warmth and brightness of the sun." It was an odd place for such an article to appear, and it was strange juxtaposed with the ad for the VD clinic. You see, 35 Dongjiao Minxiang in Beijing was the foreign embassy district that had been attacked by the Boxer rebels in 1900. At the time it was the site of a British medical clinic. Anyway, I tore out the article, but because the print was so small, I ended up with a scrap of paper that also had the details about the VD clinic.

Of course, the newspaper reported her story as though it were yet another triumph of the socialist system, but when I met Zhao Li in person, she described a lifetime of discrimination and frustration. I was using locally produced batteries in my tape recorder, and I found myself having to change them every twenty minutes or so. Zhao Li took one look and laughed. Without any to-do she said, "They're fake. You can't get real batteries here."

It was her tone of fatalism mixed with complacency that led me some time later to search out the Consumer Protection Association; I eventually found someone who was willing to talk about the epidemic of fake products in Hunan Province, south China (see chapter 10, "Consuming Habits"). Other trails to other people opened up to me in a similar way.

I transcribed my 150,000-word manuscript at home in Brisbane, Australia. The distance gave me a chance to listen carefully to every interview in an entirely different space and to think about the lives that I was in conversation with in my own world.

Compared to my first published oral history, *Chinese Lives,* a book that appeared in the mid-1980s, *China Candid* has been both an easier and a much harder project. And it has enjoyed a very different fate. *Chinese Lives* was produced to be acceptable within the parameters of early reformist China. Much of it was circumscribed by circumstance or limited by what publishers would accept at the time. *China Candid* was produced with no such restrictions, but, because of its content, despite much interest and long negotiations, no mainland Chinese press has been willing to publish it. Some of the material was never meant to appear in China, because some of the people I interviewed agreed to speak with me on the understanding that what they said was for international distribution only; furthermore, much of the material, although it reflects personal realities and historical experiences, is still deemed unsuitable for Chinese readers, or, rather, unpalatable to China's leaders.

Studs Terkel, who wrote the introduction to the U.S. edition of *Chinese Lives* that appeared in 1987, said that the oral literature of North China had been one of the sources of inspiration for his own work. To my mind he was being overly diplomatic; I have not found any trace of such an influence in his writings.

Much North China oral literature favors a repetitious narrative style. A classic example is: "Once there was a mountain, and on that mountain stood a temple. And in that temple there lived a monk. The monk told a tale, and what was the tale he told? Once there was a mountain, and on that mountain stood a temple . . ." In another traditional narrative style, the story is related from the middle, from the thick of the action. It starts with a climactic moment, then the background and events leading up to it are narrated, and finally its impact and consequences unfold. Although similar techniques might be used in these pages, the focus of Studs Terkel's own work has always been on people, individual stories, and the past. In Chinese dynastic writings and even much modern literature, although a great deal is made of the past (or, in the case of politically driven recuperative writings, the past is heavily reworked to serve present exigencies, losing in the process anything but a pragmatic and evanescent value), and although oral literature contains much incident—a universe of detail and variety—one thing that is very rare or entirely absent is people, or rather individuals. Although dynastic writings—and here I refer to the official records of history, the histories of the twenty-five dynasties dating back over two millennia—have since the beginning of the Christian era included a particular form of biography, the *liezhuan,* they are more often than not histories in which formulaic language has buried the person; or details of military campaigns, virtuous acts, or political achievement have blurred the features of the men and women whose lives they purported to record.

Starting in February 1984, I worked with the novelist Zhang Xinxin over sixteen months to produce an oral history that we called *Chinese Lives (Beijingren).* It was the first oral history of its kind produced in the People's Republic of China. Our work was initially serialized in literary journals throughout China and then published as a single volume in 1986. Subsequently it was translated and published in more than ten other languages. But in China *Chinese Lives* was never called an oral history. Rather it was dubbed "oral veritable record-style literature" *(koushu jishixing wenxue).* Veritable records, or material recorded and transcribed as spoken, was a long way away from what was called literature in China at the time. This new nomenclature was not of our invention, and it confused everyone.

At the time, the leaders of the Chinese Communist Party and their approved historians maintained strict proprietary control over the writing of all modern and contemporary Chinese history. Writing about reality was the prerogative of what many people have termed the handmaidens of the power holders. Those not so privileged, or outside that charmed circle, could not presume even to use the word *history* to describe their efforts. That's why *Chinese Lives* couldn't be called an oral history.

Among the people I searched out as part of our project was an elderly member of China's rubber-stamp parliament, the National People's Congress. I wanted to talk with him about his political activities in the 1930s, when he had participated in a social-democratic political party, an organization eventually co-opted by the Communists in the 1940s. It was one of the parties that had been active in what was called the Third Force of Chinese politics, that is, a political grouping that was neither Communist nor Nationalist (or Guomindang, KMT). We were about halfway through our formal dialogue, which I was recording, when an old friend of his dropped by. It turned out that the visitor was the head of the Central Party History Committee, the body empowered to write modern China's history.

He sat for a few minutes, listening to our conversation, before suddenly exploding. "What do you think you're doing?" he shouted. "What makes you think you can write *our* history?" I tried to reason with him, but he cut me short, banging his fist on the table. "This is party history, the history of the Chinese revolution. Apart from us, no one is authorized to write about it." He then threw me out on behalf of our host.

All history was their history. If people like me and Zhang Xinxin, not to mention anybody else, took it upon themselves to write about their past, or indeed their present, attempting in the words of a favorite party slogan "to seek truth from facts" for ourselves, then we would be showing up the farrago of myths that they paraded so confidently as historical truth. The fellow who threw me out was a historical technocrat. He knew full well that if we continued our discussion about the Third Force, we would inevitably touch on the question of Madame Soong Ch'ing-ling (Song Qingling), the widow of the father of the Chinese Republic, Sun Yat-sen (d. 1925). Shortly before her death in the early 1980s, Mme Soong was made the honorary president of the People's Republic of China. This gesture was part of the party's efforts to maintain a united front with the other political forces and parties that had been co-opted and then silenced in the 1950s. For, you see, Mme Soong was a staunch supporter of the Third Force—one of their patrons, in fact. To discuss her history and the history of the Third Force would have inevitably led us to the question of why other Third Force activists had refused to recognize the Communist Party. And one reason was that many of them were also socialists who, like members of the Communist Party, had advocated a worker-peasant revolution of the type that eventually led to 1949 and the People's Republic. But they had rejected the Communists on principle, and the reasons why they had done so would have inevitably come out if our conversation had continued. One of the central reasons was that in the 1930s, during the first power struggle in the Communist Party, there had been a bloody slaughter of the defeated faction. Some 3,500 former comrades were executed in the melee that followed. And if our dialogue had continued, it would have been revealed on the record who had ordered that mass execution: Mao Zedong, the man who later became the chairman of the Chinese Communist Party itself.

The history of the Chinese revolution, and what it has wrought over the past century, is covered in similar festering wounds and unsightly scabs. That's why, when I started working on oral history in the 1980s, outsiders were kept strictly out of things. In the officially approved genesis of the revolution, distortions are added to by falsehoods, and outright lies are presented as prettified facts. Because Mao Zedong remembered the wrong date, the Chinese Communist Party still celebrates its founding on 1 July every year. No one is willing to change it and admit that the party's party should be later in the month.

This sketchy history of mine should help you understand why, whenever I come across people who decry oral history for not being real history, I don't feel like arguing the point. All I'm left with is a question of my own: "And what you regard as being real history, is that *really* history?"

Once I was stuck on an overcrowded train and had to stand for nearly twenty-four hours. I can't tell you how much I hated China's floating population at that moment. What in heaven's name were they all doing wandering around the country, clogging up the transportation system? When I'd calmed down, I thought how lucky they all were finally to have the freedom to move about. Even the sons of landlords, people previously subjected to constant surveillance, were free to travel in search of work. But wait a second: the landlords had been exterminated in the early 1950s, and that meant that even their children would be old men and women by now. So the people who have the freedom to move around are the grandchildren of the landlords. They're the first generation to be able to get out and about in China.

Occasionally I encountered problems that seemed more intractable than crowded transportation. Take that time in Yunnan when I started work on *China Candid,* for example. Because of the sensitivity of religious issues among ethnic minority groups in the People's Republic, the local authorities tried to frustrate my efforts to talk to people. The county party secretary granted me an audience and questioned me about my visit. He solemnly declared that although I was looking for local Christians who had been converted by an Australian missionary, no Australian had ever been in those parts. The so-called Zhuang Weilian I was asking about was, in fact, an Austrian.

Of course, it was a blatant and clumsy ruse, easily exposed. I didn't confront him head-on but asked whether he could tell me what they called the species of tree that you could see growing all around the district. He said, "Gum trees!" in English. I couldn't help laughing, and he knew the game was up. Not only had the missionary John Williams brought the trees from Ipswich in Queensland, northeast Australia, to Yunnan, he'd even taught everyone what they were called in the Australian vernacular.

Although I have my regrets, I have spent a happy and eventful number of years with *China Candid* and everyone who has traveled with me.

I interviewed a man who had used the money he had made as a small trader to establish a private orphanage and take in over a dozen young children (chapter 6, "Looking Ahead"). His experience in life helped him see through my enthusiasm for his enterprise. He said to me, "You've come a long way and been through a lot to get here to see us. Of course, it means a great deal to our big family to have someone show such interest in us. But apart from your sympathy and support for us, haven't your travels, and your visit here, also helped you find a measure of meaning for yourself?" He was a deeply sincere and extremely perceptive man.

At the very least, *China Candid* will introduce you to some of the people who have lived through the first half century of the People's Republic. It is a version of China, a facet of its history, a slice of its life. Naturally, it is far from being the whole story.

Shortly after finishing work on the one hundred interviews in *Chinese Lives,* Zhang Xinxin and I got a letter from a student at Peking University. He was obviously unimpressed by our endeavor and the whole idea of oral history. The letter was elegant in its simplicity. It said: "100 = 1. You've written about one hundred people, but in reality all you've told us about is yourselves."

There are lots of clever and insightful people in this world of ours. In Chinese there is an ancient debate about whether writers spend their lives annotating the Six Classics of Confucianism, or whether the Six Classics of Confucianism are an annotation of every person's life. It's a debate in which I don't take sides.

Chairman Mao's Ark

A Hero for the Times

A Winner in the Economic Reforms

On 1 January 1993 the China Business Times *ran a front-page story under the headline "Millionaires on the Mainland." In it an unnamed government official said, "For some time now China has had not only millionaires, but also large numbers of billionaires. Some of their number would even rank among the rich in the West."*

The report celebrated the fact that "it is no longer a rarity for people to have mansions with luxuriant gardens, lawns, and swimming pools. Only a decade ago these would have been the stuff of Hollywood fantasies. Not so today."

Few of the megawealthy in China are willing to talk about how they made their money. Here is one real millionaire who was happy to tell his story. He was short and thin, dressed in a well-worn, although meticulously clean, navy blue suit. He looked just like a cautious accountant—at least until he started talking.

Doing business is not as hard as people make out, that is, as long as you're on the right wavelength. That, plus some startup capital, and you're set. There's money to be made everywhere you look; as long as you've got the right instincts you can make a pile out of whatever you set your mind to. That's why I can tell you straight, no bullshit, I've been at this game for a good ten years. Sure, I've taken my share of hits, but now I'm sitting pretty. I'm a millionaire. But that's not such a big deal these days.

Now, I'm being honest with you here. Five years ago a million was a million. You were a master of the universe. Everything was yours for the taking. But now millionaires are as common as dirt, you can buy them secondhand on the street by the pound. If I really thought I was something, wouldn't that make all the dudes with their own Boeing 737s think they were God? But everything has two sides. You can trip yourself up really easily, and every cent counts. I might only be a *renminbi* millionaire, but the people who used to kick me around all the time are sucking up to me and playing buddy-buddy now. Once you have a few bucks, you definitely feel better about things.

Doesn't everyone talk about diving into the sea of commerce these days? Even the bureaucrats in their Mao suits, they're on the make too. Take the police I used to have dealings with—yeah, the guys who reckon they're my buddies now—those guys who used to have it in for me. Well, nowadays they want to invest in my business. But when it comes to dollars and cents, it's no more Mr. Nice Guy. I tell them, "Look, fellas, we go back a long way; I know you." These guys are too slow on the ground; they're just not wired for business. Why make life hard for myself? I say, "Let me give you some advice: don't give up the day job, okay? Stay with the uniform and the government wages. Keep an eye on me from over there where you're standing, and if by some chance I get into serious shit, give me a helping hand, okay?"

Look, I don't want to bullshit these guys, so I'm straight with them. They have a hard enough job just making a living. If they're really hard up for a bit of cash, I'm happy to give them some help, a loan or a gift, whatever. I see it as sort of like taking out extra insurance. Anyway, I know they'd never dare ask for such a big slice of me—no more than ten thousand yuan or so. I wouldn't feel a thing. But if they invested in me and expected returns, that'd be completely different. I'd be at their mercy. If something went wrong, they wouldn't be in any position to help me out. And, let's be frank, I don't need their money.

What a turnaround in ten years, eh? The guy they used to fuck over as a petty criminal is on top now, and the heavy boys are begging to be friends. They dumped the whole proletarian dictatorship thing on me, and, though I wouldn't go so far as to say I'm the one who is doing the dictating these days, it's about the same damned thing. They're still driving around in their shitty old cars. Even their bureau head only has a Santana, and it's not even his own. I've bought my own, and I can go wherever I want in it. It's only right that they'd want to suck up to a God of Wealth like me. I deserve it.

To be honest, when I was an angry young man, my only fault was that

I loved a good fight. And, believe me, I was damned good at it. I wouldn't say I could beat all comers, but there was no one in South Beijing who could stand up to me, take my word for it. Back in '82, outside Yongding Men, I had a run-in with a pack of Northeast Tigers,[1] though if you ask me they were a bunch of pussies. Okay, I was a bit heavy-handed, and I put one of them in the hospital for a while. Normally I would never have got done for it, but those were bad days, right around the time of the "strike-hard" campaign.[2] I had this rep for being a brawler, so the local pigs already had it in for me. Plus the little shit I was teamed up with ratted on me and said I was the one behind it. I ended up being the evil black hand, and so they hauled me in. Remember, back then, it was "try them fast and throw the book at them"? In less than a fortnight I'd been in court and been sentenced to three big ones, and I was lucky to get off so lightly. Thankfully they didn't send me to the boondocks or anything, just a local spot for labor reform on a farm. Because I had a pretty good attitude—fuck, but I had a good attitude!—they made me a prisoner-warden, in charge of the others. After a while the government showed a bit of mercy and reduced my sentence by six months, so I was out in the summer of '84.

Apart from never having enough to eat, labor reform is pretty much just what you'd expect. Freedom and human rights are all relative, wouldn't you agree? I was twenty-three when they let me out. Yeah, I was born in April 1962. Two and a half years inside, and I'd had three birthdays. Before they locked me up, all I had was a part-time job at our local vegetable market— nothing regular—and that was gone. When I got out, I knew I'd have to start thinking seriously about the future. By then all the guys my age were married, and I had absolutely nothing. The police weren't all bastards, though. That's how come we could be friends later on. Quite a few of them said I wasn't like the usual crop of thieves and crooks. "You're just a bit too

---

1. Northeast Tigers (dongbei hu) is the wary term Beijing people use for rowdies from northeastern China, who are reputed to be fearless and vicious. Yongding Men was once the southernmost gateway to Beijing; it is now a suburb, with a multilane overpass marking the former entrance to the imperial capital. A new, shoddily built Yongding Men has been built to replace the original, razed in 1957.

2. "Strike-hard" campaign (yanda) refers to a period of coordinated, draconian police and judicial repression of social disorder, corruption, and crime during which arrests, trials, and executions are commonplace. Such campaigns have occurred with increasing frequency since the early 1980s in China, and, to an extent, have replaced the Maoist-style mass movements that were common in the past.

handy with your fists, otherwise you're an okay guy." That really touched me. Just goes to show that when they wipe the floor with you, you're happy for any small kindness. So, all right, I was a fighter, but I had a good heart. I was okay.

Can't tell you how hard it was to find a job when I got out. In those days state-run enterprises still meant something. None of them would have anything to do with me. My parents were really anxious, too, because they thought it'd only be a matter of time before I landed myself in trouble again. They used every connection they could think of and even sweet-talked the local police into keeping an eye on me. Finally I got a license to run my own stall. But to get that you need startup capital, and my dad was just a fucking coolie. We scrounged and borrowed and finally managed to get 1,400 yuan together. There was nobody with money you could approach; no one had real cash in those days. If you had ten thousand yuan, people thought you were really somebody important. Anyway, getting money out of people was real hard labor.

I started out mostly trading in clothing. You can make more profit on clothes, and you don't need any particular expertise. It all depends on how good a talker you are. If you're into something else, like watches, you really need to know how to fix the damned things. If you fuck up a person's watch, you have to pay for it. I didn't know any of that stuff, so I followed the crowd and set up in the garment business. Another thing was, my license was only temporary, so I couldn't trade in anything but clothes and small everyday articles.

Clothing was hard enough, since you had to go racing between Guangzhou and Beijing. You had to bring in the stuff from Guangzhou yourself; if you stayed in Beijing and depended on middlemen to bring the goods from Guangzhou, you'd be ripped off. Who knows how many people you'd end up paying off? If you didn't get your own supply you'd only make a few yuan, if that. It was really hard in those days; you couldn't afford to take a break. After a day in the market you'd set up a night stall and just keep going. Never got home till the middle of the night, and you'd be at it again at daybreak. And those trips to Guangzhou and back were sheer hell. I had limited capital, so I could only bring back a few hundred kilos or so at a time, as much as I could lug onto the train myself. I wouldn't waste money on a sleeper—couldn't get a ticket anyway—so I'd end up sitting or standing or crouching near the train door for the whole trip back to Beijing. By the time I got off a few days later, my legs would be swollen as big as loaves of bread. If you pressed the flesh, your finger would leave this big dent. But as the old saying goes, "Only when you suffer in the extreme can you become a superior being." With everything I've been through, I could write my own *Pioneering History*.[3]

It was when I was working in clothing that a real opportunity finally presented itself. There was a time when the authorities allowed people to import secondhand clothing. To people outside China it was just rubbish, but we started buying loads of clothing, mostly square-meter boxloads, at ten dollars or less a load. You couldn't really say it was imported; mostly it had been smuggled in—through Guangdong and Fujian at first, though later Tianjin and people along the Shandong coast got involved as well. Once they had this stuff on their hands they couldn't offload it locally, so they had to sell it on. Getting secondhand clothes into Beijing wasn't so easy, though. In the first place, they wouldn't let you ship them on the trains—unless you were willing to rent a whole freight car, that is. Guys who had the money to do that wouldn't be caught dead trading in secondhand clothes. So your only choice was to rent a truck yourself to haul the stuff all the way from the south. I'd made some buddies while working on my stall, and one of them cleared the way for the trip all the way from Fujian to Beijing without getting anyone else involved. It was cheaper than from Guangdong, and he'd even arranged the truck. The only problem was that he was stuck with a driver he wasn't all that sure about. It was a long way to travel with no real security, so he needed someone to go along with him for backup. And here I was, known to be handy with my fists—infamous in fact—and a trader in clothing as well. So he asked me to go along as his bodyguard.

To think at the time I was nearly stupid enough to let this opportunity pass me by! I told him that if there was money up front I could find a reliable guy who knew how to handle himself to make the trip. But he was in a bind because he didn't have any cash in hand. In other words, he couldn't afford to front the money. That's how I ended up offering my services, like we decided to work together. I got a few sacks of old clothes as payment. All in all, the trip went pretty smoothly. Whenever we ran into a blockade, you could usually get by with a bribe. It was fairly peaceful on the roads. We came back with a few trucks full of stuff. When we divided the cargo up, I

---

3. *Chuangye shi,* a 1960s novel by Liu Qing about the pioneers of socialism in the countryside.

didn't have time to open up my sacks to see just what I was getting—just brought it straight back home. That's when I discovered, fuck me dead, most of it was 70, 80 percent new, and the type of thing that was in fashion at the time! The only damned problem was it was all filthy, and it stank to high heaven. I separated out the stuff that was too dirty to keep—things with oil stains or bloodstains or whatever—and sent it off to the recycling station. Then I mobilized my whole family to work with me to wash and iron the rest. We ended up with a fairly impressive wardrobe of clothes. Because there was so much, we left a lot of the second-grade stuff unwashed and sold it as it was. And boy, was it a profitable deal for me! I sold the better things for a few hundred yuan each; one or two items like that, and I'd covered my costs. The rest of them—and we're talking a few hundred garments here— were pure profit. Your average piece of clothing would fetch twenty to thirty yuan a pop. Night markets were particularly good, since no one could see what they were really getting. Back then people were completely fixated with new stuff from overseas, and there wasn't much of it around. I was in a good position because I was selling bona fide foreign clothing, just what amateur overseas Chinese and tarted-up girls around town were looking for.[4]

I decided to strike again while the iron was hot. This time I went to Fujian by myself to bring back a couple of loads of clothing. I thought I'd wholesale the stuff back in Beijing, so that's why I bought so much; it made better business sense, too. Nowadays people are impressed if you can make a 50 percent profit on a deal; back then I wouldn't think anything of 500 percent. We were so hot we were just burning the place up.

You could never get away with a beautiful setup like that for long, and soon the government banned the trade in secondhand clothing. They incinerated all the clothes they confiscated. They were perfectly within their rights; anyway, the clothes really were incredibly dirty, and no one knew if they were carrying some infectious disease. I might have made a killing selling secondhand clothes, but believe me, I never wore them. Never mind the filth; it made me sick to think I'd be wearing the things some fucking foreigner had thrown away. Anyway, I'd been working on the premise that they'd ban the stuff sooner or later, so when the government finally took

4. "Amateur overseas Chinese" (yeyu huaqiao) is a term of deprecation for young men and women who want to look like wealthy Chinese from overseas returning to visit their down-at-heel Motherland.

action, I was pretty much in the clear. I didn't have much left on my hands—the good stuff had all been sold, and what was left was just stuff people had sifted through and discarded—and I was more than happy to hand it over to the authorities for burning.

It was the individual stall owners, the private entrepreneurs on the streets, who were hit hardest by the bans. By the time the clothes reached them through all the middlemen, they were already fairly pricey. They were just managing to make back a few dollars when the bans took effect. I felt sorry for them. Some of them didn't want to give in, so they kept selling the clothes on the sly. They ended up being fined or having their licenses taken away. But they were stupid to try and dick around with the authorities. You always lose when you take on the government head-on. If you want to play games, you have to learn where the loopholes are and catch them unawares, before they've woken up to your scam. If you have any sense, you'll be long gone by the time they're ready to strike.

Sure, people still trade in secondhand clothing today. They've adapted to the environment. They know the government can't keep an eye on them all the time, so they wait until things have calmed down, and they go back into business. When the market booms and the government puts out another ban, everyone lies low. After the ban slacks off, they start up again.

I made tens of thousands of yuan out of that first deal. Amazing how much you could score with just a few thousand in startup capital. Within about half a year, or more precisely about three to four months, I had nearly a hundred thousand yuan. Back then that was real money. I was crazy. Man, I went out and bought an electric cart, you know, the kind disabled people use. The top speed might have only been thirty kilometers or so an hour, but I felt like I was on top of the world. Later on I couldn't get a license for the damned thing, so I was always being stopped by the police. Since I wasn't disabled, they said I shouldn't be driving it. I took the hint, and I knew a bit about cars anyway, so I got myself a real one. We were so clueless back then; like we thought the best car in the world was a Toyota Crown. I didn't have that much cash, so I got a joint-venture Fiat. It was this dirt-gray color, with the engine in the back. It was small and cramped, and if you put four people in it you couldn't shut the doors. I might have thought it was a shit bucket, but other people treated me differently. I was the first in my neighborhood to have my own car. It had only cost me about ten thousand on the black market—not bad, considering that the retail price was around nine grand.

As for the rest of my capital, that's a classic case of easy come, easy go. I wasn't careful enough and lost it all in a bad investment.

I really have to blame the guy who first lent me the money to start up my stall. He was my dad's old friend, and he had retired from his job in a woolen mill. He was bored, so he decided to get some money together and start up his own factory with some farmers and local worthies in the country around Changping outside Beijing. The peasants provided the space and labor, while he came up with the technical know-how and some of the capital. They went into the knitted woolen shirt business, mostly producing for export. Knitwear was pretty hot at the time, and even if you couldn't get a toehold in exports, the local market was hot, too. You couldn't expect great returns, but I figured it was a safe enough investment. Anyway, I was wary of reselling because you never dealt with anything solid. But a factory that actually made things seemed real to me. So psychologically I was in tune with the project and I was easily convinced to invest, thirty thousand at first. He put together a package of three hundred thousand yuan, so I was in for 10 percent. They also made me a manager. After six months they went into production, and that's when the problems started—and everything was a problem. The biggest headache was marketing. I don't know how many sales managers we went through. Anyway, none of them could hack it for very long; there were always disagreements and fights over every fucking thing.

I could see quite plainly where the problem was: the reason they couldn't move stock was that the product was inferior. But all these bumpkins knew about was planting corn; they didn't have a clue about manufacturing. Only a complete idiot would have been taken in by our goods. And since all the raw materials were obtained at a premium on the black market, there was no way we could cut our prices. Even though our labor costs were lower than in most factories, the finished product was many times more expensive than the competition. I could tell there was no future in it, so I decided to withdraw my money and head for home. But they were too fast for me. Before I'd even got my act together, they decided to increase capital investment to keep the factory from going under. That way I couldn't get my money back and was forced to go along for the ride in the hope that I wouldn't be completely wiped out. I should just have let it go under—that's where I made a tactical error. But I wanted to salvage my thirty thousand.

I believed them when they told me they were about to strike an exporting deal and they needed money fast. I was stupid enough to think I could protect my original investment by throwing in another thirty thousand. That was everything I'd made from trading in secondhand clothing. But guess what happened? Of course the big deal fell through. After the buyer had approved our sample, the first batch was made up and they discovered that the quality of the finished product was nothing like the sample they'd seen. They produced another batch, but that was rejected too. Not only did the contract fall through, but we ended up having to pay damages as well. That's when my dad's buddy let us in on his little secret: he was so desperate to save the factory he'd given the buyer a sample made by another factory!

So that's how the factory went under. The machinery was stripped to pay off bank debts; we couldn't cover it all, so the bank just had to cope. We were left absolutely penniless, and lucky not to have been dragged into court. I had absolutely nothing to show for my sixty thousand yuan. Some price to pay to be fucked over like that. Had no choice but to accept the mess. I couldn't very well carve myself out a chunk of sorghum fields from the old peasants and take it back to Beijing as payment for my share, now could I?

It was a lesson I wasn't going to forget in a hurry, though. No matter who spoke to me about how much money you could make by setting up a business, I simply wasn't interested. Sure, running your own enterprise sounds more serious than being a profiteer, but fuck me dead if you don't actually have to produce things and then get entangled in all of the shit that goes with production, and all the people who have to get a piece of the action. No matter how careful you are, you can never be sure things won't go wrong somewhere down the line. If your main aim is to make money, my advice is to concentrate on profiteering, or what the authorities call "the circulation of commodities." Stick with circulation, stay out of production. The setup in China at the moment is ideal for traders; just keep clear of trying to make a name for yourself as an industrialist. Now, if anyone wants to get you into that, I'd say they're out to get you, or rip you off. Don't fall into their trap.

The problem here is that in recent years things just haven't been in the producer's favor. You need a stable and reliable setup and the right environment so that in eight to ten years' time you can make your money back. But, fuck, eight to ten! Who can wait that long? People these days are unsettled; everyone wants, you know, whaddaya call it?—damn, I talk about it all the time and I can't remember the word—that's it, immediate returns. Or, more precisely, exorbitant profits.

These days people love the idea of killing the chicken to get at the eggs. All they're interested in is instant gratification.

Anyway, where were we? I'd got up to about 1985–86, hadn't I? After that disaster I only had ten thousand or so yuan left in the kitty, not much to do anything real with. The rag trade had leveled out as well. Sure, you could make a living out of it, but you couldn't get rich quick any more. The prices for genuine imports coming in through places like Guangdong had gone through the roof. Then there were the "clothing towns" around Beijing where itinerant workers from the south had settled and were churning out cheap rip-offs. They had all the right labels, but their product was incredibly shoddy; it looked like clothing, but that's all you could say for it. The places that were still doing well were the local markets like Silk Street, which are mainly for cheating whitey, getting the best of the devils and trading in foreign currency.[5] It was real hard to get your foot in the door at places like that, and even if you did you probably wouldn't make much. All those stalls give the impression that it's a simple, rustic environment, but, believe me, the competition is fierce, and everyone's crooked.

That stint of labor reform really taught me a few things. The government gave me a crucial life lesson: avoid confrontation, and don't buck the odds. I knew there was no future in operating a clothing stall, so I changed tack. That's not to say I abandoned the stall; I kept that going and made over a thousand yuan a month out of it. It only cost me a little over a hundred to hire a peasant woman to run it. If she sold a lot, I gave her a little more. I used my remaining capital to get a loan and went back into profiteering. This time it was beer. The loan was easy. Everyone thought I was this rich guy and they were happy to throw a few million in my direction. Anyway, they knew I wouldn't be running off anywhere soon.

At that time the government hadn't freed up retail prices, so beer, like the stuff produced by the Beijing Brewery, was sold locally at the price fixed by the municipal commerce bureau. It was good quality and cheap booze. Beer made in other provinces, though, could be sold here at market prices—so it cost twice as much. But that same stuff was sold in its own local area at a price fixed by the commerce bureau there, and outside beer was much

5. Silk Street (Xiushu Jie) was next to the Qijia Yuan diplomatic compound in Jianguo Menwai.

more expensive. Quality-wise, I have to say, the piss they produced at small local breweries could hardly be called beer. If you drank a shitload of Beijing beer and pissed into a bottle it'd still be a hell of a lot better than their stuff.

But you see what I'm getting at? There was an opening for me here. If I got hold of all the Beijing beer and sold it out of town and introduced out-of-town beer to Beijing, I'd be able to make a killing at both ends. Of course, you had to go the whole hog and make sure there was no Beijing beer being sold in Beijing at all, otherwise the scam wouldn't work—who'd want an inferior product that cost more than twice as much if they could still get Beijing piss? A few of us came up with this idea at the same time, so we joined forces, or at least we made sure we didn't tread on each other's toes. United, we were able to wipe Beijing beer from the local market. There was only beer from other places—we got it from all over the place—even Guangxi. About the only place we didn't import beer from was Tibet. The consumer had no choice; if you don't like the stuff or reckon it's too expensive, then fuck off! As for the rest of the country, it was just the opposite—Beijing beer was all over the shop. The trick was that we'd shipped it so far from the capital that no one could afford to bring it back. Don't forget that outside Beijing it was an expensive, imported beer. You'd have to be a dumb fuck to try buying it all up at those high prices and trucking it back to Beijing, where you'd have to resell it at the low prices fixed by the Beijing Bureau of Commerce. A dumb fuck who'd probably be nabbed by the authorities for illegal profiteering!

That kept me busy for just on six months. My supply line was mostly to the northeast. At first I moved the goods by truck, but when things really took off, all I had to do was deal with consignment forms; my outlets took care of the actual shipping. For an illegal trader, I reckon I had a conscience. Most of our beer was Snowflake brand from Shenyang. It was much better than the crap produced by township breweries. It sold for a few *mao* in Shenyang, but in the summer heat in Beijing we could easily sell it for over two yuan.[6] At the time, the local beer was supposed to sell for a little over eight *mao*. But you never saw it in the marketplace because we'd shipped it all out to the provinces. And there was no way you could buy Snowflake in Shenyang for a few *mao*. If you wanted a beer you had to drink stuff from out of town, and that was two yuan a pop.

I'm not bullshitting you, but by the time the government caught on to

6. One *mao* equals ten *fen,* or one-tenth of a yuan.

what was happening and closed the trade down, I'd dealt myself out and was sitting on three hundred thousand yuan. Trading beer is a seasonal thing, after all. Who wants to drink that shit in the middle of winter? But it just goes to show how slow on the uptake the authorities can be. The first snows had fallen, and they still hadn't figured out our scam. All they knew was what they read in the newspapers, all those articles like "Oh where, oh where has all our local beer gone?" Absolutely useless. I reckon I'd actually done a good deed. They might accuse me of illegal profiteering, but I could defend myself by claiming that I was acting in support of the Central Committee, and through my business practices I was striking at the evils of local protectionism.

Of course I'd used local protectionism to my advantage. But there should be a level playing field, right? All local governments can think of is keeping their own beer prices down. Well, if it's that cheap, then I'm entitled to buy up as much of it as I want. And if I buy it all, that's your lookout. I haven't cheated you. If you're that full of local pride, then why not just establish a People's Republic of Beijing, set up a customs zone, and tax all the beer you export?

If you know where to look, there are chances to make money everywhere in our society.

With that capital under my belt, I started trading in fresh fish. Once you've got yourself a big fishery, you can really go for the money. The thing you have to be good at is weathering the storms of the marketplace. If you're only going to trade small-time, then you might as well not even bother. I've also dealt in scrap metals—copper and steel. Once I even bought myself an abandoned transformer substation and sold the whole thing to these people down south. They repaired it and put it back into service. If they'd wanted to, they could have hired people to strip it for copper wire that still could earn them a fair bit. I've also traded in complete construction projects. In some cases you need big bucks; other times, like in motor vehicle or construction projects, you can get away without any financial backing at all. You just play the middleman, and you can strip a layer of skin off everyone involved.

Frankly speaking, I'll try anything if there's a buck in it. I keep on the move, and it doesn't matter how much I score; as long as I score, I reckon I'm ahead of the game. These days I'm a bit more careful, though. There are some deals that might yield a big profit, but the risks are too great. In the old days, I would have been into it without a second thought; now I know how to let go. Take going to Russia, for example. Everyone knows you can make a pile out of just about anything there, and lots of mates of mine have done very well out of the mess in Russia. But I've kept out of it. It's just not safe. They tell me that those Russkis carry out raids on people with submachine guns. No way am I going there! Money is one thing, but you have to stay alive. More to the point, I've got a family to think of.

Commerce has been pretty lively these past couple of years, with everyone getting involved in the market economy. I'd be stupid if I was still a petty fishmonger trading in stinking prawns and rotting fish. Lately I've been trading in company names. I'm filling a market niche, really. You see, you've got these shithole companies, ones that are so run down that they have absolutely no capital apart from the general manager's one decent suit. They can't think of anything better than linking up with a bigger industry or state firm or contracting a subsidiary company of a larger operation. As for the state organizations, like ministries or commissions, or the army, they have companies under them that could really do well, but they've got bogged down through lack of managerial expertise, and all that's left is a shell. So what you've got is a situation in which two parties need to be brought together, but they don't know how to go about it. I come along and do my magic, and I satisfy both sides.

Take, for example, the National Defense Science Commission. Let's say they have a corporation called the Eastern Group—now, I'm just using this as an example, right? They don't really have such a corporation. Under the Eastern Group there's an electronics development company that has been bleeding money like there's no tomorrow. They're thinking of closing the operation down altogether. At the other end there is this pathetic electrical company run by a few hicks in Tong County outside Beijing, produces lightbulbs that burn out within a couple of days. They can't give the things away. Then I come along and introduce both sides to each other, and they're back in business. Just think about it; the company under the National Defense Science Commission can make lightbulbs that people will actually want to buy, and they'll be products of a quality that people want. So the hicks will strike it rich. As for the commission, they only have to put their seal on the documents and sign their company over to the bumpkins under contract, and pay five hundred thousand yuan a year on the contract.

See what I'm saying here? There are openings to make a buck wherever you look if you put your mind to it.

How many company shells have I traded my way through? A good twenty by now, I guess. I'm one myself, I suppose, though I've never set up my own company. Some of the shells I've traded in have actually tried to get me on board as a consultant or that kind of shit; you know, honorary CEO. You must be kidding! I'm a profiteer, plain and simple, and what I trade in is companies like yours, and now here you are wanting me to be a managing director—what, so I profit from myself? I don't think so. Anyway, none of those companies will last; if I stuck around, sooner or later I'd end up back in labor reform. My relationship with them is simple: you hand me my fee, I'll close the deal. Being in business is like being one of those out-law knights: one day you're fighting on the same side, and the next day you make like you don't recognize each other in the street.[7]

I might not have a black belt in profiteering yet, but I'm pretty damned close. I don't even bother with the business-card thing. I don't have a shop front either. Why bother? It's just a waste of assets. Anyway, you can't take it with you; it limits your freedom of movement. More to the point, when the shit hits the fan, who wants to be tied down? I still have a stall-owner's business license. I don't do clothing now, though; I'm in handicrafts these days. I've got two Sichuan girls looking after that side of business. They've both been to school and can speak a few words to the foreign devils. They're doing fine, so I can look after the big picture. I let them make most of the day-to-day decisions, like pricing and so on. Don't ask me for advice if you can decide yourself, that's what I tell them.

I've been in handicrafts for quite a few years now. It's more stable than clothing, and more profitable too. In the rag trade a street stall can't sell a T-shirt for three hundred U.S.; people would think you're joking. Some dumb-fuck foreigner comes along, and sure, it's your duty to try and rip them off, but you'll scare them off if you ask prices even higher than Yaohan Department Store prices. It's different with handicrafts, though. Take a small embroidered shoe for a bound foot, for example. You can say it was your great-great-grandmother's back in the Qing dynasty,[8] when women all had bound feet. You say you can get three hundred yuan a shoe, easy. But, since it's you, my friend, I'll let you have the pair for three hundred. How about that? You blind them with crap and they leave happy, "Sankeyou

---

7. Outlaw knights or knights-errant *(xiake)* were itinerant warriors with a particular code of honor.

8. The Manchu-Qing dynasty ruled from 1644 to 1911.

waidai ni machi."[9] They've not really lost out, either. Okay, so they've lost the equivalent of a couple of days' pay, but they've bought themselves a Chinese antique that they can show off back home. In fact the wholesale price of those little shoes isn't much more than your average T-shirt. They're all made by peasant women, hicks out there in the villages. Genuine Qing dynasty my ass. Rip the soles open and you'll find that they're lined with old copies of the *People's Daily.*

Cheating in business is commonplace. If you don't do them, they'll do you—and if they're willing to be done, then it serves them right. The crucial thing is that you have to be legal. Doesn't matter if you make the occasional mistake; just don't break the law. Keep well clear of drugs, arms, and trading in girls; most of all, don't go near politics. Touch politics and they'll fuck you over every time. So I pay my taxes on time; I pay any fees on time; I pay my insurance on time. Anything the government asks for, I hand over—whether or not they give me a receipt. I make donations to the disabled and disaster relief, and even pitched in money when the students were demonstrating in 1989. I'll give money to any cause that seems reasonable. And that's why the government doesn't regard me as dangerous. To them I'm just an insignificant guy with a bit of money. In reality, I'm a master of my trade—and being an insignificant guy with a bit of money takes real talent, believe me.

In this society of ours you have to be able to play the game. You know full well that you're screwing them senseless, but you have to let them feel they're in charge, that they're doing you over. Once you've perfected the art, you're home free.

Making your first million is both easier and harder than it seems. But no rich person in China was born to be rich, except maybe the chairman of the Communist Party. All the Mercs you see driving around Beijing today are the product of people learning the tricks of the trade and working hard these last few years. It's just a matter of knowing how to do it.

9. A Chinese phonetic rendition of "thank you very much."

2

Chairman Mao's Ark

One of the Floating Population

A retired cadre with access to internal statistics told me that there were over three hundred million people in China who were no longer living in their original place of residence. In other words, he said, "Virtually a quarter of China's population has uprooted itself. Of that number, some eighty million have drifted to the cities in search of work. They are mangliu, *the floating population of workers."*

There's a popular saying:

Beijing relies on the Central Committee,
And Shanghai on its connections;
Guangzhou leans on Hong Kong, but
The floating population lives by Mao Zedong Thought.

During the Cultural Revolution the Red Guards traveled the country by ship, train, bus, and foot, spreading the word of rebellion; they also went to Beijing to see Chairman Mao. From the 1990s on, the descendants of Mao Zedong's Red Guards—a generation who had changed China in another way—were on the march once more.

The proud citizens of Beijing dubbed the area outside the Dongdan Park in the center of the city, where itinerant workers would gather every morning looking for jobs, the "people market." They called the clothing of this floating population of laborers—Western-style suits made from low-grade synthetic fiber that were so filthy you couldn't tell the original color, and faded military great-coats—the "itinerants' uniform." The young man I talked with was a scrawny, dark-skinned fellow who, like most of the others at the people market, was dressed in the regulation uniform, the only distinguishing characteristic of his attire being an orange baseball cap.

I came to Beijing from Jianli, Hubei Province, in 1991. No one has ever heard of Jianli, but it's near the famous Honghu Lake. There was a Red Defense Force in Jianli, just like at Honghu.[1] I remember when I was a kid, the party leaders in Beijing sent a delegation to pay respects to the people of areas like ours, which had been among the first occupied by the Communist Party. It presented the local people with a huge letter of gratitude for their support during the revolution. It was red, and it had a quotation from Chairman Mao in big gold lettering: "Carry on the revolutionary tradition and strive to achieve even greater glory."

That was shortly after the Gang of Four was arrested,[2] and the old army people in our county were deeply touched by the gesture. They were grateful that Party Central and Chairman Hua—Hua Guofeng was chairman then[3]—hadn't forgotten them. In reality, though, they had been forgotten. All they left us with was that piece of paper. After the revolution, I guess it must have been in 1951 or '52, they gave us another piece of paper with some writing on it. My granddad kept it all those years. But what's the use of a few sheets of paper? The people in the old Communist areas made much greater contributions to the revolution than city people. So many lives were lost; the Communists had grown to strength and then came to power on the backs of people like us. But after he went to Beijing, even Chairman Mao didn't do anything for us, let alone Chairman Hua. Sure, they spoke about the victory of the revolution, but we were still as dirt-poor as we had been in the old society. My granddad was in the Red Defense Force, too; he had joined the revolution back in the 1920s, or maybe it was the thirties. He got wounded and everything, though he lived until 1981. When he

1. The Red Defense Forces *(chiwei dui)* were local armed forces similar to militias. The most famous was the Honghu Red Defense Force, active around 1930. Its fame gave rise to a major stage production (1959) and a feature film (1961) directed by Xie Tian. Both enjoy an abiding popularity.

2. The Gang of Four *(siren bang)* consisted of Wang Hongwen, Zhang Chunqiao, Jiang Qing, and Yao Wenyuan, core leaders during the Cultural Revolution who were arrested following Mao's death in 1976 and eventually tried for numerous crimes.

3. Hua Guofeng succeeded Mao Zedong as chairman of the Chinese Communist Party in 1976 and was himself replaced as head of the party by Hu Yaobang in 1981.

died he didn't have one piece of clothing that wasn't patched. And he was buried like that, in poverty. He said to me himself that Chairman Mao owed us, that he wasn't even as good as Li Zicheng.[4] He was more like the Emperor Qin Shihuang that you see in old operas.[5] The only thing the poor were good for was fighting for him. Once he got into power, they weren't good for anything. We were never liberated.

Generally speaking, it's only in the past decade or so that Party Central began to take any notice of us. That's particularly true of Hu Yaobang; he really traveled around the place and was pretty concerned about helping the poor,[6] and he gave us practical material support, or money, investment, and loans. Before that we were really no better off than people had been under the old society. I feel that we were just like the people you see in movies about the bad old days. The only difference is that there were no Jap devils invading us, killing people and burning down villages. In other ways, though, it was even worse than it was in the past. The home the White-Haired Girl lived in was better than the place where I grew up.[7] She had proper walls and windows, even a table and chairs. We didn't even have those, and we lived in a thatched hut with walls made out of branches, and holes for windows. And we raised ducks in it as well, for the eggs. But it's got a bit better recently with poverty relief and the reforms; people are adequately fed and clothed now, and they can be involved in small-scale businesses, and do things like keeping ducks for making thousand-year-old eggs. At least we can say we've reached the level that Party Central talks about: people are no longer cold or hungry.

There aren't that many people in my family. After granddad died, that left only my parents and us four brothers. I was the youngest, and by then my

4. Li Zicheng, or Li Chuangwang, was a rebel who led a peasant army to conquer Beijing at the end of the Ming Dynasty. After proclaiming a new dynasty and a short-lived reign, Li was defeated by Manchu troops, who took the city and established the Qing dynastic capital there in 1644. When entering the city in 1949, Mao Zedong remarked that the Communist Party must not follow in Li Zicheng's footsteps.

5. Emperor Qin, or Qin Shihuang (r. 221–210 B.C.E.), was the draconian ruler of the Qin Dynasty who created a unified empire. He was traditionally represented as a tyrant. At various times Mao Zedong proudly claimed that the rigorous rule of the Communist Party put Qin Shihuang's to shame.

6. Hu Yaobang led the party as general secretary until his ouster in 1987.

7. *The White-Haired Girl (Baimao nü)* was a 1940s revolutionary play, later made into both a ballet and a film, about the sufferings of a peasant girl at the hands of a cruel landlord. Her hair turned white as the result of her ordeal.

eldest brother had got married and had his own place. That was then; now two of my brothers are married. In our area you could do okay if you could plant rice or raise fish and lotuses, or if you lived near a township or the wharves and could go into business.[8] But in our village we don't have enough water, so people can really only grow wheat.

Since they dissolved the people's communes and everyone got small plots of land, it's been even harder. It doesn't matter how many laborers you've got or how carefully you do it, there's only so much that you can grow on that amount of land. That's why you have to decide whether you're just going to put up with all the poverty and deprivation at home or try your luck elsewhere. Yes, I know that saying that "life is always easier at home, and everything is difficult in foreign parts," but I couldn't stand being poor. I just had to get away. Since graduating in 1989—ours wasn't the poorest family, and there was no lack of able-bodied workers, so I was able to finish junior middle school—I've done all kinds of odd jobs: cutting reeds, making and selling thousand-year-old eggs, working on the docks. It was all seasonal work; when they were busy they'd call you in for a few days, and when things slackened off you'd have to move on. Apart from these smaller jobs, I also responded to all the publicity in the papers telling people how to make money by raising silkworms. I joined up with some people to make bean-curd skin too, but we ended up broke.

So after the Spring Festival of 1991, I caught a boat down to Wuhan with two friends and started my career as an itinerant laborer. Before setting out we'd heard all kinds of stories about how Guangdong had the most opportunities, so we thought we'd go there. I had twenty yuan in my pocket, a bedroll, and some food for the journey. We planned to try a trick we'd heard about and buy a platform ticket at Wuhan station, then sneak onto a southbound train and hide in the roof of the toilet. We could sleep the whole way to Guangzhou! But we soon found our information was out of date. There were too many itinerants in Wuhan already, and the authorities were onto the scam. The moment they saw people with bedrolls and platform tickets, they blocked us from entering the station. We hung around for two days, not knowing what to do with ourselves, until we finally heard someone tell us that the goods depot in Hanyang was not so strict. If we sneaked in at night and squeezed onto a freight car without being discovered, we'd make

8. The seeds, roots, and leaves of the lotus are used widely in cooking and make the plant highly marketable.

it to Guangzhou just the same, even if it took a few days longer. So that's what we did. After settling into our freight wagon, though, we didn't dare peek outside. The train kept stopping all the time, sometimes for what seemed like half a day. We couldn't even guess where we were—but we did gradually realize that we were on the wrong train.

Guangzhou was in the south, so the temperature should have been getting warmer, but we were feeling colder all the time. We had to be heading north. This went on for two full days and nights. I don't know how many stops we made, and even though we wrapped ourselves in our bedding, it didn't do any good; even our bottles of water froze up. At one stop the lights were really bright, so I plucked up my courage and took a look outside. The sign said Shijiazhuang. "Damn it, we're heading the wrong way!" I cried. "This is Shijiazhuang. We'll be in Beijing soon." My companions said we should jump off now and go looking for work in Shijiazhuang, otherwise we'd freeze in the train. Generally speaking I was the one with the ideas, so I said we should stay on the train and put up with the cold until we reached Beijing. In general, since I'd been to school and studied a little geography, they decided to follow me. They weren't really literate, and they usually did what I suggested. I knew that Shijiazhuang was a small city, and since we were on the way, I thought we should keep going until we hit Beijing. It was the capital; there were sure to be more opportunities.

Later I got a real shock when I heard that people froze to death hiding in freight cars. But we were lucky to have our quilts with us, and the weather wasn't at its coldest. We didn't go hungry, either; in fact we hadn't even finished all our food when we arrived in Beijing.

It didn't matter that we'd taken the wrong train. Any big city would have done.

At first we didn't understand the way they do things in Beijing. As soon as we arrived, we tried to register with the local labor bureau. We asked someone where it was, and that someone turned out to be a policeman. He asked what we wanted the labor bureau for. I told him we were going to register for work. He thought that was a great joke and told us off: "Fuck me stupid! A labor bureau that finds jobs for itinerants? Get the hell out of my face." We wandered around the train station for a whole day until we finally bumped into a beggar from our part of the country who told us there was a people market outside Dongdan Park. Anyone selling their labor would go there to be hired. We found our way there soon enough. I'd say there were fewer people looking for work then, though there were still quite a few thousand, men and women. There weren't many like us from Hubei, though. We stood around there waiting for six days with no luck; no one even approached us. Things were really expensive, too. A lunchbox cost three yuan, but we'd already used up all our money, so we had to go around restaurants eating the scraps people had left. We slept in the entrance of an underground station. Generally speaking, city people are very hard-hearted, and we were thrown out of the stations at night; they wouldn't even let us into the doorway.

At the restaurants they wouldn't let us in to pick up leftovers, either. First we had to wash plates for them for free. Only when we played along would they let us take the leftovers.

We stuck it out for six days, until my luck finally changed. There was this boss who had been looking for the right person for ages. He noticed that I looked pretty strong and knew what to say, so he picked me out and told me to go with him. I had to take care of myself, so I said goodbye to my two companions. Everywhere has its own particular rules. At the people market, for example, you only speak when spoken to, and you don't butt in and say you'll take a job when a boss is talking to someone else. That'd be like stealing someone else's rice bowl. If you do, there'll be a fight for sure.

The place was a small, privately run restaurant at Yongding Men. We'd get up at two or three every morning, and I'd fry crullers with the boss until after nine.[9] I'd use the break to sleep, and then after four in the afternoon I'd get up and start cutting up meat and vegetables and doing various odd jobs until about midnight. I'd have another short sleep, and then it'd start all over again. At first I just couldn't get used to this kind of work; I found it hard to sleep during the day, and at night I was always drowsy. I kept cutting myself with the meat cleaver, but gradually I got used to it. There were two other employees apart from me, both girls from Sichuan. I'd agreed on a hundred yuan a month with my boss, but I don't know what the girls got; they never told me. If business was good or we worked well, we got a bonus; if it was bad, he docked our pay. Mostly that didn't happen, though, so I usually got over a hundred and thirty yuan a month, and once I made a hundred and fifty.

Most restaurant workers earn about that much. It's a hard job, and the bosses are all pretty much the same, though they have to cope with all the

---

9. Chinese crullers, similar to churros, although not sugared, are usually eaten with hot, sweet soybean broth for breakfast.

worries and work harder than any of us. At the time I thought the job suited me, especially as I had no particular training. Although I was strong, I didn't know how to use my strength. If my boss wanted to drive me into the ground, I'd have had no alternative. Back in Jianli I wouldn't make a hundred yuan in a year, let alone a month.

What makes me angry about working in Beijing is the way the people here treat you. They think they're superior to us, even though we're the ones who do all the dirty jobs in this city for them. And it's as if we're always in the wrong. They feel free to swear at us whenever they please, and if you answer back they hit you. Sometimes they would even feel up those two Sichuan girls, take advantage of them.

I was in that job for nine months. There was this one regular, a truck driver, a friend of the boss. We called him Elder Brother Zhang. One day he said to me on the sly: "There's no future in this job, boy. If you work for me, all I'll expect is eight hours a day, and you'll get at least eight yuan." I told him I'd have to talk it over with my boss, but he said I should just slip away without saying a word. I didn't think that was right, so I told my boss. "It's up to you," he replied. "There's a hundred like you waiting for a job every day at the people market. But don't say I didn't warn you: there's something wrong with Zhang." I didn't care about that; I was in it for the pay, to make a living. So I went to work for Elder Brother Zhang.

This transportation company was run by several partners, including Zhang. He had invested quite a few big trucks in the operation. The hours were short and the pay a little better than before, though not that much, since in the restaurant we didn't have to pay for our own food. In this new job I also had to rent a place to live. I shared with six others for forty yuan a month. Food was roughly another hundred yuan on top of that. Everything in Beijing is expensive. I didn't care that much about making a lot; it's just that I felt that Zhang was right when he said I had no future working in the restaurant. Here I had a future; gradually I could learn how to drive and become a driver. You could make better money then. The drivers in the company, and the foreman, the guy who controlled the schedules, made about a hundred yuan a day.

I worked loading and unloading Elder Brother Zhang's truck. He treated me really well. Sometimes at lunchtime he'd even buy me lunch. He said that the next time he went down to Hubei, he'd take me along and give me a few days off to go visit my family. Things went along like that for a while, and since he was so nice to me I decided to tell him that I wanted to learn to drive. I saw it like I was a disciple who was approaching a master, so I thought I had to give him a gift, and before I told him I bought two cartons of Marlboros. Cigarettes are very expensive, a month's wages gone just like that. Zhang told me he knew I'd want to learn to drive, and that it was a good thing. "It's only natural that people want to better themselves," he said; there's no future in just loading and unloading trucks. He said he'd be happy to teach me on one condition. He said we'd have to become friends. I didn't understand. I told him we'd been friends all along; we didn't have to become friends. He said what he meant was that we had to become especially intimate friends. I was all alone in Beijing, and so we should get together. I finally realized that he wanted me to sleep with him, to be homosexuals. No wonder my boss had said there was something wrong with him. It had never even occurred to me. Anyway, I didn't understand how two men could do it together. He was asking too much, so I refused. So he turned on me. "Fine, suit yourself. Don't bother coming to work tomorrow."

That completely threw me, so I went to speak to the personnel officer. He told me that since Zhang had introduced me to the job, it was up to him whether I stayed or not. "Don't bother complaining to me about it," he told me. Then I went to my old boss, but he'd found a new kitchen hand ages ago. So I had no choice but to go back to the people market. I hung around for ages before I got three days' building work that paid thirty yuan. Then another three weeks passed without anyone hiring me. There are too many itinerant workers these days; some people don't find anything long-term even after waiting around for six months. They survive on restaurant leftovers. Although I'd saved up some money, that soon ran out; and since I didn't know anyone else, I went back to my old boss again. He was really happy to see me and told me that the Sichuan girls knew of a job, so I should ask them. They told me a construction company from Sichuan had got a big contract and that they were hiring people for six yuan a day, plus lodging. They asked me whether I'd take it. Of course I said I'd be ready to start work the next day. Seeing how desperate I was, they whispered to each other and then told me that if I wanted the name of that Sichuan boss and the address I'd have to pay them a two-hundred yuan "information fee."

I just didn't have that much money. I begged and cajoled for ages; I was so anxious I nearly broke down crying. My old boss spoke up on my behalf, and they finally agreed to accept a sixty-yuan advance and then another sixty after I'd been working a month. My boss acted as guarantor, and that's how I finally got the job.

We're living in a commodity economy these days, so you can't expect anything for nothing. It was reasonable enough that they wanted to be paid; it's just that they were asking too much. I didn't have it. Beijing's not the only place where it's like that. Even in Jianli, people want to be paid. Nowadays you have to pay for information on how to make money; and sometimes you only discover it's phony once you've paid for it. And that's not all: you even have to pay when you ask for street directions. You haven't had to pay because you've never asked for directions in Beijing.

I was little more than a coolie; in Beijing they call it a "work assistant." You had to put your hand to everything that the experienced workers or machines didn't or wouldn't do. They said it was an eight-hour working day, but if there was a quota to be completed it'd be longer; and if there was no quota, they still made you start earlier and finish later. They took advantage of us at every turn. We never got our full wage. First there was health and accident insurance—strictly speaking, the boss should pay for those, but he'd just take it out of our wages. What was really unfair is that he'd knock off another 25 percent on top of that: 10 percent of that was a bond that he'd keep if you quit mid-job, or even if he fired you. The other 15 percent was called a "work responsibility bond." If the construction project failed to pass the municipal quality control investigation, we would lose that amount too. In other words, we were expected to cover the company's losses. That's why I reckon things are the same now as they were in the old society. The union doesn't do anything either; it's phony. The union chairman is the boss's nephew. He made up a few name lists of members and subcommittees just in case they ever come around to check on him, but they never do. The Communist Party might as well not even exist. The boss has the final say in everything. And you don't have to pay your party fees or union fees either; he deducts them directly from your pay packet.

That was the setup. Generally speaking, I felt okay about it. They are happy to exploit you, and you're willing to be exploited. It's all about money.

Over fifty of us lived in the same big prefab dorm, and apart from a few of us locally employed casuals, the rest were all from Sichuan. No one was in charge, so people were always getting up to things, you know, like gambling every night, or bringing women in. The women would ask to be paid up front, and then everyone would take their turn doing it. In my opinion that kind of entertainment wasn't really very good. It was a waste of money, and you only depleted your own strength. So I never took part. As for other kinds of fun, like having friends over for a drink, or listening to them all talking away, or watching television, I was always happy to take part in that. I also rented books to read; historical novels are what I like. Because we were paid by the day, and you wouldn't get paid for any time taken off, I generally didn't have any days off. You'd always get your strength back after a good sleep, and I was used to having time off. I didn't want to compare myself to the way Beijing people live; they have good jobs and have a day off on Sunday, and two Saturdays off a month.[10]

I worked on three building projects with that company. Because there was no new work going in Beijing for a few months, they moved off to Ningxia.[11] By then I was earning twelve yuan a day and had picked up enough skills to be a minor foreman. After thinking about it carefully, I decided there were more opportunities here in Beijing; anyway, I had, well, you know, a girlfriend. She was from Sichuan and worked as a maid in the house of a manager in a trading company. He had a lot of money and all these connections and lived in this big apartment with four bedrooms. He suggested I go home and visit my family in Jianli and said when I came back to Beijing he'd find me a job in his company. So I decided to stay and not go with the company to Ningxia.

When I went home I took 2,500 yuan, as well as some spare cash and presents. This time I paid for my own train ticket. Generally speaking, nothing much had changed at home; everyone was as poor as ever. I stayed for a month and left some money. I don't even know whether my parents will be alive the next time I go back, but I gave them some money anyway. My nephew—my eldest brother's son—came back to Beijing with me. Lots of people wanted to come along because they saw I had money; they reckoned I was on the way to becoming rich. But I didn't let any one else come with me when I returned.

Why wouldn't I come back? In Jianli I was always cut off from everything; now that I've lived in Beijing, I know much more about the world. I know that rich guys can spend a few hundred or a thousand yuan in a karaoke bar drinking all night. If I stayed in Jianli I wouldn't be able to earn a thousand yuan in ten years. You can't imagine how much money these people have. Generally, socialism meant that everyone was equally poor, or, if they were going to be well-off, we would all be well-off. Too much

10. In 1996 the weekend was regularized as two days off a week.
11. Ningxia is an autonomous region in northwest China.

inequality is a bad thing. But in Beijing today even dogs eat canned food. My granddad was in the Red Defense Force and fought for the revolution, but he didn't even know what a can looked like. Why would I want to hang around in Jianli? We've become floating workers because of all the inequalities. I didn't ask to be born in the countryside; but I could choose to leave. If I hadn't come back to Beijing, I'd have no future.

But by the time I got back a few things had changed. They say now that if you give the Beijing Public Security Bureau a fifty-thousand-yuan "accommodation fee," you can buy yourself a residence permit. They've also tightened up the regulations on minors working, so all the entrepreneurs are forbidden to use child labor. My nephew's only thirteen, so he's way under the limit. He's officially banned from working, but I don't give a damn. As well as that, the government has supposedly fixed the minimum monthly wage at 210 yuan. Supposedly you can make an official complaint if you get less. But who believes that? I know from experience that people get away with lots of illegal things. All the rules are phony; if you're happy to be exploited, the government won't interfere.

But the biggest change is personal: I haven't been able to find my girlfriend. I went back to that guy's place, but no one answered the door. Finally a neighbor saw me waiting there and told me that that fellow had been arrested a few weeks earlier. I asked what had happened to my girlfriend, whether she'd left me a message. They gave this embarrassed laugh: "You really are a dumb *mangliu*. She'd been fucking that guy for ages. The moment the police turned up, she was off. Do you seriously think she'd leave word for you?"

I can't hate her too much. After all, we weren't married or anything. These days, even people who are married screw around all the time. I guess I don't really mind. Though I am angry about being unemployed again. But that's not her fault. I spent a few hundred yuan on her, but it's not worth chasing after her for that. Anyway, even if I did find her, she probably wouldn't pay me back. So I've decided just to drop it. She can do whatever she likes.

I couldn't keep my nephew with me, or I'd never get hired. So I went back to see my old boss, and we were in luck. We settled it on the spot: he took my nephew but only gives him food and lodging and a bit of pocket money. Then I came back here to the people market. And now you've found me. That's my story up to now. I don't know how long I'll have to wait until I find another job. At lunchtime today I went to see a fortune-teller. For five yuan they told me that I'd make it and be rich, but that my time hadn't arrived yet. I'll just have to be patient.

All the founding emperors of China's dynasties started out as part of the floating population of migrant laborers. Chairman Mao was a big *mangliu* himself. When he first came to Beijing from Hunan, Chen Duxiu's and Yang Kaihui's fathers were well-known professors.[12] They made hundreds of yuan a month, but Mao couldn't even find a decent job. He ended up earning eight yuan a month working at the Peking University library. Everyone treated him like a country bumpkin and laughed at him for his accent. But later Mao was chairman, and nobody else counted for shit.

"The East is red, the sun has risen, Mao Zedong has appeared among the *mangliu*."[13] Most people reckon it's gonna happen like that again. Lots of books have said so, too.

12. Chen was a founding leader of the Communist Party, and Yang Kaihui was Mao's wife, later executed by the Nationalists.

13. The original line in the Maoist anthem "The East is Red" *(Dongfang hong)* goes: "The East is red, the sun has risen, Mao Zedong has appeared in China."

3

The Nondissident

A Party Man Betrayed

Alexander Solzhenitsyn divided the political prisoners in the gulags into two distinct categories: those who were resolutely opposed to the authorities and the nondissidents who were ideologically pure. In contemporary China the nondissidents aren't even taken seriously enough to be thought worthy of jail. In the darkling waters of fin-de-siècle confusion, these "old leftists" [people who were part of Mao's original revolution] share an interest with the "new leftists" [neo-Marxists who combine a diluted version of Maoism with international leftist thinking] in searching for a reflection of the Maoist sun. They enjoy the full wages and privileges of their status as old revolutionaries, and the authorities don't take much notice of them. Perhaps they simply can't be bothered to deal with them. Therefore, China's nondissidents suffer from an unprecedented sense of isolation.

The majority of residents in the newly built high-rise in the Beijing suburbs were men and women who had been party members for over half a century. The apartments are larger than the average in the capital, and there was an "old cadres' activity center," actually an exclusive club on the ground floor, where the retirees could play mahjongg and read Central Committee documents.

We found a corner in the activity center for our conversation, and he motioned for me to sit on the sofa opposite him, whereupon he unzipped his dark brown jacket and said, "Let's get to work, then."

I was born in Gaoyang, Hebei Province, in 1919, the year of the May Fourth demonstrations.[1] It was a completely unexceptional place, and I wasn't

1. The May Fourth Movement of 1919 was a seminal student-led protest movement that has come to symbolize mass political awakening in twentieth-century China.

even born in the township itself, but a few miles out in the countryside. Both my parents worked on the land.

When the party determined class status for people in rural areas during the land reform of the 1950s, my father was classified as a prosperous middle peasant. You couldn't say it was exactly an accurate reflection of reality, since he rented out fields, kept livestock, and employed farmhands as well as a maidservant. Strictly speaking, he was a landlord. Around that time Party Central issued an order to cadres not to interfere in land reform—though some still did and were punished for it. But both the land-reform teams and the local peasants could easily outwit the Center. They knew it would be quite unacceptable to classify some families as landlords if they had sons working for the party in Beijing, because they'd end up being defined as class enemies. To avoid any political embarrassment, they made them rich middle peasants instead. That meant the family would still enjoy full voting rights, and, no matter how you looked at it, were still on the side of the people. You can't blame the local authorities; after all, even the families of the chairman, Comrade Shaoqi,[2] and many others were classified as rich middle peasants. All you'd have to do is take one look at where they came from, their childhood homes and lands, and you'd know that if they were only middle peasants, that meant China didn't have any landlords at all.

The chairman? Of course I mean Chairman Mao. Who else could ever live up to the title?

The classifications did have some basis in reality. One of the farmhands working for my family, for example, was also a distant relative, so he wasn't really an exploited laborer. Apart from big landlords, and I mean the really wealthy landed gentry, most landowners in China worked the land themselves as well, or were at least directly involved in managing their own property. That picture of landlords never having to lift a finger, people who could indulge their luxurious lifestyle by feeding off the blood and sweat of others, was not accurate at all. It might have held true for some infamous landlords like Liu Wencai in Sichuan,[3] but the vast majority were nothing

2. Liu Shaoqi (1898–1969) was a party leader and state president until his fall from power in 1967 during the Cultural Revolution, when he was denounced as "China's Khrushchev" and accused of attempting to restore capitalism. He died ignominiously shortly thereafter.

3. A landlord whose legendary usury and cruelty were the subject of major artistic and fictional representations such as the Cultural Revolution–era sculpture *Rent Collection Courtyard*. More recently, in keeping with the changed mood of the times, some have claimed that Liu was actually a local benefactor.

like that. It was not the same as, say, England, or czarist Russia. Right up to the time of liberation in 1949, in purely material terms most Chinese landlords had never seen electric lights, a telephone, or even running water. They were hesitant about eating foods made with white flour except on festivals and at New Year, because they thought it was wasteful. They ate coarse grains and were little better than peasants themselves. In many cases they weren't as well off as the lowly office workers you found in the cities.

They didn't have any particular advantages in terms of politics, either. Chiang Kai-shek and the Nationalists represented the interests of the imperialists and the urban bourgeoisie all right, but deep down they didn't give a damn for the landlords. They might have played a decisive role in the rural economy but, let's be frank, what type of economy was that, really? Up to the 1950s it was nothing less than a bankrupt disaster area. In retrospect, it seems evident that our party's policy toward the landlords and rich peasants, as well as the small businessmen in the cities, was far too harsh. The majority of them were representatives of a backward form of production, certainly, but expending so much bile on them was quite unnecessary and just not worth it. Regardless of whether they'd been guilty of various atrocities, they were generally all physically eliminated, and their families were wiped out as well.

At the time? Well, things were different then. At the time I think it was probably necessary to do what we did. By equalizing things throughout China in one fell swoop, into a forced egalitarianism, the party (to use the chairman's words) "won the support of over 95 percent of the people." Tactically speaking, it was absolutely necessary.

That kind of revolution, an egalitarian redistribution of wealth in which you give everyone the same amount of everything, has nothing to do with the Communist Party or Marxism. Egalitarianism is a very destructive thing, but it's an ideal solution for the lowest of the low among the petty bourgeoisie and for impoverished people in the city, as well as for bankrupt peasants in the countryside. That's why the 108 heroes of Liangshan were so keen on looting and pillaging.[4]

So then, immediately after the forced redistribution of wealth, the party expended even greater energy creating a unique style of Chinese mass agriculture. It was a system of neither public ownership nor private ownership,

4. Tales of these "heroes" are depicted in the classical late-fourteenth-century novel *Water Margin (Shuihu zhuan)* by Shi Nai'an and Luo Guanzhong.

but collective agriculture. First there were the mutual-aid teams, primary and then advanced co-ops, which were followed in the late 1950s by the high tide of socialism and the creation of the people's communes. By the mid 1960s, that is to say on the eve of the Cultural Revolution, there was only a minute fraction of private agriculture left in China. By then the whole nation was firmly striding along the path of socialism and had accepted the system of planned, intensified production that went with it.

From the early 1980s, however, after Comrade Xiaoping and his core leadership established their political control throughout China, everything was turned on its head again. I don't care what you want to call it, the fact is that they launched a reprivatization of the means of production. After that, the entrepreneurs who contracted large tracts of land or collective industries, and exploited large numbers of employees, became the heroes of the day. I simply refuse to accept what has happened. I think it's outrageous.

All right, I admit that starting in the 1950s our party made many serious leftist mistakes, but despite all of that we had ideals, and we stuck to our principles. What we were doing conformed to the objective rules of social development that predict that disparate productive forces must be brought together and that private ownership must inevitably evolve into public ownership. Granted, despite the best of intentions we made some errors; in certain cases we were even guilty of being over-hasty and implementing infantile policies. But starting with the Third Plenum of the Eleventh Party Congress in 1978, we have pursued a dangerous rightist policy. Now we've gone so far to the right that we've abandoned the basic principles of Marxism and the objective rules of social development.

The open-door and reform policies have only been in place for a little over ten years, but already we have dismantled the socialist edifice and are selling off the bricks! We are doing nothing less than selling off the iron from the great wok of socialism. Things are a complete shambles. I tell you, we still talk about revolutionaries being people who struggle valiantly their whole lives for the cause of liberation, and so, no matter what difficulties we encounter, we should just tough it out. But things have reached a point where anyone with a conscience, anyone who cares about the fate of our nation, just has to weep.

Let me say this: during all the recent efforts that have been made to "invigorate the economy," three kinds of people have been particularly enthusiastic. First there's the idle urban drifters—those shiftless people who aren't committed to anything. Then there's the people who blindly worship capitalism and the new bourgeoisie. And the last group is people who used to be counted as revolutionaries. That our veteran revolutionaries should be mixed up with that bad lot just goes to show you what a farce it all is.

The majority of old revolutionaries came from poor and deprived backgrounds; they were the bankrupt peasantry. If you could hear them talk in private, you'd learn that the reason they first got involved with the revolution was so they could get a bit of land. They became revolutionaries simply to improve their standard of living. There's nothing wrong with that, mind you, it's plain and straightforward. But it has nothing to do with the future direction of humanity as outlined by Marx and Lenin. But I can assure you that there are still people in the party who are concerned with more than just having a better life. We joined the party because we wanted to realize our communist ideals. We weren't that badly off in the old society, probably better off than most. We wanted to pursue an ideal. Marx revealed that a new epoch was dawning; he led us to set our sights on changing the world, to overthrow the system of feudal capitalism, and to strive for the liberation of all humankind. If that wasn't the case, why would we—and here you can include everyone from the chairman right down to people like myself—have risked our lives fighting for communism? But now we're the ones who've fallen behind the times. We can't keep up with their phony revolution.

They can keep up, though. No lack of enthusiasm there! You haven't seen what I've seen. By the time they retired a few years ago, those bankrupt peasants who'd thrown their lot in with the revolution right after the Anti-Japanese War or during the War of Liberation were mostly midlevel party cadres of at least the county or bureau level. Their original aim in becoming revolutionaries was to achieve a basic standard of living. Well, they got that ages ago. They even had electric lights and telephones. They'd made it. And now finally they've hit pay dirt, and they're not going to let this bonanza pass them by. They've forgotten that they were ever in the Communist Party. Who do you think has poisoned the reputation of the party, made the people despise it for corruption? They have, that's who! But they're the ones who are in tune with Party Central.

The real workers and peasants are extremely dissatisfied with how things are going these days. And their dissatisfaction is growing. Why do you think so many common people went out in the streets to rebel back in 1989? I remember 1957, when the workers in more than a dozen provincial cities and centers went on strike and staged demonstrations. And then there was the Qingming Festival in 1976. People in Beijing, Shanghai, and Nanjing poured into the streets then as well.[5] But none of that could compare with 1989. Even the slogans had changed. In the past the party's extreme leftist errors had driven people to desperation. They were hungry, but their protests were restrained, and they could tell right from wrong. They didn't want to overthrow the Communist Party, but they did want to protest against its policies. But in 1989 things were different. The situation escalated to the point that the Center had to resort to military force to clear Tiananmen Square. People died as a result, both good and bad people. The majority were good people. They weren't out there supporting the likes of Wu'er Kaixi,[6] they were protesting against the corruption of the Communist Party. Our people could forgive the party its errors, even the most extreme errors, but they cannot forgive its corruption. The people are the mother of the party. But now it's completely corrupt and feeding off the people. You can't call this damned thing a Communist Party!

I was born with a big mouth, can't help letting off steam. Why do you think I never got further in the system? I was made a level 12 cadre back in the 1950s, and it was a big deal then. If you count down the ranks from the chairman, we were up there with a few thousand others, on top of a pile of a good six or seven hundred million. But soon after that I committed "right-wing opportunistic errors," and although I wasn't demoted, I didn't get any further promotions. In the 1960s, before the Cultural Revolution, that is, I finally managed to crawl up another level. But then I was accused of being "a person in power who had taken the capitalist road." This time they weren't nearly so nice about it, and I was locked up in jail for quite a few years. When I finally got out I was still a bureau chief, and that's the level I stayed at right up to the time of my retirement. As a parting gift they gave me the perks of a vice minister. What you'd call a cheap farewell present. I never actually had the job, but they gave me everything that went with it. It's hardly surprising, really. That's the way they deal with retired old revolutionary cadres these days; it's the same thing we did to "fellow-traveler capitalists" like Rong Yiren and Le Songsheng back in the 1950s.[7] Now the

5. In both 1957 and 1976, popular demonstrations against party power and policies erupted in cities throughout China.

6. A leading student rebel in 1989 who went into exile after 4 June.

7. Former capitalists who were used by the party as exemplars of patriotism during the socialist transformation, or appropriation, of industry and commerce. Those who survived the political turmoil of the 1960s and '70s returned to public prominence in the 1980s.

party's turned its guns on us, and they've got us in their sights. They're trying to buy us off. It's a bad business. Anyway, I'll just keep shooting my mouth off right up to the day when they accuse me of "leftist opportunism." What can happen to me? The most they can do is strip me of my privileges. So let them do it.

In retrospect, one must admit that we didn't do all that well under the leadership of Chairman Mao and Premier Zhou Enlai. Although the overall direction was correct, we paid heavily for our mistakes. In some instances the reason things went wrong was to do with faulty policies at the top, other times it was because those of us implementing the policies got it wrong. Of course, if we could do it all over again, the cost wouldn't be as high. But you can't turn the clock back; we paid the price, and that's all there is to it. We might not be able to go back, but at least we can learn from our mistakes. And no matter how you look at it, we did achieve a few world-shaking things. In the early 1950s, New China was the only country in the world that could stand up to American imperialism and take it on in the battlefield. Even Comrade Stalin didn't dare do that. That alone signified that the Chinese people had stood up, and I mean really stood up. Moreover, the people at least had sufficient food and clothing at last. And they had the right to vote for people's representatives. That a country of six or seven hundred million people was able to achieve these basic human rights within the short space of a decade was no mean feat. I'm not exaggerating when I say that Hong Xiuquan and Sun Yat-sen had spent their whole lives working for such changes and had failed.[8]

Economically speaking, we also established a fairly firm basis in those years to bequeath to the people who came after us. You can ask Comrade Xiaoping himself: What did the Communist Party have in 1949? They didn't even know what real machinery looked like. What did we have? Sure, Comrade Chen Yun[9] had an operation in the factories in the northeast, and they were able to produce the *Liberation Daily* with a broken-

8. Hong Xiuquan (1814–64) was the pseudo-Christian leader who led the Taiping Tianguo (Kingdom of Heavenly Peace) rebellion against the Qing Dynasty in the mid-nineteenth century. His rebellion—one of the bloodiest civil wars in history—is seen by Communist historians as a precursor to the successful Communist revolution. The political activist Sun Yat-sen (1866–1925) is acknowledged as the father of the Republic of China, founded in 1912.

9. Chen Yun (d. 1995) was the party secretary of the North Manchuria Bureau during the civil war between the Communists and the Nationalists in the late 1940s and also had responsibility for the party's economic leadership in the northeast.

down printing press and manufacture a local currency. But that was about it. Although things were broken down and poor when Comrade Xiaoping launched the reforms in 1979, it wasn't the kind of desperate poverty China had endured in the late 1940s. We were no longer poor and blank.[10]

By the mid-1950s we had a machinery industry and an automotive one, too; by the end of the decade we had an electronics industry and television. By the mid-1960s we had atom and hydrogen bombs, and soon after that we launched a satellite—it would have been even sooner if it hadn't been for the delay caused by the Cultural Revolution. We had oil and synthetics, and we produced millions of tons of iron a year. We might still have been poor, but in just over a decade we had created an industrial base for the nation and a self-sufficient agrarian economy. People need to learn how to appreciate our past in its historical context. Even if today's achievements are impressive, people shouldn't forget that they're working on the basis we created. Without the Communist Party there would be no New China. If the chairman hadn't left behind the huge spiritual and material wealth that was built up during his day, then we wouldn't have what we've got now.

People might think they're doing fantastically today, that everything's brilliantly successful. But let me ask you, where's it leading? It might well end up like 1959, when the chairman got all carried away and we were left with nothing. I'm prepared to go out on a limb and predict that when people in the future look back at today, and review what's been happening these last few years, they might not think very much of it. We are a socialist nation. We expended a prodigious amount of energy on transforming the private economy, and now an even greater effort is being mounted to destroy public ownership. Just wait until there is nothing left of socialism, until it's the People's Republic of China in name only; they'll have only succeeded in overthrowing themselves.

Comrade Peng Dehuai had a famous expression, something he said when he was really angry: "The sons feel nothing even though they're selling off their father's land!"[11]

We are Communists. Our roots are in the working class, and because of the particular situation here in China, we also have to rely on and educate

10. In 1956 Mao Zedong had described China as "poor and blank as a sheet of white paper" on which the most beautiful things might be written or painted.

11. Peng Dehuai (d. 1974) was a famous plain-spoken general who was purged for daring to present mild criticisms of Mao's Great Leap Forward.

the allies of the proletariat, the impoverished peasantry. But now you have all become capitalists, and you're grooming your children and grandchildren to be capitalists and landlords, too. Do you still expect the proletariat to support and sustain you? And if they don't want you, what do you have left? The bourgeoisie and the petty bourgeoisie never wanted anything to do with you, and, let's be frank, you've never really done anything for them. So do you think they'll support you now? As for the intelligentsia—sorry, but I have to go against the fashion here as well. Comrade Xiaoping might have claimed repeatedly that they are part of the laboring masses, but that's simply not the case. Marxism is very clear on the question of praxis, and Xiaoping knew it. The intelligentsia has never had a solid class basis. They are easily swayed opportunists; they're always anxious about their own petty gains and losses. They are small people with very dubious morals, despite all their hypocritical talk about having a sense of social responsibility. Just as the chairman said, the intellectuals are like hair, but hair can only exist if it has skin to grow from. If the skin, that is to say the Communist Party, is not stable, then they will immediately defect to some prattling bourgeois political party. Do they care what Comrade Xiaoping has said about them? They don't take any of that seriously.

Yes, of course, nowadays you're allowed to sing a different tune; but even if we weren't allowed to speak, what could they do? Sew up our mouths? Treat us like we dealt with the landlords, rich peasants, counterrevolutionaries, and rightists? Some people say that things have really opened up economically since 1989, and that there's much greater freedom of expression, too. I'm not so sure. Take a look at who is really profiting from the economic boom. The major state enterprises, the backbone of the system, are having trouble even paying their workers—not to mention the rest of the state sector. You only have to consider the fact that primary and secondary school teachers are badly underpaid. It's actually worse than under the Nationalists. Where's all the money been going? As for freedom of expression, superficially things seem looser, but in reality we should examine people's true motives and the impact of what they say. The Communists are not the only ones who can let people speak out; so can the capitalists. Freedom of expression is not the aim; it's just a means to achieve a particular end. You make use of it so you can hear some opposing views and give people a chance to let off steam. At the moment they completely ignore dissenting views and just refuse to hear what people are really saying. They're dead set on the course of revisionism. And unless you get them really riled up, they take no notice of you. You're just wasting your breath. So what if they're giving people the freedom to let off a bit of steam? It's a utilitarian strategy that fits in with their current short-term priorities.

Of course, we can't be too extreme about this or make sweeping statements about things without taking reality into consideration. You can't negate everything. Even I have to admit that regardless of whether you're talking about people's general standard of living or how this generation of core leaders are doing, things are a bit better than before. But we shouldn't only consider the present. When you're playing cards, you have to keep your next move in mind. Wait until these reformists, that is, the newly emergent bourgeoisie, are completely in control of the nation. Wait until China produces a Yeltsin. Comrade Xiaoping left to meet his Marx, leaving in his wake a revisionist party leadership that is in charge of a system that's neither fish nor fowl, a system that pleases nobody—not the left nor the right, not the top nor the bottom. Then what? The chairman constantly warned us of the danger that the party and the state might collapse. He warned us about the perils of revisionism and the danger of the third generation of leaders betraying the revolution. His predictions have proved incredibly accurate!

Have we really failed to appreciate the significance of the tumultuous events in the eastern bloc, where the red flag fell in over a dozen countries? China is faced with two choices. Either stick resolutely with the socialist system of public ownership, and work like hell to keep it afloat and refuse to follow the West, or else let's just quit right now and let those bastards restore capitalism in its entirety. There is no third way for the Communist Party. To engage in revisionism or maintain the status quo will only hasten China's peaceful evolution into a bourgeois republic.[12] And in my view, that's not a viable alternative. The events in Eastern Europe proved that whoever goes down that road will only harm the people and destroy themselves too.

In reality, a full-blown restoration of capitalism is no answer either. To relinquish power to those bastards, the bourgeoisie, is not something a Communist could do.

I joined the revolution in 1937, when I was just eighteen.[13] The party was

12. That is, the gradual and insidious transformation of China's socialist society into a state that is little more than a vassaldom of international capitalism.

13. "Joining the revolution" *(canjia geming)* means becoming a party or state employee.

still young then; even Chairman Mao was only in his forties. The words of the national anthem describe those days perfectly: it was a time when China faced its greatest danger, as the Japanese devils had invaded. Now, or rather when we look back at the present from some point in the future, I believe we will see that our nation is facing its greatest danger once more. All the devils are back in force—and not just the Japanese. Devils everywhere see China as just one big market for their goods, a source of limitless labor and resources. They think of China as though it were a prime cut of meat. Starting along the South China coast, they have advanced to eastern and northern China. Then they've extended themselves up the rivers and along the borders, and they've already come right into the heartland, into medium and small towns far inland. But the really disturbing thing is that they're not just blindly grabbing what they can get and then leaving anymore; now they actually have a strategy for long-term control. Through investment and the manipulation of the share market, they are building up strongholds in key areas such as oil, coal, hydroelectricity, steel mills, and mines. At the same time, they are insinuating themselves into strategic economic and military areas through the wholesale rental of land.

It is obvious that we are confronting a serious crisis. The devils—including the pseudo–foreign devils like businesspeople from Hong Kong and Taiwan—have ingratiated themselves to such an extent that every time we make a policy adjustment or announce a new law or regulation, first and foremost we have to consider whether they will be adversely affected. People are always going on about "what will the foreign investors think?" There is a constant threat hanging over our heads: if we don't accept the situation, we'll scare off badly needed foreign capital. The devils are already acting as though they own China as much as we do. Can you tell me we're not facing the greatest threat to our survival ever?

After graduating from teachers' college I went to the Communist-occupied areas to do grassroots work and was appointed principal of the Eighth Route Army Primary School. I joined the party when I was still at college in Baoding, Hebei Province. It was famous for being a nest of Communist bandits. Comrade Li Yingru described it in his famous novel *Struggle for the Ancient City*,[14] which was later made into a film. It had a great impact on people in their forties and fifties now, the generation born around the time of the founding of New China. Li Yingru later worked in the General Logistics

14. Li Yingru, *Yehuo chunfeng dou gucheng*, published in 1960.

Department of the People's Liberation Army [PLA]; and because the novel had made him so famous, for a short time at the beginning of the Cultural Revolution he was in the Central Leadership Group. Then he got on the wrong side of Jiang Qing and was jailed for many years.[15] Even after the Gang of Four was smashed in 1976 and Li Yingru was long dead, some old revolutionaries still couldn't forgive him for having been involved in the Cultural Revolution. They won't abide other people's mistakes, even though they shout themselves hoarse in support of revisionism. But that's because it makes them wealthy and it's turning their children and descendants into capitalists. At least they'll die without regrets.

The Cultural Revolution really went too far. In 1966 I was still only being attacked as a capitalist-roader; by 1967 or '68 I'd become a spy. They held a hundred-thousand-person struggle meeting at the Workers' Stadium, and all of us "spies," from bureau chief to ministerial level, were put on display. There were dozens of cadres just from the ministries under the State Council, supposedly part of a huge spy network. After being struggled we were paraded through the streets so that the masses could see what all the high-level spies in the Communist Party really looked like. The struggle sessions seemed to go on forever, and the stadium was always filled to capacity with spectators. Everyone was given time off work or study, so there were lots of people with nothing better to do. It was ironic that I'd been involved in building the Ten Great Buildings that included the stadium.[16] If I'd known what use it was going to be put to, I would never have signed off on the construction plans. A few years back they held the opening ceremony of the Asian Games there. They say tickets were being scalped at US$150 each. Surprisingly, someone thought of us oldies and sent us complimentary tickets. The seats were okay, though not on the podium, of course. I went along, and as I sat there, I recalled the other times I'd been up there, even on the podium, as well as when the Red Guards had dragged me out to do a circuit of the place when I was being struggled. Now there I was in the stalls with everyone else. The past was just like a dream. It's a fascinating sensation.

Apart from the comrades in the State Council, Comrade Liu Ren was

15. Jiang Qing, Mao's last wife, rose from political obscurity to become a radical leader during the Cultural Revolution. She led the purge of the "black line in the arts," resulting in the denunciation and incarceration of numerous cultural figures.

16. Ten major construction projects were undertaken in the new socialist capital to commemorate the first decade of the People's Republic.

attacked as the head of a group in the Beijing Municipal Committee, and so was Comrade Xu Zirong in the judiciary and public security organs. All these different groups were lumped together as part of a massive spy network. But what were we, in fact? Former underground members of the Communist Party that was under the command of the North China Bureau. All of these comrades had been covertly carrying out the struggle against the Nationalists from within. If anything, we were Communist spies. There was another high-ranking clique headed by Comrade Peng Zhen, and all the people in it had spent time in Nationalist jails at one time or another. Even the comrades who had followed the party's orders to make false confessions so they could get out and return to their revolutionary work were accused of being spies. Naturally, they needed a ringleader for this conspiracy, so they picked on Comrade Shaoqi, the president of the People's Republic. It was all absolutely absurd, and it was out of control.

Of the people who graduated from my college, I suppose that by the 1960s a few dozen were high-level cadres of bureau-chief status or higher. They were scattered through all the major provinces and cities, as well as in the army. We might have been from the same college, but we never got involved in factional activities, not the way people are keen on forming cliques and gangs today. We didn't have any alumni association, let alone regional associations. It simply didn't occur to us to do so. It was enough that we were members of the Communist Party.

The only time we ever gathered in the same place was shortly after the occupation of Beijing in 1949. Comrade Ye Jianying called together all the comrades who had been doing underground work.[17] I suppose there were a few hundred people there all told. It was so we'd have a chance to see each other. There was no food provided—not even the "four simple dishes and a bowl of soup" they talk about today[18]—or even tea. Comrade Ye made a short speech, we all cried as we sang the "Internationale," and that was that. Now that I'm talking about it, it upsets me too much to go on. Just thinking about it . . . I can't say any more. That's all. I can't talk any more today. . . .

17. Ye Jianying (d. 1986), a prominent army leader from the 1920s who took a leading role in the negotiations for the peaceful handover of Beiping (which subsequently reverted to the name Beijing) during the civil war.

18. In its efforts to curb excessive banqueting, in the 1980s the Communist Party ordered that at official functions only four dishes and a soup would be served. This policy of economy was observed more in the breach than the observance.

The first thing Comrade Ye said was, "Comrades, we've won!" And he couldn't go on. Tears were streaming down his face. Tears! The harsh realities of class warfare had been incredible. But if the Communist Party is to disappear now, if the party and the state are to collapse after all of this, I'm telling you, the newly emerging bourgeoisie will kill people to maintain its ascendancy. Believe you me, they certainly won't give anyone a chance to declare, "Comrades, we've been defeated!"

When the wage system was introduced for cadres in the 1950s, there was an average of one cadre to every six hundred citizens. And that included all the bureaucrats left over from the old government, as well as those turncoats who had abandoned the Nationalists for us, who were given a phony title to keep them happy. But now, heavens above! In the 1990s the situation is completely out of control. There's one bureaucrat to every thirty-four Chinese! In the old days, when we denounced the Nationalists for all their bureaucracy, we said, "Section heads are as numerous as dogs, and the streets are full of generals." We're worse than Chiang Kai-shek's dynasty ever was! And they keep telling us that without so many bureaucrats, things would get out of hand. In my opinion, with all that overgovernment, things are already out of hand. You can't have that many dragons ruling over the waters. Sooner or later all hell will break loose.

In the late 1950s, when we established our electronics industry, the factories and research institutes were under the same umbrella. Now there is a massive computer company that controls it all, the Taiji Something-or-Other Corporation. It provides computers for rocket systems, oversees the launching and retrieval of satellites, and all the rest. What did it take to set up that operation back in the 1950s? I'm talking from experience here, because I was personally involved. It went like this: the office in charge wrote the relevant ministry a report that was under two pages long, appended to which were two technical endorsements. If you don't count the seal of the premier's office, there were only two other official stamps on it, as well as a few signatures. Nowadays, even if you only want to start up a shoe factory, you need at least thirty official seals, and you have to jump through over 150 bureaucratic hoops. Everyone who is anyone seems to have their own official seal, and you need each and every one of them stamped on your permission slip before you can do anything. They claim this is all a necessary part of proper regulation and control, that it represents a division of power and is part of the new market economy. What a load of nonsense.

They've started talking about downsizing the bureaucracy again. And how are they going to do it? By laying off state-employed cadres and getting them to go into private business. They're going to clear the way to help cadres make the transition. The present core leader, Jiang Zemin, has said: "The state can't support so many cadres. Better for you to go out and make millions in business than squabble over your five-yuan bonuses."[19] Just listen to what the man is saying! And this from the General Secretary of the Chinese Communist Party![20] One of the phony moves that's part of the downsizing operation is the closure of various bureaus at the national and provincial levels. Getting rid of some of the dead wood of bureaucracy would be an excellent idea if it wasn't a total sham. They're not closing anything down; they're just converting parts of the public sector into companies. So now the Provincial Machinery Bureau will become the Machine Company and the Electricity Bureau an electricity company, and the bureau heads will turn into managing directors. Feel free to call yourself whatever you want to, but for heaven's sake go and find your own money to invest. What they are doing is converting public assets into private property. Isn't this tantamount to pillaging the people's wealth? A brazen abuse of the common good?

Following Comrade Xiaoping's Progress through the South,[21] there was a new way of putting it. He reportedly declared, "In my view it doesn't matter if we are colonized or establish concessions under foreign control. As long as China can be made to prosper, it's all right by me." Doesn't anyone see what's wrong with this? If we really let them colonize us, what prosperity can China ever enjoy? There won't even be a China left to speak of. It won't be our China that prospers—it will be their colony. But illogical statements like this have actually been propagated in the party media, printed in our newspapers. Everything under heaven is in chaos!

19. Jiang Zemin was appointed party general secretary following the ouster of Zhao Ziyang as a result of the nationwide protest movement of 1989. He eventually became state president as well as the chairman of the Chinese Communist Party's Military Commission, a position he retained until early 2005 despite his formal resignation from his other posts in 2002, when Hu Jintao succeeded him.

20. Repeated campaigns from the early 1940s onward attempted to reduce the size of the administration but invariably failed.

21. In early 1992, in a series of speeches made during a tour of cities and special economic zones in South China—called a *nanxun,* or "Progress through the South," an expression traditionally used to describe imperial tours of the southern provinces—Deng Xiaoping called for a new wave of reform and forestalled further debate about ideological issues that undermined the pressing tasks of economic transformation.

I came to Beijing in the spring of 1942, except back then it was still called Beiping.[22] By that stage the fighting in the Communist-occupied areas was extremely vicious. Every village was embroiled in a battle for its own survival, and individuals were fighting to save their own lives. Party members were constantly on the run, hiding out wherever they could; they often had to endure cold and go without food. The enemy outnumbered us and were constantly turning up the pressure. That's why the party decided to send qualified cadres behind enemy lines in the cities to engage in a covert war on this second front. It was a strategy designed to attack the enemy while at the same time preserving some of our better people. To be qualified, you had to be able to function effectively in an urban environment. If you were illiterate and didn't know anyone in the city, you were useless. You might think it wouldn't matter and you could get away with running a vegetable stall. But there were trade guilds everywhere, and the Japs were constantly checking ID cards. Where would you get one of those if you were a country lad? You'd have no hope of taking up any constructive work. I got a job as a teacher in a church school. You see, it was absolutely normal for a teacher from the countryside who came from a landlord family to leave the Controlled Zone and come to the city to teach, especially since I had contacts in Beiping in the first place.

The Controlled Zone was a Japanese expression for areas that hadn't been pacified, where there was still strong resistance to them. The Japs got their culture from us back in the Tang Dynasty, so they knew how to play word games with Chinese, too. So they made up this euphemism to describe the situation. With the outbreak of the Pacific War, the Jap devils and white devils were finally at each other's throats, and the Japs occupied my school with the excuse that they were merely appropriating enemy property. Despite the upheaval, the school continued operating under the same principal, although now he had to be called the school director. That's exactly why I despise the Japs. They're obsessed with face and human sentiment, but they have no concept of principle. They kept the place running because they could make money out of it.

In 1944, when I was twenty-five years old, I was given the party's blessing to start going to the Japanese-run "Peking University." Even the Nation-

22. Literally the "pacified north." The former imperial capital was so named in 1927, when the Nationalist army quelled local warlord insurgents in the north of China. The city's former name, Beijing (literally "northern capital"), was restored by the newly established government in 1949.

alists regarded it as a fake university then; that's because the real Peking University had been evacuated along with Tsinghua University to behind the lines in the southwest, and together they were renamed Southwestern United University.

Shortly before the Nationalists went under, back in the autumn of 1948, they launched a massive manhunt for underground Communists. I had long since graduated from university and was working in their State Taxation Office when I was suddenly recalled to the Liberated Area under Communist control. I returned to Beiping before most people in my area did, just when the armistice negotiations were initiated. My cover was as a shop assistant. I was sent to help prepare the way for the Liberation Army's entry to the city. . . .

After Liberation I worked for a short time in the North China Ministry of Heavy Industry before being assigned to the Agricultural Ministry under the State Council. It was still called the Government Administration Council then. Following on from that I was made a senior leader in the Construction Ministry, then the State Planning Committee, and so on. . . .

Yes, to think back on it all now, you realize that there was one disturbance or political upheaval after another: the Anti-American War in Support of Korea, then Monopoly Purchase and Sale, then the Great Leap Forward, the Soviet withdrawal of technical assistance, the Three Years of Natural Disasters, and so on and so forth.[23] There were trials and tribulations in those years that you couldn't even begin to imagine. But we made it through, even the harshest times. Even the chairman went hungry and gave up eating meat. . . .

These days some old comrades are afraid that they won't get the recognition they deserve. They say gingerly that "perhaps we didn't make any positive contributions, but we did stick it out and we kept things going." What the hell is this about "no contributions"? We must not and should not undervalue ourselves. I don't know about other people, but comrades like me, who worked under the guidance of the chairman and premier on the economic front, forged a path ahead; we overcame all the obstacles in our path. Just look at all the difficulties we weathered! We have made a contri-

23. "Monopoly Purchase and Sale" refers to the state appropriation of key production and retail activity, starting in 1951, that established a government monopoly on essentials such as cotton yarn, cloth, grain, and edible oils. The Great Leap Forward (*da yuejin*) was initiated by Mao in an attempt to realize instant communism in the late 1950s. It resulted in an economic disaster and contributed directly to the death by starvation of tens of millions of people in the early 1960s.

bution—a magnificent one! It's just like that pop song, what's it called again? You know, what is it, the one that says: "The flag of the Republic glistens ever brighter with our blood."[24]

What did I study at university? I suppose you'd call me an economics major. After the victory over the Japanese, I went to various major universities—Peking and Tsinghua—ones that had been resettled in the Yunnan-Guizhou-Sichuan area. I returned to Beiping after being discharged. Our first struggle at the university with the Nationalists was to oppose political screening. I left before that had finished. During my first year in Japanese-occupied Beiping I studied pretty hard, but things were less settled the second year, so I only chose easy courses. It didn't matter what I studied—statistics, management, whatever—as long as they kept me registered and I had a student ID. As long as I had an official status, I could concentrate on my real job for the party.

My standard of living these days? Overall, it's pretty good. They adjust our pensions according to the rate of inflation, and we're always given some of the goodies they divvy up at the end of the year among the central government organs. They want to buy us off, you see. In material terms, I'm satisfied with my situation. Maybe I can't compare with those creatures who've made a fortune out of corrupt or pro-foreign activities. But at least I don't get indigestion, and I can sleep at night.

Where does the extra money come from that they give us at the end of the year? Where do you think? Naturally, it's not from the State Council. Just think of all the companies and other operations they're involved in these days, and they have control over the official seals for approving new projects, too. Why should I ask about the details? If you ask too many questions, you just make trouble for yourself. That's been my problem all along. I've learnt that sometimes you just have to turn a blind eye. And if you do get nosy, they tell you the state only provides 150 liters of petrol for your car per month, the rest comes from such and such a place. The guesthouse you go to in the summer is paid for in the following way, and so on and so forth. There's sure to be some story lurking behind the innocent-looking mah-jongg set we have here in the Old Cadres' Club. So what if you find out all the details? What do you do then? Refuse to play? Refuse to use the car? You can't honestly think all the old cadres like us should be forced to scramble onto crowded buses like everyone else?

24. "Xuerande fengcai" was an army song popular in the late 1980s.

My children are a constant source of vexation. My eldest daughter has a job with some company; at least it's a proper job, and she gets a real wage. But my son is running his own company; he even has his own employees. They're nothing more than speculators trading in various goods. They both started out with decent government jobs: one an assistant section chief, the other a manager. But they resigned. If you ask me, it's all terribly risky. But they won't listen to me; they shout me down. "What do you want us to do? Everyone's going into business. What choice do I have but to start my own company?" I've tried persuading them to be more rational about things, but they laugh in my face: "You keep telling us that going against the tide is a Marxist principle, but we don't believe that crap any more." And I get this from two cadres who were nurtured and trained by the state for years! Can you imagine what kind of fuss people who are already dissatisfied with our party and state would make if they could only hear what I was saying here?

Despite all of this, in general I believe that the future of our Motherland is bright, even if the way ahead is tortuous.[25] There may well be great vicissitudes in the future, but no matter how angry I might get, I'm not scared. I believe the chairman: "If there is an anticommunist right-wing coup, I am confident that they will never rest easy. It will most probably be short-lived."

As a staunch Communist Party man, I can say that as long as I'm alive, there's one right they can never take away from me: I will eat well and sleep soundly, and I will watch them carry out their vile capitalist restoration. I will observe their unease and, what's more, I'll talk about it just as I please!

25. This is a paraphrase of a famous quotation from Mao Zedong.

4

The Union Rep

A Worker against the Party

Guiyang had been rainy for days on end, and we were stuck there with noth-ing to do. When I told a friend I was heading to Xichang to interview old work-ers who'd been moved from Beijing to the satellite launch site there, he told me I didn't have a chance. They were especially tight-lipped, and I didn't have any contacts. Even if I ran into one, the most I would get out of him would be some polite talk. And my coming from Australia, that made it even touchier. They'd all think what I was really up to was digging up the dirt on the recent Austel satellite crash.

"If you've got to interview someone," he said, "head for Zunyi, or Anshun, or Kaili. There's lots of old guys from Beijing. In fact, I can introduce you to this union chairman.

"I met this oddball when we were organizing an art exhibition. We handed him a letter from the Bureau of Culture to hire the factory club. Obviously we were doing him a favor by bringing in some cash, but he still wouldn't agree. Before deciding whether to hire it out to us, he wanted to be sure the exhibition conformed to the Four Cardinal Principles.[1] I told him that it had already passed the censors, but he just had to give it another going over. Sure enough, he was unhappy with the first picture he saw. 'What do you call this?' he asks. 'It's junk. Forget it.'

"Yeah, the picture was junk. A pile of surrealist industrial junk—broken bits

---

1. The Four Cardinal Principles *(sixiang jiben yuanze)* were promulgated by Deng Xiao-ping in 1979 and written into the Chinese constitution. The nation was enjoined to uphold the socialist path, uphold the people's democratic dictatorship, uphold the leadership of the Communist Party, and uphold Marxism-Leninism and Mao Zedong Thought.

and pieces, busted tools. I tried to smooth things over, but it was no good. He said if I could explain what the picture meant, he'd rent to us. I'm thinking to myself, 'If I explained it to you, would you get it?' But that's what he wanted, so I tossed out some generalities just to piss him off. I asked him if he knew what 'transient as the floating clouds' meant. Well, this was it. Old. Wasted. Useless. Our only future was on the junk heap. In the past these things were useful; they had a life. They were human achievements, dreams made real. But that was all wasted. All ideals and achievements end up on the junk heap. After hearing me yakking on like this, you'd think he'd have had enough of transient fleeting clouds. But—would you believe it—the old guy was moved by my speech. He almost cried, and he kept on saying, 'I get it, I get it. Fine. Fine. Go ahead. And put this painting in the main room for me!'

"Later," my friend laughed, "the old guy treated me to a meal and poured out his sorrows. He asked if I had anything against reform. I said I wouldn't dare; the painting didn't mean anything like that. I wouldn't put my head on the chopping block."

He said he had to meet me at the street corner where his apartment block was located because the numbering on the buildings wasn't clear. He had on large gumboots and was wearing an old-style workers' uniform that was nearly as gray as the rainy sky itself. He stood under an equally old-fashioned pink nylon umbrella that he held over us as we walked along the corridor between the gray buildings. When we sat down in his cramped living room, I noticed a crudely written couplet on the wall: "Self-cultivation is for all, the Way can be found at any time." He said, "Take a good look; that's from the hand of the best calligrapher in Guiyang. I chose the couplet after searching in the library for ages; it's a famous line from the Tang poet Yuan Zhen."

Guizhou

China never had that many industrial workers to begin with; that's because we never had much industry to speak of. Ordinary folks farmed the land for a living, and they had to trade their crops for foreign fuel. Even the rickshaws were foreign-made. What mines and railroads there were had only a few workers—and they were just muscle, breaking their backs for a living. There were hardly any real skilled workers. The machinery was all foreign-made, so the workers could only try their luck when it needed repairing. Pretty much all of them did apprenticeships, learning under a master for three and a quarter years. They ended up with a license that was useless if you got injured, fell sick, or decided to quit. That's how you learnt your trade, hand to mouth.

Is what I'm saying okay? When I was young I was a hopeless speaker. But the going was good then, and a dumb mouth wasn't a problem. Later, I was the union chair for a whole decade and I never stopped yakking. On big occasions I'd have to speak in front of meetings of two or three thousand people; when little things came up I'd have a word here and there, giving the members an ideological workover. It was all good training for my mouth.

Only after the People's Republic was founded and they brought in economic planning did you begin to see decent, educated workers who'd gone to school and weren't just apprentices. I was one of them. I went to a technical school. There you didn't just learn how to do your job; you also learned some basic political principles. They even fed you and gave you pocket money. I was eighteen when I graduated, a big lad in my prime. I was a machinist and worked on the Soviet-made lathes donated by Comrade Stalin. We had to learn everything from the Soviets then, copying our Big Brother and even picking up his way of saying things. All the lathes—turners, grinders—were called "mother tools." Those damned Russian words were everywhere, but within a year or two we'd forgotten them all. China's got an ancient culture of its own, and there was already a word for everything you could ever need. The Russkis had great machines, so why not use them? We didn't have to mimic their lingo as well.

I was young then, and there were lots of workers who were older than me when they graduated. I came from a poor family. My dad ran a street stall, and I started school late in life. By the time I finished senior primary I was already sixteen, but instead of going out to find a job I went on to technical school. By now pretty much all of us in that first batch have retired; a lot of us have died. After retiring, some found other work to bring in a little extra money, and some are just taking it easy. I'm happy just taking it easy. Guizhou's got a good climate and it's quiet, so I spend my time raising birds and doing tai chi. I've thought it over, and there's nothing to be gained by going back to Beijing. Everyone's squeezed together there, cooped up in tiny apartments. But there's not many of us who've stuck by the factory. Apart from retirements, there've been retrenchments. In the past two years, lots of people well below retirement age have been retrenched. It's a cruel business, retrenchment; they use it to keep on the fitter and abler workers. No matter what an old worker has done for his country, they just don't want him, and they pack him off home. You call this reform? It's just like capitalist factory management before Liberation.

I was in my prime back then. When I got my first job assignment, there were state-owned, local state-owned, and joint state-private factories, as well as totally private ones. I'd gone to a state-run technical school, so of course I got to go to a state-owned factory. They were the biggest and the best back then. Now all it's all been turned upside down, and the private ones are the top dogs. With the state-owned factories, the bigger they are, the worse shape they're in. They can't even pay wages on time.

In those days everyone was falling over themselves to get Soviet experts. We had no heavy industry ourselves and had to start from scratch. First we tackled basic construction, turning cornfields into construction sites. The foremen and section heads all headed to the Soviet Union to study. Our factory directors learned from their factory directors, and our section heads learned from theirs. It was just like doing an apprenticeship all over again. When we first joined the factory, the party secretary and the head of the specialists' section spoke to us. We were the New Democratic China, they said—back then it still wasn't called socialism—and we workers were now the masters. What we were doing, industrializing China, meant a lot for keeping the world peaceful. Back then, they'd mention peace at the drop of a hat; it was tacked onto everything. Just like *reform* is the buzzword nowadays.

Personally, I'd sum up these decades in just four words: peace, the Leap, revolution, and reform. First there was peace, then the Great Leap Forward; next came the Cultural Revolution—family planning, practicing hygiene, smashing and looting, everything was part of carrying out revolution. When the Cultural Revolution ran out of steam, then came the reform we've got now. Now everything's about reform.

From the start, I was always pretty lucky; never really tripped up. And that's because I've always stayed loyal to the party. Whatever the party told me to do, I put my heart and soul into it. The Great Leap or the Four Cleans or whatever,[2] I was always in the thick of it. Whenever the party told

2. The Four Cleans (*si qing*) of 1964 was a rural purge of party leaders who were said to be "taking the capitalist road," that is, pursuing market-oriented policies that had been instituted to help the nation recover from the ravages of the Great Leap Forward. It was a rural rehearsal of the Cultural Revolution.

me to put my shoulder to the wheel, I did. Even when they made me union chairman, running around for everybody, acting the fat-cat cadre who had to take all their shit, I didn't hesitate then either. I joined up with the party in '56 and have always been a believer. Without the Communist Party, the best I could have been was a bum with a street stall, never even sure where my next meal was coming from. To me, the Communist Party's not just a party; it's my friend, and I've got to stick by it. So I've always been an activist, whether it's been for high-speed cutting methods, technical improvements, "grasping revolution and advancing production"—I've collected a pile of awards for it all. I must have been through dozens of political campaigns, and I was an activist every time. Nowadays people take me for a fool, just some old bastard who blindly stuck by the party. They think I'm the fool and that those slick organization climbers are the smart ones.

But the party also looked after me. I always got the promotions, never got demoted. In '63 I made level 8 seniority, and back then there weren't many people of my age at that level. And I worked my way up. Promotions then were by exam, not like it is now—by personal connections, so you need a private backer to give the okay. They considered your politics as well as your technical skills. So even if you did your job well but were always mouthing off at the party, you wouldn't just miss out on a promotion—you'd be struggled. For workers, level 8 was as high as you could get. The monthly wage was over a hundred yuan, as much as any section-head cadre.

But back then people had the right idea. They weren't competing for money but to make the biggest contribution. There were model workers for every job. "Emulate, learn from, catch up with, help, and surpass" was the slogan we went by. Not like these days when there's only one standard to judge everything: money. If you're rich, everything's great; if you're not, then everything's crap. I'll give you an example. There was one old worker in our section who really wasn't on top of his job. He never got any better at it, and he couldn't even put two words together. He slaved all day just to knock over his work quota. He'd only just made it to level 5 at retirement. The way people see things now, he was just a big, clumsy no-hoper waiting to be retrenched. But back then he was made a model worker. That's because this guy never took any leave, so naturally he was made a model for attendance. Just being in a workshop for years on end, always changing shifts, can affect your health; but he never took any leave. That's some achievement, but people now couldn't give a damn. They'd say he was only in it for the money, scared that his pay would be docked if he took time off. But that's just sneering at the way we were back then from today's viewpoint, because then they didn't dock your pay if you went off sick.

Being a model worker got you material and moral benefits. As well as the bonuses, you got a red silk flower pinned on your chest and your name went up on the honor roll. It wasn't just about money then. Old workers still keep their certificates and banners. They're worthless in monetary terms, so why keep them? Because they're reminders that once upon a time respect was more important than money, that we led a decent life.

After the spring of '65, lots of factories were moved inland as part of the country's preparations for possible war. Our factory also had to send a group to the Third Front, and we began shipping workers and equipment down to Guizhou. I'd never been to Guizhou, but I knew it was bad news. In Qing times they exiled criminals to the Guizhou-Yunnan borderlands. Still, as soon as they called on party members to set an example by signing up, I did. It turned out to be just a formality, though. Our bosses told us at the mobilization rally, "If you sign up, you mightn't have to go, and if you don't sign up, you still might have to go. So signing up is a test of your attitude, to see if you're totally in step with Party Central and Chairman Mao. But whether you end up going or not will depend on what's needed." Anyway, since I'd signed up, I mentally prepared myself for the move. And that's how it turned out: our whole workshop was moved. Before we left, they promoted me to technician level and made me deputy foreman; that was probably because I'd passed their test. Up to then I'd always been a section chief; now I was deputy, a cadre.

Guizhou really is a dump, and back then it was worse, much worse. Just like the saying: never three clear days, never three level feet of land, and nobody with three cents to their name. As part of the war preparations, our factory was hidden up in the hills. There were no villages or shops anywhere; it was just a wilderness. Our workshop was hidden in a cave. It all turned out to be a huge waste of money and effort, of course, but nobody understood that then. They reasoned that building the Third Front was Chairman Mao's idea. By sticking factories up in the hills, we'd be able to fight a guerrilla and tunnel war when the foreign devils finally hit. It was a sure bet; the chairman couldn't be wrong. But when the Cultural Revolution broke out, not even the basic building work had been finished, and the factory soon stopped production—though the truth was that it had never really started up. Anyway, we weren't working.

During the Cultural Revolution I was the puniest of "power holders," but still I got denounced as a "revisionist black element" and a scab. Later, things really heated up; the factory's leaders refused to go quietly, and the two factions beat each other to a standstill. They were going at it tooth and nail, and no one could be bothered with me. So I sneaked off to Beijing. There was no lack of escapees then. I missed out on all the fighting and killing by sneaking off like that.

I stayed around in Beijing for over two years. Got bored sick. The only entertainment then was the eight model operas. You couldn't even do a little tai chi, as it was one of the Four Olds.[3] All that was left were the calisthenics over the loudspeakers. It's easy to get sick when you're bored like that, and I got a kidney inflammation. After that my blood pressure shot up, too. Here I was, still in my thirties and already with high blood pressure.

After the PLA set up revolutionary committees in the factories, I was summoned back. My own inclination was to stay put, and there were certainly people who just loafed around in Beijing and wouldn't budge. But I was a party member, and the rule is that the individual must obey the organization: sick or not, I had to go back. Actually, they'd mobilized us to return before that. When Premier Zhou met the heads of Red Guard factions, he always went on about how all the people from the Third Front who'd run off to Beijing had to return and carry out the revolution. Back then all the leaders' speeches floated around in leaflets; you could believe them or not. I knew this one was real enough, but I ignored it anyway. Guizhou was out-and-out bedlam; the fighting never let up, and I was scared stiff they'd do me in as well. And I had this kidney inflammation. So I stayed put.

When I did finally go back, Three-Way Combinations were the big thing, but I wasn't a capitalist-roader or a revolutionary smasher, so I was stuck in limbo.[4] So they made me deputy head of a production team. The head was a PLA rep. But there wasn't actually any work for us to do. We were supposed to handle production, but the factory wasn't making any-

3. The Four Olds (si jiu)—old ideas, old culture, old customs, and old habits—were denounced by Cultural Revolution leaders in 1966, as the Red Guard frenzy to eliminate all traces of the old and bourgeois China spread in Beijing and then throughout the country.

4. The Three-Way Combinations (san jiehe) were a political arrangement during the Cultural Revolution that consisted of representatives of the revolutionary organizations, leading cadres, and the People's Liberation Army. Capitalist-roaders (zou zipai) were party members who were deemed guilty of following a bourgeois political line, and revolutionary smashers were their rebellious enemies.

thing, so I was left twiddling my thumbs. Here was this factory, over two thousand workers—all idle. The most work we got was knocking together some bits and pieces for the Second Artillery Battalion and the atomic testing site. These jobs were right up my alley. We built the scaffolding for China's first atom bomb test. That was when we were still in Beijing. We built it there, did a trial assembly, and, once we were absolutely sure there were no problems, tore it down and shipped it to the test site. They put it up again with the atomic bomb on top. And when that bomb blew, the whole thing went up in smoke.

Our factory took on jobs set down for it in the state plan. If we weren't given assignments, there wasn't enough work to go around. We got used to that, it went on for years on end; it was nothing special. Still, it'd be unfair to say we leeched off the state. We'd been moved there to prepare for war. It wasn't our fault if the Yankee imperialists or the Soviet revisionists didn't invade. And if we didn't get state support, how would all those workers get by? It all goes back to the ancient rule: "Soldiers might only fight for a day, but they must be fed for a thousand." We were military-industrial workers, and looking after us was the same thing as keeping soldiers ready for battle.

Running a country is just like running a big family. There's enough to go around for food and clothes so long as you stick to a budget and don't go overboard. Taking care of military-industrial workers was always part of the plan, and the costs had to be taken into account. Isn't there a rush now to take out home insurance? Well, for a country to take care of its military-industrial workers is just like taking out home insurance. You don't worry about the price of doing it but about the price of not doing it. You shouldn't get wound up about the cost. As I see it, our problem isn't whether or not the boss can afford to pay up; it's that our country simply isn't budgeting right. The party leadership and the State Council don't plan anything; they're not taking charge of the family. Back then, they had a plan for everything, and you spent according to the plan. Sure there were cock-ups, but at least the whole country wasn't a complete shambles. Just look at it now. Nothing is planned. We just throw up our hands and let the market go to it, liberalizing so that workers are not even getting paid. You tell me what sense there is in that.

It's not that I'd oppose reform. But I can't figure out just what this reform adds up to. Do you call it reform? Don't they say that the test of reform is in the results? Well, one of the outcomes has been to hypnotize workers with money. Their lives are getting more and more empty; now everything's about money. There's no sense of duty or being the country's masters. What reform amounts to is that if you're rich, great! But the nation isn't rich. They've changed all the rules. "There's no money, but even if there was, we wouldn't spend it on you. Look after yourselves, live by your own wits. We don't give a damn if you're military-industrial workers. We're not paying out for you any more." It's getting tougher and tougher for the factory to scrape by. The workers, the masters of the country, aren't in charge any more; now they have to scrounge around for scraps; and a perfectly good factory has been taken over by slick operators who know how to hustle for work. Your politics, or whether or not you can do your job, doesn't matter—even if you're a hopeless case, it doesn't matter—just as long as you can drum up business so the factory can pay out wages and bonuses. If you can do that, you're top stuff, a reformer. You call that reform?

I became union chairman just when the ground rules were changing. In '83 there was a push to promote younger cadres. The old chairman was a Yan'an-era cadre going on seventy. He got the shove, and I was given the job. I was forty-eight then, a deputy in the production office. Apart from a stint as section head—and I guess a section head is still really a worker—I'd never been head of anything, always a deputy. But when they made me union chairman I wasn't nervous. I knew that union work just needs the gift of the gab. The only thing they judge you by is that the workers don't raise hell—and they're not going to do that.

I've thought about union work long and hard. I've never seen what capitalist countries are like, but I know the basic setup. The factory is owned by the capitalist, the union is the workers' organization, and the two of them march to different drummers. The capitalist's job is to keep a lid on things; the union's job is to stir things up. They slug it out and eventually strike a deal. For us, the party and the state represent the fundamental interests of the working class. The factory belongs to them, so the union is still just a supporting act, no matter what. It's got to sing to the party's tune and can't ever vie for power—can't agitate for independence or undermine the regime. So our unions are just props, and the chairman is just an extra, at best. It's just like the Beijing opera *Accord between the General and Prime Minister*. The union chairman is a bit player, not the star. When a bit player tries to become a star, he's sure to be killed off and pushed into the wings.

That's how it goes. I love Beijing opera—that explains all the theatrical lingo—and that's partly why I was made chairman. A big part of the chair's job is organizing entertainment for the members, and that was just my thing. But that wasn't the main reason. They didn't have to spell out why they'd picked me to take over. It was because they wanted to shunt me aside and give my old job to someone who'd do their reforms for them. The union chair is elected at a meeting of all the workers' reps. But that's all a charade, a prop like the union. The party committee of the factory decides who the union chairman will be and sends its decision up to a higher committee for approval. So when I was nominated, the vote didn't matter. I was the only candidate, and it was me no matter what; it was a matter of just going through the motions.

Being chairman's a lousy job. Keeps you running around in circles. In theory, you're in charge of everything under you, but in actual fact you don't have a say in anything. Having nothing on your hands is okay, it's fine. But if you do want work, there's lots of it—divorces, fights over welfare, disputes about allowances, family planning quotas, registering wives and family members for household permits, New Year's and holiday dinners, organizing parties—they need you to lend a hand for all those kinds of things. Even with four pairs of hands, you couldn't handle it all—but one hand is all you really need, to hand it on to someone else. Want welfare? No money. Divorce? Go to court. Residence permit? Go find the police. If someone refuses to do their job, I can't really do anything, either—best if you send some gifts and try to get things done through unofficial channels. Really, though, I like helping people. I put in a lot of effort to do everything I can for them. Even if people these days are more selfish than we were, it's tough going for ordinary workers. In the past, things were organized; there was somebody to take care of everything. Now there's new people in charge. Apart from making money, the bosses try their level best not to get involved in anything. They're not bothered about what they don't see. To them, a worker is just a worker, just labor power. At most the leaders might go and see a worker who's seriously ill in hospital, or give his body a send-off when he dies. Even then, they still treat it as a burden, something to be fobbed off on someone else. They all say they're too busy, pass the buck, so you've got to pester them to do their job. They only do it when you beg them to. They're all reformers, though; all they think about is setting up joint ventures and making money. They have no sense of comradeship with the workers, no feeling for the proletariat. If this is what society has come to, workers have to become selfish. It's a dog-eat-dog world now.

The union never had much say over things like family planning, labor insurance, housing allocation, and such. The factory has offices to look after these things, so we've always been left to do the odd jobs—things like maintaining the bathhouse, the canteen, the club, and the library. Now we don't even run the bathhouse. All I've got left is a library that nobody wants. The bathhouse was leased out and is open for outside business. The club's also been leased out and screens videos all day. Tickets for the dance nights bring in some money. The canteen's the same; now it's run as a restaurant and handles its own takings. Once all of this was part of workers' welfare from the state. When you reform them into businesses, aren't you robbing the workers in broad daylight?

But what can I do about it? Accept it, that's all. The ones who've taken out leases on these things are the success stories now; they've got the support of the party secretary and the factory director. So what's the use kicking up a fuss? It wouldn't even cross my mind to undermine the party and the state. If I did go against them, wouldn't that make me an agent of turmoil?[5] But these reformers who are enjoying all the limelight are nothing like cadres. They're a shady bunch—dining out all the time, playing mahjongg, taking their female secretaries out for those karaoke sessions. And it still calls itself a Communist Party!

In the past weren't we always shouting that we had to "oppose and resist revisionism"? I'd say that this garbage is revisionism.

We've already had the share system for ages. Our factory was real keen on this particular innovation. But, remember, when you're desperately ill, you'll try any quack remedy. Like I said, there wasn't much work to do when we were a military industry. After we shifted to civilian production, there still wasn't any steady work coming in. We'd do anything as long as it could turn a buck. Mostly it was producing cheapo-brand car bodies and chassis. There still wasn't enough work; we just had to make do. After the turmoil of '89, nobody was buying anything; even when they did, they wouldn't pay up. All the state-owned firms were tangled up in triangular debt. You know: I owe you, you owe him, he owes me. We're all caught in this debt spiral, and going to court over it is a waste of time because everybody's broke anyway. By '90 or '91 the factory couldn't even afford to pay basic wages. The workers were all sent home on leave. Ours wasn't the only factory. We're all in the same boat. All of China's large and medium enterprises got caught in the same mess, and nothing's changed since then.

5. *Dongluan,* a term used to describe both the ructions of the Cultural Revolution era and the mass protests of 1989.

My wife works in a woolen mill, and things are even tougher there. A while back they handed everyone a pile of yarn and told them to get out and sell it. Whatever you managed to sell counted as your wages. They gave their workers stuff that their marketing division couldn't get rid of after running all over the country trying to offload it. And these workers who'd never sold a thing in their lives were suddenly expected to become salespeople, and they didn't have a clue. They had to sell the stuff on the sly as if they'd pinched it. They didn't have retail licenses, so they were scared stiff the police and commerce officials would catch them and squeeze them for a fine. Later they ran out of yarn, and so the factory started handing out wool ends instead. Who's going to buy wool ends? That's the raw material that hasn't even been made into yarn. What the hell are you supposed to do with it? Start your own spinning mill? We used the wool at home to make four big quilts. They're really warm, but they weigh a ton.

Nowadays, even the weather stinks. For years we never had floods in Guizhou. There's not three feet of flat land, so how could it flood? But in '91, when everybody least expected it, there was a huge flood. Just when everyone was making a fuss about resisting the drought, we were hit by a once-in-a-century flood. That was in July, when I was on holiday, staying with my in-laws. They said it would never touch them. They lived on the third floor and couldn't be flooded. But the same night they told me this, the water reached the third floor. Zunyi was covered by a sea of water. Now, seriously, Zunyi's no ordinary place. It's where Chairman Mao was elevated to supreme leadership. Before the Zunyi Conference, Chairman Mao wasn't the chairman, just Committee Member Mao. Zunyi was where he assumed the throne. I'm not one for superstitions or rumors, but they say the floods hit because the old man was angry. He sent the flood to warn us to stop messing around.

Not long after the flood, our factory was "reassigned and reintegrated." That's a new expression. Sounds harmless enough, but it means being swallowed up by a big conglomerate. It's surrendering to the market and ditching the socialist planned economy. Anyway, we became a subsidiary plant of some motor vehicle corporation. These days you count yourself lucky if someone wants to swallow you up. There are lots of factories out there begging to merge with profitable enterprises, but nobody wants them. Soon after the merger, they started sacking people; pardon me, I mean "rationalizing." But that's just another way of saying sacking people. Old, sick, and disabled people are the first to go. The most they get is a small payout, then it's thank you and out the door. Struggling along on bald tires and worn-out shoes, you're only good for the junk heap. All those contributions you've made for the nation, being the class that is master of the country—that's all gone now. These days you've got to live by your own wits. In the first year the motor corporation offered shares, and of course we went along with it. You've got no choice when you're not your own person. But I'll tell you, the whisper is that there've been closed-door meetings where they've predicted that the market will take a dive this year. There's a glut of vehicles, and the corporation—not just the factory—will be hit hard.

Now I'm still the chairman, but it's a sham. I'm up for retirement in a year, and I won't let them get rid of me a day sooner. But I'm not on the job either. I'm at home sick with high blood pressure. It's not that I'm malingering; the doctor made me take leave. Anyway, all I've got to look after is an office and a derelict library. Nobody cares if I show up or not. If there's any business to deal with, there's someone else in the office—they haven't all dropped off the perch yet. These young union cadres love to drum up business for themselves. They always want a say in management. They think they can more or less pass for bigwigs themselves, spokesmen for the working class. If that's what they want, let them go for it. Wasn't it all over the papers last year about how a union in Yunnan sued a factory on behalf of its workers, and won? These youngsters felt their backbones stiffen when they read that—they were thinking, we unions have a job to do and the power to do it. Delusions of grandeur! That court ruling was a stunt to keep the workers happy. How could it be true? "Stability and unity" means keeping a lid on everything.[6] No one can make waves. That's the real principle behind politics in China today.

Way back, I learned to take things the way they are. I'll stay on as the union chair till my time's up, and when I'm put out to pasture I'll become chair of the poker society. The retired cadres have their own activities center, but the union club has been leased out, so the retired workers have nowhere to go. They were bored witless, and so they found a nice sunny wall where they play cards. They say that when I retire I can be the chairman of the board. That's how it is. I've been loyally following the party all my life, and now it's come to this. Who'd have thought it?

When they introduced this share system, they allotted me some first-issue

---

6. Stability and unity (*anding tuanjie*) were promoted by the party after protests in 1986 and 1989 and used as an excuse to crush opponents and dissenting opinions.

shares. Do you know what first-issue shares are? I didn't. Anyway, I didn't want them. I told them I wanted none of it. I couldn't get what those flashy pieces of paper were for. I didn't want them. They sell you some lousy shares, then tell you you're part owner of the factory, get out there and work. Who would be dumb enough to believe this is still socialism?

For me, the 1950s were better than now; so were the '60s. That was when the workers really were in charge.

5

The People's Deputy
A Congresswoman

We met in her high-rise apartment on a hot and humid day. She was dressed in the outfit favored by Beijing's suburban high-school teachers: a sky-blue, short-sleeved blouse, light gray slacks, and sandals. The difference between her and a teacher was that she didn't gesticulate when she talked, although throughout our conversation she constantly used pencils and pens, a magnifying glass, and tea glasses to represent the people, places, or events that she was describing.

Like all the deputies to the National People's Congress, she entered the Great Hall of the People without even the pretense of an election campaign. Although she's a parliamentarian with Chinese characteristics, she's distinctive in a number of ways . . .

The first thing I noticed when I sat down in the Great Hall of the People was how hard the seats were. They were not nearly as soft as I'd imagined. Honestly, I'm not joking, that really was my first reaction. The next thing I realized was that there was no portrait of Chairman Mao above the rostrum. Before then I'd never given a moment's thought to the inside of the Great Hall. Why on earth should I? But I'd always had this impression that there was a portrait of Chairman Mao front and center. Later, I learned that it had been replaced by the national emblem after the first session of the National People's Congress. After all that, I was lost in my own thoughts.

Are you recording what I'm saying? I'm not scared of being published. Now that I'm a member of parliament, my biggest worry is that nobody ever hears what I have to say.

Anyway, so there I was lost in my own thoughts, and in particular I was thinking about the Communist Party's Ninth Congress. It was 1969, and I was still at university, though there weren't any classes. The factional battles had just eased up, and the propaganda teams had us studying Mao Zedong Thought day in, day out, doing "struggle-criticism-transformation."[1] We were to vote for delegates to the congress, and lists of local candidates were announced by the leadership; we debated them at what seemed like endless meetings and then sent the list back up. Eventually, Party Central issued the final list of national candidates for us, the broad masses of the people, to discuss. In due course this too was sent back up to the center. It went back and forth like that a few more times. No one had any idea who these candidates were, but we were expected to attend all the meetings nonetheless. Even non–party members like me—including all the grannies from the neighborhood—had to be there. It really was democracy run riot, nitpicking over each and every delegate this way.

Later it struck me just what a terrible thing it was, a mockery of public opinion and a violation of the sincerity of party members. It was sham democracy because there was a rule handed down to us along with the list of candidates: "I will trust whoever Chairman Mao trusts." To object to anyone on the list was tantamount to opposing the chairman himself. That would have been absolutely suicidal. So, each step of the way, all the candidates Party Central had put on the list were approved unanimously. But even after all that rigmarole, the lists were sent down to us yet again; the line was that Chairman Mao wanted us to look them over one more time. Naturally, they were endorsed unanimously. This time around, and this was the clincher, everyone had the right to discuss the party delegates. In other words, the Party Congress had taken over the functions of the National People's Congress as well. They had the gall to say this was an "expression of the monolithic leadership of the party." In effect, the National People's

1. After the tumult of the first years of the Cultural Revolution, institutions of higher education were occupied by Mao Zedong Thought Propaganda Teams made up of workers and soldiers ostensibly sent to restore order. According to the Communist Party's 1966 decision on the Cultural Revolution, "struggle-criticism-transformation" *(dou pi gai)* was an avowed process of purification that entailed "the *struggle* and overthrow of those persons in authority who are taking the capitalist road, the *criticism* and repudiation of reactionary bourgeois academic 'authorities' and the ideology of the bourgeoisie and all other exploiting classes, and the *transformation* of education, literature, and art and all other parts of the superstructure which do not correspond with the socialist economic base."

Congress, the highest elected organ of government, was cast aside, as was the nominal head of state, the state president who headed the National People's Congress. This all justified Mao's eventual claim at the Ninth Party Congress that "our power has been given to us by the people, by over 95 percent of the nation." That is to say that the chairman of the party's Central Committee did not have just party members to thank for his position of power. The whole country had taken part in the discussions leading up to the congress; that meant that his position didn't even need to be rubber-stamped.

The Ninth Congress was the darkest page in the history of the Chinese Communists. Mao even had a clause inserted into the Party Constitution to the effect that he had personally designated Lin Biao to be his successor. It goes without saying that this proposal too "received the unanimous endorsement of the entire nation."

So there I was sitting in the Great Hall musing about all of this. Then I started thinking about how, within the space of four short decades, the capital city of Beijing had been transformed from being a cultural and political center of just one million people into this congested industrial city of over ten million people, its skies forever blackened by toxic pollution. Naturally, being in the construction industry myself, I'd figured out the answer long ago. We all knew what had gone wrong, even if nobody was willing to say it out loud. It all started in the early 1950s, when the party leadership declared that "the proletariat must dominate the population of the capital." I don't have to explain how they formulated that theory, do I? Later they learned that there could be another set of rules. They started with general elections—not direct elections—democratic consultation, fixed-candidate elections. Then they created a National People's Congress—not really a parliament—one that was stacked with progressive workers from all fields and ethnic minorities and a few other characters, including the relatives of the last emperor and stooges from Hong Kong.

I was sitting there mulling over all of this just before the official opening of the congress. I couldn't help it getting entangled in all of these thoughts because that was the story of my life up to that point.

Until I found myself sitting in the Great Hall of the People, I'd really never been a political animal. I'm a civil engineer by training. I'd never been a people's delegate; I'd never wielded so much power. My job was to try to build the best housing possible in the best places available, and I loved it. Not that I could do much good there, either. In the past ten years, tower blocks have mushroomed all around Beijing's public parks: the Forbidden

City, the Temple of Heaven, the North Sea Park, and especially the Summer Palace. It's a serious problem. Just go to the highest point in the city, Coal Hill, or the Fragrant Buddha Pavilion in the suburbs and look around. You're surrounded by huge, gray matchboxes on every side, blocks of twenty or more stories. To the layperson, urban planning might seem simple enough, but it's not. It not quite a science and not quite an art; and it's inextricably bound up with politics. Fortunately, I don't have the right qualifications to be in the planning game. If I were I'm sure I'd go crazy. I'm a perfectionist, and no matter what I do it's got to be the best. It's an irritating flaw, I know. There are only two kinds of civil engineers. One is the perfectionist. The other belongs to the school of "it's all the same pile of dirt to me," people who are happy to fly by the seat of their pants, satisfied with the buildings they put up as long as they don't fall down. There's no such thing as the commonsense civil works engineer somewhere between these extremes. Perfection is impossible; if you strive for it, you've lost before you even start. You're always in retreat—from Waterloo to Paris, then from Paris to Elba, and finally to solitary exile on some tiny island. Every step of the way is a recognition of defeat. Even so, you still believe that next time you'll do better.

As for politicians, they have one simple ground rule: we need to maintain stability, and stability means more housing. "I can't let the people kick up a stink because of housing problems. So, sorry, I couldn't care less about all your expert mumbo-jumbo, that stuff about high-level winds and illumination, or even emergency evacuations and fire prevention. And this scenic corridor business that you worry so much about doesn't mean anything to me." That's the rationale of a politician. Sure, in the first decade of the People's Republic they built the Great Hall and the History Museum—those and the other Ten Great Buildings of the Great Leap Forward—but it was all window dressing. In the same period of time, the average living space per person in Beijing shrank from 4.7 to 3.2 square meters. Later, in the 1960s and '70s, it crept back up by one tiny percentage point, but, right up into the 1980s, when you started seeing these high-rises being crammed together, things were actually worse than before 1949. Now, after a decade of mushrooming high-rises and the urban sprawl eating up farm land—and all of it is good land, mind you—we've just about reached seven square meters per person. A great achievement without doubt, but it's come at a high cost. Whether you think the losses outweigh the gains or vice versa depends entirely on your point of view. Objectively speaking, I'm one of the winners. I've got a three-bedroom apartment, and finally I have my own work space. But no matter what direction I look in, I'm surrounded by gray walls. In Chinese we say that someone who has no place to turn "bumps into the four walls."[2] Now we're blocked in on six sides: four walls plus the floor and ceiling. I'm standing on the ceiling of an eleventh-floor apartment, and above me is the floor of a thirteenth-floor apartment.

Ordinary people are nowhere near as well off as me, though. Seven square meters per person means that a family of three can barely even squeeze into the tiniest one-room apartment. That's why illegal constructions have sprung up along every street in the old city. Apart from the hundred or so traditional-style courtyard houses that have been put under official protection, all the other old courtyard compounds in Beijing are full of jerry-built shacks.

But the Chinese are a patient people. I'd imagine that in any other country people would have been up in arms about all this long ago.

I've lost count of all the elections for people's deputies I've voted in. One every few years, I guess. I remember the very first election well enough. I was a youngster then, still in primary school, and it wasn't for a people's deputy. We were electing our own class monitor. Everyone was handed a ballot paper, but there was only one candidate and he'd been selected by the teacher. He was a born organizer who did well in school; he also came from a pretty good class background. Naturally, he was elected without a hitch. It was a fixed-candidate election, with only the one name on the ballot paper; how could there be a hitch? So I've known ever since I was small that elections are only a formality, a show in which my vote didn't really count. That's the setup we've grown accustomed to and accepted; for us it's a sensible system, one we've been used to all our lives.

The first time I voted for a people's deputy was in our local district. The candidate was a librarian at our university, an "advanced worker." I think she was something in the Women's Federation, too. Anyway none of the university students knew much about her, but that didn't matter, and she was elected without question. That was the last I ever had to think about her. For all I know, she was elected in just the same way from the district to the next level up, and then to the next, right on up to the National People's Congress. That was the Third National People's Congress session in 1964. There's a line people use about indirect elections, they're like buy-

2. *Si chu peng bi.*

ing an old cow blindfolded: you can't tell whether it's really a heifer or a bull.

Now things are gradually changing. The major development is that the scope of direct elections is wider than ever before. People's deputies at county level and below are now elected directly. The National People's Congress has five levels: villages and towns, counties and county-level cities, provincial-level cities, then provincial and national levels. Nowadays there are direct elections for the first two. Another big change is the introduction of multicandidate elections. There are a few more candidates, maybe one or two, than there are places to be filled. Multicandidate elections may look like only small-change democracy, but they've made a difference all the same. At least it's given certain people the fright of their lives.

Still, it's hard to think of any really major changes in the actual electoral process itself. Some might say there have been, but I wouldn't know anything about that.

No, there haven't been any basic changes, none at all. As I see it, there are only two ways to make fundamental changes: to introduce universal direct ballots and allow election campaigning. Up to now no one's been game to touch either of these big issues. I'm particularly interested in the question of election campaigns. A multicandidate election with no campaign is not a real election. It's illogical. I'm an engineer, and I don't have a head for politics, but I do have a good grasp of logic. I know that not even the greatest genius can build an illogical house—one with the front door on the roof. If they did, sooner or later it'd have to be demolished.

I'm also interested in direct elections, but I keep a level head about it. Put yourself in my shoes. It's obvious that full, direct elections, if introduced immediately—that is to say permitting the elections of deputies to the National People's Congress through Western-style elections—would be like trying to shore up a tottering building. Nothing would be left standing after you'd finished. No, I don't want to indulge in simplistic language to discuss such a serious issue. It's not a matter of whether or not you "dare to," or "can," or whether it's "good" or not. Simplifications only encourage crude emotionalism. Certainly you can accuse the Communists of not daring to introduce direct elections, but they'll reply that it's not a matter of not daring, it's just that they can't. Bickering over who had the guts to do it would be endless. And in the midst of it all some compromiser would pop up to say that it's not that we don't dare or can't, but that direct elections are just plain bad. Such carrying on is completely pointless.

Of course, I think direct elections are a great idea. I might sound disingenuous here, especially since I wasn't elected by a direct vote. After all, if we had that system I would never have got into the National People's Congress. Nonetheless, I think direct elections are a good thing. Here we are in a new century, and, regardless of whether you're talking about federations, constitutional monarchies, democratic republics, or whatever, they all have direct elections of some kind. Even countries that still have big problems with democracy and human rights, or difficulties with such basic things as feeding and clothing their people, at least they have direct elections. Of course, we can claim that China's different, that we're a socialist country with a people's democratic dictatorship. But what does that really mean? Marxism-Leninism comes down in favor of rule by the majority; it states that elections must guarantee freedom of expression and a free vote. Even Lenin argued that the highest legislative body should be elected through universal, direct, and fair elections. "Only universal, direct, fair elections can be said to be democratic elections." Those are Lenin's words. Let me check my notebook. Yes, here it is: *The Complete Works of V. I. Lenin,* volume 18, page 273. Now, upholding Marxism-Leninism is one of the Four Cardinal Principles laid out at the beginning of the Chinese Constitution. So you can't say that Marxism-Leninism is wrong here.

But no matter how attractive the idea is, I don't think we're going to be having direct elections here any time soon. I'm realistic. This isn't like building houses; you can't demand perfection here.

"China is the most populous country on earth, and at present holding direct elections would be extremely difficult. As for equal representation, peasants would make up 80 percent of the population, and so the majority of deputies would also be peasants, and that would not be any good. Such an outcome would be out of keeping with the present trends and requirements of the revolution. Furthermore, I would argue that, given the current educational level of the people, it would be impossible to have elections by secret ballots."

This is the standard response to the issue that is taken from a speech made by Premier Zhou Enlai in the early 1950s. Now, half a century on, it still holds true. It is possible that China will always be the most populous country in the world and that peasants will always be the majority of the population. And there will always be illiteracy. No, I'm not being sarcastic. Zhou Enlai presented the facts fair and square, and facts they remain. Talking about it now makes me even more aware that they remain the facts.

However, I still believe that the principles of universality, directness, and equality in elections are basically right, even if you only think of them as window dressing. China can't go on forever selling itself short on the standards of truly democratic elections.

As I said, I'm a perfectionist. Now that I'm a deputy, I want to do the best I can. To start with, I've been reading up on certain issues and thinking them over. The only thing that some deputies can remember, apart from the fact that they're "parliamentarians," is that they're protected by parliamentary privilege. The minute they open their mouths, you can tell they're amateurs. I don't want to be like that. But the more you look into things, the more there is to learn; it's a bit overwhelming. I've really been floundering. Perhaps I'll eventually have to beat a retreat to Elba myself.

The National People's Congress only meets once a year, unless there are extraordinary circumstances. When we're in session, we listen to all the government reports, review the budget and any proposed laws, approve official appointments and dismissals, and so on. We pass resolutions on all those things, of course. It's all decided by ballot. Apart from the annual congress session, delegates also make tours of inspection that mean we spend a couple of weeks trotting round the country "investigating things." All told, we must spend about thirty days or so, forty at most, on congress-related business. For the other ten or so months we work at our regular jobs. Peasants go back to the fields, workers go back to smelting steel, and soldiers go back to war. Hang on, that's not right; there are no wars to fight at the moment. Okay, soldiers go back to *prepare* for war. That makes all of us nothing more than amateur parliamentarians. It would be pretty much impossible to expect us to be engaged fully in the running of government.

I feel there are three pressing problems that need to be addressed in our system. Unlike direct elections, these issues aren't an ideological minefield. Even some simple changes could make a big difference.

In the first instance, our "parliament" is simply too big. There are close to three thousand deputies. Even if each one was only allowed to speak for one hour and we met every day for a year without a break, still not everyone would get a turn. Three thousand divided by 365 equals 8.2 hours. Calculating it on the basis of an eight-hour working day, that still leaves you 0.2 hours short every day. And that's with all the holidays and weekends thrown in. It would be impossible to put in even more overtime. As I said, the congress meets for only a few weeks every year, twenty days. The present solution is to divide the congress into three tiers: the congress in plenary session, provincial-level delegation meetings, and small-group meetings. The only real chance a deputy gets to speak is at the group meetings. There are hardly any opportunities to address the plenary session.

The exchange of information between small groups is managed entirely through internal congress bulletins. That means you might speak for ages on a particular topic at your group meeting, but when it appears in the final briefing bulletin it's only a few short lines, sometimes not even half a line. "Deputies Zhang, Li, Zhao and Liu believe that . . . ," followed by some wishy-washy summary. Some deputies will have spent the year slaving away working at the grassroots level and will have a lot to get off their chests. They prepare their speeches with great care and energy, weighing up every phrase and idea. But after they've spoken, all they get is one line in a mountain of documents that most deputies don't even have the time to plow through.

Furthermore, the National People's Congress is the highest organ of government; it shouldn't be a museum for the humanities. Now, I know that it's crazy to agonize over the background of every single deputy. And it certainly makes sense for each region and ethnic group to have their own deputies, but I don't see why we need to be any more specialized than that. Film actors, stage performers, Beijing opera singers, Western opera singers, folk singers, ballet dancers, I've seen them all in this congress. I suppose I've seen all the celebrities I've ever heard of in this one place. Now it might look like broad democracy, you know with deputies from every field in attendance. But in reality these people don't have a clue about even the most basic issues, like how the price adjustment index is calculated. Nor do I, for that matter! If this is the highest organ of government, then it should stick to the practicalities. It should be organized along the lines you use when building a factory workshop; you need to place maximum stress on rationality. The way things are at present, with a congress that's this big and clumsy, one with so much haphazard duplication, you're undermining the whole effect of the thing. That's why I think the number of deputies needs to be significantly reduced. Get rid of all of us, and bring in deputies who can serve full-time for a term. Give them the chance and the time to speak out and debate. Introduce professional politicians, and get rid of "dilettante deputies" like me.

Moreover, ordinary citizens don't have the right to sit in and observe the proceedings. Special seats are set aside for official observers, but they're not open to the public. Whatever the reasons for this, I don't think it's a good thing. People can only visit the Great Hall of the People when we're not in session, and just look around an empty hall—and they have to buy a ticket even to do that! It's farcical, isn't it?

Apart from everything else, we need access to a good library. Maybe I'm being too much of an egghead just mentioning this. But if I want to look something up during the congress, it's extraordinarily difficult. We simply don't have access to adequate information resources, and that hampers our ability to review proposals effectively. Many documents are only issued while congress is sitting, and none of us is a walking encyclopedia. How am I supposed to vote on something I don't even understand? For instance, what's the definition of "negative growth"? Or what do you make of the rule that candidates for vice-premier must have "qualifications equivalent to a college graduate"? If you've got a degree, then you're a graduate. If you haven't, then you're not, no matter what you say. But if you are a "college graduate" but you don't have a bachelor's degree, what does that "equivalent" really mean? We need to be able to get answers to questions like these. Of course, many proposals come with materials and diagrams attached, but sometimes they only give you one side of the story—in other words, the reasons why you should vote for it.

I think of myself as being civic-minded, not a person with a servile attitude to power. Obviously, my attitudes have been shaped by my life experiences. If I had been a People's Deputy in the 1950s or '60s, I'm sure I'd have been the same as everyone else. I'd have marched off in whatever direction Chairman Mao indicated, even if it was straight into a muddy ditch. But times are changing. I was born and grew up along with the People's Republic, and I've learned from its history. I went hungry when I was in high school,[3] and at university during the Cultural Revolution I was beaten up for supposedly belonging to the anti–Zhou Enlai May Sixteenth Clique.[4] In 1976, Hua Guofeng, a man who didn't understand the first thing about architecture, got away with ordering the building of the Chairman Mao Memorial Hall with the words: "First dig out a big square foundation on Tiananmen Square and we'll take it from there," before they'd drafted

3. As a result of the great famine induced by the economic policies of the Great Leap Forward.

4. A fictitious extremist Red Guard group that was supposedly founded on 16 May 1967 and plotted to unseat the premier, Zhou Enlai. A decade-long purge ensued, which was particularly vicious during the early 1970s.

any plans at all. Then he proceeded to build the Memorial Hall we have now. The 1980s might have been the era of reform, but things were just like they were in the old days: a certain very diminutive leader [Deng Xiaoping] happened to look up at the ceiling when he was inspecting residential housing in Beijing and remark off-handedly: "Don't make them so high, we've got to save on building materials." As a result, we had to slave through the night to revise the plans for all new housing developments in the city by reducing the ceiling height. History's taught me a lot. It's taught me that to cling to the ramblings of one man—for a billion people to follow him blindly—just won't work now, and it never will again.

There aren't that many deputies like me. That's a fact, and I have to acknowledge it. It's also true that Chinese citizens, especially the more radical ones, younger members of the intelligentsia, for example, might entertain various extreme views about the National People's Congress. But if you ask what impact Western media opinion has on us, I have to say, sorry, we Chinese aren't here just to collect bouquets from foreigners. It doesn't even occur to me to wonder what the West might think about our affairs. Of course, I'm aware of the fact that they don't rate us very highly, but any fair assessment of the situation today, be it Chinese or foreign, will concede that things are changing.

When a deputy finally stood up in the Seventh National People's Congress and said: "No, I disagree," I was an outsider, just an ordinary TV viewer. I didn't give it much thought, let alone understand its real significance. These days I think that even ordinary viewers will have seen that things in the Great Hall of the People, like things everywhere in China, are changing for the better. The biggest difference for us is that though we might still be just a rubber-stamp parliament, we don't actually have to give you that stamp of approval any more. Sure, representatives with a civic consciousness like me may still be in a minority, but at least we're here! We're not just mindless cogs in some voting machine, the way Westerners think we are. We're not, and we never will be again.

The evidence is there for you to see. When Jiang Chunyun was put forward for a vice premiership, many deputies voted against him. Although it was still only a minority protest vote, and it was too small to block his election, it was still far more than anyone expected. The Communist Party certainly never expected it. "I trust whoever Chairman Mao trusts" just no longer holds. Sorry! In the Great Hall there's no point accusing me of not maintaining solidarity with Party Central.

I remember when the secretary of our party branch came to see me with what he said was some good news. The party committee of my academy had decided to propose me as a deputy for the next National People's Congress. "This is an indication of the trust that the party and the people have in you," he said. It was supposed to be an honor not only for the academy but for all Chinese intellectuals.

I was completely taken aback. With so many old geezers and grannies in the place, how come they thought of me? He told me, "But don't you see that this shows how highly we think of you? Party Central and the United Front Department of the Beijing Municipal Party Committee have both stipulated that we need even more young and energetic intellectuals getting into the Congress this time around."

Moonwalking

6

Looking Ahead
The Founders of a Private Orphanage

It was the Lantern Festival, the fifteenth day of the first lunar month of the New Year. When he showed me out after our conversation, the small city of a million inhabitants was filled with the noise of firecrackers and the flashes of fireworks. There were explosions all around us.

The streets on the way back to my hotel were lined with stalls selling fireworks, some with a hundred crackers on a string, others with as many as a thousand, or even ten thousand. They were all wrapped in red paper, while the colorful fireworks were in small cardboard boxes, waiting to be bought, taken home, and released from their lonely isolation.

> *Jingsha, Hubei Province. The city used to be called Shashi. Although the name was changed on the maps in the mid-1990s, people still call it Shashi.*

We started working towards setting up our orphanage in 1987, and we took in our first child in July 1988. We accepted five children in that first month. In 1989 we hung up our sign, "Shashi Private Orphanage," although we didn't get permission from the government until March 1990. Even then we were only authorized to set up a children's art class, not an orphanage. The Bureau of Civil Affairs of the Shashi municipal government finally gave us verbal permission to operate as an orphanage in July 1993. The de facto recognition of our existence made it possible for us to go public. In reality, we'd already been operating for five years and had more than ten children in our care. Over the years we have taken on twenty-one children, and there are twelve with us at the moment. Altogether we have fifteen, if you add the three children my wife and I have. We provide them all with food, clothing, accommodation, school fees, and medical treatment, as well as kindergarten teachers when necessary, or wet nurses, and home tuition. We are really just one big family. All our children get on well together, and they are a lively and loveable bunch. But as you've seen, they have a fairly basic life; for China it's an average to good standard of living, but it's not particularly luxurious. That's the story of the orphanage and our present situation in a nutshell.

But I'm talking about us, not just myself. My wife, Yao Zhongying, has contributed both her youth and her love to establishing and building up this orphanage. At the same time, the support of people throughout our city has been crucial in making it possible for us to keep going.

"Alone I go upstairs and stare out along the distant path." What we've gone through can best be summed up in this one line of classical poetry.

I was born in 1953 and I'm a Hui.[1] I was born and raised here in Shashi, but my family was originally from Nanyang County in Henan Province, so that's recorded on my documents as my birthplace. After four years of primary education at Qinglian Gang, I graduated from Shashi No. 4 Middle School in 1970.

My only brush with fame was in 1966, when I was twelve. The Cultural Revolution had just started, and they were holding mass meetings to denounce the Three-Family Village all over the place, including at our school.[2] While the rally was going on, I heard someone crying out from the direction of the big pond next to the assembly ground. They'd obviously fallen in the water. I ran over to the pond—it was actually more of a stinking, watery garbage dump—but anyway, I jumped in without a second thought and helped the boy out. I was in sixth grade, and he was in first year. The local paper ran a story about it, and they even called me a "little hero." We soon lost touch, though. Last year an old teacher of mine came by and said that I should try and get a hold of a copy of the paper, as it could prove useful. I wasn't that enthusiastic, but I asked him to go

1. One of the Chinese Muslim ethnic groups.

2. The Three-Family Village (sanjia cun) was a group of three writers (Deng Tuo, Wu Han, and Liao Mosha) who, in the prelude to the Cultural Revolution, were accused in the mass media of a plot to undermine socialism and Mao Zedong Thought through the publication of supposedly satirical essays in leading Beijing newspapers.

and look it up in the library and make a photocopy for me if he had the time.

I didn't really learn much during my time at middle school. There were no proper classes as it was the Cultural Revolution, but that didn't stop us graduating, in 1970. On 3 March that year, I was sent off to work on a farm with Advance Team No. 6 in Gongan County. Our production team was later incorporated into a state farm. Life was hard in Gongan, and as my parents were already quite old, they couldn't give me any help. My father was a worker, and my mother was unemployed, so they didn't have any of the right connections, and I couldn't get out of the place. I couldn't even wangle a job in a factory. Anyway, after the state farm had taken me on I was formally classified as an agricultural worker, and that meant I wasn't supposed to leave the land. That really upset me. I felt I was being discriminated against because I came from a Muslim-Hui family. Added to that, my father had got into some political trouble, and that made it even harder for me to get back to the city. He used to be a soldier and had got into the habit of being very straightforward and upfront about what he thought. When the Red Guards went to our mosque they began destroying everything, including the special coffins. My dad couldn't help himself. He told them they could talk about rebellion all they wanted, but that if they destroyed the coffins there wouldn't be anywhere for us to go when we died. The Red Guards weren't going to take any of that, and they denounced him as a counterrevolutionary. You see, Hui funeral customs are very different from the Han. We don't approve of cremation. The corpse is washed and dressed in white before being placed in a coffin to be taken to the burial site. Then, after the body is interred, the coffin is returned to the mosque so it can be used again. So those coffins were an integral part of our religious rites and customs; everyone has to use the same ones, no matter how wealthy or poor they may have been in life. They were sacred ritual objects.

I stayed in the countryside for two years, right up until I was arrested on 20 May 1972. On 15 January 1973, I was sentenced to three years of labor reform for wounding someone in a fight. Yes, I'd been involved, but I was only helping out a friend; I wasn't the main one in the fight. But because of my father's status and the fact that we didn't have any well-connected friends who could protect me, I took all the blame. They packed me off to a labor camp. Here's the court's written verdict on my case. They tried me for attempted murder. Look at this:

COURT VERDICT

People's Liberation Army Martial Law Committee,
Public Security and Procuracy of Shashi, Hubei Province

Case Summary: Attempted Murder

Accused: Xu Yongfu, male, 19 years old
Family status: Poor peasant
Personal status: Student
Permanent address: 15A Yingxi Street
Present address: Working in the Advance Team No. 6, Yugong Commune,
    Gongan County since February 1970

The accused, Xu Yongfu, in collusion with Wen Houjun, Wei Guangyuan, and
Li Huaxi, took part in fights and injured people with wooden clubs and planks
with nails in them on three separate occasions in the second half of 1969, at the
savings bank on Jiefang Road, at Bianhe Road, and at the docks, respectively.

Of particular severity was the incident that occurred at the Peasant's Friend
Restaurant on Yingxi Street around midday on 15 November 1971. The accused, armed with a bricklayer's cleaver, struck Yin Jie a blow on the head. He
fled the scene of the crime during the investigation of the incident.

Xu Yongfu's crimes are of the utmost seriousness. We hereby sentence the
accused to three years' imprisonment from 28 May 1972.

People's Liberation Army, Martial Law Group Overseeing
the Public Security and Procuracy of Shashi, Hubei Province
15 January 1973

Strictly speaking, it was a miscarriage of justice.[3] But nobody would take
up my cause. I tried getting my name cleared after the Cultural Revolution,
but the authorities said it was too minor a breach of the law to be worth both-
ering about. And anyway, they said, the public security and court systems were
under army jurisdiction at the time, so the army had the last word on everything. It was all so long ago, they told me, I should just drop it. After all, they
said, lots of people were killed in the Cultural Revolution, and all I got was
three years' labor reform. So they told me I shouldn't attempt to get the case
reopened or overturned, as it was just too insignificant to warrant such a fuss.

---

3. *Cuo'an,* that is, trumped-up charges leading to persecution during the Cultural Revolution that should, by rights, have been overturned after 1976, when many sentences passed
by the military authorities were officially negated.

I spent my three years working in a forced labor team at a state farm in Jiangbei under the jurisdiction of the Shashi Penitentiary. At first they locked me up with serious felons, though later they put me in a team with common criminals. They could justify it either way: I had been accused of murder, so I should be put with the hardened criminals. On the other hand, I was only a would-be murderer, and I'd only got three years, so they could put me in with common petty criminals. Life in jail was relatively good, considering the times. The place was run quite scientifically, and discipline was very strict. And it was a lot better than being sent off to work as a peasant on a state farm. At least in jail you always had enough to eat.

After my release in 1975, it was virtually impossible to find a job. The Cultural Revolution wasn't over yet, and the economy was weak. Factories weren't working at full capacity, and no one was allowed to start their own business. People who did have jobs had nothing better to do than spend the whole day in the office reading the paper. Obviously, there weren't any openings for someone with my background. So I had no choice but to go for the most menial work, in transportation. My local Shengli Street Office gave me a part-time job with their transportation team.[4] I started on 28 May 1975 and stayed with them for over ten years. They were pretty decent and basically didn't discriminate against me because of my criminal record. All in all, I suppose I enjoyed the same opportunities as everyone else who worked there. They eventually took me on full-time, and I gradually worked my way up the ladder, becoming the team accountant and eventually team leader. Finally, I was made the head of the whole transportation division. In September 1986 I started doing some part-time study, first senior college and then television university. In 1992 I passed the provincial exams and was awarded a graduate diploma in business and government administration management. Here, take a look for yourself.

DIPLOMA

Certificate No. 9207015

This is to certify that Comrade Xu Yongfu of Nanyang County, Henan Province, has successfully passed the examinations for Business and Administra-

4. Street offices or street committees act as the party and government's eyes and ears in local areas. They are in charge of monitoring (and, in the past, strictly controlling) the lives of people in their area.

tion Management. Having satisfied all academic requirements, he is hereby awarded this certificate of graduation.

The Higher Education Committee of Hubei Province
December 1992

I don't know what to say to that. Sure, maybe some people might find it hard to believe that someone who'd been in jail would want to start up an orphanage—or that someone with a diploma in business management would want to either. I don't know what other people think. But we decided to found an orphanage, and that's all there is to it.

When I started out in transportation, I made over a hundred yuan a month. And that was when money was really worth something. Relatively speaking, it wasn't a bad wage.

I got back here in 1975 and made the bricks for rebuilding our house. I even had to find the coal I needed to fire the bricks. Originally, our family lived in a broken-down old place. We took a photo of it before tearing it down; the picture is still hanging in our bedroom. We finished the house in 1979, and I got married in 1980. My wife came from the country, so she didn't have a city residence permit. Coming from the countryside is supposed to be something bad, and the way most people look at it I'd married beneath myself and lost face. On top of that, people thought our marriage had left me economically disadvantaged because she didn't bring any grain or oil rations with her. But things were beginning to change when we got married in 1980. They'd just launched the economic reforms.

After our wedding, we started up our own small business. My wife is an incredibly hard worker, a person who can put up with extraordinary deprivations. In the early years she would grind beans for soy milk at three o'clock every morning. When it was ready we took the milk to the main bus station by handcart to sell to travelers. When we'd sold it all, she came home, while I went off to my day job. We sold the soy milk for three *fen* a bowl, or five if you wanted sugar in it. It wasn't very profitable; the most we made from a night's labor would be enough to buy a pack of quality cigarettes. We don't smoke or drink; we don't even drink tea. I wouldn't presume to criticize anyone else for being extravagant; I've just never had the habit. Although we are doing okay now, we still only ever have soft drinks. Back then, most people had a hard life like us, and usually they couldn't even afford sugar in their soy milk. So she made her money selling paupers soy milk—without sugar, three *fen* a bowl. Let me tell you how incredibly strong my wife is: the morning before she gave birth, she made a batch of soy milk during the night and pulled the load from our place up the big incline to the bus station. I remember her saying to me, look how big my belly is, but I can still pull our soy milk cart. That's how we've done so well for ourselves, managing to fix this place up and making some extra money, because we are both hard workers. We should be well-off considering all our efforts; we've worked for the money we've made. If I couldn't improve my lot with all this work, then I'd say that any talk about succeeding through your own efforts was a big lie.

We sold soy milk and ice blocks and then ran a restaurant and a video-game parlor. After seven years of work building up our capital and re-investing it back into our enterprises, we had enough money. We wanted to do something useful, and that's when we set up our orphanage in 1987. Why not?

Once we had money, we didn't think of showing off or comparing ourselves with other people. No cars, big new house, or extravagant eating for us. At first we didn't know what we were going to do; we didn't have any definite plans. Initially I asked the party secretary of our local Shengli Street Office whether I could be allocated another job, such as in the street committee, which was in charge of old people who had no one to look after them, as well as latchkey children, not to mention the various social problems and crimes that you get at the grass-roots level. You see, I'd decided that I wanted to do some social work.

But the leadership wouldn't agree. The party secretary was very happy with the way I was running the transportation unit, so naturally he didn't want me to quit and go into social work. He probably thought I was being silly. In local government you have lots of paternalistic people who just want to control you because they like being in charge. It makes them feel important. But they couldn't control what I was thinking; every individual wants to realize their potential and affirm their self-worth. We're always looking for a means and an environment in which to express ourselves. Look, here you are, having traveled so far to speak with me. Apart from showing your support and love for our big family, and witnessing for yourself how we put our ideals into practice, aren't you also searching for a means to prove your own self-worth? Everyone wants to shine, to get what they really need and want. People's aspirations and hopes can't be repressed.

The leadership might not have been able to accept what I wanted to do, but I could sense that we were living in a different age, one that was more suited to ideas like mine. It is a more reasonable age. In the past they might have thought I wanted to change jobs so I could engage in criminal activity. They would have felt compelled to reeducate me and force me to accept some punishment so that I could be reformed. Don't break the law, they'd tell me; don't oppose the leadership. Anyway, that's what my father always taught me.

I believe society needs me to be a good person, but what does it mean to be a good person? It's hard to do the right thing; sometimes other people won't let you, or won't allow you to be the type of good person you know you should be. Not that this could stop me. It's very hard to stop people from trying, especially if you think you can force them to comply with what you want instead of being reasonable. Since they wouldn't let me work with the street committee, I thought, what about starting up my own orphanage? A private orphanage—how about that?

I suppose I'm just one of those obstinate types who always gives the leadership headaches. But although they were annoyed with me, I really felt like I was the one with my nose out of joint. Just take my attitude to family planning, for example. I'm very backward. According to the regulations, as a member of an ethnic minority I'm allowed to have two children, but we went and had three: one daughter and two sons. Of course the leaders were furious. I accept that I was politically backward. Even though I agree in principle that family planning is a good thing not only for China but the whole world, I think it's a bad thing for individual families. Anyway, since I figured that high-level cadres can have more kids—and that's something I've seen with my very own eyes—I thought, why can't the common people? They can afford to have more kids, so I reckoned that since we could afford it too, we should have more. I knew I was breaking their rules, but I did it anyway. That's just the way I am. And, of course, they punished me for it. I was fined six years in a row. They docked 20 percent of my pay right up to the time that I went on unpaid leave, and then I wasn't taking their money any more, so they didn't have any way of fining me. It was a pretty heavy punishment, but I was always optimistic about it. That's just the way I am; nothing can change me.

I applied for two years' leave without pay at first, and then at the end of that I extended it for another three years, then another five. Look, here's the contract.

Contract for Leave without Pay

Comrade Xu Yongfu, head of the Shengli Transportation Team, has applied for leave without pay so as to establish a private orphanage. The leadership of the Shengli Street Office has reviewed this request and hereby approves Comrade Xu's application. In granting permission we would like to make it clear that:

1. We support Comrade Xu Yongfu's efforts to establish a private orphanage and to that end have agreed to his request for leave without pay starting from 1 September 1988 and terminating on 31 August 1990.

2. During Comrade Xu Yongfu's period of absence his pay, bonuses and all welfare benefits will be suspended.

3. During this period of absence, if Comrade Xu Yongfu is unsuccessful in his attempts to establish an orphanage, he will be regarded as having voluntarily relinquished his job dating from the time of his original application for leave without pay.

Shengli Street Office
Shengli Transportation Team, Shashi City
Signed and sealed by the applicant, Xu Yongfu
27 July 1988

They certainly underestimated me, not to mention the fact that they obviously didn't trust me. They thought I was going to run off and get involved in some money-making scheme. They're just too suspicious. That's why they stipulated that I could only go back to my old job if I got the orphanage up and running; if I didn't, I would automatically lose my job. It's a very harsh and impersonal way of dealing with things, very insincere. We're all Chinese, but all Chinese like to think the very worst of each other; they can't believe you're acting out of good faith and that you're not trying to get away with some scam. No matter how unreasonable I felt it was, I had no choice but to do it by their rules. If I didn't comply, they simply wouldn't have let me go. You see, there is this little oasis in my heart, and that is what I'm working toward, so I can put up with all these petty annoyances. So I signed the contract and affixed my personal seal. I was sure that things would work out. It was already July 1988, and the preparations for our orphanage were well under way. We had bought beds, quilts, and various other basics, and we were getting the rooms ready, so things were pretty much in place. By this stage I couldn't have stopped even if they'd wanted me to.

That's right, I'd started making preparations well before I'd even signed their contract. I figured that since I was doing it all with my own money and my own time, I could just go right ahead without waiting for their permission. So we were on the way to that oasis, only we didn't realize what a marathon journey it would turn out to be. In 1987, government policies were put in place that would allow us to proceed, so we went to the home of the vice mayor in charge of civil affairs to arrange for official permission. He not only agreed, he expressed his personal support and thanked us on behalf of the people of Shashi for what we were doing. That was all well and good, but we didn't have anything from him in writing. We needed written permission to proceed because, although we had enough money to cover our expenses, it was absolutely vital that the children should have the right household registration and medical coverage.[5] These were things that money could not buy, things that were entirely in the hands of the government to allow or refuse. Although the vice mayor had been very supportive, when we went to the Bureau of Civil Affairs to complete the formalities, our application was passed from the head of the office to a department head, who then gave it to a low-level functionary to deal with. Those documents moved back and forth for two whole years, right up to July 1989, by which time we already had more than ten children in our care. It was at this point that they decided to hold a meeting and declare that the original bureau chief was being replaced by a new person, and this fellow refused outright to give us permission for the orphanage. He said he couldn't possibly agree to a private orphanage. At the time I asked him whether this was his personal opinion. If it was, we would continue our discussions in the Bureau of Civil Affairs. However, if his refusal was based on a decision passed down by the bureau as a whole, then I would have to go above the bureau, to the city government, to pursue my application. Furthermore, I pointed out, we were no longer waiting for permission to operate a private orphanage, since the said orphanage had been in existence for some time. He didn't really want to deal with me at all, and so he said

5. Urban dwellers were required to have residential permits allowing them to live in a city; in the past, these were also required in order to obtain rationed goods such as grains and cloth.

of course he was only expressing a personal point of view. Be that as it may, he reiterated, I really don't agree with you running an orphanage.

Given the situation, I had no choice but to seek a meeting with the party secretary of the Bureau of Civil Affairs. He told me, "Listen, young Xu: you're right, but the bureau chief does have a point. You see, the whole idea of running a private orphanage is a very sensitive one, and there are certain policy restrictions on such activities. Let me tell you what I suggest: continue as you have been doing, and we'll just wait and see." Now, I realized he was being decent about all of this, because we all know there are lots of things in China that you can get away with doing as long as you don't talk about them. The party secretary hadn't refused us permission outright, he had just observed that neither I nor the bureau chief was in the wrong. That meant, since I wasn't in the wrong, I could continue with the orphanage; though, by the same token, since the bureau chief was also in the right, permission would not be forthcoming. In other words, we could both carry on as before. The upshot of all of this, however, was that they rejected—or perhaps just ignored—our applications for household registration and medical coverage for our children. I was absolutely livid, and what made me even angrier was what they called a Three Nots decision regarding our orphanage. That is, they decided not to publicly promote it, not to allow reports about it to appear in the media, and not to support it. I didn't particularly care about the first two prohibitions, since we were doing it because we thought we should, not because we wanted the authorities to say nice things about us. But to refuse us any support meant that they were denying the children residence permits. That made the future very bleak for us indeed. It created an insurmountable obstacle to our going ahead. China's a socialist country in which everyone has to have a registration permit and ID; if a person doesn't have the right documentation, that affects their access to health care, schooling, and employment. Life becomes impossible. Don't forget you can't even buy an airplane ticket without an official ID card these days.

We had no choice but to do it the circuitous way. Initially we applied to the Education Bureau for permission to set up a kindergarten and an art class. We thought the crucial thing at this stage was to get the official go-ahead for a school so that the orphans could be classified as our students. As such, they would have legal status during their school years. So we started by setting up a small art class, and then a kindergarten. Why the art class? That's because I think that apart from providing children with food and clothing, you need to equip them with some useful training, or at least a hobby, so they can be useful members of society. We didn't have the wherewithal to teach them violin or piano—either to employ instructors or buy the instruments—but for an art class all you basically need are pens and paper. Something else that I'm sure you'll appreciate is that it was easier to apply for permission to run an art class than a school, and, as a result, in March 1990 we were issued with an official license. Four months later we got support for the kindergarten. Here's the document.

License to Operate a School
Issued by Shashi City

Shashi Education Bureau

Doc. No.: 011

Name of Unit: Shashi Spring Morning Kindergarten-level Art
Specialization: Art tutorials for infants
Address: 31 Yingxi Street, Shashi
Responsible Person: Xu Yongfu

The Education Committee of Shashi City
26 March 1990

The classes were taught and tutored by the chairman of the Shashi Artists' Association and a professor in the art department of the Normal College. And not just for our children; the classes were also open to outsiders during the winter and summer vacations. After the course had been running for a while, we organized an exhibition so that the teachers and pupils could review what they had been doing, as well as allowing interested individuals in the wider society an opportunity to see what had been achieved. It was a chance to let everyone feel there was a future to our enterprise, that there was a reason to feel good about it. A reporter with the municipal radio station came along so they could do a story about the exhibit, but the Bureau of Civil Affairs got wind of it and told them not to broadcast the report. Obviously, the Three Nots were still in place. Even the reporter was very annoyed, and he told them that this was real news, it was an art exhibition, and he should be free to report it. He asked the bureau what right they had to interfere with his performance of professional duties, and they responded that he didn't appreciate the complex background to the exhibition. They told him that I was an ex-con who was up to some scam. The reporter told me all of this, and I admitted that I had done time, but that was back in 1973, and we were now in the 1990s! I said I'd paid my debt to society in full and that I had full civil rights; furthermore, education is a legal activity! The authorities might pursue their Three Nots policy, and there was nothing I could do about that, but my art classes had official support. The teachers and students had applied themselves and produced this exhibit; now what right did the authorities have to interfere? It was just too much.

A new Bureau of Civil Affairs chief was appointed in April 1993, and he immediately gave us permission for our orphanage. He said that the vice minister of the Civil Affairs Ministry in Beijing had said in a recent speech that not only the state but also collectives and individuals could also operate social-welfare projects. I was delighted, because it seemed that finally we had some protection. But by July of that same year, I still only had verbal approval for the orphanage from the bureau. Again I asked for something in writing; I tried to reason with them by saying that even a shop needs a retail license, and that without an official document our children couldn't get residence permits. Once more they said just keep on with what you're doing and leave the issue of getting it in writing for the time being. After another eighteen months, we still didn't have a license. None of the children had household registration or health coverage.

Nearly seven years had passed. Our first seven years had been spent building up the capital we needed to get started; this second seven years had been hard in another way, and yet still we didn't have a license. Our orphanage was itself still an orphan. The government simply wouldn't let us register.

"Alone I go upstairs and stare out along the distant path." It makes me worry, it really upsets me. I've tried to see things from their angle, and I realize that the Bureau of Civil Affairs probably thinks that we're up to no good, that somehow we are using the orphanage as a cover, or that we are trying to blacken their reputation. But I feel fully justified in pointing out that there are so many abandoned children in the society who have nowhere to go, no home, that the government's reputation is black enough. It's hardly what you'd call sparkling!

We had no elaborate agenda when we started the orphanage, just three simple reasons. The first was historical: my father was an orphan, so whenever I see an abandoned child I think of him. Now that it is within my power to do something about it, I feel that I have to. The second reason is that I want to give something back to society. The Shengli Street Office helped put me on the right path, and they treated me decently. Regardless of what they really think about me, I feel I want to do something to pay them back and carry my share of the social burden. Third, I want to do my utmost to be a good person as I see it.

No, we didn't just pick up any of the children who are with us. People sometimes mistakenly think that. Our children were with the relevant government organizations before coming to us. They were all taken to the government—say, for example, to a street committee, a family-planning committee, or whatever—after someone had found them. Take this little girl, for instance. She follows me around whenever I'm at home. She was the first abandoned child that we took in. Her surname is He. On 8 June 1988, someone found her and took her to the Shengli Street Office. They handed her on to the Bureau of Civil Affairs, but since they don't have jurisdiction over an orphanage or a similar organization, they instructed the Shengli Street Office to "absorb her locally." A fellow by the name of He Yonggui working for the office decided to take her because he already had a son. But after a few days they realized that she's intellectually handicapped, and so his wife demanded he get rid of her, threatening to divorce him if he refused. So He Yonggui took her back to the street office. This was just around the time when we were starting up our orphanage, and even though we still weren't officially established, he brought her to me and I decided to take her. She wasn't even a year old then, and now she's just started attending a special school.

"Absorb locally" is a terrible expression. It's so inhumane. But at the time there wasn't an orphanage in the whole of Shashi. They party had been in power for over forty years, and for all that time the Bureau of Civil Affairs has been telling people to absorb orphans locally. At least now they've got their own organization, an orphanage that is run under the auspices of the No. 1 Social Welfare Center. It has a big entrance with two different plaques on it. They put all the old people without families, the seriously disabled, and orphans in there together. Of course it's number one; don't forget, the authorities still haven't officially recognized our existence. They were registered first, so they are entirely within their rights to call themselves number one. Whether they do a good job is not a subject that I'd like to comment on. You can go and see for yourself. They are very properly organized; even the nurses are cadres.

I simply don't understand how anyone could just abandon a child like that. Since children are generally found at the main bus station or the docks or left at hospitals, we presume that most of them are abandoned by people from the countryside. Some are actual orphans. For example, the mother of one of our children ran off with another man, and then the father hanged himself in despair. Another was orphaned after a murder-suicide: the family was wrangling over some property, and the father went to the aunt's house one night and turned on the gas heater; when the apartment was full of gas, he lit a match. Don't we have a responsibility to help such unfortunate children?

When we started out, people circulated a lot of unpleasant rumors about us. They said we were hiding something or using our orphanage to make property claims, using our welfare operation as a cover for a real-estate scam. But you can see for yourself that our orphanage is in our own house. The government has never given us a square inch of land, and we've never thought of trying to get anything out of them. As it became evident that we had nothing to hide, the rumors died out.

The place was originally only one story; the five-story building we're sitting in now was built on the original land the year before last. In 1993 the boiler in a nearby factory blew up and, praise be to Allah, although we were hit by over three hundred kilograms of debris it only destroyed our roof and ripped out a wall. None of the children was hurt. The factory gave us 37,000 yuan in compensation, and by putting in another 200,000 yuan we were able to erect this building. It's over five hundred square meters, and since we have both bedrooms and classrooms here, it means that the children can go to kindergarten in their own home. Before this, some of the kids were sent to other kindergartens, and although they were treated all right, it wasn't the same as if they were here. The state kindergartens have too many children to deal with, so ours didn't get the care they needed. One has to appreciate the fact that orphans are probably going to be both slightly physically and psychologically disadvantaged, so they need more attention and care than even the average child. Outside kindergartens really can't manage the job; they are big collectives, and you can't expect them to provide the special care that our children need. But because we have our own place now, all that's taken care of.

We rely entirely on our own earnings; that's about four thousand yuan a month. The average wage in Shashi is three to four hundred yuan, so of course compared to others we make quite a lot. Obviously, if we were poor we wouldn't be running an orphanage; but it's because we are pretty good at making money that we can afford to support this large family of ours. It goes without saying that we'd be comfortably off if it was only our nuclear family of five, but we couldn't live happily knowing that there were abandoned children out there in need of a loving home.

It takes about three thousand yuan a month to cover all the bills, including nannies, kindergarten teachers, and so on. We put aside what little we have left over to purchase new equipment or to save up for the future, that is, for example, to pay for the children to attend middle school or university. You always need some money on hand to deal with emergencies, like when one of the children is suddenly taken ill. A serious bout of illness might require a few thousand yuan. Because some of our children are physically weak, we might expect that they'll have to be hospitalized a few times in any given year.

We make most of our money from our garbage transportation business, as well as renting out retail space and video games. We bought the shop space back in 1981 and originally ran a restaurant out of it. At the time, real estate was very cheap, and so we got it for only three thousand yuan. Now we rent it out for nearly two thousand yuan a month. Garbage disposal earns us another thousand or so. We employ five people and have a tractor and a truck. The bottom has fallen out of the video-game market, but at its height we had over twenty machines. We've sold most of them off but still have five in operation.

We get donations, but that's a fairly rare occurrence; we've certainly never gone around asking for them. We've received a few hundred yuan from the Shashi Women's Federation and another couple of hundred from a machine-tool factory. The participants in the Five-Good Family Conference of Hubei Province gave us a collective donation of 1,400 yuan, while the Red Cross gave us 4,000 yuan worth of stuff the year before last, and another 1,000 last year. A lady in Hong Kong heard about our work and wrote to me offering financial support. She told me she was sixty years old and had heard that I was pretty extraordinary, and that the only way she could show her support was to send money for the orphanage. You understand, of course, that there's no way I could accept a donation from her, and despite all of her letters I have had to refuse her kindness. I'd be happy for her to come and visit us, but we don't dare take anything from her because we're afraid we could never explain our connection with her to the authorities. Of course, someone who gives you a lot of money would also be buying the right to have a say over how that money is spent. This big family of ours would have to hold board meetings. That would be a real worry, so that's another reason why I've declined her help. We're not like an ordinary social welfare institution that relies entirely on charitable donations and government grants. We have to use the wealth that we have generated ourselves and do as much as we can with it. It's easier that way, cleaner.

Apart from monetary donations, people have also given us things, mostly clothing and food. We don't accept everything, however. For example, old school uniforms donated by teachers and students; though we're certainly grateful for their kindness, we have had to return them because our children also have a strong sense of self-worth. They wouldn't want to wear hand-me-down school uniforms, and I wouldn't want them to either. When our children go to your school, they are not going as orphans; they have a family, and I am the head of their family.

No matter what you do, whether it's your private work or when playing a public role, I believe you must maintain the same standards and principles. Our children have to be able to feel they can go into the future with their heads held high. At no stage do I want them to feel as though they are second-rate or inferior to anyone else, or that they have to rely on the charity of others, on their leftover love or secondhand things.

All of our children, whether they are our biological children or not, live, eat, and dress exactly the same. They are all our children, and we treat them equally. Each one of them has the same opportunities to share in what other people have given us. Look at the jacket my son is wearing at the moment, for instance. That was donated. It fits him, so he gets to wear it. Yes, you're right. If he was upset at the thought of wearing something that had been given to us, it would have been a very bad sign.

Our children are very conscientious. Generally speaking, they all do well at school; and those who haven't reached school age yet are lively and adorable, too. Our own daughter is in her third year of middle school and is doing very well. She's been getting an average of over 90 percent on her tests, and she's even a class cadre. She's the first up in the morning, and we don't have to worry about her at all. My son, on the other hand, is not doing so well. When we first started the orphanage, we had to have our own seven-year-old live with one of his teachers for some years. He's only recently come back to us. It's our eldest son's turn to live outside now; it's sort of like the changing of the guard. He loves fooling around, and his school results have been terrible, so the teacher is going to keep an eye on him for us and help him with his studies. People say that we are so occupied with our orphanage that we've had to pay a teacher to take care of our own son. But I think that's unfair, because we're paying the teacher for all the effort he's putting into helping our children improve themselves, and he's really devoted to us. I'm not exploiting him. It's true that there was a time when we were really overstretched; we had five or six babies, plus the disabled little girl and another child who was in hospital, so we really couldn't cope. That teacher was a real godsend.

The kids are still at primary and middle school, so they haven't had any problems with the household registration system yet. The law states that children are to be assured of nine years of compulsory education, so you don't have to worry about where you're being taught. The head of the Shashi Education Committee has a special interest in our children, and, apart from making sure that they can all attend local schools, I have been trying to arrange a special school for our girl with the intellectual disability. I want her to go to an experimental school run by the Normal College, and, although the cadre from the education committee was very supportive, the person in charge of our case wasn't. Sure, we had permission from the top to enroll her in the school, but this lower-level bureaucrat wouldn't process the application. He said some pretty awful things; he said that we only wanted her to go to the special school because it would be good publicity for the orphanage if she did well. I tried reasoning with him and made the case that if she did well she would be a credit to our socialist system, a blossom that had flowered in the nurturing warmth of the Chinese Communist Party. He still refused, but I just wouldn't let it go. He accused me of trying to start a fight, and I must admit that we got into a bit of a scuffle. The police were called, but they ruled that he was in the wrong for provoking me. This petty bureaucrat wasn't going to give in that easily, so he claimed that I had wounded him and demanded that I pay him a hundred yuan for medical expenses on the spot. What a dreadful person! Even the police felt completely at a loss, so they suggested I just pay up and be done with it. But the upshot of it all was that our little girl still couldn't get into that school. Another one of the children successfully passed the entrance exams and got in without any trouble. The annual fees are three thousand yuan, although tuition in some things is free. It's a quality establishment and very well run, and compared to an ordinary school it isn't that expensive; in some ways it's even cheaper. The general rule in Shashi is that the worse the school, the more expensive it is; that's because, on top of tuition fees, they pile on various other charges and levies.

So that's the situation we're faced with: I can't get the authorities to do what I want them to, but they can't make me do anything against my will.

What they say doesn't count; what does count they won't come out and say. There is no reasonable explanation for the way things are done, it's just the way it is, and somehow, for better or worse, it works. We've had visits from both the mayor and the vice mayor, and although the mayor supports our enterprise, he can't force the Bureau of Civil Affairs to do the right thing. Even if the head of the Education Committee approves your application, you're stuck if the section head or officer in charge of the case refuses to support you as well. That's simply the way things are.

Not counting my own daughter, the eldest child is twelve, the youngest three. As for their surnames, some are called Xu, like me. Both my daughter and eldest son are called Xu. If we know what the child's original parents' names were, then they are called by either their father's or mother's surname, like Liu. Or they might get their name from a family that has previously taken care of them, as in the case of He Xi, who spent those few days with He Yonggui. It wasn't long, but we shouldn't forget that connection. The rest are all called Lai, because we don't know their family names. My younger son is called Lai, too, but that's because during the war with Japan, my father was seriously wounded in Shanghai and was saved by a captain by the name of Lai Zhichun. He carried him on his back for forty *li*[6] to a hospital where he was saved. Lai Zhichun himself was killed in the Battle of Tai'erzhuang at the end of the war, so we decided to name our boy after him as a sign of our gratitude. The other children have the surname Lai because the word also means *to come,* so it signifies that for various reasons they have come to us and become members of one big, happy family.

I suppose all of the orphans are originally from Han families, but they are all brought up as Hui. When they first start attending school, I tell each child that although they are probably Han, we have specified Hui on the enrollment forms where it stipulates ethnicity. I also tell them that the state gives children from minority ethnic backgrounds special treatment, such as allowing them into university with lower test scores, and that's why we are taking advantage of this now. I say, when you grow up you can decide for yourself whether you are Hui or what, if any, religion you want to believe in. If they agree, then I'll fill in the form saying they are Hui; if they don't agree, then I'll leave it blank. The children always reply, "What dad says must be right." So up to now they have all been registered as Hui.

My wife spends all her time here. She has a complete system for nursing

6. An itinerary measure, or distance. One *li* is roughly a third of a mile.

and taking care of the children, and she is better at doing the housework than I am. She is a Han, but she respects our Hui beliefs and customs. I also respect hers, and when she goes to her mother's house, she can eat pork.

I feel that I'm living a very full life, and I believe that we're spending our money in a positive and constructive way. I believe that with this money we are buying gold. Of course I don't want the children to pay us back; we won't need our orphans to take care of us when we are old. But I believe that in the future they will contribute to society; they will grow up to be people who are emotionally healthy, people with a sympathy for others and a strong sense of responsibility.

It's not up to me whether our orphanage continues to operate. It depends on whether people feel there is a social need for it. If things continue to develop and progress as they are doing at the present, then I'm sure we'll be able to continue our work. As for what will happen after our children have finished their education, whether they can get to university or find jobs, that is still a matter of residence permits. We have to rely on the efforts of people who sympathize with the weak to resolve this problem. I am confident that all people of good conscience will be concerned with the fate of these children and will help them forge a path forward. As long as there is such an ocean of love, our children have a bright future. From the government's point of view, they have to admit that orphans constitute a very small number of people in the society as a whole, and if they really make an effort, these children can be helped. It is easy for us to help them cope with any economic difficulties they have because we are doing better all the time. At present I'm planning to open a teahouse. The building was finished last year, and we're decorating it at the moment. It's two stories. Next time you come I'll take you there.

I've never been to a mosque, but the Koran says that one good deed is worth seventy trips to the mosque. My father complains, but my excuse is that I'm too busy. When I found this quote in the Koran, I told him that Allah had given me permission not to go—at least for the moment.

Even if there is a major change in China, I don't think it will necessarily affect our work. I believe that every society needs some form of welfare and social work. Moreover, our orphanage is a big family; no matter what happens, the family unit remains the most basic and worthwhile way of protecting life and self-worth that humanity has developed so far.

So, although there might be various pressures on us, I am optimistic.

7

Getting Organized
The Parents of a Stolen Child

Two Children Lost, Mothers' Hearts Broken

My name is Tu Xiaofeng, and I am a teacher at No. 19 Middle School in Nanchang, Jiangxi Province. After eleven years of marriage I became pregnant, and after eight months of careful bed rest, specialist treatment, and a caesarean, I was able to give birth to a son, Yang Nan. But when he was just six years old the unimaginable happened: left unattended at the entrance to our home for less than half an hour, he disappeared without a trace.

At approximately one P.M. on 7 July 1994, Yang Nan was playing with a friend, a boy by the name of Xiong Hui [4 years 10 months, the son of an employee of No. 11 Middle School], outside the dormitory building of No. 19 Middle School when both of them went missing.

> Yang Nan, male, six years old, approximately 111 cm tall. Shiny black hair, slight build, with a large greenish birthmark on his abdomen. He is bright and lively, speaks Mandarin, and before his disappearance attended kindergarten at the Design Institute of the Department of Metallurgy, Nanchang Municipality.

Since Yang Nan's disappearance, our whole family has been in a state of deep depression. We have done everything in our power, both physically and materially, to locate him, but to no avail. His grandparents have not been able to withstand the shock and have fallen ill, while his parents have been in constant torment; they are in tears all day, and can't eat, drink, or sleep. Yang Nan's father has suffered a number of chronic conditions for some years, and his health has further deteriorated since the loss of his beloved son. He has fainted many times and now weighs only forty kilograms, a mere shadow of his former self. This agony has aged me too, so much so that I'm like a different person.

Yang Nan's parents are sincerely appealing to all people of conscience: If you have any clue as to the whereabouts of Yang Nan or Xiong Hui, please get in touch with us at once. We are willing to pay a reward of twenty thousand yuan, or more, for the recovery of our boy. Pity Yang Nan's ailing grandparents and his suffering father. Sympathize with the agonies of his mother and return our beloved child to us. We will gladly compensate you for any expenses incurred. If that is not enough, we are willing to arrange to become relatives with you so that we can maintain contact and both families can share Yang Nan.

We appeal to the public to offer us your hand in support and help save this shattered family!

Address: No. 19 Middle School, Nanchang, Jiangxi Province,
Postcode: 3300006 Tel.: [0791] 6239900 or 6238577

This announcement was carried in all of the major print-media outlets in China—both newspapers and weeklies—for months on end.

Similar notices appear regularly in all of China's newspapers, including the Chinese Red Cross press. They may be shorter, or may announce the loss of a baby or small child. For readers bedazzled by the endless good news about the latest successes of the economic reforms, or whose eyes are more easily drawn to advertisements for Japanese electrical goods, such notices—short pieces written in the blood and tears of parents—are all too easily overlooked. Perhaps it is just that they have become so common that they can no longer arrest readers' attention.

I spoke with the mother of a missing child in her apartment on the outskirts of Xi'an, capital of Shaanxi Province. The comments in brackets were made by an official who works for the Office for the Prevention of the Kidnapping and Sale of Women and Children.

Our organization is a voluntary and unofficial group. We have organized ourselves spontaneously and have a specific, short-term aim: our sole interest is to find our missing children. It doesn't matter whether they are simply lost or have been kidnapped and sold; we just want them back. We have no other agenda, nor any political dimension. We are desperate parents who have lost their children. That's why we have joined together in the hope that through our joint efforts we can get our children back.

That's why we don't even have a real name for our group. At first we thought of calling ourselves the Fellow Sufferers' Association, but then we felt that the expression *fellow sufferer [nanyou]* doesn't really sound right, since we are victims, and especially because it usually implies that what people suffered together was a jail sentence. But then some of us began calling the group the We Love Our Children Association. That's more accurate, and it describes who we are and what we are about. But after a while we still felt We Love Our Children didn't feel quite right; the word *children* is often taken to mean just sons and could easily lead to misunderstandings.[1] That's why we agreed with the suggestion that we call ourselves the Missing Children Association. Finally we had an appropriate name.

We had to band together because instances of child kidnapping in Xi'an have become so common that parents are often so reluctant to leave their children that they don't go to work. They only feel safe when their children are right there in front of them. Even after work, they worry about letting their children go out to play, even if it's right in front of their own building. When we started our group here in Xi'an, on average one child was going missing every week. These lost children were virtually impossible to find, since they were being sold out of town. My own daughter went missing on the way to school, which is only three hundred meters from our house. She disappeared in broad daylight. Bai Jianrong's son disappeared at the zoo; Li Maiqin vanished from right outside their door while playing; Li Jingzhi's son was carried off right opposite the Xi'an Municipal Public Security Bureau! Our children aren't safe anywhere. Even at home they may be in danger, as a number of children have been kidnapped right out of their own homes. They say that the government, the Women's Federation, and the public security bureau are all there to protect us and deal with the extraordinary level of social disorder we are experiencing, but in reality they are all equally powerless to help us find our children. We have no choice but to find inspiration in that line from the "Internationale": "There is no such thing as a savior. Rely not on gods or emperors. We must save ourselves!"

1. In this context the Chinese for "we love our children" is *aizi,* the word *zi* meaning either *child* or *son.*

[Official: Parents who have lost children do suffer terribly. We completely sympathize, and as members of the Public Security Bureau, we are doing absolutely everything within our power to help. We have indeed saved a number of kidnapped children. During these operations some officers have been wounded; others have even lost their lives. When a child goes missing, there are two possibilities: one is that they have simply got lost, the other is that they have been kidnapped and sold. If, after a certain amount of time has elapsed, they still can't be found, we conclude that in all likelihood they have been kidnapped. In recent years the number of such cases has increased dramatically. Yunnan, Guizhou, Sichuan, Jilin, and Heilongjiang are the provinces worst hit by this blight; the most seriously affected cities include Xi'an, though it is not the worst. The majority of "buyers" are peasant families living in Henan, Hebei, Jiangsu, and Shandong provinces. It goes without saying that these are not the most economically developed regions of the country. As for the frequency of kidnappings, all I can give you is the relative number of cases over recent years: if in some seriously affected areas there were, say, one hundred cases in 1990–91, then that increased by 100 percent in 1990–92; that is to say there were more than two hundred instances. Following this, we concentrated our energies on striking back at these criminals, and we achieved some initial successes, with 1992–93 seeing an increase of kidnappings of just a little over 10 percent. Now, as for just how many cases did occur in 1990–91, I'm afraid that is a state secret. Very well, if you insist, I can give you a vague figure to illustrate my point. For example, for the year 1990–91 in Guizhou Province, there were over four hundred kidnappings. Over a third of these involved the violent kidnapping of babies and small children.]

When a member's child goes missing, we report it to the police immediately. Then we put flyers up all over the city, at the train and bus stations, as well as at the airport. Some parents have made tens of thousands of copies. Parents who are economically better off might even broadcast their pleas on TV and have them published in the press. Some parents are actors, so before each performance they will read out the details of their lost child and appeal to the audience for help. Some have even quit their jobs and become itinerant peddlers, moving from town to town in the hope that one day they might bump into their child, or at least find some clue as to their whereabouts. We have mobilized friends and relatives throughout China to help with finding information. No matter what they discover, whether it seems reliable or not, regardless of how far they have to travel, our members will go and follow it up for themselves. We have done everything we can think of, and most of us have been more or less reduced to poverty by our efforts. Our common experience is that when confronted with this implacable social problem, the individual and the family are completely powerless. All of us have simply felt that we had to join forces and express our frustration to the authorities. Although our notices and flyers may not have led us to our children, at least we have found each other.

In December 1988, on 10 December to be precise, over twenty parents met for the first time. We were all strangers. Our number included workers, cadres, and teachers as well as peasants; some were parents, and some were grandparents. Regardless of these differences, when anyone spoke about how they had come to lose their child and their efforts to find them, everyone wept uncontrollably. It was a room full of tears, and those tears united us as a family. The reason we got together that day was so we could make a collective approach to the provincial government and appeal for aid. We ended up establishing this support group.

The secretary general of the provincial government, Song Haiyuan, met with us. Before he even had a chance to open his mouth, one of us cried out: "Be our benefactor! Save our children!" Then they knelt down in front of him, and we all followed suit. He was obviously very moved, and he pleaded with us to stand up. "Your concerns are our concerns," he told us. "We will do everything we can to coordinate efforts being made to help find your lost children." He certainly sounded sympathetic, but in retrospect we realized that he was treading very carefully. He emphasized the need to "coordinate efforts"; he spoke of helping us "find" our "lost children." He said nothing about the criminals who were stealing our children for profit. What particularly annoyed me was his line that "your concerns are our concerns." What's that supposed to mean? This appallingly lawless state of affairs is the government's responsibility, after all, not ours. After that, a journalist wrote a news story reporting that we had all found new strength and hope after meeting with the secretary general. It claimed that we all felt the government had our concerns at heart. What a load of nonsense. I certainly didn't feel any of the strength or hope that reporter was talking about.

After leaving the provincial government headquarters, we went to the provincial public security office. The person who met with us there also offered his sympathies but immediately discouraged us by saying that the situation was very complex and that we couldn't expect any results in the short term. Then he asked us: "Are your children lost, or were they kidnapped? Now, if they just went missing, then that's the jurisdiction of the Third Bureau; but if they were kidnapped, that'll be a matter for the Sixth Bureau."

How could we possibly answer? If they were simply lost, how was it that after all the extraordinary lengths we had gone to, we couldn't find them? But, of course, we had no proof that they had been kidnapped either. That didn't matter, he told us; the smallest clue would be sufficient. But we didn't have any leads. If we had, we would have followed them up ourselves.

[Official: Of course, for the parents of lost children this is an impossible question; but from the perspective of the public security system, it is a rational division of labor. They can't just lump everything together. In Xi'an, for example, these cases are handled with the utmost seriousness. The Third Bureau issued a nationwide appeal for support, and the Sixth Bureau followed up every lead related to its criminal investigations. Unfortunately, none of these efforts have had the desired outcome, although, as the old saying has it, "Though nothing has happened, it is not for the lack of will." In our job, no matter how much you do, how much you might care, if you don't get results, no one will appreciate you.]

A few days later we went to the provincial Women's Federation, where we were met by the chairperson and the head of the Department for the Protection of the Rights of Women and Children. They too were sympathetic, but all they could suggest was that they would speak to the provincial-government and public-security people on our behalf. They did, but nothing came of it.

After the New Year we repeated this round of visits, and they all told us they would do what they could, that they'd look into it and make representations on our behalf to their superiors. That's when we began to lose all hope. All we could do was support each other and try to look after ourselves.

The first time we took to the streets was on 8 March 1989, International Women's Day. There were only fifty or so of us, all parents of missing children. We didn't want to create any disturbance, but we had no other choice. It was the only way we could focus attention on our plight, in particular to make the government realize the extent of child abductions. We also hoped to alert parents to the need to be vigilant, to warn them to protect their children so as to avoid the tragedy we had all suffered. It really shocked people to see how many people had had their children go missing. Because the media didn't report kidnappings, many people simply hadn't realized how many children had disappeared in Xi'an. They couldn't believe that such incidents were occurring in broad daylight in a socialist nation like China. We marched for over an hour and covered about two kilometers. As we walked, many parents who hadn't lost children joined our ranks tearfully with their own children.

Our slogan was: "Keep an eye on your kids." Our banner read: "Save the children, protect your kids" and "Children aren't merchandise." We also handed out leaflets with the details of our missing children.

By the time we reached the provincial-government headquarters, they had set up a police cordon outside to maintain order. An official asked us to go inside, or rather invited us into the reception area and spoke to us one by one. The basic tenor of his remarks was that we should present our grievances to the government directly and not resort to these methods.

But we *had* gone directly to the government. For the sake of our children and so that the central authorities could be made aware of this horrifying trade in kidnapped children, we even traveled to Beijing. The first time was in March 1991. Our delegation consisted of eight parents whose children had been kidnapped. First off we went to the Reception Center for Complaints and Appeals to the Central Committee of the Chinese Communist Party and the State Council. Yes, that's what it's called: the party and the government share the same space. We were received by a man in his forties who was wearing a suit. He kept his hat on throughout the interview.

—Where are you all from?

—Xi'an.

—And how many of there are you?

—Eight altogether.

—And what's your business?

—Our children were all kidnapped.

—Go see the Ministry of Public Security. They are the relevant governmental instrumentality. We can't help you here.

—We've come to Beijing especially to inform the central government of our plight. Child abduction in Xi'an is an extremely serious problem.

—I'm aware of that, and also the fact that you staged a demonstration. Speak to Public Security.

—The situation in Xi'an is disastrous. Please take a look at these documents that we've prepared.

—If you have any extra copies, you can leave one with us. Then I suggest you go to the Ministry of Public Security.

Right next door to this reception room was a Reception Center for the Standing Committee of the National People's Congress. We thought we might as well go in. Again, we were greeted by a man in his forties.

—Where are you from, and what business do you have?

—We're from Xi'an, and our children are missing.

—Missing? All eight of you have lost children?

—We're not the only ones. We have here the names of forty-eight families who have had children stolen. This is a list of the people in our support group.

—That serious? Have you been to the Reception Center for Complaints and Appeals to the Central Committee of the CCP and the State Council?

—Yes.

—Very well, then. I suggest you now go to the Ministry of Public Security.

—We're not here to try and deal with any single case of kidnapping. What we want to do is inform the Standing Committee about the dire situation in Xi'an. We have come all this way; the least you could do is give us an opportunity to talk to you.

—Very well. Come back at 1:30 this afternoon.

At the appointed time we were received by two people, a man and a woman. We sent two representatives to talk with them, our main point being that the instances of kidnapping were so frequent that the authorities had to take urgent action. The discussion was fairly general, and when we'd finished it was obvious that they were in sympathy with our situation. They undertook to make a thorough report to their superiors but concluded with the following words: "You really do have to go to the Ministry of Public Security. They're the ones in charge of cases like this."

So we went to the Ministry of Public Security, where we had a dialogue with six people. The upshot of all of this was: "We will report the information you've provided us to our superiors. However, you will have to refer to your local authorities for the actual resolution of these cases."

The whole exercise had proved to be incredibly instructive. We all realized that the earth is round; after all that agonizing effort, we ended up right back where we started. We had done everything we could, and we had achieved nothing. Our children were still missing.

According to the Constitution, "marriage, families and children are protected by the state." The law clearly states there is a crime called "abuse of the freedom of citizens and their democratic rights." The Decision on the Strike-Hard Campaign against Wrongdoers passed by the Standing Committee of the National People's Congress is even more explicit: "The ringleaders of gangs who engage in kidnapping or are guilty of serious crimes related to kidnapping will be sentenced to death." With all these laws and stipulations to protect us, why are so many children still being stolen and sold? The problem is that there are laws, but they are not adhered to. I simply cannot accept that this plague of kidnapping—in particular that involving children—cannot be brought to a halt. I believe that if they caught some of the people doing it and executed them—shot a whole lot of them—then the others wouldn't be game to carry on.

[*Official: Things are not quite that simple. She does not appreciate the difficulties we encounter in the legal process. It is precisely because we must act within the law that we cannot simply execute all the people we catch who are engaged in the trade in children. In actual practice, these would be our biggest headaches: in the first place, there's a difference between selling children and simply kidnapping them. According to a 1983 decision of the National People's Congress, "those guilty of extremely serious cases of trafficking in human beings can be sentenced to death." Now, that covers the selling of children, but not kidnapping; that's a crime dealt with in Article 184 of the Criminal Code: "Those guilty of kidnapping children under the age of fourteen from their families or legal guardians will be imprisoned or detained for a period up to but not exceeding five years." In reality these people are clever, and they have divided the trade up between those who specialize in kidnapping children and those who sell them. In one year, over a hundred and fifty traders were arrested in Gaotang County in Shandong alone. Not a bad catch, eh? But all of them were either kidnappers or sellers; no one did both. That means that after going through due process, not one of them was executed.*

Second, how do you determine what an "extremely serious case" is? The lack of any fixed standard makes for a really confusing situation. The crime might be the same, but it is judged differently depending on where you are. Is selling five people serious? Or is it only three? Or is it only "serious" when the victims are injured? What kind of injury counts as "serious"? The same crime will be viewed very differently in different places—and it's particularly difficult in "disaster areas" where people are extremely worked up about the issue. Ironically, if there are too many cases in one area you tend to see people getting lighter sentences.

Third, it is extremely difficult to take legal action against people who buy the children. Trafficking connotes a two-way exchange; there is a seller and a buyer. Naturally, if you can control the buyers, then there won't be any market for the goods. In 1991 a presidential decree was issued that stated: "Those who purchase or detain kidnapped women and children are to be sentenced to up to but not exceeding three years' imprisonment or detention." Prior to this decree, buyers could only be reeducated through criticism. Although now there is a legal sanction, there are still problems. For example, what if the kidnappers never told the buyers that they were taking possession of kidnapped women or children? They might claim that these children were born outside the quotas permitted by the family-planning policy. Of course, an adult woman or an adolescent would be able to speak out on her own behalf, but what about little babies who can't defend themselves? Thus, often the buyer really wouldn't know where the child came from. Another possibility is that prior to the kidnapper's being arrested, the buyer might claim that they were never told that the child was stolen, so that when a case comes to trial, you can't legally prosecute them. So there are two loopholes for buyers. If they're good at stonewalling, they can easily get out of three years' detention. Thus the threat of imprisonment is not all that effective in practice.

Fourth, we are seriously underfunded and understaffed. Traders in human beings work all over the country, and although the actual cases may be fairly straightforward, there are lots of complex leads to follow up. According to the law, you have to obtain all the evidence of an alleged crime within two or three months following the arrest of a suspect, and that's a real problem. The procuracy isn't interested in your practical difficulties; if your investigations haven't been completed within the stipulated time, then the suspect is released.

Fifth, regional protectionism often makes it difficult to recover a stolen child. The police are constantly coming into conflict with the local people in the place where the child is located. All right, let's forget it. I'll come straight out and say it: What actually happens is that the police often come into conflict with local party committees and governments. There have been cases where these local overlords have trashed police vehicles and beaten up or even killed police officers. Quite frankly, all too often we feel just like these parents do—that we are chasing our own tails and never getting anywhere.]

Anyway, that was the upshot of our efforts at petitioning the Center. Thereafter, some people decided to appeal directly to society as a whole and try to get some public sympathy for our cause. They wanted to stir up public outrage at these barbaric crimes so that pressure could be brought to bear on the authorities. They began getting signatures from people working in various departments, factories, mines, and schools for a petition. Most people were sympathetic, so they soon had tens of thousands of signatures; a lot of people even wrote a few words on the petition to express their outrage. What happened after the petition was presented to the government? Silence. We weren't directly involved in organizing the petition; we just didn't have the time or energy.

Regardless of whether the appeals were directed at Beijing or at local authorities, the whole aim of the exercise was to get the government to take this matter seriously, and to act sternly, rigorously, and quickly to strike out at these traders in human beings. The key was to bring enough pressure to bear on the authorities. Naturally, if they had been elected democratically, they would have been more responsive; but they are not from among us. They were not elected by the people who sign petitions. If they sense pressure on them, then they respond; if not, then they go to work as usual, completely untroubled. As long as they don't engage in corruption, they will be regarded by the party as good cadres. That's why I said earlier we are a spontaneously formed, temporary, voluntary, and unofficial organization. Our sole aim is to find our children. If you still think we are a lobby or pressure group, then you're wrong. I'd never even heard the expression *lobby group* until we formed our organization and someone told me that's what we really are. But we aren't. In the first place, we can't bring any real pressure to bear on the authorities. Second, we don't have any political program or agenda; nor do we wish to make trouble. Some people do think we want to stir things up; they regard any street demonstration as troublemaking. But that's their problem.

Since people think we are a lobby group, I thought I'd better look up the term. The dictionary defines such expressions in the context of Western-style politics. It goes without saying that the political setup in China is quite different, so the term really has nothing to do with us. That's why we have nothing to do with the concept. As I see it, lobbyists negotiate with members of parliament or congress who then may act on their behalf or bring pressure to bear on the government through parliament. We might try lobbying the National People's Congress in Beijing, but don't be fooled by the superficial similarities between them and parliamentarians. Our congressmen and -women act rather differently. They won't even see us. When we went to the capital, we didn't get to meet a single member of the NPC. The functionaries who did deign to speak to us chorused, "Go to the Ministry of Public Security and your local authorities."

Although we enjoy universal suffrage and every citizen has democratic rights, in reality our vote doesn't threaten them.

Another thing I'd like to mention is something that many of us have discovered since losing our children. We have learned how complex our society really is. We have finally realized that in our socialist country, although there are people who are sympathetic and who have a strong sense of decency, there are also many vile creatures who have fed off our agony, people who can't even be called human beings. Many of us have been cheated. After putting out our flyers and pleas, many of us have received letters from people telling us that they had clues as to the whereabouts of our children. These people said that they'd like to help, but since they themselves were destitute, they'd want to be paid for their information. And that was the most direct form of deceit. There have been cases where someone claims that they know where your child is but dare not tell because they're scared of the kidnappers. They arrange a rendezvous with you and promise they'll secretly take you to where your child is. The place is invariably a station or a wharf in another town. You arrive in a strange place where you don't know anyone, and they get you to pay them some money for traveling expenses and then take you off to buy tickets. Then, before you know what has happened, they've lost you in the crowd. Or there are people who lure you to some out-of-the-way place to rob you, knowing full well that since you've come to find your child, you're sure to have some cash on you. Then there are those who claim they're practitioners of *qigong* or that they have supernatural powers, or pretend they have connections with the kidnapping ring. They too try to rip you off. Some pretend to be part of the mafia. They call up claiming that they have your child and say that unless you pay a huge ransom they'll kill the kid.

I've been cheated three times. It's not that I didn't have my doubts, but even when you're suspicious, you have to go and check out a lead, just in case it's the real thing this time.

[Official: What's even worse is that some cheats pretend to be working for us. They claim that the child has been found in some other place and offer to pick the kid up and bring him back to Xi'an. Then they spin some line about how

the family that the child has been with has spent thousands of yuan to buy the child, plus all the money they've had to fork out on feeding and clothing him and whatnot. To ensure a trouble-free trip and the safe return of the child without argument, they suggest that the parents cover the buyer's expenses. Of course the parents agree. Even if it means they have to sell everything they have, they get the money together somehow. Then, when they're on the way to get the child, the cheat will find a way to steal the money.

This might not be the right time or place to mention it, but there's another type of situation that involves parents hiding their own children with friends or relatives and then reporting them missing or kidnapped. They make a big show of it and get us involved so that we expend a huge amount of effort searching for the missing child. What the parents really want to do is get around the one-child policy and have a second child, a fat and healthy baby boy. They don't dare flout the family planning law openly, so they do this instead.]

One. Although we have done absolutely everything in our power, we have only recovered one child so far. It might only be one, but all I can say is that at least we have found one. Maybe in the future we'll find another, and then another. Maybe not. Even if we never find another child, at least we have found this one. Do you understand what I'm saying?

My profession? I'm an accountant.

Some people believe there must be some complicated story behind the loss of a child, there must be more to it than we let on. But there isn't. One day she went off to school as usual, with her satchel on her back. It was a badly made satchel; the school made them all buy one. It was less than a year old, and it was already falling to pieces. She simply never came back.

8

Shine

A Prodigy

China needs its prodigies. As early as the Tang Dynasty, there was a system whereby children under nine years of age who had completed their "higher education" would be sent to the imperial court. Today, among the reports in the media that fall under the categories of "Revitalizing China" and "Pride of the Nation," you often come across stories about three-year-old calligraphers or five-year-old "living computers" who know by heart all the place-names on the map and can recite over three hundred classical poems. There are even legends about little Ph.D.'s who still wet the bed.

According to a report in the Beijing Youth Daily, *there are a hundred thousand little piano prodigies hammering away at keyboards in Beijing alone. They appear in public before even reaching school age; in other words they are fulfilling, or rather have already fulfilled, their own future.*

The interview was conducted in the green room at the auditorium where the National Musicians' Association tests young pianists for certificates of proficiency.

I'm nine years old. I'm on level 5; today I'm taking the test for level 6. If I pass, that'll mean I can perform in big hotels. My teacher says I won't have any trouble. I'll be fine as long as I don't panic. Level 6 isn't really called "hotel level"; it's called "commercial performance qualification." That's how the grown-ups put it, anyway. But it really means you're good enough to play for money in hotels. I'm not going to do that, though. I'm still a kid, and my family doesn't need me out there earning money for them. Besides, there's the law, and we've all got to obey the law. It says I'm not old enough to be working.

There are ten levels altogether. If I don't get to level 10, then I'll never get to be a maestro. I think it'll take me a long time to get that far. I don't think I can do it in the next few years. It's too hard. Dad doesn't agree. He says I have no ideals. He says a soldier who doesn't want to become a general isn't a good soldier; you've got to rise to the challenge.

I wish I could be grown up right now. It's boring being a kid. I don't like practicing the piano at all, but Dad won't let me go out and play. I have to practice every day. I finally get through all my homework and he goes, come on, come on, be a good boy now and practice your piano. When I don't practice hard he hits me. Not hard; he couldn't do that, and anyway he wouldn't dare. It's against the law to hit people, even people in your own family. He's got to obey the law. He's just threatening me. You know the word "threaten"? The characters for it are really hard to write. Our teacher has only taught us the first one, but I can read both of them. I can read about a thousand characters.

Dad says practicing the piano is like going out to play. He says I'm learning a skill that will help me make a living and having fun at the same time. Mom says it doesn't matter if I can't make a living with it. She says it's a sign of culture, and high-class people don't go running wild when they're children. She makes me learn English as well as piano. I've been studying English for six months already, one lesson a week.

I started piano when I was five, so I've been doing it almost five years now. I practice two hours a day. I have lessons at my teacher's place on Sundays, so I have to practice longer on Saturdays. It doesn't matter if it's the middle of winter and it's snowing, I still have to go out for my lesson. Some of the other kids come from rich families with cars. We don't have a car. Mom takes me on the bus. My teacher is a real pain. She's a famous pianist. She takes a few students on Sundays at eighty yuan an hour. We also have to give her gifts at New Year and on festivals. She's such a pain; she can tell right off if I practiced hard or not. If I don't play well, she says, "You didn't practice, you haven't made any progress at all." Dad gets all upset if she says that. He never asks if it's really true; he just yells at me. He takes my teacher's word for it. "You haven't made any progress; you can't have done any practice." He's so sure about that; and he threatens me, too.

He thinks that since I'm just a kid, I don't have any dignity. All he does is lecture me, telling me to practice harder and harder. He says the harsh winter brings forth the fragrant plum blossom. If you don't work hard, you'll be a complete failure.

In fact, I'm already working as hard as I can. I go for a run every day when I get up. I didn't do that well in phys. ed. at school—last semester I just passed, but Dad says I have to do well in everything, so I can't do badly in phys. ed. He goes running with me every day. Well, not every day. If he's been doing night duty at the office, then I get to slack off a bit. That happens at least once a week. He has to sleep at the office. So if he's not at home to keep an eye on me, I get a bit of time off. When I come back from my run, Mom has breakfast ready. We eat, and then I go to school. As soon as classes are over, I come home and do my homework, then we have dinner. Our teachers give us heaps of homework. Sometimes I can't get it all done before dinner. After dinner I'm allowed to rest for a while. They let me watch the TV news, then I have to practice, and I keep going until Mom calls out that it's time to wash up for bed. Every day is the same. And they still say I'm not working hard enough. It really makes me mad.

Dad's bigger then me. Getting mad doesn't do any good; he's still the head of the family.

What do you mean, kids are "little emperors"? That's all lies. We don't even get any time to play; they just make us work harder and harder. The harsh winter brings forth the fragrant plum blossom and all that. It's no fun at all being a kid.

I think hard work's for grown-ups. But what can I do? Look around at all the drifting laborers and street vendors. When they were my age, they were running around wild. They didn't get an education. If I mess things up now, I won't achieve anything. I'll end up like them. Mom says the competition is only going to get worse. There are so many only children these days who can't do anything for themselves that it will be a real problem. If I don't make something of myself, I won't even be able to be a street vendor. All those drifters from the country would be better at it than me.

I know I'm only young, but I know a lot about how things work. My parents scrimped and saved to buy me a piano, and they still had to borrow money. It was all so I would have a good future. They'll spend anything on me, for my future. They'll take me to concerts at two hundred yuan a ticket. Two hundred yuan! Think about it. That's four hundred yuan just for me and Mom. It starts at 7:30 and finishes some time after 9:00. It's not even two hours, and that's half my dad's monthly salary gone.

If I pass this level, I'll do level 7 next year. If I fail, I'll do level 6 again next year.

Why do I have to study piano? Don't ask me. Ask my dad. He's here, but he doesn't want to make me nervous, so he won't come in and watch. He's waiting for me outside. He can't play piano. He's a policeman.

[Not long afterward I got a phone call from his father. The boy had passed the test with flying colors and was about to take part in a concert for young pianists. "He'll be playing in the Beijing Concert Hall. One solo piece, and one accompanied by the Central Symphony Orchestra! The Central Symphony Orchestra! What do you think of that? When I was his age, get this, I wouldn't even have been allowed in to listen."]

9

Moonwalking
A Differently Abled Young Woman

Most of the interviewees in this book are people I encountered only during my various trips to China. I might have jotted down some notes before leaving Australia about the sort of people I wanted to talk to and where I might find them, but I constantly revised my list. Some turned out the way I planned; others fell by the wayside. But Zhao Li was the exception to the rule. Before I'd arrived in China, I'd decided I had to interview her. She was one of a very few I really wanted to see.

I'd read about her in the Beijing Evening News. *The article on her appeared on page 10 of this popular paper, directly underneath an advertisement for a venereal disease clinic run by the Tiananmen branch of the Armed Police.*

I clipped out the article and stuck it in my notebook. It gave the name of Zhao Li's school in the northeast. That's where I found her.

Anshan City, Liaoning Province

When I was little, I didn't know I was disabled. I knew I couldn't use my hands. But it never occurred to me that when people spoke about the disabled, they were talking about me. When I was in fifth grade, some reporters came to our school. My teacher said to them, "You can see what a strong spirit this handicapped girl has." That really upset me. It shocked me. I went home and asked my mother, "Am I handicapped? How could I be?" Up to that moment, I thought I was just like everyone else. I was shattered.

I was a difficult birth. There were complications—in fact, you could probably call it malpractice. But you know what it's like with hospitals. The victim of malpractice can never get any satisfaction. Anyway, when I was only three days old, my mother discovered that the nerves in my arms were paralyzed. I couldn't move them at all. That was 1974. Today I can only move one little finger, and that only slightly.

I can't grip anything with my hands, and I can't move my arms. I'm not the same as other people; I am handicapped. It makes me different. It's the cruel reality I have to live with.

From the time I was a child, I've used my feet to pick things up, to wash my face, to put on my shoes and to eat. We lived in a village in the mountains and, when I started going to the local kindergarten there at the age of five, I learned to write with my feet. At first, I'd make these huge, ugly, messy characters. The teacher would guide my foot with her hands. But my feet were so small, they just wouldn't do as they were told. I'd get pins and needles after writing for a while, and then my foot would grow tired and hurt like the devil. I only learned to draw and paint later on, in high school, in art class. I took art because I wanted to learn something useful. Later, before the university entrance exams, I took extra lessons in the painting department of the Shenyang Art Academy. I don't like Shenyang. It's all tall buildings, and the sky is always gray. Kids from small places like me find big cities awfully cold.

I chose to study art because I liked it, but also because I had to consider my future career, and art seemed like a viable choice. An artist needs inspiration; a real work of art has soul, and although I might paint with my feet, I think I do better than most people who use their hands.

I started primary school at the age of eight. It was the school my mother worked at, and although she taught both my older sister and my younger brother, I was never in her class. I always did well and was in the top five in my class. Despite my disability, I was very strong-willed and worked harder than most. So I didn't just keep up with the others—I could do better. The school was in the mountains, and our village grew subsistence crops like corn, sorghum, and soybeans. What I'm saying is that it wasn't a very rich place. Our family was very poor, too. My father had spent five years in the army and was a party branch secretary for thirty years after that. He was very upright and honest. At that time cadres weren't corrupt at all, and our house was the most dilapidated in the whole village. I'm not trying to make him out to be some revolutionary model or anything, but he was dedicated to the village and the party. He even spent my mother's paltry savings on the village. So you can imagine that he's not very happy with how things are going now: the way party officials carry on, feasting and drinking at public expense and doing whatever they can to further their own interests. It makes him so angry he cusses all the time, but what's the use? Things are the way they are. Nowadays he's just a simple salesman and a good father.

After primary school I graduated to junior high. The school was quite a way from home, and the road went through the mountains. Some classmates boarded at school, but I couldn't do that, so I commuted. We didn't get out of class until nine o'clock at night. So after a day of school, I had to make my way back home in pitch dark. It wasn't an easy time for me. The main reason I couldn't board at school was because I couldn't go to the toilet by myself. I still can't. Like some other handicapped people with a similar problem, I try not to eat or drink too much, and to take as little water as possible.

In primary school I took part in physical education classes like everyone else. I'm physically very active. But since I couldn't move my upper limbs, I wasn't able to maintain my balance when running. I fell down a lot, and it was hard to stand up once I'd fallen over. I couldn't support myself with my hands and arms, so I had to use my head and shoulders instead. You can just imagine what it was like. So as I grew up I had to learn to keep myself in check. Seeing others run around, I always wanted to join them, but eventually I gave up on physical education classes.

It was a very average high school, the kind that doesn't get many students going on to university studies. Even those who weren't handicapped found it hard getting into a university. You can have all the confidence you like, but you still don't get many opportunities. Although I came first in my year in senior high, I knew it wasn't certain that I'd make it to university. Our school was too mediocre, and that was a fact. On top of that, there aren't a lot of universities or courses willing to accept handicapped students. In the end, only one person from our class got into Liaoning University.[1]

We handicapped people have to expend more time and effort to achieve our goals. But if you give us an opportunity, we'll know how to value it and work harder than anybody else to take advantage of it.

For senior high I went to Tongze High School in Haicheng. My family moved nearby to look after me. Entirely because of me. My mother hadn't

1. The major institution for higher learning in Shenyang, the provincial capital of Liaoning.

yet retired, so she asked to be transferred to Tongze. As a primary-school teacher, she wasn't qualified to teach there, so they gave her a job in the school office. It was the same thing with my move to Anshan—my whole family came with me. There are just some things I can't do for myself. I'm like a snail—wherever I go, my home comes with me. I'm so happy that I have such a wonderful family. My mother is now working as a cleaner at the teachers' college I go to in order to earn some extra cash. My father's got a job as a salesman, selling boiler parts. They're not easy to sell.

In high school I heard that Changchun University had an art department in its special learning division that specialized in teaching the handicapped. That was another reason I decided to do art; I thought it might increase my chances of going to university. I've wanted to go to university since I was little. I looked upon a university career as though it were an unassailable mountain peak—and I was intent on climbing it. I imagined I'd be able to smuggle myself in there by way of the fine arts. Once I got in—once I was in that university atmosphere—I thought I'd get lots more opportunities to study anything that interested me, such as literature and English. But the year I took the entrance exams, in 1994, Changchun University wasn't accepting any students into its special learning program.

So I tried for a university in Dalian instead. I won't tell you which one; I hate even saying the name of the place now. I applied to do fashion design in their applied arts program. The supervising professor learned that I was disabled just before the exam and that I use my feet to draw with. He was full of admiration and didn't say anything about not letting me take the exams. He did advise me, however, to have a talk with the head of the school first. This man proved quite courteous, even amiable, but what he told me was this: "Not everyone who draws with their hands can get into our university. Given the fact that you use your feet, you can't possibly make the grade." At the time, I thought that as he hadn't even seen my paintings, he had no right to tell me I wasn't good enough. I was confident about my abilities and felt my work would stand the test, so I replied, "Just let me take the exam. Give me a chance. That's all I ask." Seeing my determination, he agreed.

The examinations were to be held in Shenyang. But before the exams, I ran into a bit of trouble. The day before, we had to register and see the examination hall. From where I was staying I had to walk over an hour to get there. I'd just arrived in the big city and, being from the country, I'd bought new leather shoes for the occasion. After walking to the exam hall and back that first day, my feet ended up covered in blisters, right in the places where I hold my pen and painting brush, so just picking up a pen was agony. The exam the next morning was portrait sketching. Half an hour in, I still hadn't finished the first sketch (and I hadn't done a good job), I was so tense. The university administrators and teachers were curious about me; they kept coming over to see how I was going and saying things like, "Look how this kid paints with her toes." This made me even more nervous. I'd always been quite confident about achieving whatever I set out to do, and wasn't afraid of showing anyone. But now, what with my nerves and the pain, I had to change feet, and now they were standing there saying, "This kid's feet are better than hands, she's completely ambidextrous." It was driving me completely crazy, and I simply couldn't concentrate.

But I finally managed to finish, and I thought I hadn't done so badly after all. In the afternoon, we were tested on colors. The supervising teacher from the academy praised me on the spot for my sense of color. I mumbled some pleasantry like "You're too kind," but I was thinking, it's true: it's not bad at all. That made me feel a bit better. On the second day, we had a test for design, and I did well. Afterwards, I felt as though my skills had been recognized, and I began to relax and felt confident and hopeful again. I thought I wouldn't have to try out for another university, that I'd be accepted, no problem at all; I just had to wait till they gave me my qualifying certificate, then take the other general exams, and that would be it.

But things didn't work out that way at all. Other people received their entrance certificates. A week passed. I didn't receive either a qualifying certificate or notification that I'd failed. I was completely distraught. Although I still felt pretty good about how I'd done, ultimately you just don't know. After I'd suffered for a week, the certificate finally arrived, but at the same time the principal of my high school called me in for a talk. He said that the university had contacted him to say that although I qualified in the fine arts exams, they didn't want to enroll me. Even if I passed the other exams, he said, the university still didn't want me.

I was shocked. They rejected me, they said, for two reasons. First, they felt I wasn't suited to study art. Second, foreign guests often visited the campus, and it would be bad to let foreigners see me painting with my feet; it would damage the school's image. They thought my presence would make their university lose face!

The door to a university career slammed shut in my face then and there.

I was devastated. What could I say? I'd done my best, and yet ultimately it had nothing to do with my level of accomplishment; they simply were not going to accept me. Wasn't that just a way of telling me to bow my head to fate? My only problem is that I can't use my hands; but I can use my feet. I could paint with my feet as well as other people painted with their hands. Why wasn't that good enough?

Even though I was very depressed, I pulled myself together and decided to try again. I didn't have any time to waste. I'd failed this time, but it wasn't because I couldn't do it. I owed it to myself to try again. Several days later, I took the entrance exams for this teacher's college, Anshan Normal University, to do applied fine arts in the fine arts program. I passed, and they accepted me. I'd got through that doorway to college education.

To be honest, Anshan Normal University was the only choice I had. When signing up for entrance exams, other people would list as many different preferences for universities and subjects as they could. At least they were allowed to dream. If they didn't get into one program, there'd be others they could try for. I had very few choices; the disabled aren't allowed to dream. I had one last chance, and that was to get into this teachers' college. There are so many universities and colleges in China, and they all clearly specify that a basic condition for entry is that the applicant be physically fit. So I didn't even bother applying. No matter what I do, I can't make the grade on that one.

Actually, Anshan Normal University had the same stipulation—but it wasn't far from where we lived, and the teachers there knew of me. They'd seen me on the Spring Festival TV broadcast painting with my feet. And, as they put it themselves, "This kid's got guts." They made it clear that they'd welcome my application to enroll. I actually didn't do that well on the exams this time; I certainly didn't come in first or anything, just around the median of the students they accepted that year.

I was so excited. I truly valued the opportunity being given to me. At the same time, I couldn't get too worked up about it. You can understand that, can't you?

Whenever the local TV station recorded its Spring Festival special, or when there was some meeting of Women's Federation representatives, they'd ask me to go and perform—not just my painting, but also everyday things like threading a needle with my toes, washing my face, getting dressed and so on. They loved it. Every time someone would say the same thing: "Look, she's more agile with her feet than we are with our hands." Of course I hated that. What did they think I was? I eventually got used to it, or rather, became numb to it. Fine, I thought, if that's how you get your kicks, then I'll entertain you. Call it my contribution to society, a service to others.

When I'm walking down the street, I do my best to hide my disability. I want to appear like the rest of you. But I'm not, and if you look out you can see me—the girl who's got her money and her ticket in her teeth getting on the bus next to you, the girl who never carries an umbrella no matter how heavily it's raining or snowing, the one who is soaking wet yet forges on regardless. That's me, the real me.

I don't like sitting still. When I'm feeling down I go out and kick a ball around with the boys. I like that. If I can work up a good sweat, my mood improves tremendously. I played volleyball in high school, but where the others used their hands, I used my feet. I can't swim, though. There's a girl like me in Japan, Noriko, who's famous all over the world. She uses her feet for everything, too. She loves swimming. I don't. I'm afraid of the water.

West Willow Village put up the money for my university tuition. Last March I was still in high school, getting ready to take the exams. The leaders of the village saw me perform at a meeting to celebrate International Women's Day. Seeing how determined I was, they sought out my principal and asked him how I was doing in school and what our family's financial situation was like. When they heard how poor we were, they donated twenty thousand yuan toward my university tuition. Without that money, I wouldn't have been able to go. It was such a worry. My father hardly earns anything at all, and so I'd have had to rely entirely on my mother and sister's salaries. My family was prepared to scrimp and save for my tuition. From the time I entered middle school, I never had any new clothes; I wore only my sister's hand-me-downs. But we still weren't able to save much. To get together the vast amount of money for university tuition would have been virtually impossible.

I'd never had anything to do with West Willow Village before that. I only knew that there was a clothing market there that was famous throughout China, but I'd never been there. That's why I had this idea of going into fashion design, in the hope that I could do something useful for the village in return for their kindness. They never made any demands on me about that, but I believe that when you drink water you should remember who dug the well. I hoped to be able do something for them. But my hopes were one thing, reality was quite another. My presence would have disgraced the school, and so they didn't let me through the door.

That was in 1994. We all thought that the village money would cover my basic expenses, but actually it wasn't enough. In addition to tuition, I had to buy a lot of reference books. They are really expensive, sometimes as much as several hundred yuan. Then there were paints and brushes, and those are really expensive, too. I couldn't afford them—but you can't do without them. I scraped and saved for half a year, and rented some of the painting materials I needed, but I still spent 5,500 yuan. With things as they are today, I know I'm going to need at least thirty thousand yuan to make it through to graduation. I'm still about ten thousand short. I plan to find whatever part-time work I can manage after class, maybe doing a bit of interior design, for instance. Don't look at how we live here, with our borrowed furniture. I can create beautiful homes for other people.

I have to pay full tuition. That amounts to 2,800 yuan a semester, and there's no waiver for me. What with that and other expenses, I had to hand over 3,700 yuan when I enrolled. It's not a rich school, and the administration does their best to look after me. They've done everything they could possibly do. The teachers and students are so warm and supportive, too, and are constantly looking for ways to help me out. The departmental secretary knitted a pair of woolen socks with no toes, so that I can paint without getting cold in the winter. She invented the pattern herself. The department has also made two special desks for me to use, of different heights, with chairs to match. I said one would be fine, but my classmates insisted. One of them used to be a carpenter, and is very skilled, so he knocked them together in no time.

No, I don't think I'll ever have a boyfriend. I'm disabled, remember? That'd be looking for trouble. I've got lots of good friends, but I'm not someone who knows how to go out and have a good time. I'm not like other people, partying and fooling around. It's not in my nature to do that. If I could do something about my hands, or if I was financially independent, and could hire someone to look after my daily needs, maybe then I'd think about starting a family. I'd never let a boyfriend or husband look after me that way. It would be too much trouble for them, or they'd get sad about it. I couldn't make them very happy.

I've always felt that if I were a man, people would look at me differently. They'd speak of my determination as being really admirable, or even great. But I'm a woman, so what they say is that I'm ugly. Sure she's got guts, they say, but she's handicapped, physically defective, ugly. It's not enough for a woman to be great—she's got to be beautiful, too, if people are going to love her. Isn't that right?

I wanted to tell you something else about the time of the university exams, but I got distracted. That time when I got to Shenyang, I found a very cheap room in a hostel. It had a bed and nothing else. Only after I'd moved in did I learn how far it was from the classes I would be taking at the academy in preparation for the exams. Half an hour's walk at least, and even further to the examination hall. That would take one and a half hours. If my family had been able to afford it, they'd have helped me find a room closer to the school. But we just couldn't manage it.

My family did everything they could to look after me. My mother left my brother a carton of instant noodles and came with me to Shenyang. Having such a fantastic family has been so important for me. They were all waiting for my news; they were all doing their utmost to help me, standing by me as I tried to overcome the obstacles that life has put in my way. Because of this, no matter how tough the going gets, I can still carry on. There was an exam preparation class in the morning, one in the afternoon, and one in the evening. I felt I had to make up for lost time, so I went to all of them. After I walked home, carrying my easel on my back, my mother would wash my feet. I'd be asleep before she'd even finished. Walking doesn't bother me, but to paint all day and then do all that walking was hard on my feet, and they were showing the strain. Then add to that my idiotic vanity, the day of the exams, wearing those dumb leather shoes. So my feet decided they'd had enough and broke out in blisters.

The exams began at 7:30 A.M. So early, and so far from where I was staying, too. I couldn't afford a taxi. I worried about this half the night and finally got up at 3 A.M. So far from home, I was nervous about spending any of our savings, and besides, whether I passed or not, who knew what sort of money I'd need after that? I'd met some girls who attended a private school across the road from the hostel. They were really lovely, and when they saw my blisters the first day, they were concerned about my feet and said they'd take me to the exams. And they actually appeared shortly after I woke up that morning. They'd brought along a pair of soft-soled shoes for me, too. I was so moved. They had two bicycles and wanted to push me all the way there on the back. I said no, I'd walk with them, and that if they'd only take me as far as where some of the other people in my class were staying, that would be fine. We could go together to the exam hall. By then it was about 4 A.M. The streetlights were still on. It was quiet and cold on the street. There was no one in sight. It was like something from a poem.

After an hour and a half's walk we arrived, but the others were still in bed. They said they'd call me a cab and catch up with me there. But the cab driver got lost and took me round in a big circle, and then another one, and still couldn't find the right place. I was a nervous wreck. In the end, he took me back to where we'd started. By then my friends were up.

The cab driver hadn't turned on his meter, and he demanded thirty yuan for the trip. I talked him down to twenty-five, which was still twice as much as it would have cost to get a cab to the examination center from my hostel in the first place. He hadn't taken me anywhere, and if I could have reasoned with him I wouldn't have had to pay. But what could I do? No hands, and my feet tied up in shoes—I couldn't even open the cab door myself.

There will always be prejudice. I never wear short-sleeved clothing, to make it less obvious that I have a disability. The moment people notice it, they look at me differently. It's just a fact of life. There's nothing you can do about it. People can be so hurtful. When I'd just started in senior high school, a classmate noticed my disability and shouted out, "Eew! How come they let deformed people come to school too?" At the time I was terribly upset. Later, in retrospect, I could sort of understand her reaction.

It's not just high school students. It was university administrators who felt that having a disabled person around would shame their school. It's bad in restaurants, too. People don't just stare; they say things like, "What's wrong with this kid, how'd she injure herself like that?" Sure, you could say they're expressing sympathy, but it means that I can't just sit wherever I want; I have to find some corner where no one will notice me. Unless it's absolutely unavoidable, I just don't go out to eat.

In theory, mental health is more important than being physically sound. But in actual fact you can see what people's priorities are from the way they look at someone like me.

Although my situation is like this, I know I'm incredibly fortunate compared to so many other people with disabilities. I am totally aware of it, totally. I've seen a lot of disabled people who suffer much worse than I ever have. For example, I have a friend who did very well in school but wasn't accepted into high school because of his disability. They wouldn't even give him the opportunity to educate himself, to let him find a way to raise a family and make a living for himself. All he ever wanted was some education, so that he would be better equipped to compete in and serve society. Lots of disabled people are denied this chance. They're really unlucky, but they're still fortunate compared with the ones who end up begging on the street. I really feel like I've been terribly fortunate.

I'm still living with my family. As for having an independent life, well, I'll still have to overcome some pretty serious obstacles. I can't shop at the supermarket, can't put up an umbrella when it rains, can't put out a hand to hail a cab, and I need help to go to the toilet. There are some quite specific things that other people can do easily just by lifting the proverbial finger but which I just can't do. Things that wouldn't even occur to most people, like how hard it is for me to buy shoes. I need shoes that don't lace up, that you can just slip into, with a relatively soft sole and uppers, shoes that keep your feet pretty warm. But no one makes shoes exactly like this. And there would be no market for them, as only disabled people need them. Sneakers are good, but they all come with laces. I have to wear them very loose, otherwise I can't get out of them. But if they're that loose it's impossible to run, and they're not that warm either. I'm eternally searching for a pair that will suit my needs.

Up till now, the most painful thing that's happened to me is nearly being shut out of university. But that's just up till now. In the future, when I start looking for work, I think it'll be even harder. I'm still going to school now, and people do their best to look after me. They're willing to lavish their concern and care on a student, especially "a kid with guts" like me. But in the workplace things are very competitive, and that's real life. Out there, people are only interested in how efficient you are, what you're able to create, and how well you're able to look after a client's needs. So the true test as to whether I'll make it in the world will come once I'm out in the workplace, on my own.

China has 1.2 billion people. With such a big population, it's not realistic to expect that just because you're disabled, they're going to look after you. My greatest wish is simply to be treated as an equal. I hope that this society can improve a bit and give people like me a chance. I hope that other disabled people will have an easier time getting into university and not run into the sort of obstacles that I did. I hope—I hope that people don't have to wait till the end of their lives to realize how regrettable the things they have bequeathed to the future might be.

Do you think my hopes are too unrealistic?

I love dancing. I do an excellent moon walk. Sometimes when I'm dancing I get so excited that I feel a little crazy.

Can you do the moon walk? Even normal people don't need to use their arms for that.

Unlevel Playing Field

10

Consuming Habits
On the Flood of Fakes

On 19 May 1995, the Beijing Municipal Technical Supervision Bureau under-
took a quality inspection of Chinese national flags being sold in six stores on
Nan Xinhua Street in central Beijing. Of the six different kinds of flags in-
spected, only 6.2 percent were found to be of acceptable quality.

Changsha, Hunan Province

Changsha's always been chaotic, even from when I was a kid. That was during the Cultural Revolution. Chairman Mao was the Red, Red Sun who
rose out of Hunan Province, and Changsha was the city where he came to
"strike the waters" when he was young.[1] He used to go swimming from the
Shuilu sandbanks, right here in the city. Little wonder that we were destined
for chaos. But that was long before the appearance of the market economy;
it was a different type of chaos from the kind we have now. No one needed
a Consumer Protection Association then; as long as Chairman Mao was
protected, everything else could slide.

There weren't that many people in our extended family, though friends
were always coming and going. But that's all changed. Now both time and
money are precious commodities. Time is money—who wants to waste it
socializing?

My father was born and bred here. He had a bit of schooling before
becoming a soldier. After being discharged, he taught primary school. I was

1. This is a reference to the last line of Mao's 1925 poem "Changsha": "Remember still/
How, venturing midstream, we struck the waters/And waves stayed the speeding boats?" See
Mao Tsetung, *Poems* (Beijing: Peking Foreign Languages Press, 1976), p. 2.

one of his pupils. We were constantly subjected to his substandard Mandarin, both at home and at school. He'd never been to a teachers' college, and he never did learn to get his tongue around Mandarin pronunciation. On those grounds alone you could claim he was a bit of a defective product himself.

I suppose you might say I was born in the right place at the right time. As a kid, I was just old enough to be dragged through the Cultural Revolution. My dad was very straight, and apart from *Quotations from Chairman Mao,* all he gave us to read was endless stuff about Lei Feng, so we could "learn from him."[2] He's another famous son of Hunan. Nowadays, when people from other provinces are ripped off or sold inferior-quality goods here in Changsha, they'll act mad and shout: "But Lei Feng came from here! Aren't you ashamed that you're cheating people?" Our shop owners aren't fazed by that. "Don't give me that," they say. "Lei Feng's not from Changsha, he's from Wangcheng County nearby. That's the county where the hicks are hopeful *[wang]* of making it in our city *[cheng]*. Get it?" But even Wangcheng is no law-abiding paradise these days. They're even better at cheating shoppers there than we are in Changsha, and they hide the con behind shop fronts that tout themselves as the "Lei Feng Store" or "Lei Feng Markets."

Naturally, we soon grew tired of reading about Lei Feng and his revolutionary heroism. Our father got us to learn poetry, too. After we'd memorized all of Chairman Mao's poems, he selected some suitably edifying Tang dynasty poems for us as well, politically healthy verse that he believed expressed antifeudal sentiment or gave voice to the suffering masses. The last thing ideologically correct people back in the Tang dynasty would do is sit around writing decent poetry, so again we were given fake and shoddy goods. Any poets who were critical of their times—and acceptable to my father—were invariably people with frustrated bureaucratic careers or who had failed in love. So, apart from mass demonstrations and struggle meetings, we had virtually no entertainment as children at all. Watching all that jumping around, people screaming and shouting, was the most fun we could ever expect.

In fact, the place has always been awash with inferior and second-rate

2. A famous "red Samaritan" Communist martyr. Famed as a loyal student of Mao Zedong Thought, the PLA soldier Lei Feng died in the early 1960s and was made into a national paragon and role model. In 1963 Mao declared that all should "learn from Comrade Lei Feng," and something of a war of civility has been fought in Lei Feng's name intermittently ever since.

products. These days people buy imitation wines with counterfeit money and then come to us to complain. It was the same in the Cultural Revolution. Phony revolutionaries were going around denouncing fake reactionaries—and then, after it was all over, they'd appeal to the Central Committee of the Communist Party to be rehabilitated. Things may appear to have changed, but the same old chicanery continues. China is rife with fakes; it's our social pathology, and it's been that way from long before the Cultural Revolution. My dad's standard Chinese was so bad he couldn't differentiate between the words *fu* [good fortune] and *hu* [lake],[3] but just because he'd helped fight the Americans in the Korean War, they made him a Chinese language and literature teacher. But that's nothing. You can find worse phonies than him throughout our history, past and present. You don't need me to tell you that.

Of course, the sheer scale of fraud these days is unprecedented. We make fakes, we sell fakes, we trade in counterfeit currency, and we buy imitation goods. Everyone is a victim, and everyone is cheating everyone else. The whole society is trapped in a vicious cycle. We're all caught up in an endless revolution of revolutions.

There's always a counterfactual reality about anything and everything in China today. *In fact* has become just a catchphrase for the whole society, because, in fact, things are never what they appear to be. When people say what, in fact, is happening, at least you know you might be getting a little closer to the truth. But what I hate most about the use of the expression *in fact* is the tone of voice people use. It's as though they're leaking you privileged information: I'm treating you with particular respect and letting you in on a secret, the truth. But that's not really the case at all, because there's always sure to be much more going on than they'll ever admit to you when they say *in fact*.

Let's take jasmine tea, for example, a product everyone uses. The average consumer really can't tell the difference between good and bad jasmine tea, although there are nine grades, Grade 1 being premium quality. In fact, however, over and above Grade 1 there is a Special Grade, and that's further divided into three subclasses: Special Number 1, Number 2, and Number 3. Then there's something even better than Special Number 1; it's called Special Superior Grade. Apart from all of that you also have provincial-level premium quality teas, ministry level, national level, expo level, convention

---

3. In the Hunan dialect the sounds *h* and *f* are not distinguished.

level, and a whole range of other quality varieties to consider like "special selection" tea, "special choice," "imperial quality," "national banquet quality" tea, and so on. No matter what kind of tea you buy, they're all advertised as the best possible quality. In reality, none of them are really top-notch. Even the stuff you buy for a hundred yuan a tin is only special because of the pretty packaging. The quality of what's inside may be no better than what you get in a ten-yuan pack. And that's not to mention imitation and inferior-quality teas. That's when things get really complicated; there's no end to the skulduggery that goes on. Believe me, you can pick and dry leaves from any old tree and sell them as tea.

Or take the Sichuan hotpot that's so popular with people in restaurants these days. It's so good you just have to keep coming back for more. Ever wondered why you get a craving for it when you haven't had it for a while? It's because they put opium pods in the soup.

Then there was the case of a Jeep Cherokee that just fell apart at the seams after only a few thousand kilometers. Great, everyone thought, we've finally got one over the Americans. But it turns out that they had one over us after all: the car had been assembled in an underground plant here. It was 100 percent "Made in China."

Counterfeit money is so widespread nowadays that even the hicks with their stalls in the cities have their own ultraviolet-light counterfeit detectors. The only problem is that a lot of the devices are substandard themselves and often can't detect fake currency.

Lately my daughter's school has introduced a new regulation making it compulsory for all students to buy new satchels. They're badly made, but the manufacturer gave the school a special deal so they could offload them. If you don't buy one, you'll be banned from school. Now, my daughter has an attitude that she's inherited from me. She started arguing with her teacher over this scam, but the reply she got was simple: "Don't give me a hard time about it. Isn't your mother in the Consumer Protection Association? Lodge a complaint with her. Anyway, I haven't been paid in ages, so it's not as though I'd care if the school fires me."

My husband turned forty this last Spring Festival, so he bought a bottle of Wuliangye grain wine to celebrate.[4] He knew it was fake after the first sip.

4. The spirit of choice among Chinese wine aficionados. From Sichuan Province, Wuliangye, literally "the essence of five grains," is even more highly prized than Maotai, its famous Guizhou cousin.

Impossible, I said innocently; there's a quality guarantee stamp on it. Anyway, I thought to myself, since he'd never had such good liquor before, he probably couldn't tell the difference. But he was adamant: it was definitely fake, 10 percent proof at most. So I went along to see the manager of the store where he'd bought it, and they said: "Of course it's fake. Since you're from the Consumer Protection Association we'll give you your money back. But, take note: we weren't selling it at the usual market price!"

I didn't make the grade for university—see, even I'm a fake. I knew I wouldn't make the cut, so after applying to a few technical colleges I ended up going to a business school to do accountancy. After graduating I initially had a job in a department store and then got into an accountancy firm. But I have a problem: I like speaking my mind, and I rub people the wrong way. I'm not cut out to be an accountant in the present age of reform and openness. I know I might have a propensity for talking out of turn, but professionally I'm absolutely straight. In practice that means I can't satisfy people's demands to "be more courageous and take bolder steps."[5] I don't think I was born like this; it probably has more to do with all that antifeudal Tang poetry my dad made me read as a kid. All those lamentations about the uncertain political fate of bureaucrats in imperial China left a deep impression on me.

Anyway, eventually, with a bit of help from my friends, I arranged for what they call a "human resource transfer." That's how in 1991 I ended up in the Consumer Protection Association. I knew that the job called for enthusiasm and a sense of duty, as well as a pretty broad-ranging knowledge of the market and consumer products. I'm actually a bit out of my depth here. But, to be honest, I'm one human resource that I don't think could usefully be transferred anywhere else. I've learned to go with the flow, and I'm satisfied with my lot in life.

Everyone complains about things being shoddily made and says that pirated goods are flooding the market. But all the talk in the world won't make any difference. To make a convincing case, you need statistical evidence. We've carried out a survey of the major shopping centers and manufacturers, and our findings indicate that even though 75 percent of factory output passes quality inspection, about 55 percent of everything on sale is

5. A 1990s slogan referring to the need to speed up economic reform. The interviewee is hinting that she was not prepared to go along with the corruption rife in the business world.

substandard. That 20 percent differential illustrates how many things—and I'm talking about brand-name products—are being churned out by second-rate underground factories.

The most common imitation goods you find in the marketplace are cigarettes, wines, electrical goods, clothing and medicines, and all kinds of drinks and sodas. Shoddy products, on the other hand, are not type-specific; you find them everywhere. No matter what you buy, and it can be as big as a building or as small as a nail, it may well be an inferior and shoddy piece of work. Even the raw materials used to produce it might be fake.

Even though consumers' rights are subject to such serious and constant threat, there are people in the government who argue that "we're still in the initial stage of socialism,[6] so it is unreasonable to be too demanding. People will just have to put up with what they get. The process of economic reform throws up all kinds of inequities, but this situation is preferable to refusing to reform, or allowing people to have money but leaving them with nothing to spend it on."

Others are more straightforward about our role: "The Consumer Protection Association is duty-bound to support the government's position and defend the party's enterprise. You should avoid cheap sensationalism and not complain about the downside of our market economy. You could easily incite consumers, and that may well have a negative effect on our hard-won environment of political stability."

Of eighteen kinds of soft drink available on the market, sixteen are either fake or of poor quality. Phony Coca-Cola, imitation Seven-Up. Some people collect old bottles at recycling stations and fill them with well or river water, then they foist them on the public as mineral water. They knowingly threaten public health for the sake of a quick profit. For the authorities to tolerate the situation might mean that we can boast of political stability, but I'd argue that it's a stability achieved at a very high price.

You might have noticed that the sign outside our office reads "Consumer Protection Association," so you'll be thinking that we represent and protect consumers. But take a good look around and you'll find that what, "in fact," is behind that sign is something entirely different. While we may look like a consumer watchdog, in reality we're actually a political guardian. For those of us who work here, it's a living hell. It's not that we can't do the job;

6. The "initial stage of socialism" (*shehuizhuyi chuji jieduan*) is a political euphemism for the arrant capitalism of China's economic reforms.

it's a question of what the job is actually supposed to be. You'd be wrong if you thought it was to protect the interests of consumers. We're just a pressure valve for the government, a safety zone they've provided so consumers can let off steam. Nothing more than that. What I'm saying is that even the Consumer Protection Association is a fake. It has nothing to do with our willingness to serve the public. Whenever there's a conflict of interest between consumers and the government, you know there's no competition. The government and party are going to win every time. As we say here, keep the customers happy, but stay on good terms with the authorities.

政府和民众权力的不平衡.

We're not a popular, nongovernment organization. We're an official body set up to mollify the masses. Any group that isn't strictly illegal has to fit into the system one way or the other. They don't want any renegade groups out there engaged in guerrilla warfare with the people's government. So, monks are on a par with department heads for salary and conditions; *qigong* masters are the equivalent of army captains; even the chairperson of the Private Entrepreneurs' Association has the official rank of section head.

Our boss, for example, is a vice bureau–level official. Everything works in his favor, and he knows how to play the system, how to put the right spin on things. So what if the quality of our products is so appalling? He'll argue: "Even America doesn't produce one hundred percent quality goods. It's ninety-eight point something percent at most. Now listen here, comrades, America leads the First World, while China is the head of the Third World. If the disparity between the First and Third Worlds is only some forty percentage points, then I'd say we're doing pretty well. So, if you're ever approached by any journalists, that's the line I want you to take. We have to encourage the media to explain things to the consumer."

Then there's the times he suddenly gets all conscientious. I don't know who's been after him, but he'll come rushing in all flustered and demand: "Have there been any complaints directed against Sony or Matsushita? Get everything you have on them—TVs, fridges, sound systems, the lot. We need all the evidence we can muster because the focus is on the Japs at the moment, and we have to give it to them good."

Minor scams are as numerous as flies, you can never swat them all. The big ones are like tigers, though; not only can they maul you, they're even a protected species. But consumers aren't idiots. Even though they know what we're really all about, they still have a bit of confidence in us. Everyone wants a hero who will respond to the needs of the society, someone who will come along and set things right. That's how come Wang Hai became such a popular figure. "Wang Hai attacks the fakes!" He got on TV and radio and then in all the papers; he became a nationally recognized figure. He sure made life hard for corrupt businesspeople, and for a time there his name was on everyone's lips.

Wang Hai had it all worked out. He went around buying up shoddy and poor-quality goods, and the moment he got a receipt for the transaction he'd turn on the vendor and exclaim: "You've sold me an inferior product. I want to see the manager!" But he was a bit of a fake himself, 'cause he'd work out which shops to hit, carefully avoiding the actual manufacturers, the tigers.

Anyway, the minute the manager turned up, Wang would say: "You can compensate me or I'll see you in court. It's your call. But let me warn you, there's nothing I like more than a good fight." Shop managers aren't stupid. They know you'd have to be insane to take on a person like Wang Hai, because he's the kind of fellow who wouldn't hesitate to make your life hell. Who could be bothered to play his game, either timewise or in terms of your reputation? "Stability above all," as the saying goes. So invariably they'd give in, admit liability, and pay up. But the moment Wang got his compensation, he had proof positive of malfeasance, and he wouldn't let go. He'd squirrel away all these mini-scams until he had enough under his belt to make a real splash in the media. But after a few headlines, that was the end of it. Even someone like Wang, who appeared to be a hero flying in the face of our chaotic society, proved to be nothing more than a phony himself.

If we lived in a slightly more normal environment, a scam artist like Wang Hai would never be able to get away with it—let alone become a national celebrity. Nor, for that matter, would people make a national celebrity out of him. He's been in the right place at the right time, so he's been able to make a name for himself.

What more can I say? It'd all be a waste of breath . . .

11

Fringe-Dwellers

A Nonofficial Artist

In the late 1980s, some of Beijing's freelance artists began moving into the villages in and around Yuanming Yuan, northwest of the Chinese capital. Yuanming Yuan, the Garden of Perfect Brightness, was for over 150 years the garden palace of the Manchu-Qing emperors. It was destroyed by an Anglo-French force in 1860 and subsequently plundered by generations of local people. As something of a wasteland, Yuanming Yuan seemed like an ideal—and cheap—haven for the wandering artists who came to Beijing in search of fame and wealth. For a time many found a home in Fuyuan Cun Village—the "West Village"—a spot that once housed the Jesuit missionaries who worked for the Qing court as artisans.

In the early 1990s, the West Village (or the Yuanming Yuan Artists' Village, as it came to be known), grew in notoriety. Home to a number of the most successful post-1989 artists, the village promised its inhabitants spacious and inexpensive accommodation as well as relative freedom from official harassment and interference. Its spirit of camaraderie was a draw not only to aspiring local and out-of-town wannabes but also to the foreign patrons interested in discovering the up-and-coming talents of China's unofficial arts scene.

On the eve of 4 June 1995, the sixth anniversary of the Beijing Massacre, police sealed the village and ejected the artists living there. The dispersed talents found various new abodes, including the East Village in Tongxian County, although some eventually found their way back to the Garden of Perfect Brightness.

Let me show you something. Just take a look at this joker's name card. He's damned well put "homeless artist" on it. Homeless, my ass. He's even included an address and phone number! He's worried people won't be able to find him, and that he might miss out on making a deal. Even the homeless are printing name cards these days. It's fucked.

When things were just starting out, this place wasn't too bad. It could have become an ideal spot. Maybe. Back then the artists who came here were so poor they had no alternative. They were a bunch of itinerant, unemployed workers who just happened to be a bit literate; a pack of fuckwits who felt it was cool, like normal, to be artists who were out of sync with the rest of society. They thought they could really say something through their art, or at least more than complete illiterates could.

So they just hung out here. It was fun. Of course, no one ever pretended they weren't interested in making a buck or two. Everyone here wants to cut a deal. There are only two types of people in this world: those who want to be famous and those who want to make a fortune. But that's okay, though in the beginning I'm sure it wasn't this bad. Doing deals has become a real science, and people around here are pros. They've got the game down pat. They've turned alternative art into their own form of planned economy. They've got their sights set on fame and gain, doing the squeeze and then slipping away overseas. Let's face it, you have to know about the nuts and bolts of this business, and not just be able to waffle on about abstractions.

At first people really didn't need to understand about making a deal. Remember all that stuff about "long live mutual understanding" in the eighties? What a crock! Well, personally I reckon everyone has shit for brains, so how can they possibly understand me? Everything's been perverted now. The artists around here might make a big show of being macho men, but the minute they open their mouths all you hear is some girly crap about nobody really understanding them, like they'd just die unless you show them some sympathy. That's absolutely fucked. It's just like Mao Zedong Thought; once you start, you can never get out again.

Anyway, this big act is all for the benefit of the art dealers, publishers, critics, and reporters, as well as those complete fuckwits: the foreigners and people in the official National Artists' Association. Sure you can argue that they're fish and fowl, with nothing in common; on one side you have the establishment, on the other the people outside the system. But in reality they're all the same; they have the power to grant you public recognition and the power to exploit whatever value you have. It reminds me of that song by Ai Jing: "Let me get out to that glittering world; put a big red stamp in my passport." Well, the artists here all reckon they're pretty tough people, but they don't have anything like Ai Jing's free spirit. The only reason you're interested in being "understood" is that, as she says, "He can come to Shenyang, but I can't go to Hong Kong."[1] You want to be able to travel on your own terms. Now that's what I call being practical.

In my opinion there's only two good things about this lame village nowadays. The rent's cheap, and lots of foreigners hang out here. Whenever you've got a good supply of foreigners, it means you've got major access to the latest market info and the international art world. The downside is that once they're here, they won't ever leave; they're always in your face, trying to promote you and fucking with your head. What's any of that got to do with being an "independent artist"? It's bullshit.

What you've got here now is a group of people who only ever talk about getting into the annals of contemporary art history. Everything they do is priced at eight thousand U.S., and they write autobiographies. When do they have any time to paint?

I reckon Liu Wenjun's got the right attitude. He just paints beautiful girls in the traditional style of commercial calendar art. He knows where he's at: I want to make money, your village is famous, and there's lots of foreigners here, so there's a market. Fine—I'll move in and set up shop. Lots of people in the village criticize him for lacking depth. But he was trained in aesthetics; how can you say he lacks depth? So maybe his paintings aren't that profound, but what do those morons who criticize him know about anything? And why should he try to be profound just to impress a bunch of dumb fucks?

Sure, old Liu's got his limitations. He's going about things in a fairly convoluted way. He argues that once you've made enough money, you can concentrate on being a serious artist. But that's not necessarily the case. Enough is never enough. By the time you've made enough money, you'll have lost your original inspiration. But, all that aside, he's been doing really well out of his art. People are always lining up to buy his stuff, and he can really churn it out, too. All he has to do now is sign a painting someone else has done and he'll be able to sell it. That's what they say, anyway.

1. From Ai Jing's song "My 1997." The line quoted refers to the fact that Ai's boyfriend, a Hong Kong music producer, could travel freely to China, but Ai Jing, who is originally from Shenyang in northeast China, could not go and visit him in Hong Kong. See Geremie R. Barmé, *In the Red: On Contemporary Chinese Culture* (New York: Columbia University Press, 1999), p. 137.

Nowadays the rent's not that cheap, either. The farmers around here aren't idiots. They're always raising the rent. Everyone wants a piece of the action.

Sure, there are still vestiges of primitive communism here. People always say that when they write about the village. They say poor artists here can always get a meal from their neighbors. So what's the big deal? It only means that people don't make a fuss about who they feed. Well, not too much of a fuss; you still have to make a living. But what's really a problem is developing the exploitative attitude you need to survive. You have to take advantage of every opportunity that presents itself, and when the occasion demands it people can sink pretty low. They guard their turf and won't let anyone else get a look in. That's when you can forget all the talk about primitive communism. Opportunities are few and far between; that's just the way things are. People around here are united by poverty; they're locked together in its vise-like grip. It's no wonder that in the end they invariably try to do one another in. It's fucked.

But, yeah, there are people who are always working, painting, taking pictures, writing poetry. Most of them have been on the road for years. Now that they've got something like a nest, they really get into making stuff. But that never lasts long, and what they produce is, well, you can just imagine. They plagiarize their own lives; their creativity is based entirely on a desire to reproduce themselves. Some people are truly pathetic. As one of them said to me, "I've been bumming around for years, but now I've made it to Beijing I've finally learnt the knack."

They love being "creative," but whatever they do is the most straight up and down, the most fashionable fucking crap in town. And do they ever think they're wonderful! It's like they've arrived. One look at their stuff, and you can see it's the same tired old crap that's been on the market for ages.

It's hardly a surprise that some people ditch painting altogether and just hang out. It's all talk; they talk up painting and rave about poetry. They fuck people over with all their talk. And those are the good ones. The people who end up as "art activists" are really bullshit. They think they're out there working on our behalf, buttering up the establishment, getting into bed with mainstream artists and foreigners. They can eat and drink up a storm, and for them life is real sweet. Of course, it's nothing to be surprised about. As Chairman Mao said, "If the conditions are ripe, take advantage of them; if they're not, then create the right conditions and take advantage of them." It's a cool gig, and if you're good you can get away with it. People never think they don't have the talent—and once you're in there you can't go back. You just have to keep bumbling on.

What do people live off? I guess it's the same wherever you go: some sell their work, others rely on grants or get by doing odd jobs. Some artists here make quite a decent living from their art. The type of artists I was just talking about can't move their work. But that's no surprise. Anyway, they're too fixed in their ways to change. They can't get any foundation money—you know, there are no foundations. So they suck on the big tit of the National Artists' Association. If you can make it with the association, then sooner or later you can say goodbye to this place.

You still have to be an old fart who practices socialist realism to be on the Artists' Association payroll. You might think they're hopeless, but they're the ones who get all the funding. What can you do about it? We're free all right—free to do odd jobs, paint ads, calendar posters, trite pictures for foreigners, portraits of the wives of the new rich. And if it comes to that, you can make a living moving bricks. None of that has to affect your attitude. But if all you do is paint whatever keeps the foreigners happy, copying the kind of dreck they like, you end up thinking you're actually doing worthwhile work. You kid yourself into believing you're the real thing. That's when you're really fucked.

There are some artists who are really talented, but they're all mixed up. Those fucking foreigners give them ideas about what they should be painting and keep them up to date with the latest market trends, and those dummies just churn out the work to order. It's a perfect blend of mental and physical labor; sort of collaborative creativity. And they're told that this is the only way they'll break out of Asia and make it on the world stage.[2] These artists are real pros. They play the field: politics, philosophy, the mysterious Orient, you name it. If it'll sell paintings, they're prepared to screw over anyone, even their parents. They just want to be wanted. But their work ends up being all the same. Bloodless.

You can't just blame the artists, though. The foreigners around here are really fucking destructive. They might have money, but they're dumb. And they're the ones who start the new fashions. They know how to play the international scene, but getting involved with them really fucks you up inside. They're nothing more than a money tree. Every time you need more

2. "Break out of Asia and go international" *(chongchu Yazhou, zouxiang shijie)* was an official slogan promoted in the 1980s to celebrate the internationalization of Chinese sport.

U.S. dollars you just have to shake 'em down. But it's not only a matter of getting cash out of them; they can make you, and once you're out there in the marketplace, the payoff in residuals is phenomenal. All you have to do is keep producing steadily, and you'll be rich and famous.

A lot of the people in the village have been to art school. Some even come from artist families; it's in their blood. But they'd be better off if their parents were just your average morons and not artists. At least normal people have a sense of proportion, but artistic families really think they're a big deal. Their kids go to art school and learn how to be arty. School can't teach you how to be an artist, it only gives you the basic techniques, the foundations of the trade. You get a shitty education for four years, then they assign you to a work unit, end of story. No wonder people want to do a stint here after they've finished art school. They come here to find something new, play at being an independent artist for a while. Long on ambition and short on talent, you say? Actually, it's quite the opposite. They're trained to be technically competent, and they sure can paint, but they don't have what it takes. No feeling. They can't tell good art from bad.

You want to know about me? Forget it, you can't write me up, I'd never get a drink in this town again, man. You said we'd just have a freewheeling conversation. Nothing's free. If those fuckers knew what I'd been saying about them, or that I'm the one who's said all this stuff, they'd do me. Don't let all that tough-guy business fool you, underneath it all they're absolute wimps. They know how to keep themselves from getting hurt. Independent? That's a joke. Independence is PR. In reality we're always backbiting. Everyone here's an expert at engaging in "class struggle."

I bummed around China for a few years before settling here. Then, before you know what's happened, this village becomes Hippieville, China. The place fills up with people who want to get in on the act, they think this place is on a different plane from the rest of society. When you've got cash, you buy booze; when you run out of booze, you cry. If you run out of money you can sell empty beer bottles, and if you can't find any empty beer bottles you go hungry until you think of some way to make a fast buck. It's great. An absolutely artistic lifestyle.

But in reality it's not like that at all. If you hang around here for a while, you soon discover that we're fringe dwellers. We're on the edge of the social order, but not outside it at all. You're actually involved in the same game as everyone else, and the same rules apply. What's the big deal about being part of it? You can't blame anyone in particular. It's just the way the marriage between reality and ideals pans out. It's petty fucking bourgeois, don't you reckon? It's normal.

But I'm still here. Where else can I go? Everywhere's the same. Things are marginally better here. At least the Beijing beer and Erguotou aren't watered down.[3]

But everyone puts up a good front anyway. On the surface it looks like things are happening, but really I think it's all over. Things peaked back in 1992, and everything's been fucked ever since. "The bird of my youth has flown away and will never return." It's gone, man. Some of us have become major money-spinners, some have turned into pseudo-foreigners.[4] Some are living off the rich or shacking up with foreigners, and some are still hanging out and doing the same old crap, forcing their stuff on everyone who comes within range. Then there's the shitheads who've only just discovered the place. That guy you just met has only just arrived. He's a poet. The minute he came he started talking himself up, says his ambition is to overthrow Bei Dao.[5] Fuck me dead! Bei Dao? Didn't he slink off to Europe and disappear off the map ages ago? Then there's the ones who are prepared to "sacrifice themselves for a righteous cause," or the ones who get successful and then try to notch up some moral victory by facing down the authorities. That's some of the fucking fantastic types you see around here.

Naturally there are people here who work for the Ministry of State Security.[6] Of course there are! Don't think we're just fluff! They take our artists' village very seriously, and they're constantly working on ways to infiltrate or co-opt us. You've got to pity the poor bastards who have to infiltrate this place, though. Here they are, people with carte blanche to harass anyone they want—anything they want, they can get—they get sent here to deal with us! It must be the pits! They mostly rely on co-opting people. Some artists are so fucked up, they'll cave in the minute you show a bit of interest in them. Yes, I could point them all out to you—it's obvious who they are—but what would be in it for me? I sort of sympathize with those guys

3. A popular and cheap Beijing rotgut made from sorghum.

4. Pseudo-foreigner *(jia yangguizi)* is an old term of contempt for Chinese who ape foreign, particularly Western, manners and lifestyles.

5. Bei Dao (Zhao Zhenkai) was a noted and internationally recognized nonofficial poet who rose to prominence in the late 1970s and left China in the late 1980s. For many years Bei Dao was a Nobel hopeful. In October 2000 the playwright and novelist Gao Xingjian, a French national, became the first ethnic Chinese writer to be awarded the prestigious prize.

6. China's KGB.

playing at being cops. They're pathetic little people. You can hardly expect them to stand up for themselves, or to sacrifice themselves rather than submit to official pressure. If you think they're above it all, that only proves that you're a stupid prick, and you thought too highly of them in the first place. In my opinion, some Yuanming Yuan artists keep up with the trends and want to make a name for themselves. The repressive political situation works in their favor. Others are technically competent artists who cozy up to the government because it makes them feel secure. But it's a real dumb move to become a government stooge. You're no better than a lackey. Now, if you wanted to become an official, you'd have to do something pretty spectacular—but if the Communist Party has got nothing on you to start with, they don't even need to co-opt you. They can hire you as one of their running dogs.

Some people understand that acting up is the only way to make sure of a big future. But it's a career option that doesn't suit everyone. Like, I know this guy in the city who comes out here occasionally to check out the action. For a while there he was really hoping to create some kind of disturbance so he'd be picked up by the authorities. Once he set up a stall opposite the China Art Gallery in central Beijing to exhibit his "black paintings."[7] He wanted a confrontation with the government, but nowadays the authorities are as cunning as you are. When old Ma Desheng and the Stars were detained for putting on their "black" exhibition outside the Art Gallery in 1979, it was really explosive.[8] Now here you have this wannabe lining up his works along a wall in an alleyway, and the authorities simply ignore him. They didn't want to give the kid a break. They didn't give him a chance to make a stir or get a name for himself. How would it feel to be treated like that? The guy just overplayed his hand.

The farmers around here don't care about us. They're pretty dumb, and all they care about is getting their rent on time. So what if they sometimes spy on us for the police? All they can report is if we're at home or not, who we've been fucking, and who stays the night, stuff like that. They don't understand anything we talk about.

7. *Heihua,* a term for supposedly antisocialist art made famous by a 1974 exhibition of "reactionary works" by older artists who had previously been denounced.

8. Ma Desheng and his fellow nonofficial artists formed a group in the 1970s called the Stars. Their antics and exhibitions elicited a furor, and for a time the Stars were China's most famous dissident cultural group. Most of them subsequently took up residence overseas or became migratory artists.

The police have a very simple take on us: we're unemployed vagrants, or people who refuse to take the type of jobs available to us. They think we're destabilizing elements, so they're always finding an excuse to call us in, "have a chat," "make friends." But they're really dumb, they'll believe anything you tell them. For example, they saw this one painting that showed some people having a group photograph taken in front of Tiananmen Gate, with Chairman Mao's picture in the background. So those dummies ask us why all the people have their mouths open? It simply never occurred to them that the fuckers might just have forgotten to close their mouths when the picture was being taken. Anyway, the artist told them that the people in the picture were laughing with happiness because the economic reforms had helped them make money. The cops actually believed it. Later the artist told the same story to this shit-for-brains reporter from the New China News Agency. He swallowed it whole and said it was a really good artistic theme. You'd have to be a complete idiot to believe you can help these fools understand what you're really on about.

Before old Grandpa Mao became a cult figure again in the early 1990s, this dummy in the local police station asked me, "How come you're wearing a Mao badge lately?" What did it have to do with him, I thought to myself, but I spun him this line about how when Chairman Mao was alive, everyone was real poor and their clothes were falling to pieces. Now that people have money, I thought I'd ask the old man to go around with me and see the peasants all wearing suits, and city people in their stonewashed jeans, and even the police in their woolen uniforms. Wouldn't that make old Mao happy? And you know what? That fucking cop believed every word![9]

Don't flatter me. I haven't mastered all the tricks of the trade. The guy who really has it down to a fine art is Yan Zhengxue. He's just about got the whole game sewn up. Old Yan is not only a "homeless artist" but a representative in the People's Congress as well, and he's even a player in the Artists' Association. He loves talking about democracy, but he's managed to get himself made the head of the Artists' Village. Whenever he gets a chance he launches into his "Catch-22" lecture: "don't get drunk and make trouble; don't fight amongst yourselves, and don't say reactionary things in front of officials. The way ahead is long and treacherous, but as long as you're straight with yourself, you can afford to make compromises." Heaven

9. For more on the revived reputation of Mao, see Geremie R. Barmé, *Shades of Mao: The Posthumous Cult of the Great Leader* (Armonk, N.Y.: M. E. Sharpe, 1996).

help us! Straight with yourself? He couldn't be straight if he tried. Old Yan really does believe the road of life is long and arduous, and that you've got to advance with great care and determination. The fucker even wrote an autobiography called *The Path Is Long and Treacherous,* solemnly recording his history as a struggling artist. It was serialized in *Fine Arts in China.*[10]

Old Yan has it all down pat. But don't get me wrong; I'm not making fun of him. There's only one thing I can't stomach. Like I said, this artists' village started out as a refuge for literate itinerants. Many of the people who moved in wanted to get away from things and find a way to keep the establishment, society, and the masses at arm's length. But Old Yan has used this place as a base to do quite the opposite. He's been bending over backwards to get society to recognize the village's legitimacy, to get it on a more legal footing, to make a reputation for the place. To do this, he's always trying to create artistic happenings. It's sort of like something out of *Death of a Salesman.* If nothing's going on, he tries to make something happen. Of course, it hasn't been easy for Old Yan. So I suppose on one level he's the most well-adjusted person in the village, and the most representative. He's a hard worker, too. Once he's set on a course, he applies himself to achieving his goal through hard work and clever manipulation. Nothing tires him. Pity you'll miss him this time; he's finally been nabbed by the police.

It's all a lot of fuss about nothing, really. Old Yan got into an argument with a bus conductor for not buying a ticket, and then the police got involved. Yan was ranting on in his broken Mandarin, and the local cops thought he was just some out-of-town hick, so they beat him up. Then they discovered that he was a people's representative who lives in the Artists' Village. That really threw them. They tried to buy him off, gave him some money to keep quiet about it, and he pretended that was the end of the matter—but the minute they released him he held a press conference and told the whole story. He got all his foreign and pseudo-foreign friends to attend. You can imagine the stink it caused. The story got into papers all over the world: "Chinese police assault independent artist." The case ended up going to court, and the policeman who'd beaten him up was jailed for a year or something like that, and the chief of the local cop shop was dismissed as a result of the case. Then the police decided it was payback time. From then on they were looking for any excuse to get Old Yan. They bided their time,

10. *Zhongguo meishu bao,* 1985–89, edited by Shui Tianzhong, Li Xianting, Gao Minglu, and others.

and about a year later they arrested him on charges of stealing a bicycle. They packed him off for reeducation before he knew what hit him. Who knows if he really stole the bike? Even if you're willing to believe the police, what's the big deal? So Yan went riding around on someone else's bike for a while. It's not exactly a capital offense. Anyway, people are always stealing bikes. There's even a gang of louts from outside Beijing who specialize in bike theft. Lots of bikes have disappeared from our village. So why did they have to make an example of Yan Zhengxue? It was really underhanded.

We've been drinking and talking all this time, and I still haven't asked you, how many U.S. dollars can you make from an interview like this? If it's a few hundred, then I suppose it's worth it. Artists ask a lot for their paintings, but at the end of the day we only get a few hundred bucks in hand. A few grand would really be a lot. Art dealers play dirty, especially those two bastards from your Australia. Don't be taken in by all that talk about them only dealing for fun on the side. If they actually hook a buyer, they split the proceeds with the artist sixty-forty. Of course, they take a 60 percent cut. The Japs are even worse. They think they're doing you a big favor if they buy one of your paintings and think they can fob you off with a good feed.

But tell me, how are those people who've gone overseas in the last few years really doing? When they come back, they act like they're visiting a disaster area; they treat us like we're poverty-stricken clods or something. When you see them next time, tell them something from me: they probably haven't had as many expensive foreign meals in the West as we've had here in China. And what gives them the fucking right to come back here and lord it over us?

But don't get me wrong. I have a very strong self-critical sense. Talking to you today, I've only been posing as an objective observer. Observers see things more clearly. They think they can do things better than everyone else. But ultimately it's a state of mind that leaves you really frustrated. The observer's role is dumb; you can't escape reality either. In actual fact, the observer is really hungry for an opportunity to do what everyone else is doing. Isn't that right? So in the future I should copy what the writers do: fuck myself over, cry out "please don't treat me like a human being," and then mock all the "comrades, friends, leaders, and honored guests" who come my way.[11]

11. *Qianwan bie ba wo dang ren,* the title of a satirical novel by the Beijing writer Wang Shuo, published in 1989. See Barmé, *In the Red,* pp. 89–95.

Everyone's drifting. You might marry some foreign woman and move overseas, or get co-opted and join the National Artists' Association, get involved in advertising, make cliché paintings, or get thrown into jail. None of it's a real answer. You're just choosing a different form of drifting.

But, fuck it, there's that "but" again—but it's something to be a drifter here.

12

The Computer Bug

The Software Pirate

Diannao chong (computer bug) is the name for everyone from computer geeks and hackers to software pirates and specialists. That's what they're called in Thieves' Alley in Beijing. Thieves' Alley is in China's Silicon Valley in Zhong-guan Cun, part of the university district in the northwest suburbs of the capi-tal. Colloquially, people refer to it as Electronics Street (Dianzi yitiao jie), but for the pros it's just Thieves' Alley (Pianzi yitiao jie).

Thieves' Alley is one of the homes of the massive Chinese pirating industry, and this is an interview with one of the early masters of the trade. He's called one of the Four Heavenly Kings of Pirating (papan jiemi sida tianwang zhiyi), and he has an attitude and ego that goes with his title.[1]

He's in his early twenties, and if you met him you'd think he was just another typical Westernized Asian businessman. In gray suit pants, Adidas shoes, and a bomber jacket, he's wearing the uniform of the young business toughs of Beijing. This computer bug is no nerd: he doesn't wear glasses, and he sports a crew cut favored by the I-mean-business young men of North China. A handsome young man with a sharp tongue and biting wit, he's always poised to answer his mobile phone.

What type of computer do you use? And what about software? Don't take it personally, it's just that if I'm dealing with a computer illiterate I need to know, so I can work out how much information you can handle.

---

1. The Four Heavenly Kings *(sida tianwang)* are the door guardians traditionally placed at the entrance to a Buddhist temple, although in contemporary parlance the expression refers to a foursome of Canto-pop singers: Aaron Kwok (Guo Fucheng), Leon Lai (Li Ming), Andy Lau (Liu Dehua), and Jackey Cheung (Zhang Xueyou).

Lately I've been working on a CD-ROM version of *The Story of the Stone*.[2] Mostly for fun, really, because I don't expect to make any money out of it. In that novel there's a character called Jiao Da, who realizes that apart from the two stone lions placed at the entrance of the Jia family mansion, nothing and nobody in the place is innocent. It's the same here on Thieves' Alley. No one's clean, we're all in the muck; the only difference is some people can play the game and some people can't. And among those who can play a good hand, you have to know who's a true winner and who are the losers. Everyone pirates software, and people are into putting together phony hardware, too. If you're really good, you do serial numbers and all.

I studied at Tsinghua University,[3] specializing in computer databases. It was boring as hell, and I barely managed to avoid turning into a machine myself. DBP, DBA—it's all about data-based machines. That wasn't for me, so I dumped it after graduation, and I hooked up with a small company to get some money together. If you specialize, you just end up in some government research job or working for a big company. It might sound all right, but at best you can only make a few hundred a month. It's chicken feed, and you end up sitting in front of a machine all day long doing what people tell you. You've got to be kidding!

At my present company, or rather at our company, I'm the development manager. That means I manage my own development. I'm really nothing more than a glorified wage slave, an employee. There are only ten people in this company; one boss, eight managers, and that secretary sitting outside. She's called the office manager. We've all got fancy titles. It's good for business, and our main business is selling hardware. Small companies like ours can only push software by selling hardware. Although I've got a reputation as a pirate, that's what I do after hours.

I've been with this company for more than a year. The pay is okay, a steady two grand a month. But there's not always stuff around to pirate—not stuff that'll make a profit. A decent interior-design application like CCHD 6.0 contains more than a thousand ready-made 3-D images of interiors. A licensed copy sells for 2,700 yuan. But I can strip it down in a little over an hour and make as many copies as I want. Actually, I was working on that a few days ago. I was doing it for a friend, so I charged only six thousand yuan, less than my normal fee.

2. A popular traditional novel written by Cao Xueqin in the eighteenth century.
3. China's self-styled MIT, near Zhongguan Cun in the university district of Haidian.

It was cheap at the price. My friend can sell my pirated version for ages and make back what he spent on me many times over. To employ me for an hour costs about a hundred yuan; the rest went to buy my skill. Someone else might not have been able to break the program code in ten thousand hours. Anyway, I didn't learn what I know for free. I have to make back the money I invested in going to university.

The way I see it, pirating software is no big deal. The Four Little Dragons[4] created all their wealth and prosperity by pirating. Tell me what those little shits in Hong Kong have ever invented? Nothing. They're just a bunch of pseudo—foreign devils who started out as tailors and cobblers. Everything they know about computers comes from having learned how to pirate stuff.

PCs are made up of parts from everywhere. Open up any machine, and you'll find components manufactured in a pile of different countries. Plus there are always a few things without any labels made by guerrilla outfits. It's the same for software. I rip you off, then you rip me off. Popular software products—regardless of who developed them—all contain some fishy things. Everyone's got a bit of everyone else in them. So much intermarriage has gone on over the years that nowadays everyone's related.

It's ridiculous for these stinking foreigners to pick on China like they do. We're just following the general trend by pirating some of their stuff. And they're up in arms, carrying on about intellectual property infringement and making a fucking stink about us all over the world.

Those foreign devils are just plain unreasonable. Actually, they've been ripping off us Chinese for ages. What's all this stuff about intellectual property? Whose ancestors got everything going in the first place? I don't think there are any cut-and-dried answers, but just ask yourself: What's the basic element of computing? Binary notation! Zero and one, positive and negative, open and closed. That's the theory of yin and yang. Everything in the universe is made up of yin and yang, and of course it was us Chinese who discovered that. And, not only did we get the idea first, we were the first to apply it. In printing we invented movable type, a concept that's based on being able to disassemble a matrix of text and put it together again in a different order. They've just learned how to do that recently.

But let's forget the hardware aspect of all of this. What about electricity and magnetic fields? Who discovered magnetism? Pardon me, it was the Chinese! If we hadn't discovered that, then what would you do with your

4. Hong Kong, Taiwan, South Korea, and Singapore.

data? How would you record it? And while we're at it, let's talk about hard copy. Obviously, you need paper for that—and where did that come from? If it weren't for Bi Sheng,[5] those foreigners would still be writing on parchment. Can you cut parchment into A4 size and print on it? I don't think so! Those fucking foreigners simply haven't figured out how much they owe us in copyright fees, and they make a fuss about *us* infringing copyright. When China was advanced, they were free to rip us off left, right, and center. Now that they've managed to get ahead of us a little, it's a different story! As soon as they strike it rich, they begin lording it over everyone else. Where's the sense in that? Well, I'm going to go right on copying whatever comes my way.

They can hit China with as many sanctions as they want. Anyway they're only punishing the state; it can't touch any of us. At least the foreign devils got that right—the Chinese government is the one to go after. Boy, do they make a heap from pirating! You can make a packet if you pirate really clever software. But only the government can get away with it. I couldn't copy programs for heavy-duty machines, even if I wanted to. I don't have any originals to work with; we don't have the know-how either, or equipment, or access to a market. There's no alternative—we just have to sit back and watch the government making the real killing.

The authorities raided us a few days ago just to give the Yanks some face during the latest round of Sino-U.S. intellectual property talks. Go for it! All they got was a few disks. We still have software coming out our ears. Our cops were just putting on a show for the Yankee devils. If they really wanted to enforce a ban, they'd go hit on the National Defense Science and Industry Commission or the Academy of Sciences. All we get are their leftovers, a few kindergarten-level PC disks. The government has been breaking the same laws we have. If they don't give a damn, why should we be scared? Besides, if they really got me, I'd play dumb. I'd say I was just ripping off the foreign devils to help the Communist Party and the people save some money on advanced technology from abroad!

In the case of more professional software like CCHD 6.0, for example, the market is limited, so you can't sell a pirated copy for more than a third of its retail price. But if a state organization or company buys it, you're looking at helping them update their system or establish one from scratch. We're not just talking one-third anymore. They need the works, and we

5. The legendary inventor of paper.

charge them an arm and a leg. And why not? State-run companies aren't worried about money. As long as their middlemen get their commission, you can do what you want. Small private companies are more uptight about the bottom line, but that's no problem; they're computer-illiterate, so you can tell them they need a whole pile of software, and they'll believe you.

Once there was this company that got a 386SX clone and thought they'd be real cool by running Windows. But obviously, Windows can't do much all by itself. They reckoned their outfit was an international trading venture, so they came crying to us that they needed top-of-the-line English software. I was at a bit of a loose end at the time, so I helped our retail people do them over. I talked them into buying the full package: WordPerfect, Word, ClarisWorks, Lotus Notes, Excel, as well as the Chinese systems WPS and WPS-NT. Who cared if there was a lot of overlap? They all had different icons, so they looked pretty convincing.

Of course, we'd pirated the whole suite. But the place is oozing with that type of cheap shit, so you can't even get a third of the original price for it. We sell it for 10 percent of the retail price, or even less. We just have to sell more to make a profit. In fact, if you want a new version of Windows and you bring your own disks, our company will charge only ten yuan. Bet you can't buy Windows where you come from for a dollar and a quarter! Really, that's what we sell it for. It's one of our favorites—once customers get hooked, they have to come back for more software. If you're lucky, they want more hardware, too. Windows is a real money-spinner—everyone who gets it comes back for more.

Software companies do their level best to foil us. But they're people just like us computer bugs. I can unlock anything they care to come up with; it's just a matter of the degree of difficulty, and of course whether it's worth my while. . . .

My first job wasn't on Thieves' Alley, it was with an advertising company in Beijing's Eastern District. That was back in 1992, while I was working my way through my third year of university. At the time, my dad was only making two to three hundred yuan a month, and when he saw me make a few grand for one night's work, it blew him away. He said to me, "You never know when you're going to make that much again, so you'd better not let your girlfriend spend it all." But he could tell I could make that kind of money easily, and he hated my guts for it. He always reckoned he was better than me, but that he simply hadn't had my opportunities. The old prick hasn't got anywhere in life, and here was his sperm really making it.

And I sure am making it. I'm making a killing, and I've got a bit of a reputation for what I do. They call me one of the Four Heavenly Kings of Pirating here in Beijing. My old man just can't believe it.

He was one of those "radio nerds" when he was a kid. The way he tells it, he could have got into Tsinghua University if it hadn't been for the Cultural Revolution. But the most amazing thing he ever managed to do was to assemble a six-valve superhet that actually came out with some sound. He's kept the thing, too. For him it was a milestone, whether he ever got any noise out of it or not. According to him, back in the sixties this was cutting-edge stuff. A four-valve regenerative detector was a middling achievement, but that was only a reflex receiver. There weren't even any IF amplifiers then. A six-PNP crystal valve, add a voltage-doubler rectifier, that gives you fourteen PNs. All I have to do is use the bits and pieces of a CPU and I can leave him for dead.

Before I went to college, I didn't take much notice of people in my dad's generation. You can forgive them for not knowing anything about computers, but I never spoke a common language with them. At the time of the June Fourth Incident back in 1989, I was in my last year of middle school. I went out to muck around in Tiananmen Square for a few days, but I didn't burn any military vehicles, let alone kill any of our blood brothers in the People's Liberation Army. Besides, only a moron would ever admit to taking part in the riots, unless of course they'd been caught by the authorities. That's when I realized they were a completely different generation from me. They were geriatrics; they're past it.

My parents were freaking out because they were afraid I'd get into trouble in the square. "Politics is really complex," they said, "You don't understand. Whatever you do, don't get involved." Fuck that for a joke. They didn't even stop to consider whether I was actually into politics or not. Those kids who got mixed up with politics were idiots or plain fools. I just went along for the ride.

My parents were old Red Guards. When the Cultural Revolution broke out, they were just finishing middle school. Then they were sent off to work in the countryside and didn't come back to Beijing until I was in primary school. But my mom and dad don't see things the same way. My mom is a teacher and is the timid-housewife type. My dad was a small-time gang leader in the Red Guard movement. He's still a bit of a leader, but now he's in local government. He's not so timid, but he reckons he takes the long view, sees the big picture. He said if the protesters in 1989 were too extreme they'd be asking for trouble, and that no good ever comes of rebellion. Anyway, my parents weren't happy with the lives they had, and they didn't know how to give me a meaningful life either. Pretty pathetic.

When I started university, the leftists were back in favor. They made all college students do military training. We lived in army barracks for months. But the more training we got, the worse we became. Geez, the government is full of idiots. They're always talking about trying to reform the way people think. Well, that's pretty dumb, if you ask me. The way you think is already all programmed in your head, like a big mess of documents. You might be working with a fucked-up application, but it's got its own internal logic. You have to pick out what you can use so it can give you what you want when you want it. It's impractical to try and change it according to some master plan, document by document. It's more labor-intensive than starting all over again.

If I started acting like our shit-for-brains government and spent all my time trying to change things, then everything would always be going wrong. I'd always be crashing. Then I'd make some more changes and crash again.

My approach is just to copy, without changing anything. I'll leave your mistakes where they are. I won't even touch the trademark. It's not worth changing things. I'll sell whatever the market wants. I just have to make sure I can outsell everyone else.

Generally speaking, I've been in the right place at the right time. After my third year at university in 1992, I was pretty much free to do what I wanted. I had a chance to exploit my talents to the full. Didn't have to worry about a scholarship or finding a job. You have to rely on yourself, and that's just what I've been doing. That's why I'm completely different from my parents: I don't owe the Communist Party anything, and the party doesn't owe me. The party makes money its way; I make mine my way. It's all money after all. We've just got a different approach.

My parents' generation lost out because they had some sense of duty to the state and the people. Even if there hadn't been a Cultural Revolution and my dad had been able to go to Tsinghua, he'd have been useless. They spent their lives creating a Buddha they could worship. They were stupid enough to do that, and now they've ended up totally passive. It serves them damn well right.

I'm only responsible for myself. It's not my duty to save the nation or save the people. I couldn't do it even if I wanted to. I'm clean and serene. All that propaganda about "the people sending me to university," "serving the people"—it's a load of old crap. I couldn't even be bothered to ignore it. I got into university because I passed the entrance exams. For me it was an investment, pure and simple. Once I graduated, I didn't have to pay anyone back. You think you can rip me off because you're the state and claim to represent the "people"? Forget it! No way!

We're not living in a moral society, and sure as hell not a moral age. As the saying goes, "Only when you have enough to eat and wear do you think of frugality and shame." We're at the stage of accumulating capital. We're going through a baptism of blood and fire. It's much too early to start going on about morals. Anyway, I'm sick of being poor. When my parents were sent to the countryside, they handed me over to my grandmother. They didn't give me a cent for seven, eight years. At best they'd come back to see me once a year. Then, when they moved back, we didn't even have a real home, and we were dirt-poor. This society's never given me anything. I don't care what they say now. Sorry—it's too late.

Sure, sometimes I have a bit of a conscience. Once I heard a talk by Wang Yongmin, a famous designer of Chinese-language programs. He told us that when he started out, he didn't even have a computer of his own. He had to get people to write out the programs in longhand. Then he finally got some people in a state organization to let him use their equipment after hours. It really was pretty moving stuff. All the people in the room were experts, so we knew what it meant for someone to build up a sophisticated Chinese-language program from nothing. If you had to do it all in longhand, it'd take the equivalent of thirty people-years! But I got over being impressed and thought to myself, hell, now this guy's a millionaire. If the opportunity comes my way, I'll rip off his software, too.

I'm more clued-in than your average computer bug. I like reading and going to karaoke bars when I have the time. I've even read some Freud! But those brain-dead characters who waste their time in research institutes or big companies are satisfied just to interface with machines all day long. If the authorities really wanted to carry out a campaign against pornography, then they should go after those computer dweebs. They love reading porn and watching skin flicks. All they know how to do is write programs. They have difficulty relating to people. They have pathetic lives. So they spend their leisure time reading about people screwing each other. Even in their free time, they pirate other people's lives.

I'd prefer not to go into much detail about my income. My salary's about twenty to thirty thousand yuan a year. Then there's my "gray" income on top of that. I don't do too badly. I can afford to buy a car, but I can't buy an apartment yet—that's the income group I'm in. Luckily my girlfriend has a place of her own. Her dad works in the government housing administration, and he got it for her. We all have to live off what we've been given, and what her family can get is housing. Her dad can rip off housing, cars, and villas from the state. It's easy to do, and completely legal. That's what they mean by the saying, "The dog that barks doesn't bite; the dog that doesn't does."

Here, I'll give you a disk, you can use it as evidence against me. You're into IBMs, so I'll give you an IBM disk, though of course I've got a shit-load of Apple ones, too.

You really think I'm stupid enough to let you use my real name? If my name appears in print, I'll sue you for defamation.

Take a good look. These CDs are all pretty crude. All that stuff printed on the case is crap. But don't worry: you won't find the name of the real producer anywhere. In fact, you won't even find the words "Made in China."

13

Unlevel Playing Field
Confessions of an Elite Athlete

Before taking part in the Olympic Games or any major sports competition, Chinese athletes and their coaches undergo an intensive briefing in PR skills. They study an official question-and-answer booklet that bears the title You Must Respond Accordingly. *The correct answers to a range of questions contained therein are de rigueur for athletes when giving interviews or in any official or private exchange with outsiders. Of course, if the athletes also happen to believe what they are saying, it's an added bonus.*

For China, athletics has little to do with sport per se. It is not concerned with either physical health or personal wellbeing. For the Chinese, athletic competitions are a struggle between political systems. They are a heady opiate administered to salve dreams of national glory.

Sports grounds are the battlefields of peacetime. When the Chinese discuss sport, they speak in the language of intense military engagement. As Chairman Mao taught his people: "Fear neither hardship nor death"; "Base everything on tactical considerations; storm and obliterate the enemy's positions; fight tooth and nail; sport is combat," and so on. When athletes retire, they even call it being "discharged."

But despite the language, the struggle itself is not conducted according to the classic Maoist style of a people's war.

China has over 2,600 counties, only one-tenth of which have a sports field of any description or a swimming pool. Of the sports fields, only a few have running tracks, and virtually none of the swimming pools are tiled. This is the momentous result of some twenty years of economic reform.

In the early 1980s, only eleven counties and cities had the wherewithal to provide people with regulation sporting facilities. You might not believe it, but only one high school in the whole country had a swimming pool at that time. If you calculate the amount of space per capita devoted to sports in China, it equals about 0.2 square meters. That's about the space a chair occupies; one-sixtieth of the space available in Australia or the United States.

Given these constraints, the masses are hardly in a position to engage in people's warfare. Therefore the authorities have developed a strategy to "concentrate our superior forces" for training to "break out of Asia and go international."

In the years that the People's Republic of China has existed, over a hundred thousand professional athletes have been trained. Their work on behalf of the "population superpower" of China has garnered the nation no more than three hundred championships and thirty Olympic gold medals, and that includes a few dozen ping-pong championships.

This interview was conducted in 1995 with a member of a Chinese national team at his winter training ground. In accordance with his wishes, his identity and the locale at which the interview was conducted have been concealed.

Don't say who I am, and don't let on what sport I compete in. If anyone asks, whatever you do, don't let on that I was the one who spoke to you.

We're under special discipline. The leadership forbids us from talking about what goes on here with outsiders. If you blab to the press, you can be held legally accountable.

How would I know where these rules come from? Probably the National Sports Commission,[1] or maybe it's the Athletics Training Bureau in the commission. Anyway, it means you'd better not say anything out of turn; and when you do talk in public, you have to be sensitive about who, when, and where. You can't just go rambling on to journalists, either Chinese or foreign. You can only give interviews in the presence of a representative of the leadership. If you give an inappropriate interview or say anything out of line, you have to take the rap.

It's even stricter when you travel overseas. During pretravel induction they issue a booklet containing all the questions foreigners are likely to ask, along with all the correct answers. They tell us to learn it all by heart. If something comes up that's not in the book, we're supposed to reply, "I can't say for sure," or "I don't know," or "Please refer that question to our PR officer." And that's not only when we travel internationally; even before major

1. Since 2003 this organization has been called the State General Administration of Sports.

competitions at home, like the Asian Games in 1990, they prepare a special booklet for us. If you don't believe me, I'll find one for you.

I'm sixteen years old, and I've been an athlete for eight years now. I was accepted into a youth amateur-athletics college when I was in my third year of primary school. It wasn't really for amateurs; it was actually semiprofessional, though we did go to a few classes, too. Then I joined a professional team. At first I was in our provincial "hope team." Yeah, that's what they called it back home, the hope team. In some provinces they call them "youth training teams," or whatever. It's all much the same thing. We were part of the professional establishment, even though we were just kids. Later on I was selected for the national team. They say we're all students in a sporting academy attached to the Beijing Sports University, but that's only for external consumption. In fact, we're athletes. We never go to classes; we're professional athletes.

They say most people who enter major competitions have to be students or people with other employment, not professionals. If you're a pro, then people aren't going to want to compete with you. That's why we have to disguise ourselves a little; we can't let on to outsiders that we're really professionals.

That means I've only had a primary-school education. When I try to write a letter, I can never manage to fill a whole page. And don't ask me how many mistakes I make. Math? I can't do anything that includes brackets. Anyway, there's no need. Now that we've all got direct dialing, you can ask for whatever you want; you don't have to write it down. You don't have to write home any more, either. If you're a champion, no one cares if you're illiterate. You can have anything you want. If you're lucky and win gold in the Olympics, then everything's taken care of. Not just moneywise; you can become an official as well. Take the women's volleyball team, for example. Except for the players who ended up going overseas, the rest are now all department or section heads in the bureaucracy. If that doesn't work out, you can always go into advertising or start your own company. You can trade on your reputation as a champion like Li Ning, the Olympic gymnast, with Li Ning brand sportswear.

I've taken part in three major competitions: two world championships and one Olympics. I wasn't in great form, so I didn't win any medals. But it's not really about athletes competing. What it's really about is comparing drugs. If the drugs you're using aren't any good, you don't have a hope. We

Orientals are biologically different from foreigners; we've got the skills, and our reflexes are quick, but we just don't have the stamina. Relatively speaking we need to use drugs, and they're pretty effective, too. I'm not making this up. It's the drugs that compete, not people. Our women athletes grow beards from all the hormones they take. Before competition they have to "shave" with depilatory creams.

When you take part in international competitions, you can see that for the foreigners it's just a competition, might even be fun. Win or lose, it's only a matter of a little more or less sponsorship money. It's different for us. It's really intense. "The Motherland and the People are waiting for you to fight a victorious war. You must achieve glory for the nation!" And it *is* just like going to war, too. The pressure is immense. It's not the cushy job people think it is.

They put the fear of God into you the moment you get on the plane to go to the Olympics. They let the athletes who they think will take gold in the competition travel first class. Then if you don't do well, if you fail to "break out of Asia and make it on the world stage," they throw you out of first and stick you in economy on the way back because you don't deserve it.

I was too young to go to the Seoul Olympics, but I heard the older athletes talking about it. The long jumper Zhu Jianhua and the male and female volleyball teams all got to travel first class to Korea. But none of them won gold, so on the return trip all those super-tall people had to scrunch themselves up into the seats at the back. Their first-class seats went to the kids who'd got gold medals in swimming and gymnastics. I didn't believe them at first, but later I found out for myself. I saw it with my own eyes when we came back from Barcelona. First class for gold, business class for silver. As for those of us who didn't score a medal, we were all herded back into economy. They inspected your medals as carefully as your passport. It was that strict!

Back in Beijing, the medal winners got off the plane first, with their medals round their necks and big armfuls of flowers. They were ushered straight into the VIP lounge. If you didn't have a medal you could do whatever you wanted; no one gave us a second thought.

The most sickening thing was the official celebration banquet. Everyone got different food; the medal winners sat there with new dishes being brought to their tables all the time. And the worst thing of all was the group photograph. We weren't arranged in order of height but according to medals. If you didn't have one, and if you were short as well, then you ended up in the back row hidden behind the gold and silver medal winners. No one cared what you looked like anyway.

Then there were the letters we started getting. Things like, "Why aren't you dead? You've lived off our blood and sweat all these years for nothing. You couldn't even get sixth place! And you still have face enough to go on living? Why don't you go hang yourself?"

But if you'd taken your drugs and actually won a medal, and then were found out and disqualified, no one would write to insult you. The publicity people would hush it all up in China, so people wouldn't know anything about it. Even if they did find out, they'd think it was quite okay; it was just a shame that the foreigners had found you out. Actually, a lot of people wrote in offering secret traditional recipes that they thought foreigners would never be able to detect.

What I'm saying is that neither the party nor the people will let you lose. If you do, your family will never be left in peace. I messed up at the Olympics and didn't get a place, and so people back home started abusing my mom and dad for having produced a birth defect like me, someone who had lost face for the nation. Someone slashed my dad's bike tires, too, and my younger brother was beaten up. He was so freaked out that it was ages before he dared to go back to school.

Then there are people who celebrate when China loses. They're not necessarily bad. There are people on this street who let off firecrackers whenever a Chinese team loses—at least they did until the municipal government banned fireworks in 1993. They weren't in the sports commission, just local citizens. Though there are actually people in the commission who celebrate defeats, too.

When the Olympics were broadcast live to Beijing, some viewers applauded whenever the Chinese team lost. They really used to hate the women volleyball players. Every time they lost, people would shout, "We warmly celebrate the Chinese team retreating back to Asia and going local."[2] They wanted to embarrass Yuan Weimin.[3] Haven't you become a fat-cat official for your reputation in getting women's volleyball onto the international stage? Well, we're going to give you a hard time over it.

2. A satirical reversal of the official 1980s slogan to "break out of Asia and go international" (*chongchu Yazhou, zouxiang shijie*).

3. A former volleyball coach who was promoted to vice chairman of the sports commission.

Nowadays people tend to despise Ma Junren.[4] His people did pretty well at the Olympics this time around, and when they returned from Barcelona they made a big deal of being ideologically sound as well as physically superior. The line went that they had dared to go all-out to win and were going to make China a track and field superpower. But then in the world championships they only won a single medal. Within a few days people were making jokes about it. "Hey, our troops weren't completely wiped out. After all, there's a fundamental difference between one medal and none at all."

Every competition is going to have winners and losers. Our problem is that we just don't know how to lose. People treat it like a crime. We don't know how to win, either. When we do we act like we're masters of the universe, and we make everyone else hate us.

There was this guy, a bicycle repairman we were all friendly with, who wrote this article about it. "The national strategy to pursue gold at all costs is proof that we are not a strong nation. The state invests over ten billion yuan in its athletes every year, just so they can win gold, to make face for ourselves. It's not only not worth it; it's ludicrous." I think he had a point. But the leadership responded by saying that this guy was undermining our morale. In the past, he would have been denounced in an official campaign or something. They don't do that these days, but his "poison" still needed to be purged, so they said that if he turned up here again, no one was to take any notice of him or talk to him. But what had he done wrong? China *does* care too much about winning medals. We treat winning gold like the be-all and end-all. One gold medal in the Olympics, and you can get a new apartment and a car. It's literally a pot of gold: it's worth tens of thousands of yuan to an athlete. It's got a price tag on it no one can miss, and we need as many as we can get. If you score a few you can become a bureaucrat, sell ads, make music videos, do karaoke songs. Even the Olympic sharpshooting champion Xu Haifeng has made karaoke recordings. If I won a medal I'd be set. I'm better looking than him, aren't I?

"The state invests ten billion yuan annually; you shame the nation if you lose." It's statements like that that really put the pressure on you. But personally I don't feel that I've ever let the country down. I'm in a sport that relies on youth and early training. Competitors in the All-American opens

4. The famed coach of "General Ma's Army" of runners from Liaoning Province, whose international disrepute eventually led to him and his "army" of athletes being dropped from the Chinese squad for the 2000 Sydney Olympics.

and European championships are high-school students. We're not like middle- or long-distance runners who are still in major competitions right into their thirties or forties. In my sport, if you haven't won a medal by that time, you've had it. That's why, when Chinese gymnasts or divers compete in world title competitions, we occasionally encounter foreign protests. There'll be people holding up placards at the airport, and our interpreters will tell us on the sly what they're saying. They're protesting against the exploitation of children and adolescents in athletics. They attack the people in charge of us for exploiting us for personal gain.

I think the protesters are right. We are exploited as kids. Regardless of whether I win a medal or not, I reckon the state has treated me unfairly. Anyway, I'm not like some people who think they're something special even before they've been in competition, acting like they're masters of the universe.

Everyone thought that the weightlifter Old He was going to win a gold medal. Based on his usual performance, he certainly could have been a medalist. Anyway, as soon as he hit the athletes' village he started acting like a prima donna. He said that being forced to walk everywhere was too draining, so the leadership bought him his own car. Everyone else had to go on foot, including all the foreigners, or travel in buses. He was the only one with his own vehicle. It attracted a lot of attention. Everyone ate in the athletes' canteen, too, but he said that prior to competition he needed a special diet, so the leadership sent people out to buy him the ingredients for a special ginseng chicken soup. They even had to buy a wok for his personal use. And in the end he still lost. You can just imagine how much all the people at his beck and call hated the guy. But we all knew that it would have been a major political incident if he had been refused all that special treatment and then lost.

Of course, special soups won't win you medals, but they have their place, and they're risk-free. They can't find any evidence of drugs in your urine because it's all Chinese medicine, no hormones. But forget about Old He's ginseng soup; it's General Ma's turtle broth that really seems to do the trick. Ma Junren says the reason that his people scored at the Olympics was that, apart from doing the correct ideological work on them, and giving them the right amount of training, he made them all drink his secret soup. They call it "Chinese essence of turtle." They say it's made with a whole bunch of Chinese herbs, and you have to cook it for several days. It's supposed to contain like over fifty amino acids. That's what they're called, isn't it? Anyway, they say it works wonders. I've never had it myself; not everyone is allowed to. They say the General Ma Chinese essence of turtle that you can buy in the shops is just a brand name and nothing like the stuff they make for athletes. The secret formula is really supposed to work, but only his team members get it.

I'm used to exhausting training sessions since I've been doing them since I was a kid. But it's still a really hard slog, incredibly tiring. I haven't had much of an education, so I can't really describe it to you in so many words. Just help me out and make up a few things to give your readers an idea. It's like, I often feel so exhausted I wish I could just drop dead on the spot. If I happen to take a fall, I try to lie there on the ground for as long as I possibly can, even if it's only for a few seconds. But our coach is a real taskmaster. He won't let you die; he needs you to win medals for him.

The second you fall down he's standing over you screaming his head off. "What kind of fucking attitude is this? If that's the way you want it, just go home and play with yourself." So you have to drag yourself up and get back to practice. "Call this hard? The Long March was hard. Ask an old revolutionary what hard is." This is the only place in China where people still carry on with all that Cultural Revolution stuff.

As long as we can improve our performance and our fitness, I can handle all the training. What I really hate is when the scientists come along to record training sessions on video so they can analyze what you're doing wrong. Then they decide what you've got to concentrate on. Whatever it is, you have to practice it until you improve. My brain goes numb whenever I see those training schedules. I just want to lie down and die.

A couple of years back they said I didn't have enough stamina in my back, stomach, and leg muscles, and no matter how good my technique got, it would still affect my performance. So, during one whole winter training season, they made me concentrate on running, jumping, throwing, and weight lifting. Then they decided that my stamina was being undercut by a lack of lung capacity, so whenever I exerted myself I'd be short of oxygen. So they made me concentrate on running. Every morning after warm-up I had to do laps on the running field. Twenty kilometers a day was just for starters; after a couple of weeks they started upping the mileage bit by bit. Pretty soon I was running a marathon every day. I was exhausted. But after the run there was the next thing to work on. If all I'd had to do was run, it would have been great—but the coach would say that running was all well and good, but I couldn't let my specialist training go. He'd quote the old saying, "Only when you suffer in the extreme can you become a superior being." "Anyway," he'd say, "young boys can take a bit of punishment."

There are times when you're so exhausted and thirsty that it takes you ages to build up the energy to go get yourself a drink, even if it's only a few meters away. The only thing in your body that is still active is your brain. I react to overtraining like that by throwing up. You're completely exhausted, they make you work some more, you throw up, but they don't think you're really sick, so they make you carry on. Sports scientists say that you need about six thousand calories a day, but actually you can get by on two or three thousand, even if you have to work out extra hard. If you tell them you're so tired that you have wet dreams, they say you only lose five to ten calories of body heat when you come, so don't worry. Just keep training. I don't think they really think of us as people. They're all university graduates with higher degrees. They reckon athletes are all brawn and no brain, so they despise us. Well, even if we are, that's because the state requires it; it's not because we wanted it that way.

Our coaches are ignorant like us—they don't know about science either. All they're doing is "drawing tigers by looking at cats." They haven't got it quite right; everything's all out of proportion. They tell you, "I won gold by doing it this way, so you're going to get exactly the same training." It's like they're your master, and you've got no choice at all. "If I say go right, then you'd better not go left." When they were athletes, the policy was the same as the old People's Liberation Army approach to military training, Three Proceed-Froms and One Maximize. "Proceed from the difficult, the serious, and the practical needs of competition and maximize training." Back in the 1960s they bumbled along with the most primitive policy of self-reliance; and now they're applying exactly the same principles to us. They say that regardless of all the talk about reform, the old method of revolutionary enthusiasm and heroic hard work is still the way to go. In fact, it's to their advantage to make us achieve. That way they can get more money in bonuses and they can get promotions, too. If you ask me, that's what they're really in it for. Those old homespun methods and science on top of that—we can't get away with anything. It's murder.

Our coach says, "You've hardly started working out, and already you're saying you're tired and in pain. Is that fair to China? Is it fair to me? If it's too hard for you, then get out! But I'll tell you something: no one back home will want you unless you take a medal with you." Ain't that the truth! The scientists might think it's all about applying scientific methods, but our coach only cares about you putting up with pain and hard training, turning sweat into gold. Then there's all the layers of political commissars in charge of our ideological purity. They're always going on about the need to arm ourselves spiritually, the importance of the human factor in victory; how every threat must be neutralized. All day they're telling us that we have to achieve or else. Win glory for the nation or else!

We're forbidden to marry, and we're not allowed girlfriends. We're not even allowed to go out shopping. No eating between meals, no drinking beer. No staying up late, no chatter or gossip, and we're not allowed to get to know people outside. . . . There's like a million and one restrictions. At major competitions and in intensive precompetition training, there are even more rules and regulations. You're not allowed to do anything! You can't meet friends or relatives, leave the training camp, have time off, watch TV, or listen to the radio, let alone read the papers. They reckon that would distract us. So much for "breaking out of Asia and going international." We're not even allowed to know what's going on overseas!

Chinese athletes weren't particularly disappointed when we didn't get the 2000 Olympics. It's the same competition no matter where they hold it; and going overseas is better for us than staying at home. If we're on home turf, then the spectators would be Chinese, and I can just imagine the type of pressure they'd put on us. And then there were all those companies that offered to train teams under contract for the Olympics. That type of thing has actually been going on for ages. When government money started getting tight, they called for industry sponsorship. They call it "official athletics with popular support" or "privately outsourced official athletics," and they've created club teams with it. I don't know why they think it's a "reform." It's really bad news. We haven't gotten anything out of it. The state's still there putting pressure on you to "win glory for the nation," but now you've got pressure from these capitalists as well, expecting you to be successful so you'll make their companies famous. They're even worse than the government, because they pump up the pressure even for local meets, not just international ones. The pharmaceutical companies are the worst. They divide the teams up—you're this brand, he's that brand—and then put their ads up all around the stadium. It's cool if it's Sony or Nike, there's no loss of face competing under the logo of a major multinational. But making me play for some drug company whose slogan is "Just one application and the embarrassing soreness will be gone forever" makes me feel like I'm living proof of their VD cures or something.

In my opinion, sport in China has nothing to do with improving the standard of public health. It's all about earning gold medals and winning glory for China. It's completely different from the spirit in Mao's day, "Develop physical education and improve the people's health." They might still use the slogan, but nowadays it's all about training specialist athletes and forcing us to win gold for the state. The people have got absolutely nothing to do with it. But the physical condition of the athletes actually deteriorates with all that overtraining; by the time they quit the squad they're either permanently injured or sick. The women in Lang Ping's medal-winning volleyball team were all a complete mess when they retired, yet they're held up as being the model for all the rest of us. We're all supposed to emulate them for not leaving the court when they were injured and not crying even when they were seriously hurt. It's got better propaganda value if you get gold despite an injury.

The authorities are always going on about how the hope for the revitalization of China rests with us. The whole nation has its eyes on us. We're soldiers fighting a political war, a war to inspire the whole Chinese race. With this kind of emotional blackmail, plus the sheer physical demands of our training schedule, the pressure is so great that I sometimes think about killing myself. My family mean well, but they're still adding to the pressure: "You're the only one in our family that has really made it. Don't quit, whatever you do." There are actually people who can't cope with all of that and they do end up killing themselves or intentionally get injured so they can get out of having to compete. I've got this friend who generally performs pretty well. She's one of the best in the world at her particular sport, though maybe not the very best. Anyway, she could win medals in an international championship. It's not like running, jumping, or throwing; her type of competition depends on how you perform over a period of time during a match. Like, if you start out badly, there's no way you can turn that around. And how you play is very much influenced by the crowd's response. If you're playing on the opposing team's home ground, for example, and the crowd applauds when you miss the vital shot. Anyway, this friend of mine wasn't playing her best one time, and she was faced with a final on the home ground of the opposition. The pressure was just too much, and she was convinced she couldn't win, but she was equally terrified of losing. So she secretly injured herself. She told the leadership that she'd been attacked by an enemy agent and they'd also broken her racket. She shouldn't have done that. Our athletes are pretty uneducated, and she thought they would be fooled—but they saw through it right away. They declared that she was self-ish and ideologically unsound, that she was psychologically unfit and an embarrassment to the nation. So they threw her out. Things like that make people want to defect when they're overseas. It happens a lot. There have also been cases where frustrated athletes have killed their coaches. There's no way they can keep us from finding out about things like that. But we're forbidden to discuss it. They hope you'll just forget all about it.

In fact, I'm not scared of the spectators, I hate them, in particular the overseas Chinese who come to watch major international events. When people back home insult you after you've lost a competition overseas, it's not that big a deal; after all, everything we eat and use comes from our own people. But the overseas Chinese! If we win we're national heroes; if we lose we're nothing more than traitors and scum. They have it pretty good overseas, but they always have this inferiority-complex thing going. They hate foreigners and they see us as representing China in their own war with the white man. But they don't love China; they only love themselves. They're not there for the competition; they're there to see the flag of the People's Republic of China go up. They're waiting for us to make them feel proud. So if you can't get the Five-Star Red Flag up there, if you don't make them feel like big shots in front of all the foreigners, then you're nothing more than a big traitor.

I don't think you can say all drug taking is bad or inappropriate. We orientals—us, Japanese, and Koreans—are racially Asian. We're naturally smaller, and our endurance is not as good as that of foreigners. If we don't take drugs, we'll come off second best. Take the ball sports, for example. Whether it's soccer, basketball, volleyball, tennis, or badminton, given the standard size of the field or court, it's obvious that shorter people will have to run and move about more than taller people. That's particularly true when you're on the defensive. If you're not quick enough, no matter how good your technique is, you just can't keep up. If you can't get to the ball, you're dead. Given that you don't have the same stamina as foreigners, you're burning up more energy. It doesn't make any difference if you do really long, intensive training sessions or train at high altitudes. You're still not the same as those foreigners; you're racially different. If you don't take drugs, then you're going to lose out for sure. With drugs, at least you can keep going a bit longer. Track and field, swimming, winter Olympic sports, it's the same for all of them. Even sharpshooters take drugs.

The situation is a bit different at competitions inside China, though people still use drugs when necessary. Everyone else is taking them, so if you don't eat a little "chocolate" too, you'll miss out. Sure, it's not real chocolate; all chocolate can do is give you a few extra calories to burn.

You're absolutely forbidden to take anything without supervision. What if something goes wrong? Who's going to take the political responsibility for it? Provincial and municipal teams are more casual about such things, more flexible. You've got more freedom there to make money and take the drugs you want to. You can earn money by taking part in local competitions, representing other people. They get the placing, but you get the cash. Say, for example, you're in the hope team of Guangdong Province and, according to the regulations, you're only allowed to represent Guangdong. In reality, Guangdong can lease you to Guangxi Province, or Shandong, or even the Datong Coal Mines, the Aeronautical Corporation, or whatever. Anyone who can pay can hire you for a while. But you can't get away with that at the National Sports Competition, because athletes have to represent their own provinces and cities, and everyone's watching everyone else to make sure that's how it's done. But no one cares in intercity and interprovincial competitions. So you go out and hire someone from a place that's not participating in that meet. If you don't, your side is going to lose.

The principle's the same as taking drugs. It's an open secret. It happens at every level except the National Sporting Competition. It goes on at other national-level events, such as sports meets for workers or farmers, at intercity games and the national student games, too. The same athletes are there at all the games—whatever competition it is, you'll see the same faces. We all know each other. And drug taking is commonplace. You can take anything you like, as long as you don't get caught. Anything at all, including strange and secret formulas, Chinese or Western: royal jelly, turtle essence, placenta fluid, immunoglobulin, you name it. When I was in the hope team I took them all, one after another, match after match. Semen and menstrual blood are about the only things I haven't tried. Back then they still hadn't come up with turtle essence. They gave us an aphrodisiac, "Treasure of Youth," to keep us alert. The most disgusting thing was using fluid taken from dead babies. They got the bodies from the hospital. They say it only works if it's a baby boy from an unmarried woman.

I don't think the homegrown recipes really work all that well. The more you take, the less effective they are. As far as I'm concerned, the best thing for improving your stamina is still norephedrine. Those little white beauties are miraculous. If you take them when you're exhausted, they'll pick you up every time. The only problem is that they can be detected in drug tests. So in the national team we're not allowed to touch them.

Members of the national team like me don't have a clue what drugs we're being given, regardless of whether they're taken orally or by injection. The team physicians say they're vitamins, so that's what we call them. They're always being changed; there are always new "vitamins" to take. We have all our meals in our own canteen, and the nutritionist gives you special medicinal food, with who knows what supplements. Duck with *Rhizoma gastrodiae,* venison with *Lycium chinensis,* they're nutritional supplements, and they're not against the rules. Who knows if there's anything else mixed in there? As long as it can't be detected, nothing you take is illegal. If something is discovered, the officials deny all responsibility; our doctors claim that we don't even have those drugs; and the athletes say they never take any drugs. We deny everything. Just stick with the facts. All the foreigners can do is strip us of the medals. Among the scientists, there are people who are specialists in drug research. In particular they work on drugs that increase your stamina but can't be detected by the foreigners. Obviously their research is less than perfect, otherwise the foreigners wouldn't have been able to strip our swimmers and winter athletes of all those medals.

Sure, there are some people who get their own drugs and take them on the sly. Female athletes tend to go for Chinese medicines, because male hormones are detectable. But none of those foreign testing instruments can tell if you've taken Male Precious or Golden Gun Power Pills. You can find aphrodisiacs like these all over the place, especially at stores like Garden of Eden and Real Man.[5] And they're good quality, too. The stuff you get elsewhere is often just fake, and it often contains additives like Western drugs. That makes them dangerous because you don't have a clue what's really in them, and they might be detected in the drug tests. I know all about this stuff because I went shopping with a friend—she was too scared to go to Garden of Eden by herself. She was afraid they'd ask her what a girl of her age wanted to buy that stuff for. Of course no one asked her anything. As long as you can pay for it, they'll sell you whatever you want, even if you're only a three-year-old. I really didn't want her taking anything like that, because it makes you really aggressive. But the pressure was on her to win a medal, just like me, so she couldn't leave anything to chance.

It just isn't worth it in the end. All of that effort just for the sake of a few

5. Beijing sex-aid shops; see chapter 14.

medals. And even if you win one, all you get as a reward is an IOU. When they give you a big red envelope at the victory awards, it's always empty. All you get is a certificate; the cash is supposed to come later. But before you've seen a cent of it, people from back home are all over you asking for donations. There are the people from the primary school, and even people with cancer come and search you out. If you've got a conscience, you have to borrow money to help them out first. So from that point of view, all that work to win a medal and then all the stuff that happens afterwards, it really isn't worth it.

But this is all I've ever been trained to do. I don't know how to do anything but go for gold. Some of my old classmates went off to technical schools, and some are taking the university entrance exams. Even if I could start all over again, I wouldn't even be able to get into high school. Once you're in this game there's no turning back; like it or not, you've got to fight to get a medal. Once you've got that medal, you're set. If I haven't won by the time I retire, then the rest of my life will be screwed. My ideal is to win a medal. The moment I get one, even a bronze, I'm out of here. I'd never hang around for the next Olympics.

I'm nearly seventeen. And as that karaoke song goes, life is a one-way highway. I'm using my youth to gamble on the future. I've just got to win a medal no matter what.

Heaven's Narrow Gate

14

A Life of Sex
Dr Sex

She works in the Garden of Eden, Beijing. All of the employees wear white coats, like doctors in hospitals, including the part-time shop assistants. Many of them are out-of-towners with strong Hunan or Anhui country accents. They haven't had a chance to acquire the polite hypocrisy of city folk yet, and they ask all customers the same question: "Are you going to buy that?" They get paid according to how much they sell.

She was wearing a white coat as well, and leaning on the counter that featured blow-up girl dolls and massage paraphernalia. She had a long chat with the friend who had taken me there to make the initial introduction and then suddenly seemed to notice me. "You're doing oral history, so does that mean you want to record me? Do you want me to speak in English or Chinese?"

I was a barefoot doctor in the Cultural Revolution. You know, someone whose skills were pretty much limited to applying mercurochrome to whatever injury was presented to me. When I came across cases of syphilis, I didn't know what it was, so I treated it like it was some allergy-related dermatitis. I didn't know a thing about sexually transmitted diseases. I was sent back to the commune to practice after just a month-long "red doctor class" at the county health bureau. It's what they called a "daring induction" into on-the-job training. It wasn't until many years later that I discovered, no, that I *realized* how many cases of venereal diseases I'd seen then, gonorrhea in particular. I'd treated them as though they were ordinary urinary-tract infections or children's conjunctivitis. In the 1960s China claimed it was the one country in the world that had completely eradicated venereal diseases.

That, as it turned out, was complete nonsense. Now the authorities are a bit more realistic, and they admit that STDs have reached virtually epidemic proportions.

When I went to study in America, I was astounded to learn how strictly medicine was controlled, even the right to write a prescription. They require very high qualifications for their doctors and pharmacists there. I'd never even heard of such a system; in China it was simply nonexistent. After a month of study, a barefoot doctor was qualified to write prescriptions, though maybe not for every kind of drug. We were also allowed to do just about anything short of taking up a scalpel, though if you were brave enough, you could have a go at cutting someone open as well. Things are a bit better these days, but the system for approving medical qualifications is still pretty haphazard, and even then it's only really enforced in the big city hospitals. They're a kingdom unto themselves, and they reign supreme within their own walls. But just go outside the gate and you'll find the streets full of advertisements promising cures for everything, including cancer and venereal disease. Not one of the so-called doctors behind the advertisements has even the most rudimentary qualifications. Some are probably illiterate into the bargain. And this is a major city. In most county townships, health bureaus have their rules and regulations, which means medical practitioners don't actually have to have graduated from medical school to prescribe treatment. Of course, the situation in the villages is even worse. China's got to be the most lax country in the world with regard to the regulation of pharmaceuticals. So long as you've got the money to pay for them, you can go into any pharmacy and buy antibiotics, hormones, contraceptive pills, and whatever else you fancy. Take what you want; you're your own doctor. Technically, you need a prescription for some medicines, but that's just a formality. The in-house doctors will offer enthusiastic service, and since their income goes up in proportion to the pharmacy's profits, they'll write out a script for whatever you want. They'll be happy to offer free advice on top of it: one bottle of tranquilizers only contains one hundred pills, so you might as well buy two at the same time; the more the merrier.

You really are your own doctor. You'd think that with all this competition—including the street quacks—genuine medical practitioners would have a hard time. But that's not the case at all. Take us, for example. We operate as a sexual-health clinic, with a focus on tonics and contraceptives, and a sideline in other health-care items that may or may not be related to sexual or reproductive health. We're a business, a medical clinic, and a pharmacy; or, if you prefer, not solely a business, a clinic, or a pharmacy. While we've had occasional hassles over ideological issues in the past, we now enjoy as much latitude as you could want.

To be quite honest, although the quality of Chinese-made sexual medicines and aids is not particularly high, and in some cases the medicines are totally ineffective, virtually no one complains or demands their money back. When it comes to anything related to sex, people are too embarrassed to kick up a fuss. They feel they'd lose face if they came in and said: "Look, I used your medicine but I still couldn't get an erection." They'd rather cope with the fact that they've been had, write it off as bad luck, and forget about it. Some sex shops only trade in bogus medicines, for both men and women. Now, we're not like that at all, but we know that there are a lot of crooks out there underselling our quality products with their rubbish. When other people sell crappily made sex aids, it hurts our business, too. But we're operating in a very large, albeit special market, so there's lots of room for everyone.

I never thought I'd end up studying medicine. When I was little, I dreamed of being a pilot. Lots of girls wanted to be pilots, even though at the time there were probably only a handful of female pilots in the entire country. One of them came and spoke at my school. She told us how Chairman Mao had sent her up into the blue sky. I'd just started primary school, and the minute I heard her talk, I decided that when I grew up I wanted to fly a plane, too. To fly MiGs, Soviet-made planes—I must have been really brave! The Cultural Revolution began when I was in my second year of high school. Overnight, the kids at school organized themselves into combat teams.[1] Some of my closest friends formed one, too, and we all headed off to Beijing. To us, making revolution was like a game. When we got back to Guangzhou, we roamed around, keeping up with the action. We went out to protect the Trade Fair; we opposed people who were pretending to be revolutionaries but were really plotting to bring back the old order; we also supported the Hong Kong people against the British imperialists and got involved in the Hundred-Day Armed Struggle.[2] We were there through all of it. It was incredibly good fun. When 1969 rolled

1. That is, rival Red Guard factions that fought with each other in the name of defending Mao Zedong Thought and saving the revolution from revisionism.
2. Major ideological struggles in Guangzhou, some of which resulted in violent conflict.

around, the city leaders had had enough of us, so we were all packed off to the countryside. We were supposed to unite with the workers and peasants and reform our political thinking there.

Conditions in the villages were incredibly primitive. We had to fetch our water in buckets, and we only had small kerosene lanterns to read by. Following a day of hard labor, we'd huddle around the feeble light to study the works of Chairman Mao, pretending that we were trying to reeducate ourselves. But it was hell. Our only link to the outside world was the radio, but it was a struggle even to get batteries. They were so precious to us that when they ran out we'd lay them on the doorstep in the hope they'd soak up some sunlight and revive. After a day of sun baking, they'd work for a few minutes before going flat again. The next day we'd repeat the routine. The climate of northern Guangdong Province, where I ended up, was really peculiar. Most of the time it was overcast. The East was red all right, but the sun never seemed to rise.[3] We became desperate. It wasn't as though there was anything else to do at night, either. So I know everything there is to know about batteries. The worst brands were Red Guard and Beijing; they'd give up after just a few days, and they leaked out muck as well. They could damage your radio if you weren't careful. The best was Eveready—a hangover from the "old society"—but they were extremely hard to find. It was amazing that they didn't change the brand name during the movement to "Destroy the Four Olds."[4] It was pretty funny too, because it was a classic sexual double entendre: "Take me now, I can do it anytime." Eveready—get it?

People were always carrying on about the evils of sex—how bad it is, how dirty. For years you couldn't even talk about it. You did it, of course, but you weren't supposed to discuss it. But here was this naughty brand name right in front of us, and no one ever cottoned on. How ridiculous is that? Things have changed a lot in recent years. Now we've got Girlfriend brand tissues, Concubine liquor, Night Fragrance underwear—sex is everywhere you look.

I had what they called a good attitude. That meant I didn't shrink from

3. "The East is red, the sun has risen" is the first line of the Maoist anthem "The East is Red."

4. An attempt to eradicate all vestiges of the prerevolutionary and revisionist past in the early phase of the Cultural Revolution. Red Guards generally took the call to wipe out "the old ideas, culture, customs, and habits of the exploiting classes" as an excuse to destroy the physical evidence of the past, from shop signs to cultural artifacts.

hardship or complain, and I obeyed the cadres' orders. That's how I got recommended for training as a barefoot doctor. They could have made me an accountant, a storeroom attendant, or childcare worker for all I cared—so long as I didn't have to slave in the fields all day, I was happy. By then my ideals had come crashing down to earth, and I'd learned to be pragmatic.

For two years I worked as a barefoot doctor. This earned me a recommendation for university study. At the time there were no entrance exams; everything depended on your class status and support from the poor and lower middle peasants.[5] I waited two years for a chance to go to university, but I wasn't too hopeful because my family was classified as middle-class; I was Little Miss Bourgeoisie. But things changed a little in 1973. The medical schools began enrolling experienced barefoot doctors, and there was a quota for people they considered educable despite their class background. That's how I became a "worker-peasant-soldier" student.[6] I was at Guangdong Medical College when they arrested the Gang of Four in 1976. My former classmates, who were still down on the farm undergoing rural re-education, tried to escape to Hong Kong by trekking over the mountains or even swimming. I was busy studying, learning how traditional Chinese herbs like isatis root could prevent encephalitis and pneumonia. In 1981, I passed the exams for overseas study. Then everything changed for me. I spent the next six years in America becoming a genuine doctor. I got a higher degree in clinical medicine and decided to return to China to serve my country.

Of course I thought about staying there. I don't think any Chinese person who's gone abroad hasn't considered staying. Both the standard of living and the conditions for research are far better in America. You're asking me about politics? Do you really think someone like me has anything meaningful to say on the subject?

Certainly it's a crucial issue. There it's up to you to create optimum living conditions and a good work environment for yourself. If they're not that good, you can only blame your own incompetence or lack of opportunity. Here, it's all out of your control. You can try to keep out of politics, but politics won't leave you alone. America isn't the only place that's different from

5. Everyone was assigned a class status depending on their family background; the poorer the better. Those who came from a superior, "exploiting" class, as this woman did, were barred from college or only allowed to attend university if recommended by representatives of those with "good" class backgrounds.

6. That is, a student supposedly with a worker, peasant, or soldier pedigree.

China in this regard. Throughout the capitalist world, politics is conducted on a more mature level, more openly—a lot more openly—than in China. It's a bit like sex. I'm not claiming that either politics or sex is entirely healthy or particularly clean in the West, but at least they're both regarded as normal activities; they're not repressed like they are in places like China or the Islamic countries. Normality is an ideal in itself. You can't judge sex or politics by the standards of hygiene or healthiness. Is oral sex hygienic? Hardly. And that's just too bad, since it is both normal and enjoyed by a lot of average people. It enhances sexual pleasure, and that's not a bad thing.

I decided to return despite the inferior conditions in China. I'm not claiming that I'm possessed of lofty ideals or an advanced ideology. Measured by Chinese standards, my ideology isn't very progressive at all. I returned because I was on a scholarship, and my visa specified that I had to leave upon the completion of my studies. I couldn't change to another type of visa there. Many Chinese people will go to extreme and undignified lengths just to stay on in the United States. Some even go into hiding. Not me.

My specialty is obstetrics. There's not a huge demand for people with higher degrees in that field; most obstetric staff in hospitals are midwives and nurses. Now, I know that what I'm about to say goes against popular wisdom, but personally I don't believe women are all that suited for this kind of work. Assisting at births requires a lot of physical strength. There's blood everywhere, and there's more noise and stress than you'd get flying a plane. Women aren't suited for the job, either psychologically or physiologically. I know if I was having a baby, I'd want a male doctor, someone with a cool head and strong hands.

I say *if* because after having seen so many births I have no desire to go through all that myself. I think it's the same everywhere—female obstetricians would be the professional women least likely to want to have children. Even less, say, than ballerinas. It's not just giving birth; it's all that nurturing and education as well. Too much trouble, if you ask me!

It was easier to do research work in 1987. You had more freedom to choose your own field of study and the direction of your research. Now, except for the areas specifically targeted as priorities by the government, there's no money available for research at all, not one cent. So, as a researcher in the Medical Research Institute after I came back to China, I decided to focus my work on what interested me most—female sexuality. It's a topic that goes hand in hand with sociology, so, to take a line from the novelist Wang Shuo, before I knew what was going on I found that I'd become a folk sexologist.[7] I'm a big reader of novels, and I always read a few pages before falling asleep. Wang Shuo's novels are very entertaining, though a bit too phallocentric for my taste. He's even more contemptuous of women than contemporary Chinese society is as a whole.

We just don't seem to be able to face up to the fact that Chinese women are also just women, people, not just baby machines or incubators for female illnesses. This is the conclusion of the first stage of my research, the part that relates to the broader society. I don't think the medical conclusions of my research would be of much interest to the general readership. Too technical.

And I'm not prepared to discuss specific cases. I've got to protect my intellectual property until I'm ready to publish my case histories and statistical research. However, I can tell you that extreme domestic violence, sexual perversions, impotence, abnormal sexual psychology, ignorance, and the horrific treatment of homosexuals in China are all far more pervasive than I had ever imagined. I was also completely surprised by the number and complexity of the cases.

I haven't actually reached any real conclusions yet, particularly with regard to the medical and scientific aspects of female sexuality. What I've managed to do over a few short years couldn't possibly have any immediate practical applications in clinical medicine. But it's certainly proved what I've always known: that those reports that there's a magic cure for frigidity, the one that claims that through a simple surgical procedure they can allow women to experience orgasms so intense they'll scream like a stuck pig, are unbelievable. They simply don't stand up to examination; like most aphrodisiacs, they claim a ninety-something percent success rate, but then they would, wouldn't they? My research doesn't really have any clinical applications, and it doesn't fall within the ambit of the government's research plans. It's certainly not aimed at developing some new drug. If it was, pharmaceutical companies would leap at the chance to invest in my work, no problem at all. But things being as they are, it's a case of sorry, no money for you. No one is willing to put a cent into the kind of research I'm doing. So if I refer to "this stage" of my research, it's not a theoretical stage, just an unavoidable one.

7. Wang Shuo was a Beijing novelist who came to fame in the late 1980s, when he published both satirical fiction and maudlin love stories. His original line was, "Before you know what's going on, you find that you've become a writer." He later became noted as a screen and TV writer as well as an occasional literary critic.

Anyway, this is where I've ended up. Our store is part of a chain. We have branches in lots of cities, though a few other outfits have been pirating our name. We've brought lawsuits against them.

I'm just a shop assistant, really. What you see is what I do every day. I provide consulting services for the customers. Part of it is recommending the various products sold here, but I don't exaggerate their effectiveness. I certainly wouldn't advise anyone to buy China-made Indian Miracle Oil for instance, or God of War rings (which don't do a thing for you), or Superman condoms. If I did, then I'd be going against my medical code of ethics. What I will do is give advice about contraception to people having premarital sex, give out information on how to get an abortion, reassure people on issues such as whether masturbating to orgasm will affect your memory, suggest medicines suitable for older people, advise paraplegics on how they can make love, and so on. These are areas within the range of my professional competence. I help people attain pleasure for its own sake and have more fulfilling sex lives. It's a philanthropic enterprise; and it's a job that brings me personal satisfaction. It also provides a lot of original material for my research. And it brings in money. I need the money. I'm still plugging away at my research, and recently I was able to hire two university students to work part-time categorizing my case histories and compiling statistics.

I left my state job voluntarily. My field of interest was outside the national plan. They didn't cut off my salary or anything, but I thought it would be better to search out other opportunities. It wouldn't have been difficult to switch to some topic that was targeted for funding. Some people might be content to work at something they don't really believe in just for the sake of a full rice bowl and a guaranteed job till retirement, but I wanted to pursue my interests. There were several choices open to me. The most profitable would have been to work in pharmaceuticals, developing new medicines. The pharmaceutical companies are more than willing to fork out money for research into cure-alls for sexually transmitted diseases. You've seen those wretched doctors in the TV ads saying things like: "Just one application and your dirty little secret is no more." One application? That sort of thing simply eliminates the symptoms while allowing the disease to take root—and then you're really in trouble. Another road to easy money is selling so-called cures for impotency: Golden Gun Power Pills — Stick-'Em-Up and Keep-'Em-Up, A Man's Most Precious Treasure, that sort of thing. But money isn't my only concern. So I chose to work here in this shop. I don't need to make any immediate decisions about my future. For now I'm enjoying access to all these case studies, free of charge. It would be a real shame to waste such an opportunity.

The worst you can say about me is that having returned from America, I've got big ideas and the will to carry them out, or that having gone to all the trouble to get an M.D., it's a shame to waste it on the business world. In fact lots of people think my job is shameful, as though the instant that sexual medicine leaves the confines of a hospital or research institute, it becomes a harmful, corrupting force. They act as if I'm abetting prostitution or something.

I don't care what they say. The truly shameless ones are those sanctimonious hypocrites. They tell you to control yourself by taking cold showers, or try to keep people's sexual behavior in check by telling them scary stories. If that doesn't work, then "beat the dog behind closed doors."[8] Practice self-reliance—not only can you feed and clothe yourself, you can even achieve orgasm on your own.[9] It's all right so long as no one finds out what you're up to. Now, in my book, *that's* shameless.

I've always advocated a more open attitude and the legitimization of sexual services and shops like this in China. If you ban the sex industry, it just goes underground. The best approach is to welcome it into society and allow it to serve the people openly. All the people. It's a good thing, since it gives people sexual choices. It is not in conflict with all the official ideological campaigns promoting the "Five Teachings and Four Beautifuls" or defending China against Western "peaceful evolution."[10]

Sex shops have existed in China for some years now. They started out selling sex aids and aphrodisiacs, though recently they've taken a more professional direction; so we have sex chain-stores like this one. For the moment, the authorities employ a policy of peaceful coexistence. They don't encourage us, but they don't stop us either. So long as we pay our taxes, they turn a blind eye to where the money comes from. Who knows how things will

8. Masturbate.

9. A parody of a famous Yan'an-period Maoist exhortation for people to work with their own two hands to produce enough to eat and wear and thus frustrate the wartime blockade of the Communist bases.

10. Five Teachings and Four Beautifuls [and Three Loves] *(wu jiang si mei [san re'ai])* was a campaign launched in the early 1980s to promote civility, hygiene, and political rectitude. "Peaceful evolution" connotes the supposed United States–led Western strategy to quietly subvert Chinese culture and politics and turn the People's Republic into a bourgeois democracy.

work out—there's an economic and political side to everything. Anyway, so far, so good. Maybe in terms of the big picture they find it expedient to let us keep going. Heaven only knows.

Generally speaking, apart from underground porn, most of which is of very poor quality, there's nothing you can get in the West that you can't find in our shops, whether you're talking about sex aids or medicines. Among the items we can display openly are this Big Mouth inflatable woman and battery-operated vibrators and dildos, including this one with its G-spot and clitoral stimulators. The larger models are for vaginal insertion, and the narrower ones for the anus; they can twitch, vibrate, or wiggle. In America, you can only get some of these things by mail order or in out-of-the-way shops in red-light districts. Then, on top of that, there are our very own Chinese national treasures, sexual aids that you simply can't find in your Western red-light districts, like secret prescriptions from the imperial court and folk medicines that have been handed down from generation to generation, as well as newly developed drugs that combine Western pharmaceuticals with Chinese herbal ingredients. Now all that's left to do is for them to take the final step and make it all legal. What's the point of keeping things shady and ambiguous?

We don't trade in erotica. We don't sell pornographic literature or videos. That's for the street-stall hawkers. Possession or sale of that kind of thing is against the law in China—but if you look at it from a scientific standpoint, there's no reason why pornography shouldn't be given some kind of legal status, so long as it's kept out of the hands of underage readers. It's just a tool. The women in the magazines are sexier than men's wives; they don't talk back, or secretly look through their wallets, or have bad breath. So what if men fantasize and masturbate over them? How is that going to undermine socialist ideology? The negative side of pornography is that it demonstrates a lack of respect for people, particularly women. It doesn't respect sexual science either. They call it unsocialist, but in fact it's equally anticapitalist. The authorities are a lot more afraid of peaceful evolution, and that's what's really behind their antiporn campaigns.[11] They also say porn is detrimental to the healthy development of the next generation. That's a medieval way of thinking, a hangover from Confucian dogma that you ought to segregate the sexes completely. They'd be far better off legislating an age limit. The legal age for marriage in

11. During antipornography campaigns (*saohuang yundong*), which are a regular feature of life in China, contraband political and religious materials are also confiscated and destroyed.

China has to be the highest in the world, twenty for women and twenty-two for men. So why not take this as a standard and set the legal age limit at, say, twenty. That'd do, wouldn't it? Give people a chance to take responsibility for their actions. They have the right to vote; give them the right to choose as well. The authorities could demonstrate that they have confidence in the people. They can't treat everyone like children forever.

Some policies aimed at effecting a higher degree of social control are actually quite dangerous. For instance, in the case of sexual assault, they urge women to fight their assailants with all their might, regardless of the consequences. And they're overzealous in enforcing the laws against prostitution, so much so that they often jail both the prostitute and the client. They treat people with sexual deficiencies, like exhibitionists and peeping Toms, as though they were major criminals. I could name a lot of other examples. This sort of heavy-handed treatment often brings about the opposite result from what's intended. It can only lead to a continual increase in serious, violent sexual assault and the burgeoning of a criminal sexual underground. That will make society even less stable. If society is unstable, the whole state apparatus is built on shifting sand, so how can the regime be stable? It doesn't create a very solid foundation for the nation or political authority, does it?

My husband says I'll never grow up, that I'm living in a fantasy world. But he leaves me alone and doesn't interfere. He figures I am what I am, and nothing he can do will change me. He's a doctor in a hospital. The situation in hospitals has gone downhill in recent years. It's very corrupt, and a lot of doctors are on the take. The patients all slip them bribes for better service. He's a follower of Sigmund Freud, and he thinks he can understand me by using all those theoretical platitudes. According to his analysis it's because I never achieved my childhood dream of becoming a pilot that I've become obsessed with self-fulfillment, I'm always looking for trouble. He says, "If you want to go out and cause mischief, feel free. Ideally nothing will happen, and the worst-case scenario is that you'll be picked up by the police. I promise I'll take food to you in jail. I wouldn't mind; I've always wanted to see what it's like on the inside."

I'd love to sit Jiang Zemin and the other leaders down and give them a lecture on sex. Really! I'm not joking. Zhongnan Hai isn't the Garden of Eden.[12]

12. Zhongnan Hai (the Middle and South Seas) is the government and party compound, located in a former imperial villa complex by a group of lakes in the center of Beijing, from which the People's Republic is ruled.

Anyway, they're just people like the rest of us. Besides, they've got a tradition of inviting guest lecturers. Never mind whether it makes any impression or not; as the old saying goes, "The ruler must be courteous to the wise." All I ask is that they listen. You have your prescriptions, I have mine. If mine is right, take my medicine; if not, then I don't want a cent for my advice. How about that?

My husband says the party will never take any notice of me. He's more practical than I am. He thinks that what I'm doing falls outside all the categories. It's neither fish nor fowl; not really medicine, not really pharmaceutical research, and not really sociology, either. He thinks my idea of lecturing the leadership is a pipe dream and mocks me: "If the party listened to you, it would be like in *The Three Kingdoms,* where Zhou Lang comes up with what he thinks is a brilliant plan and ends up losing both his wife and all his troops." That's what he's got out of watching the TV serialization of *Romance of the Three Kingdoms* every night.

Anyway, it's all talk. If I were the authorities, I wouldn't let me in there to make mischief either. It's a pity, though, mainly because I wouldn't get to use my opening line: "Although you are all leaders of the party and the country, and have all raised children yourselves, our first lesson today goes back to the basics of sexual knowledge—what is a man, what is a woman . . ."

When people say that freedom of the press and sexual liberation are safety valves for the release of antisocial energies, it seems to make sense, but it's not the whole story. Our nascent sexual awakening is just the first wave. The Chinese people are finally realizing their humanity, though not in the sense that's understood by the party or the state. If they can't accommodate what is happening, then the people themselves need to develop an awareness of human rights, and that may well begin with an awareness of the rights of women, as well as a heightened environmental consciousness, then concern about ethnic issues, and regional consciousness. All of these things will nudge the society as a whole towards a true awakening, and once that happens, there'll be no turning back.

So I sincerely believe that women's rights, the environment, and ethnic and regional conflicts will be far more important in forcing China to reform than the events in Tiananmen on 4 June 1989. This may well be the crisis point that ushers in a new, more enlightened age.

15

Time as Money

A Shenzhen Hooker

Shenzhen South Cinema is screening a film in which Jackie Chan, China's Rambo, is lying in wait for some gutless American. Outside the theatre, prostitutes, "wild chickens" in local slang, solicit anyone who pauses on their turf even for a moment.

Shenzhen was the first of China's Special Economic Zones, a model for the Deng era. Over the decades it has also boasted the fastest-growing population and the highest rate of inflation of any city in China.

Shenzhen was a legend in its own time. It spawned the first wave of government officials and red capitalist comrades who could "travel by plane, have foreign sweethearts, spend Hong Kong dollars, and earn Chinese people's currency." It's still legendary today. You know what they say: "If you never work in Beijing, you'll never know how paltry your own position is; if you never go shopping in Shanghai, you'll never know how poor you are; and if you don't go chasing after Hainan girls, you'll never know how little stamina you have." From a Shenzhen perspective that's nonsense, something only someone with no experience would say. If you come to Shenzhen, you'll realize you've got no status and no money—and you'll fall down on the last front as well.

She was wearing a yellow nylon top, a black imitation leather skirt, and white Goldlion brand socks with the tops folded down.

You want to talk? Why not buy a ticket and we'll go inside. We're all struggling; no one wants to be lonely. Our karma's brought us together. Come on, treat me to a film. It won't ruin you.

Where do you think I'm from? Hengyang, Hunan province. My family lives in the city. My dad works in the municipal government; he's a cadre. A lover's booth will only cost you eighty yuan; that's the official price, it's posted over there. I don't get a cut or anything. Besides, I can see that you are no mere laborer, sir; you're a white-collar worker, a big manager in a company. Eighty yuan is nothing to you. Invite me to see a film, just to keep me company. It'll make both of us happy, okay? Eighty yuan is small change to someone like you, like ten yuan would be to me. It's nothing.

The police won't take any notice of us. Just sweethearts seeing a film together, healthy entertainment, outside their jurisdiction. Every major hotel is surrounded by a cordon of whores; there's more than enough to keep the police busy. They get set quotas for how many wild chickens they need to round up; so long as the quotas don't go up, they leave us alone. We're not exactly big business; it's not really worth the trouble.

Come on, let's go in. Give me a hundred yuan and I'll buy the tickets. The twenty yuan change can buy me an ice-cream. I won't ask for any more after we're inside. I've said one hundred up front, and that's it. If you have a good time and want to give me more, that'd be very nice. If you don't have a good time, you don't have to give me any extra. I won't complain. We were meant to meet. It's up to you whether you give me more or not. You'll soon find out how good I am. I've got a great body, satisfaction guaranteed. I work this cinema every day. It's no scam. I guarantee you'll be satisfied. This is Shenzhen after all. The first place to have an open door; we've got the most experience when it comes to trade and fair play. We have professional ethics, too.

You want to go somewhere else to talk? Where? It's too dangerous hanging around the hotels. I don't want to go there. They're swarming with police, and the local mafia is in there as well—they don't like you bringing your own girl in. If you don't take care of things beforehand, you might get past the cops, and *you'll* be fine, but the girl could land in big trouble. Bars and cafes are even worse. They've got their own hostesses to look after the customers. I operate out of this cinema, and that's it. It's no good trespassing on someone else's turf and stealing out of their rice bowl. If you don't want to see a film, all right, treat me to a meal, then. There's a Vietnamese restaurant above the cinema. Take me there. It won't cost too much.

This is Shenzhen. Here, time is money. If you want my company, you want me to have a meal with you, then you've got to pay by the hour. Cash in advance, no exceptions. It's nothing personal, but I've come across men who get the service first and then do a runner. You've got to pay sooner or later, so you might as well do it up front. Thank you. Sorry to be like this. That'll do just fine. If you need extra service, we can talk about that later, but this will cover everything for now.

Shenzhen is in Guangdong Province, so everyone speaks Cantonese. You have to speak it, even if you're not that fluent. The clients don't always understand Mandarin, and if they're unhappy they'll make trouble.

A hooker's a hooker. Who cares? Doesn't worry me. In this business you have to have some street smarts. I can read people pretty well. You just want to have a chat, a few laughs, write a book, just give me a tip. That's fine. So long as the police don't get me, I don't care what you write. Hong Kong people have taken pictures of me. So I've done that, too. If they don't catch you at the time, you're safe.

Yes, I really am from Hengyang. It's not easy for us Hunanese girls here in Shenzhen. We've only got a few choices—this cinema, Spring Breeze Road, or Happiness Street. It's not too bad over on the streets, you work out of the hairdressing salons, while we work the streets. All of us are hookers just the same. There's a hierarchy, though: Big Whites, Shanghai girls, girls from the northeast, then the girls from Sichuan. . . . Big Whites are brought in from Russia. My friend says they can earn several thousand Hong Kong dollars in just one night. You earn according to the pecking order; girls in the salons and us only make two or three hundred a pop. You might do several guys a day. Depends on your luck. The girls there have a harder time than us, but they've got more opportunities. They have to split their money with their pimps, though. We have to be out in the open, but we get to keep everything we earn. Most of the girls who work this theater do it part-time. They're moonlighting, like me.

I work days on an assembly line. I couldn't really tell you all the things we make. It's always changing. They're all circuit boards, all different sizes, for TVs and computers. The supervisor tells us what they're called, but I can't really remember. My job is to slot in the components. The pay is okay as long as I do it right. I don't really care what they're called. It's hard work, though. If you don't mess it up, you can earn over a thousand a month. That's not much by Shenzhen standards, but it gets me a Shenzhen ID. If you don't have one, the border guards can make big trouble for you every time you come back after a visit home.

It's not like I come here every night after work. Sometimes I do other things, like see friends, go shopping, have a meal with people from my hometown, whatever. This is Shenzhen; you've got to have other interests, and sometimes you have to take a break. You can't spend all your time just working, eating, sleeping, and going to work again. So I don't necessarily come here every night, though I'll usually stop by just to check out what's happening. With luck, I can earn more in one night here than I get in a month at the factory. But that sort of opportunity doesn't come along every day. It's only happened once or twice. But most nights I'd get at least a hundred. I'm not boasting. Really, it's never less than a hundred. I'm willing to work hard at it, so I can earn good money. This is Shenzhen. Things have been wide open here for a long time. If you work hard and the price is right, you can't go wrong. Some girls do it cheaper than that; they're mostly junkies who need money for the next fix. You can have them for fifty a pop, sometimes twenty. I haven't heard of anyone doing it for less than twenty; that's how much the cheapest bag of heroin costs around here. But whatever you do, stay away from those girls. You can't get quality goods at that price. Junkie whores are filthy; they've got AIDS.

I haven't really counted, but I suppose I'm here at the Shenzhen South Cinema over a dozen, maybe twenty nights a month. It doesn't matter if I've got my period. This is Shenzhen. It's not like where I come from, where they use pads, and you've got blood everywhere. They've got tampons here; you just stuff one in your hole and off you go. It's dark in the theater, and they can't tell. If they can, well, they've already had their go, so I'm hardly going to hand them their money back. But I look after myself. My body is my capital. I don't work on the one or two days when my period is at its heaviest.

You know how it works. The cinema doesn't want to know what's going on in the lovers' booths. All they care about is turning a profit. They set up booths so that people can grope. If they tried to control what you did in there, they wouldn't make any money. Anyway, it's me that's being groped, not them, so why should they care? Once someone has paid, they can feel as much as they like. Or we can go somewhere else and have sex. But that has to be arranged beforehand and paid for in advance. That doesn't happen every night. It's not that easy to turn tricks at the Shenzhen South. Most of the guys who turn up here are workers, or people on business from the inland provinces. They're all pretty tight with their money. They can't bear to spend all that money on a fuck, so they usually settle for a hand job.

You only get twenty back from a hundred when a ticket is eighty yuan. Twenty's not enough for a grope. Are you sure you want to hear all this?

Once you do, you won't want to come back. I've got to pay my rent tomorrow. Four of us share a room, and we pay three hundred each. It's far too expensive. I have to earn three hundred today; if I don't I'll be out on my ear. So after dinner, we should still go into the cinema. . . . Thank you. That's the same as I'd get for "seeing a movie."

First I give them twenty yuan worth. When we sit down, I lean against them and cuddle and kiss them on the mouth. Before you know it, their hands are all over me. You sure you can put this stuff in your book? Are you into writing pornography, you know, books they sell underground? Anyway, then I guide their hand under my top, and let them feel my tits. I've got a good body. You can see how good my capital is even when I've got clothes on. My tits stand up without a bra. They're not the kind that turn into little flat bags the second the bra comes off. I'm not kidding. A few strokes of my breasts and the guys get all excited, and want to move down. I say: "Don't! Please don't touch me there!" But they're all hot by now, and are dead set on going further. That's when I tell them they've got to pay more: "For a hundred, you can touch me anywhere you want. Just one hundred." I breathe hard and everything, like I'm real excited, and I keep talking to get them going though I still won't let them into my pants: "Come on, only a hundred, please, hurry up, please, do it to me. I can't stand it, please hold me, I want your fingers inside me, I want them up my cunt, please." If they won't fork out any extra, I just get up and go. This is Shenzhen. They're not going to chase after me. Anyway, they've copped a feel. Why would they bother?

My tits are real. I'm not kidding. They're naturally this big. Some of the other girls have big ones too, but they're fake. They were like little potatoes before the operation. Now when you feel them, they're hard and heavy. This is Shenzhen; things opened up here long ago, and people know how to have fun.

I can earn twenty yuan in ten minutes. That's sort of all right. Some are happy to pay extra, and then I let them finger me. You know, we're both sitting down, and I squeeze my legs together, so their fingers can't get in too deep. They can only feel the lips of my cunt. Some horny bastards will force their way inside, and it's like four or five fingers isn't enough, they want to shove themselves right up there. I pretend I can't stand it: "The pain is killing me. Stop or I'll scream." That scares them. If I don't threaten them, they'll stick their whole hand up my hole and start playing with my cervix. In fact, I'm real loose down there. I've got a big mouth, and as you know, that's a sign that a girl has a big hole. When I had an abortion, the doctor at the Shenzhen Hospital said I was big. This is Shenzhen. You can have an abortion if you can pay for it, no one gets uptight. So long as you haven't actually had a kid, a loose cunt is good for men. If your cunt is too tight, they come before they've really enjoyed themselves. It's no fun, like guys sticking it up each other's assholes. There's only so much liquid in a prick, and once it's spent, that's it, game over. It's like you don't get full value from it. Guys who really know how to screw, they love women with loose cunts who haven't had kids, because you can fuck for a longer time. They like to fuck me for ages and ages, until the bed is soaked in my juices. They only come when they're good and ready. And then, as you know, some want to start all over again. But if they're not fully hard, they'll never get it into a tight cunt. It drives them mad. When that happens, other girls have to use their mouths to get the guy hard enough, then he rams it into her cunt as soon as he can, and in a few moves he's shot his load a second time. It's a real drag. But my cunt is loose and wet, and I can take a soft prick inside and make it hard. It's more of a turn-on for them than using your mouth, and I can make the second fuck last even longer than the first.

I'm not kidding, I'm a really good fuck. I've got a better body than other girls, both upstairs and downstairs. Stick your finger up me and see how big and wet my cunt is. I'm already creaming my pants, I'd like to fuck you that much. Don't worry, we'll just sit a bit closer. The waitress won't be able to see what's happening under the table. Don't you want a little feel? I promise I don't have any diseases. If you want to do it for real, we don't have to use a condom. . . .

Do you believe in fate? You only meet people whom you're destined to meet. Let's get out of here. The waitresses'll get fed up if we sit here too long. They know I'm a hooker, but they don't quite know how to get rid of me. Let's take a walk. You can buy me a little present. Spend a little money on me—you won't miss it, it's nothing to you.

Look—even this late, there are hookers out waiting for customers. It's not easy working this strip. There's less than a hundred of us. Just a few dozen really. Going in, scoring twenty yuan, coming out again. . . . I don't let them keep their fingers up me forever. I wait till they've got such a hard-on that they can't stand it, and then I ask if they want to go somewhere to fuck. Guys from the inland are penny-pinchers, and they won't spend extra for a fuck. The workers who've been in Shenzhen a few years know the ropes, so when they want a fuck they go straight to the barbershops, saunas, or brothels. It's safe and cheap. They only come to the cinema for cheap kicks; they check out a film, have some tea, get a hand job, and go. Men can't argue with their pricks. It's their prick that doesn't want to say goodbye. But if I let them, they'd just keep at it till the film's over, or till they've ripped my cunt apart. As you know, this is Shenzhen. Time is money here. So if they say they don't want a screw, then you have to get the waterworks going so you can finish up as soon as possible. I make out that I'm so turned on that I'm about to come: "Yes, yes, just like that, shove it up me, oh, yes, that's it, way inside." While I'm talking I work their cock as hard as I can, and they come in a minute. A guy who's just come goes soft faster than his prick. Once the prick's nodded its head, I don't have to say a thing, they've already pulled their hand away. I can stay or go—it doesn't matter. It's all over within half an hour. I've made my hundred yuan and can go out and score again. It's not tiring, either. I'm fit. Fucking them doesn't tire me out at all. When they stick it inside, I fake an orgasm. I squeeze my legs and use the lips of my cunt to grip the root of their cock. The faster they come, the sooner I can get on to the next job.

I'm not kidding, I can't come even without a condom. Men are useless. If I want to come, I have to do it myself. It's not just men. My girlfriend can't quite get it right either, and I end up seething with frustration. But when I masturbate, I can get off in an instant. It's like dying for a few minutes; it's bliss. My friend is the opposite to me. She has an orgasm every time a guy fucks her. She doesn't have a proper job, works full-time in a brothel. She's so tired out by it that she's really skinny, and her complexion's gone all dark. What can she do? We're all in it for the money. So she's just got to put up with it. We see each other all the time. Every time we get together, she wants me to play with her. Hooking is a business, you sell your cunt to men for money. But it's different with friends, it's just fun. Helps you relax and feel good. It's our time off, after all. Women have to have their fun somehow. You've got to try everything—why not?

If you don't count my regulars, tricks are usually guys from the inland here on business. They don't know where to go for fun. The cinema is right in the city center; they come down here and have a look around, have a feel, and, "Wow!" they think to themselves. "Here's this real big-breasted chick. If I don't do it with her I'll regret it." Sometimes I can borrow someone's apartment, but it's often not convenient. That doesn't mean I'm going to let them go. We can do what you and I were doing—wander around a bit. This is Shenzhen. It's not hard to find a place to do it outside. There's always some corner of a building, or maybe by the railway tracks. I lift up my skirt, and they don't even have to take off their pants. All they have to do is whip out their cock and we're in business. They can stand and enter me from behind too. I squeeze hard and they're done in a few minutes. If that's not good enough for them, I know some clothing-stall owners who'll let me use their changing room for a small commission. What else can you do? You know, I wouldn't miss a chance to turn a trick. It seems to make a big difference to men if they come in my hand or my cunt. It's all the same to me; the only difference is the extra two hundred yuan I get for my cunt. It'd be a shame to let that go.

It's not like that with regulars. They love my breasts and what's between my legs, and they find it hard to get me out of their mind once they've had me, so they're always bringing money my way. They really know how to screw, too. I lie on the bed and open my legs, and before we've even begun my hole's wide open, loose and wet and warm. They stick their prick into my big cunt and thrust away; they don't come for ages. They love it. After a while, I mount them and let them play with my breasts, and give them my juices to taste. . . . All of that takes time, so you definitely need someplace to go. The flat I use is rented by a friend of mine. It's over there, third building to the left, fourth window, the one with the fluorescent light on. When that light's on, it's a signal that no one's at home. If they're at home, they leave a regular light on, or it's dark. I'm not kidding, there really isn't anyone at home. Let's go up there and hang out for a while. It's fine, don't worry. We're friends now, aren't we? If you feel like it, just give me a bit more money. If you don't, that's okay too, we can still go up. We can talk up there. No difference, really.

Since we've come in, why don't we fool around? You know, I believe in fate. It's a matter of luck. If you won't fool around, then I won't have done any business tonight, and that's bad luck. If I hadn't come out to work it wouldn't matter, but I did, so if I can't find a man I'll be out of luck for a few nights. It's true. I won't be able to get any customers. What do you mean I'm superstitious? This is Shenzhen. Everyone's superstitious here, except the party secretary and the mayor. They believe in revolution. They know what's going to happen tomorrow and the day after. They know where their money's coming from. I'm not kidding. It might not matter much to you, but if you won't do it with me then it's really going to bring me bad luck. . . . It's no fun talking about this.

It's the same for everyone; we're all in Shenzhen for the money. We're all working our fingers to the bone, you know that's true. I can see that. You don't need me to tell you.

I've been doing this for three years now. It was simple, really. There were ads from Shenzhen in our local press for female workers, aged eighteen to twenty-one, middle-school graduates. I fit the bill on both counts, so I came. At first I was really timid. I worked hard for the boss all day, and at night I sat in our crowded dorm watching TV. It didn't take long for me to realize that, well, you know, this is Shenzhen, and I'd never get rich just working in a factory. The girls who get rich become either the mistresses of Hong Kong businessmen or hookers. All you have to do is drop your pants, and you can make more in one night than you do in ten days at the factory. No one told me what was what, but I could see for myself. This is Shenzhen; the door's been wide open for a long time. Women can only sell their bodies when they're young. If you can make a buck, who cares about the rest? I know I'm a dark-skinned country girl, not suited for work in the big hotels. I could never compete with Shanghai girls with all their foreign languages, or those tall girls from the northeast. But as for the hicks from the provinces, with their mini-potato boobs in plastic bras, even they charge two or three hundred yuan for a lay at one of the barber shops. I'm a natural with my equipment: big jugs and a big cunt. I won't be young forever, so why should I let all this go to waste, and not make it work for me? If a woman doesn't earn, she's losing out.

I'm not joking. You're not young forever, and a woman loses out if she's not earning. Counting from now, if I work for three years I'll be twenty-six. I won't get such good money after that. If you're selling ginger, the older the better; if you're trading in pussy, sell it young. Men like it young and tender; the younger it is, the more you get for it. Men love saying "Fuck your mother!" *[cao ni ma]*, but if you really offered them your mother, they wouldn't be interested. They'd rather fuck you. Besides, you know, if you're twenty-six or -seven when you return home, even if you've got a bit of money, it's going to be hard to find a good husband. They like to marry early where I come from. If you're still unmarried at twenty-five, you're considered a hopeless old spinster. No one wants you. Besides, men are smart; once they know my age and how long I've been in Shenzhen, they'd never believe I'm clean, that no one's fucked me already.

All right. You're pretty sharp. So I'm not actually from Hengyang, I'm from a mountain village near there in Hengshan County. Once I've saved two hundred thousand, I'm going back home. I'm not kidding. I'll do it this year. I've got over a hundred thousand stashed away already. I don't flash my cash around in Shenzhen. It's not safe. Of course I'm going back. Why wouldn't I? This is Shenzhen. Everything opened up here too early. Two hundred thousand is peanuts to people here. You can't rely on friends here, either. Sure, we're sitting in my friend's flat, but, you know, it's a pretty casual thing. Women can't trust other women.

You could get hauled in by the cops; you could earn enough and leave, if you're lucky; you could become some rich man's mistress, though that really just means prostituting yourself for a few more years. However you look at it, no one can stay in this game for long. This is Shenzhen. Men take on mistresses like they raise birds. The bird is good to look at, and it's fun. But a cunt's a cunt. If you're going to be a mistress, if you want to be a concubine, you've got to be more than just a good fuck—you've got to be able to handle yourself in company. I know I'm not classy enough for that. My body is my capital, men just love to fuck it, they get what they pay for, and when it's done, it's done. I'm not really someone they could exactly take out in public. Who'd keep someone like me? As my friend says, you could dress me up like a movie star, but I'd still be a streetwalker from the countryside. I'm still pretty rough, outside and in. There's nothing I can do about it. I am what I am. So I've got my goal of two hundred thousand, and when I've made that much, I'm going home. I'm not going to work any more, either. I'll be a changed character. I'll find myself a good man, settle down, and have his child. I'll give him the money and let him look after things. I'll be proper and well-behaved, the way a woman is supposed to be. Everyone knows I came to Shenzhen with nothing to my name. They'll know I've made a fortune in just a few years, and I'll be a hot property. It shouldn't be too hard to find a reliable man. With that kind of money I could open a restaurant or a small shop. Once I've got a man, I'll discuss it with him. It's a big decision, so he should be the one to make it. I think a restaurant would be good. Doing business in the village at Hengshan, you could make a lot out of the tourists.[1] City folk don't buy anything from little shops, but they need to eat. You'd earn heaps with a restaurant.

That won't be a problem, either. I can take care of it real easy. I just won't tell my man, that's all. It's Shenzhen; here you cross the river by feeling the stones.[2] It's not such a big operation, repairing the hymen; it only takes a

1. Hengshan in Hunan Province is one of the five sacred mountains of China and a major tourist destination.

2. Deng Xiaoping declared that the capitalist-style experiment of creating "socialism with Chinese characteristics" was like "crossing the river by feeling the stones," that is, a process of trial and error.

few stitches. I'll get it done before I leave. Five hundred yuan and I'll be a virgin again.

Give me a big hug, will you? The way I'd hug myself. You know, if we hug each other before parting that counts as fooling around, and that'll bring good luck to both of us.

If you come back, give me a call. If you can't reach me, you'll know I've gone back home.

16

Little Sweetie
A Thoroughly Modern Mistress

In the 1990s there was a trend for young women to become the mistresses, or little sweeties (xiaomi), of nouveau riche businessmen. It represented the revival of one of the most venerable career options open to women in China.

She was a friend of a friend. When she heard I wanted to interview a little sweetie, she volunteered without hesitation. She asked me to meet her in the coffee shop of a big hotel. She'd just bought a new hat. She told me to look for the girl with the prettiest headgear, and that would be her.

"You know how they're always going on about the need to save the symphony, save the ballet, save poetry, save the theater?" she observed. "Well, forget that. These days, artists have to save themselves first!" With a cold gaze she observed the members of a state theatrical troupe struggling to entertain the travelers bustling in and out of the hotel lobby. "They really know how to choose the best places for begging."

I don't mind. Write whatever you like. I mean it. I couldn't care less. We meet, we talk, we go our separate ways; and anyway, you're not out to make me look bad, are you? It's not that I'm so much more open than other people; it's just that I've got a clear conscience. If some girls are embarrassed about becoming little sweeties, that's just a reflection of their own hang-ups. I don't think like that at all. It's not like I'm a prostitute. I'm free to choose my lovers. It's wrong to equate a little sweetie with a common hooker. But if people want to think like that, let them. So long as they don't go making trouble for me, I'm not going to get all worked up about it. You'd have to be pretty common to say a thing like that, anyway. If they can't accept me, that's their problem. What this society needs is tolerance.

Okay, let's start here. My birthday is 29 February. I was born in Chongqing. Does that sound suspicious to you—29 February? Lots of people think I'm joking, and then they suddenly remember that there's a leap year every four years. It really annoys me when they ask how I celebrate my birthday. It's so irritating. It's as though I ought to have known better than to have been born then because I can't have a birthday every year. Morons. I'll tell you this right off—one of the things becoming a little sweetie lets you get away from is crass idiots like that. If ninety-nine out of a hundred people in your circle are upper-class types and then you get this one guy begging you for money, well, that's still a big improvement on getting stuck with the plebs all the time. That's not living, that's just surviving. It's a pig's life, a dog's life.

I come from a large family. Three generations living under one roof. From my current perspective, Chongqing looks like a small town. Of course, when I lived there, it seemed so big and modern. In fact the people there have some pretty backward ideas, and the city itself is a dump. No sooner does a new building go up than it starts to fall apart. Filth and poverty everywhere you look, and yet the poor sods who live there think they've never had it so good—big wonderful Chongqing, the provisional capital.[1]

Everyone in my family always got along very well with each other, and, like most Sichuanese, we were very hospitable. We always had friends or relatives dropping by or staying over. I'm not talking about now, of course. These days people are just out for themselves, so greedy and untrustworthy. Who'd open their door to a stranger today? Hospitality seems like an ancient custom now. It's as distant from our lives today as classical Chinese music, or Western-style chamber music that no one wants to listen to anymore. We had a third-floor apartment with a view of the river. Although there were six of us squeezed into two bedrooms, we all got on fine.

My father's originally from Shandong. He can't speak Sichuanese; he thinks it's a barbarian tongue that he could never learn no matter how hard he tried. Not that he ever really did. He spent over ten years studying medicine and has been teaching for at least that many years again. He's a good man, kind and loyal. Too much so, really. People like him are selling their hard-won knowledge too cheap. If he were a bit more savvy, he'd have

---

1. During the Sino-Japanese War, the Nationalist authorities evacuated the capital, Nanjing, in Jiangsu Province, and relocated the seat of government to Chongqing, Sichuan.

become a surgeon, and we wouldn't be in the financial straits we're in now. "Professors, professors, profess yourself poor," as they say. He's a classic. I had teachers like that. Not all the old teachers are as lovely as my dad, of course, and believe me, when the old ones get up to mischief, they're even worse than young louts.

My mother comes from a good family. Direct descendants of Confucius, or so she says. She couldn't tell you how many generations ago that was. It's wishful thinking, if you ask me, but she basks in the reflected glory. It annoys me at times, but you've got to feel sorry for her.

Her name is Kong Qingyun. The character Qing is supposed to be the Confucian legacy, something to do with generational hierarchy or something.[2] It's like some big deal, proves she's a member of the old aristocracy. Whenever I see a "von" in some German name attached to a piece of Western music I think of her. She's taught me that all the "vons" are about as second-rate as most of their poxy music. However grand her ancestry is supposed to be, she's still only a primary-school teacher.

Gee, no, I've never heard of the Anti-Confucius campaign. What year was that? Oh. I wasn't even born in 1973, so I don't have a clue what happened then, or what my mother thought of it all. Why'd they criticize Confucius? The old man's been dead for ages. You wonder why Jiang Qing would even bother.[3]

I was a little girl when the reform and open-door policy began.[4] But it didn't really have much effect on us. All those teachers in my family were really out of it. Whatever upheavals were going on, all my parents could ever think about was how to wangle a raise or a promotion. That's what they

2. The direct descendants of Confucius receive the first character of their given name from a piece of writing, and the character each generation takes for its name follows from the one before.

3. The Anti–Lin Biao Anti-Confucius campaign, which was launched in 1973 and continued into 1974, was sparked by the spectacular demise of Lin Biao, formerly Mao's "closest comrade-in-arms" and chosen successor. Jiang Qing's attack on Confucius was a thinly veiled attempt to discredit Premier Zhou Enlai, then Mao's second-in-command and not one of her biggest fans. Lin Biao died in mysterious circumstances in September 1971 while supposedly attempting to flee China with his family. As the *People's Daily* said in its editorial of 2 February 1974, marking the joint denunciation: "Lin Biao fervently advocated the doctrines of Confucius and Mencius. His reactionary ideology was identical with that of Confucius and Mencius, and both wanted to restore the old system."

4. The economic reforms were officially launched in December 1978 under the leadership of Deng Xiaoping.

thought the reforms were all about—just getting a raise. They were obsessed with it, too. It never occurred to them that there was more to it than that; that in the future (or rather in the present now) you wouldn't actually have to be a salaried worker fighting for a raise or a promotion. There would be other options. So they're still exactly where they always were. They've got none of those experiences other people are so proud of—like my boss, for instance, things to do with profit and loss, and large-scale risk and adventure.

We never lacked for basics like food or clothing, and my parents put a lot of effort into my education. They've always believed that genius is born of hard work. You know that fable about the blind musician who practices all his life and counts up every broken string, believing that when he breaks his thousandth string, he will see again? The one Chen Kaige made into his film *Life on a String*. Well, my parents thought if I practiced like that, I'd get to be the star of the Central Symphony Orchestra. They're even dumber than the blind man in the story. And anyway, I'm not blind. It didn't make any sense at all. But it didn't bother me either. I was the princess of the Youth Cultural Palace and the top student in a key high school. Chongqing doesn't even have an orchestra, so I had to leave home to study at the conservatory here. But their "development strategy" got results, and I'm certainly none the worse for it.

The conservatory turned out to be filthier than those old derelict buildings in Chongqing. They're so cash-starved that they'll do anything for money. If you gave them, say, thirty thousand yuan, they'd rush off and snap the 1001st string for you. Even though it doesn't do you any good if someone else does it for you—you have to do it yourself—that's what they'd do right away. It all comes down to money.

Don't think I wanted to be a little sweetie. Not at all. If I were rich, and my boss were a poor student, then it'd be up to him to fake being in love with me just the way I do with him. You know, even as a child I never really had any fun. These days I really treasure memories of my folks quarreling over money. The rows got worse and worse until they were throwing things and hitting each other. When I think of them fighting over a few yuan like that, I feel really happy, content. It was our version of *Days in the Radiant Sun.*[5] I think people probably had a better time than that in the Cultural Revolution.

5. *Yangguang canlande rizi*, a 1995 film based on the novella *Dongwu xiongmeng*, by the novelist Wang Shuo (published in English as *Wild Beasts*, 1991). Directed by Jiang Wen, the film follows a group of young friends during the Cultural Revolution.

You know that song that goes, "Oh, the past, the past, I feel so confused when I try to talk about times past"? Makes me sick. It's so vulgar, but it does contain a kernel of truth.

If they had really cared about my well-being and my future, then they should have got their act together and earned some serious money. You know, if my dad had become a surgeon, he could have used those twenty years of education and carved out a path for us in blood. I don't mean it that way, of course. It's the principle I'm talking about. Not that I want to be dependent on them. It's just that I feel so bad for all of us. In today's society, you've got to get out there and struggle—isn't that what I'm doing now?

Hawk your fish while it's still alive. That's the lesson life has taught me. "Don't just sit around, or you'll be waiting till your hair turns gray." We live in a society of base desires. Lots of young women are in my situation. Look at how many cars are parked at the school gates every evening. Check out who's at the wheel, and you'll know what I'm talking about.

The pretty boys are getting in on the act too. It's not like there aren't any old women with money, you know. I once had a real boyfriend. He couldn't handle it when I dropped him, and he ended up driving me crazy. Now, he just makes me sick. He's all slicked up and gets down and dirty with a rich old bag from Taiwan.

There is a limit to what you can tolerate, you know, and I really think he's gone too far.

It's not really anyone else's business, of course. But there's no harm in talking about it either.

My boss is in manufacturing, a plastics company. He's a self-made man and a real con artist. These guys who start with nothing and make it big all like to have artistic girls as their little sweeties. It makes them seem less uncultured. In fact, he's so vulgar you could die. Practically illiterate. When I met the old bastard, I knew he had a wife. She's as stupid as he is. But his marriage is his problem. Men go after beauty, and women go after money. We all go for what we need. It's not like I want to marry him. I don't really care about the wife so long as she doesn't come knocking on my door looking for trouble. Doesn't bother me at all.

My feelings for him are based solely on the fact he's got money. If he didn't, I'd be out of there in an instant. It's all out in the open; he knows the score. He's not *that* stupid. To get that much money out of conning people requires some smarts. Don't ask me about the details. I don't ask him about his business, and he doesn't tell me. If he tried to, I wouldn't listen anyway. I'm not his wife.

A classmate introduced me to him. I'm serious. It's like, you scratch my back, I'll scratch yours. We like to help each other out. I've introduced men to other girls myself.

The fruits of battle have been pretty good. In just over a year, my uncultured oaf has handed over a small apartment with two bedrooms and a lounge, and the papers are all in my name. Not everyone gets that kind of deal, but the sweetie always comes out on top. The men are idiots. Self-righteous hypocrites can drone on about morality all they like. I don't have to wait till they point the finger: I'll readily admit to being shameless. "Yup, I'm a shameless tart. What the hookers sell retail, I deal wholesale." Okay? But I forgive them. Their relationships are no different. Your primary teacher is wholesaling for your professor—but they're in a nonprofit racket. In today's world, relationships between men and women are on the market wholesale. Love may represent the spirit, but material things are what it's all about.

As for the future, ask me later. For now I'm not complaining. Life's all about seizing the moment. It's no use worrying too much about the future. And why should you? Tomorrow can only be better than today.

If there isn't a 29 February, I celebrate my birthday on the 28th, if I feel like it, that is. And why shouldn't I feel like it?

17

Heaven's Narrow Gate
Christians Who Overcame

Sayingpan is located in the almost inaccessible mountains of northern Yunnan Province. Even today the area cannot be reached by train; there is not even a paved road to the district. In 1904, an Australian China Inland Mission missionary by the name of John Williams came to work in this village of some twenty thousand souls. He stayed for forty years, establishing the South-East China Theological College and the first modern hospital in the region. He also devised the first phonetic writing system for the ethnic groups in this area, based on the Roman alphabet. He incorporated many English words into the language that are still in use.

Today some fifty thousand people live in Sayingpan and the surrounding area. Most are Yi or Miao people; the majority are Christians.

Christianity was first preached in Shimenkan, and that marked the introduction of the gospel to our land here in the Yunnan-Guizhou borderlands. The missionary was from England, and before coming into the mountains he had lived among the Han. He worked mostly with the Miao people. The gospel was brought to us Yi people by an Australian missionary called John Williams. He came to China in 1904; there used to be a tombstone on his grave with the details. During the uproar surrounding the Great Leap Forward, when we were supposed to liberate our thinking,[1] the Communists con-

---

1. At the start of the Great Leap Forward in the spring of 1958, the general line *(zong lu-xian)* adopted by the party was "to go all out, aim high, and achieve greater, faster, better, and more economical results in building socialism" *(guzu ganjing, lizheng shangyou, duo kuai hao shengde jianshe shehuizhuyi).*

vinced the people that they should destroy it. Rev. Williams was called home to be with God in 1944, just before the Japanese surrendered, so he was buried here. He had been with us for forty years; that means two or three generations had grown up with him. Even some local chieftains accepted the faith.

No one who studied at his theological college is still alive, and all the people who studied his teachings are dead. A few people who saw him are still alive, though. I was a child during the Japanese occupation, but I heard him preach the Truth and sang hymns that he taught us. After the surrender I went away to study at a regular school, or should I say a Han school, for three years. But after coming back from that I haven't been away again. At first I worked the land, and I also had the job of recording everyone's work points. Then, after that, I was, how should I put this, kept under surveillance. In other words, I was a bad element, a reactionary.

Although Sayingpan isn't a large area, the work of the church was extensive. There was the theological college, the school, and the hospital. Doctors came from America and Canada to serve here; they were all brothers in Christ. All the buildings have survived. Shimenkan received the gospel first, but Sayingpan soon overtook it.

Yunnan surrendered peacefully; there was no war of liberation here. At first the Communists didn't interfere with the church. They said they wouldn't carry out land reform in ethnic-minority areas or interfere with our religious beliefs. But once they had settled in, the changes began: land, religion, and all the other kinds of interference. It really started during the Korean War with the launching of the Three-Self Patriotic Church Movement.[2] The churches in Shanghai united and cut off ties with foreign missionary societies, and they wanted to force the rest of the nation to follow their example. Foreign missions were seen as a form of imperialist aggression. By this stage the Communist Party was everywhere, bringing in the people they wanted and excluding people they didn't want. The churches had a complex history, and the Han people in the congregations had been unhappy about the influence of the foreign missionaries for many years. Even though they shared the same beliefs, many people had ungodly thoughts, and there were deep-seated grievances.

2. The Three-Self Movement *(sanzi aiguo yundong)* dating from April 1951 promoted the need for "self-rule, self-maintenance, and the self-promotion of missionary work" among Christian churches. This was a party-inspired strategy aimed at breaking links between the indigenous churches and overseas Christian organizations.

So they started exposing and denouncing people, that is, they lied and said that our foreign ministers and brothers and sisters in the congregation were really spies. Even people whom he had brought into the faith attacked Father Williams as an imperialist spy.

We are all children of the Lord, and faith knows no boundaries. However, from the time of the Three-Self Movement they started running the churches in the same way as the Communist Party, with a strong sense of national differences. The church became a national church and excluded all outsiders. This was the most fundamental transformation that occurred, more than even all of the beatings and confiscations of church property that came later. The worst thing was this Communist approach, based on the ideas that "although we may all believe in Marxism, Stalin's party is Stalin's, and Mao Zedong's is Mao's alone." They used this method to divide and rule. They controlled Christianity in China by encouraging this kind of national independence. There have always been those who use their temporal power to persecute believers. Look at the exodus from Egypt, for example, and that time of the great darkness. But none of those with blood on their hands have profited from their acts. The Lord is a just God.

Mao Zedong wanted to destroy Christianity by exploiting people's own wicked thoughts. He encouraged the evil in people and used their weaknesses to kill others. But the Lord is just, and Mao did not prosper as a result. That is why later he had to resort to blood and fire to achieve his ambitions. In the end, however, God's justice prevails.

When the Antirightist Movement began in the cities,[3] people here in the mountains shouted all the slogans, too, but nothing much came of it. The real damage had already been done. That happened during the Democratic Reforms of 1956, when all the leading figures in Yi society were overthrown. Minor leaders were attacked for one crime or another; the more important people were given phony official titles in the city but were deprived of any real authority. It was the same as being overthrown; they were cut off from the land and their own people, and the positions they were given were useless. The socialist tactic was to bureaucratize native leaders and eliminate

---

3. The Antirightist Movement, or the Struggle against Bourgeois Rightists (*fandui zichanjieji youpaide douzheng,* simplified as *fanyou douzheng),* followed a call by Mao for people to "let a hundred flowers blossom and a hundred schools of thought contend" in February 1956. The resultant clamor of criticisms of the party was such that in June that year a counterattack on so-called bourgeois rightists (that is, critics of the party) was launched, leading to a devastating nationwide purge.

indigenous tribes. The majority of new cadres were also Yi people; that's because there weren't many Han in the area that they could use. But the real power remained in the hands of Communists from the north. We call them the red Han. The Yi cadres were all political activists who supported the Communists, militiamen, or people who thought like the Communists. A new dynasty was established; the sun now rose from another direction; such changes are inevitable. But the power holders have no right to divide people into classes, for we are all equal in God's eyes, and no right to encourage people's sinful nature.

During the Great Leap Forward they sent new work teams from the city. Whenever the Communists started a new movement, they would send work teams; they were the representatives of the power holders. With each new movement they would get rid of a few of the people in power, even if they were people they had originally put there themselves. Then they would encourage the evil desires of a new group and satisfy their lust for power. This time around they came to crush superstition and liberate thinking, and in the process all the graves of the old missionaries were dug up. They threw the bones into the ravines. The missionaries weren't supposed to be representatives of imperialism any more; this time, the work teams said they were the devil incarnate. They said that the old foreign devil John Williams had never done anything for us, while in the space of eight short years the Communist Party had given us everything. They said that we would soon be entering the heaven of communism. This movement gave them an excuse to confiscate all church property. They set up a middle school in the theological college and tried to convert everyone to the godlessness of communism.

Shimenkan is quite different from Sayingpan; there aren't any Protestants there now. When they established the people's communes during the Great Leap Forward, their slogan was "overthrow Shimenkan, liberate little Taiwan." The people agitating for liberation in Shimenkan weren't Han, or even Communists; they were the Catholic Miao people that the Communists had incited to rebel. Then, during the Four Cleans in 1965, the Communists turned on the Catholics. That's how they always did it: they used the right hand to attack the left because the left had done too little to support the party; then the left hand would be encouraged to strike back at the right hand because the right now had all the advantages.

They sent in a Four Cleans work team in 1965 to propagate the socialist education campaign. They said that the Protestants had been involved in underground activities. That was quite unjust, for we still had our churches at that time and were not doing anything in secret. The Communists hated Christianity, but they had not forbidden us to go to church. If you can worship out in the open, why would you need to go underground? But what they really meant by "underground activities" was breaking state laws. We would not accept this charge, so they beat us; they hung us up and beat us. Before the Four Cleans was even finished, the Cultural Revolution broke out. The first revolutionary act carried out by the middle-school students and militiamen in our district was the destruction of our churches. They smashed everything in the buildings and sealed up the doors with big red strips of paper. They said everyone in the congregation was reactionary and that even those in the Three-Self Movement were reactionaries. So they rounded up all the ministers and church officers in the Three-Self Patriotic Church Movement, locked them up with us, and beat us all. Until then our main crime had been that we'd disagreed with the Three-Self Movement, which made us an "illegal religious movement." But now the members of the Three-Self Movement were supposed to be even worse than us; they were accused of being spies.

After a few weeks they realized that they weren't going to achieve their ends just by detaining the church leaders and sealing the churches. People were holding services in their homes. So they ordered everyone to hand over their Bibles, and if you refused they'd raid your house and confiscate all your belongings. Then they lit a big bonfire and burnt all the Bibles. "How will you believe in your God without your books?" they asked. They thought Christians were idolaters. All the people who had hidden their Bibles or organized worship in their homes were taken in and beaten because they were "underground church leaders." Anyone who held a service in their house was denounced as an "evil church boss." This group was supposed to be the worst of all, worse than us and the Three-Self people, because they were active reactionaries.

The only thing the Communists knew was violence. In the fifteen years that they had been in our mountains, they had tried all kinds of methods to wipe out Christianity, but it hadn't worked. Now they had to resort to blood and fire. Of course, they didn't call it violence; they said they were "touching the soul."[4] Detaining people and torturing them was their way

4. *Chuji linghun* was the expression used by Marshal Lin Biao, Mao's close comrade-in-arms, to describe the need for everyone to be touched by the revolution within the revolution.

of "touching the soul." You have to pity them; they had no other means at their disposal.

I was also tested. They hung me up by the arms and beat me with rods. When you fainted from the pain they would throw cold water on you. In the winter they'd tie you up and pour cold water on you and put you outside to freeze. They burnt you with cigarettes and hot coals. They did the same things as persecutors always have; and they asked the same question, "Why doesn't your God come down and save you?" We were beaten by students, militiamen from the commune, and middle-school teachers as well as the police. These poor souls were just blind followers. We cannot blame them for what they did.

Not one of us cried out, "Forgive me! I don't believe in God any more." God is always with us, and our persecutors had no power to forgive us. We didn't give in to them. We do not hate those who followed blindly; we should reach out to them and help them. If we were to learn hate from them, we would lose our own faith.

I was locked up, released, locked up again, and so on, back and forth for as long as the Four Cleans lasted, about four years. At the height of the movement, they had over one hundred people incarcerated, but many more were simply beaten and released. Except for a few leading members of the Three-Self organization who were carted off to prison in the provincial capital, the rest of us were eventually released in 1969. We were regularly arrested just before Christmas, beaten for a few days, and then released. The same thing happened at Easter. It was their way of keeping us from attending church services.

After our release we were classified as bad elements and subjected to what they called mass dictatorship; that meant that commune members and militiamen could enter our houses whenever they felt like it, twenty-four hours a day, to check up on us. The police, what we called the public security agents, would call us in to report whenever the mood took them. They'd ask whom we'd seen and whether we'd engaged in any illegal activities. It was illegal for a group of us to sit together or buy a wireless. Christians were only allowed to own small radios that could only receive two stations, the Yunnan provincial one and the Kunming municipal one. All foreign gospel broadcasts were banned. They said those were "enemy radio stations" run by spies and paid for by the Nationalists in Taiwan. Without even asking permission, they installed loudspeakers in all of our homes which constantly broadcast programs that praised Mao Zedong and denounced Christianity as an evil doctrine that was in league with Liu Shaoqi and Confucius. It was illegal to turn them off. After Mao died they changed the official line and said that Christians were in league with Jiang Qing and that she was plotting a Christian restoration.

By then there were no churches or Bibles in either Yi or Chinese. Because of the imposition of the Three-Self Movement and then the Four Cleans campaign, there hadn't been any qualified ministers for years. But we had our faith. We held services and prayer meetings with the other Christians who had not been jailed, either in our homes or out in the open. At the services, the older people who had some education or knowledge of the faith would be asked to speak and explain things. That's how we learnt about the Truth. Some of the ministers and church leaders in the Three-Self Movement were still in jail; others who had been released obeyed the Communists and were too scared to hold services. That's why many of believers who had originally adhered to the Three-Self Movement now came over to us. Just before Easter in 1970, we elected our own ministers, people we felt had the qualifications to lead. I was one of those selected. Shortly after Easter, I was detained and beaten again, along with a few others. After our release we began conducting baptisms. We were in God's grace, and the desires of our persecutors were brought to nothing.

In 1979 they sent another work team in, and this time they told us that some of the things they had done in the past were wrong and they had to be rectified. However, other things were correct, and they would continue as before. Now, they told us, the Communist Party was granting us religious freedom, but they told us to support the Three-Self Movement, to be patriotic, and not to participate in any illegal activities. In effect, what they were telling us was that everything would be the same as it had been before 1964 and that if we didn't adhere to the Three-Self Movement, we would be breaking the law. That was ridiculous. Our faith doesn't require their permission; freedom was not something they could bestow upon us.

Many years have passed since then. You can see for yourself that Christianity is flourishing in Sayingpan as it never had before. As you travel around the villages and towns, you will find that there are over a hundred churches. The old ministers' graves have been rebuilt, and we have our theological college again. They did their best to destroy what remained of it before giving it back, but we're rebuilding it.

There have been many other changes over the years, the most important being that the church is not underground any more. We are out in the open.

Another thing is that now the Communists have difficulty getting people to go to their meetings, so they have to come to our services to make their public announcements. They don't talk about ideology or class struggle any more; now they want to tell everyone what taxes are due and what fees have to be paid on the following Sunday. The Communists say that Christianity has been resurrected in the Yunnan-Guizhou borderlands. This has a lot to do with things here in Sayingpan. We are what they call a disaster area. In a sense, they're right: they spread the seeds of disaster here, and now they are now reaping what they have sown.

The followers of the Three-Self Movement are increasingly friendly to us. We passed through the trials of blood and fire together, and regardless of what the Communists may think they have achieved, we now practice our faith openly. The members of the Three-Self Movement know that it is useless to argue over the legality of our activities. The Three-Self leaders are a bit different from the congregation in this respect, and they still talk nonsense from time to time. Sometimes they will claim that we have no right to lead our congregations, that we don't understand the Truth, and that we are not really Christians. During their services, their ministers also say wrong-headed things about "constructing Christianity with Chinese characteristics" or pursuing the family-planning policy, "two children per Yi family; one child for every Han couple."

We are still facing many difficulties. The most serious is that a church cannot go for decades without a real minister. We need a minister. You can't go to the theological college if you don't belong to the Three-Self Movement. The movement runs them all, with a bit of financial support from the Communist Party. They promote "patriotic Christianity," which we believe to be a contradiction in terms. Another problem is that the number of Christians is constantly increasing, and so is the number of pastors. Some are actually ex–party members; others are still in the party, even though they are believers. Some ministers who were once party secretaries occasionally say foolish things. But if we tried to set up our own theological college, the Communists would interfere. That's a big problem. Finding teachers would be hard, and then there are the financial and material difficulties, too. It will be a real test to overcome all of these, and it will take time.

Because the Communists preach hatred and class struggle, more and more people are abandoning them. So the power holders have no choice but to make some concessions. But they still haven't understood the basic truth that what our world needs is love, not their hate.

They have forbidden foreigners from coming to Sayingpan for forty-five years. They have built some very high walls between people. But we have always been able to hear the gospel over the radio, from both Korea and Southeast Asia. Even during the trials of blood and fire we could listen to the broadcasts. We kept our shortwave radios hidden. During the decade of the Cultural Revolution we had no Bibles, but we copied down the Truth that was sent to us through the airwaves. The gospel over the air sustained us in our faith.

You must tell our brethren outside: we know about the hand of friendship you have extended to us. God be with us all.

Mastering New China

18

An Army on the March

The PLA Means Business

We met in the sumptuous but tacky restaurant of the hotel he managed at a naval port on the island province of Hainan in the South China Sea. He was a captain, but as it was Sunday he was in civvies, including an oversized T-shirt favored by international tourists that read "I've climbed the Great Wall." We talked in the hotel restaurant, the walls of which were decorated with photographs of the Communist Party leaders, Hong Kong red capitalists, and assorted international travelers who had "inspected the work of our hotel," "given direction" to the hotel management, or simply spent the night.

We weren't interrupted, and for a man with over a thousand people under his command, he seemed far more relaxed than the average hotel manager.

Look, the situation is like this: every operation has to make money any way it can. It doesn't matter whether you're an enterprise or a government organization, the standard of success in our society today is whether you can pull in the bucks. Money equals efficiency. If you can find money, anything is possible; without it, you aren't going anywhere.

It's the same for the armed forces; after all, we're not living in a vacuum. Nowadays, on top of the traditional seven bare essentials for setting up a household when you marry—kindling, rice, oil, salt, soy sauce, vinegar, and tea—you're expected to provide the latest necessities, too: tobacco and alcohol, not to mention a house and a car. Even a senior officer like myself can't afford to cruise around in a jeep all day. You're not going to find a fortune lying around in the streets waiting to be picked up. As for the slogans like "Support the Army, Love the People," they only apply on the five public holidays every year. The rest of the time it's a case of: if you want something from me, flash me some cash. If that's the way it works, you've got no choice but to get in there and make some money.

I'm not saying that we wouldn't survive if we only relied on the state. Although they say the military budget is shrinking every year, it still stands somewhere between twenty and thirty billion yuan. You could do a lot worse than count on that kind of blue-chip business. At least you know you're not going to starve. The party has never said it won't take care of its troops. There's always a potential threat—a new world war or counterrevolutionary rebellion at home—and, as long as these two threats exist, the authorities would be stupid to cut off the military. The rationale behind maintaining a standing army is that there are those rare occasions when you're really going to need it. As long as the army's there to clear up the mess, things'll be fine. Twenty to thirty billion is enough to keep us fed and clothed, but the big question is, how well are they going to look after us? Is anyone going to put up with subsistence level? No way! Everyone wants a decent standard of living, and why should we be any different? People seem to think that soldiers aren't like other people. They think we should keep up with the old revolutionary traditions of hardship and deprivation. All I can say to that is, get real.

Now I couldn't say whether it's right or proper for the government to call on the army to get involved in business and go off into the marketplace in our uniforms. It doesn't seem rational, but the question we have to ask ourselves is, what would happen if we didn't? We're not living in rational times; we have to face reality, and the facts of the matter are that the army needs money to do things, and we can't do anything without it. This is more the case for us than most. Now, our unit has an excellent reputation, so you'd think we'd be doing very well with generals popping in and out all day. To tell you the truth, we've been little more than a nonprofit organization. Our style of management was even more hidebound than that of units at the bottom of the chain of command. We needed to get out there and find investments more than anyone.

That's why I just said I can't expect you to really understand what I'm saying, because you haven't had the personal experience. In the old days, we could expect a steady stream of gifts and offerings from our subordinates. "This 250 kilos of prawns is from our recent major production activities. Please divide it up among the comrades in command, logistics, and the politics departments." These days the game is completely different. The lines of command are very clear, and the guys below have sussed out who has the real power. Now they divide the prawns or scallops or whatever into small parcels and take them straight to the home of the commander who can actually be of use to them. No need for the comrades to divvy it up among themselves anymore. I'm not saying there wasn't a measure of selfish calculation in the past, but back then it was also to do with comradely sentiment and the desire to build up your networks. Now it's purely about connections and getting what you want out of other people. All consideration has gone out the window. It's the same in local commands as well. Back then, the commanders would present the units with New Year's gifts of pork and beef; now all they get is a terse note: "We regret that productivity is down this year. We are pleased, however, to be able to invite all comrades to watch a movie." What's past is past. Things are different now. You can't go around judging things by yesterday's standards.

We got into this game relatively late, especially in comparison to those under our command. Naturally, the ones who got out there first made the big profits, but initially we were very hesitant, worried that we'd land ourselves in trouble. We were like most people at that time; we wanted to be bad but we just didn't have the balls. Later on, probably around 1987, we got some inspiration from what other people were doing. The air force, for example—they had opened their airports to civilian traffic and were even flying commercial routes themselves. The headquarters of the General Staff in Beijing had gone into the hotel business and was running mining operations to boot. The Chengdu Military Region Command in Sichuan were producing everything from cars to booze, and they were pretty good at it, too. No one ever rapped them on the knuckles. Quite the opposite; they were praised for being short on rhetoric and long on practice and ended up as a model of excellence in reform. That gave us the courage to give it a shot ourselves. We realized we couldn't just turn a blind eye to what our subordinates were getting up to and expect to keep what they gave us by way of presents to keep in our good books. So we decided to get our act together and fend for ourselves; the key was "self-reliance."[1] We were under a lot of pressure from our subordinates too, because what they could do business-

---

1. *Zili geng sheng,* an old Maoist slogan popularized in the Yan'an period of the early 1940s, when the army engaged in productive labor to beat the enemy blockade.

wise was limited by their rank. To mobilize the necessary resources, they needed support from people like us further up the ladder.

It might sound like we got in at the deep end, but in fact we were fairly cautious at first. What if something went wrong and the brass upstairs turned nasty? We could find ourselves up on charges; and if we lost money there's no way we could have made it up. Of course, those concerns were dispelled ages ago, and we've learned a lot along the way. We soon discovered that there wasn't going to be any serious fallout from our superiors, and we weren't going to be running up huge debts. Still, we didn't know that when we started out, so our initial effort was really pretty pathetic. We started with a hospital. It was our piddling little camp infirmary with a little over a hundred beds, and we opened it up to the public. They only had the capacity to treat minor things, your standard aches and pains; it couldn't handle surgery or anything serious like that. Because it was in a military compound, we could hardly allow civilians to come in and run around all over the place. Fortunately, it wasn't far from the compound wall, so we decided to make a special gate with direct access to it. It began turning a profit for us right away. Think about it: the doctors, nurses, medicines, and even the building cost us nothing. Everything was laid on at government expense, so there was no capital expenditure involved. It was a win-win situation; so what if it was fairly small-scale? Another reason it turned out to be so profitable was that it got a name for treating STDs. All those moral degenerates came straight to us. And, it doesn't take much in the way of expertise to treat VD. Give me a white coat and I could do it myself; all it takes is daily shots of penicillin. But our success didn't come from the fact that we had a better treatment than anybody else—we didn't—it was because people felt safer dealing with us. You see, your local hospital would be obliged to maintain a medical record on each patient, and that includes details of their treatment for STDs; but as a military hospital we were not required to keep any information on our patients, or what they were prescribed. Anyway, we didn't want to keep a pile of scrap paper with all that useless information. So after each visit we'd hand all the info over to the patients, and they could do whatever they liked with it. By the time they stepped out the door we'd already forgotten their names. That was one of the keys to our success. Do you understand what I'm saying here?

That first breach in the wall really opened our minds. Our next project was more like demolishing the wall altogether. Making a hole, tearing down a section of wall, or demolishing the whole thing is all pretty much the same thing really. The demand for commercial properties at that time was far greater than the supply, and here we were with all this overgrown and unused land inside our military compound. So why not pull back our wall a few hundred feet and build a row of shops along the perimeter and then rent them out? It would be like getting money for nothing. Looking back on it now, it still seems like a good decision. We were making a profit right away—and a good one too. Even better was the fact that we didn't have to get into wheeling and dealing ourselves; we just sat on the sidelines and collected our rent. All we asked of our tenants was that they pay on time and not go bankrupt. This ensured us a steady income. Without wanting to sound arrogant, I must say that it was all my idea.

Now that we were out there in the market, we were constantly refining our strategy. Initially we'd done the demolition and construction ourselves, but that was before we realized it was a seller's market. We didn't have to go to so much effort; all we needed to do was paint a white mark along the ground to mark the extent of the demolition and leave the rest to the people who wanted to set up shop. But there was a legal hitch to our plan. In the first instance we could claim, one way or another, that we were simply utilizing idle resources, regardless of the fact that we'd just built the shops and were renting them out to local people on short-term leases. There was no clear-cut prohibition on that kind of thing. But the second option—letting the lessees do their own demolition and building—was a different kettle of fish entirely. You were illegally renting state land for personal profit in clear violation of government regulations. Who'd dare carve up state-owned military land for rent? You wouldn't, and I certainly wouldn't. So we had to come up with an explanation of what we were up to. We called it a joint venture between the army and local business. Local business carried out the construction work, but the land remained in our hands. The fact that our partners did the work was in strict accordance with official military policy to give wholehearted support to economic reform at the local level. It was an officially sanctioned, mutually beneficial agreement with us, offering a short rent-free period before locking them into long-term leases.

It's what they meant by the old Great Leap Forward slogan: "The greater your daring, the higher the yield."[2] The only limit is your imagination! Let's face it, government policy may be inflexible, but people are endlessly adapt-

---

2. *Ren you duoda dan, di you duogao chan.* The slogan encouraged a belief that human volition itself could increase agricultural productivity.

able. Once you've got your eye on the prize, there's no defense that can't be breached.

I worked on the logistics of these construction projects from the time we opened our hospital to the public. I was also responsible for finding the cash for our operations. It was only natural that there wasn't a consensus, initially at least. A few comrades said some pretty nasty things to my superiors about how I was doing the job; they said that I was engaged not in military construction but demolition. I suppose you could say they were right; I did tear things down, but only in order to bring in money for us. I could just as well have asked them, "And what constructive solutions do you lot have?"

Let's be frank, before we "enlivened the economy," our military budget was little better than starvation rations. The top brass were incredibly strict when it came to giving the green light to any construction projects, and if you built anything too flashy, the party bosses on the Central Military Commission would come down on you like a ton of bricks and issue army circulars nationwide criticizing your errors. Before we were allowed to engage in business ventures, even the top brass—and I'm not talking about field commanders but high-ranking generals—didn't even have air-conditioning. At the height of the summer, when the temperature outside was in the high thirties, it would be even hotter than that in their offices. The old boys were melting away and would have to sneak off to hide in the cool of the computer room. So when my comrades went off to complain about me, it proved to be completely pointless. The old comrades had just begun to enjoy the delights of air-conditioning; were they going to be interested in mean-minded complaints? What were those guys trying to prove? Did they think that everyone had to stick with traditions of simplicity and suffering forever? What would we be proving by forcing the army command to live in the same ovenlike conditions as the enlisted men? That we were pursuing central party policy? They were completely clueless. They thought they'd get a pat on the back—but they were lucky to come away without a severe reprimand.

The soldiers? What, the average soldier? I can tell you what they got out of it: a few better meals in the canteen, an improved dormitory for family visits, and a color TV for the enlisted men's club. Even the men on guard duty would get a payoff. But you know as well as I do that the real beneficiaries of the reforms are not going to be the common masses. Just the same as in civvy street.

The leadership was totally supportive of our endeavors. We were told that no one should doubt that the reforms were on track. In other words, we had to be prepared to take even greater risks. If we got it right, we should continue on course; if some things went wrong, then all we had to do was correct our errors. We were not supposed to fixate on the mistakes; it was a case of learning on the job for all of us.

At the time I was a deputy regiment commander, so my opinions didn't carry much weight. That's why it was so important to have the backing of my commander and, more crucially, the head of logistics. This old guy would say that when he was a young soldier, Chairman Mao had told them that the army wasn't just a fighting force but a team of workers and a production brigade as well. It was true then, he said, and it's true now. For years, comrades in construction have just been spending money—in fact they've got it down to a fine art. Now we have a chance to make some money back, and there's nothing wrong with that. If anything goes wrong, he told me, I'll protect you. They'll go for those of us at the top of the ladder, they won't bother with you small fry. If the Central Military Commission tears off anyone's insignia, it'll be mine. So don't worry.

Looking back on it now I realize that if we hadn't taken risks, or rather if our leaders hadn't dared to make some tough decisions, we wouldn't be enjoying the fruits of our labors today. Think about it, we were just a common army unit, but before you knew it we had our fingers in a number of pies—from tires to travel, fisheries to retail, we were even operating a large hotel. Suddenly, we were into anything that could make a buck, and all it would have taken to bring the whole thing crashing down was one word from above, one casual remark about us neglecting our duties. Looking at it from our present perspective, it was no big deal, of course; and if the military commission was going to take it out on anybody, it would be our superiors. They'd gun for the big boys—not your major generals but your three- and four-star generals; so, in fact, they'd be after people of their own rank. But that's not how we saw it at the time. Things seemed really serious then. You can claim that a hero will always emerge when there's a big challenge to be met, but you've got to have the guts to be that hero, or to sit back and let that hero do the job.

Of course I'm telling the truth; I'm a professional army man, and you can take my word. The central military establishment runs the so-called Five Greats: there's Baoli Enterprises, run by General Staffing; Kaili, run by the Politics Division; Xinxing, operated by Logistics; Xiaofeng, run by the National Defense Science, Technology, and Industry Commission; and

Beifang, set up by the Ministry of Armaments. These five companies are involved in every kind of business you can imagine, from trading in weapons on the international market to running teahouses, and everything in between. Their interests extend into anything you can make money at. Large, small, it makes no difference. Then there's the Three-Nine Group, the leading conglomerate in the military world. It started out as a part of the General Logistics Department, but now it's connected with the Central Military Commission itself. What do they do? What *don't* they do? Everything from huge real-estate deals to women's bras. There's a saying: "Wherever there are people, Three-Nine is there too." They started out as an army pharmaceutical company producing Three-Nine Stomach-Ease indigestion tablets. They made all the right moves, and so did we.

As for the hotel, well, you've seen it for yourself, and there's not much I can say about it. Hotels are pretty much the same the world over: a place to eat and sleep, somewhere you can get a drink or have a dance. But our in-house tourist program, now that's something special. No, that's not what I meant! "Prostitution equals prosperity,"[3] that racket is an open secret, and it's pretty much par for the course in our line of business. Why should I deny it? I'm sure you've noticed the girls hanging around the hotel entrance. They can do whatever they want outside. It's none of my business; extramural activities are under the jurisdiction of the police. Where do they take their tricks? I have no control over that. And why should I? What am I supposed to do, go up to people and say, "Excuse me, miss, but you look like a hooker. Would you be so good as to get out of here?" Anyway, not that many of them come in, unless their trick happens be staying here. Our room rates are too high for casuals, and if they're only making two or three hundred a trick, that certainly won't cover it.

But if I catch them at it in the hotel, then of course we'll take the appropriate measures. There are state laws prohibiting prostitution on hotel premises, after all. Just because we're a military venture doesn't mean we're above the law. The thing is, we have so many rooms that the staff have more than enough on their plates as it is; they don't have the time to go around checking on who's doing what where. Then, of course, courtesy and consideration are basic professional requirements for our employees. It would be quite inappropriate for staff to go knocking on guests' doors to see

3. *Fanrong changsheng,* a play on words. The saying means "to thrive and be prosperous." The word *chāng* means *flourishing,* but if read *chàng* it means *prostitution.*

what's happening inside. It wouldn't be good for business, either. All we can do is rely on the local police. If they come and see how long guests have checked in for, do room searches and make arrests, that's all entirely up to them. It's not as if I'm going to go round inviting them: "Dear Comrade Policeman, would you kindly drop by at two A.M. and do a door-to-door search? Break in if no one answers the door, and arrest the occupants if they're screwing"?

Some people think that just because we're the army, the police don't dare set foot in the place, and that we provide a safe haven for illegal activities—prostitution, gambling, drugs, whatever. That's a misapprehension. We live in a socialist country that has a rigorous legal system. Everyone's equal under the law, and as protectors of the law the police don't care if you've got the support of an army general. If you've committed a crime, you'll be arrested even if the president of China happens to be your patron. Isn't that right?

I've been floating in the sea of commerce for eight years now, and I'd say I've met just about every type of person you can imagine. Just let me say that if I didn't have the necessary communication skills, I wouldn't be sitting here in front of you today. *Dico ergo sum.* Isn't that one of the central philosophical propositions facing mankind? I went to university as a soldier in 1979 and returned to my regiment in 1983. Though I was an architecture major, like all the students back then I was fascinated by philosophical issues. We were the last generation of idealists. If I could take a step back and review my life to date, my only regret would be that I've betrayed the ideals I once held dear. But let's not get into all of that. To talk about it nowadays seems really very petty bourgeois. It's a dead letter; talking about it leaves a nasty taste in your mouth.

The tourist packages we provide are our real strong suit. Perhaps you feel like a boat trip. It's the kind of opportunity that doesn't come along every day. Sure, you might have traveled to Europe or the States on a luxury liner, but have you ever been sailing on a warship, a real warship? When you get out to sea on one of our army tours, you can do some shooting, too. Take your pick: we have pistols, rifles, artillery, machine guns, you can even fire a torpedo if you want to. Anything you want, as long as you can pay for it. For a torpedo? If you've got, say, twenty thousand U.S., we can do business. Perhaps you haven't got the nerve to play with real weapons, okay, so how about some water-skiing? What's the big deal about water-skiing, you may ask? Well, have you ever tried skiing behind a PT boat? It's so fast you'll think you're flying. Believe me, it's an experience you'll never forget. If you want to go for a spin in a military aircraft, that can be arranged, too. Even though we can only offer helicopter rides at the moment, it seems to keep the customers happy. The list of joyrides we can offer is mind-boggling, just one thing after another to add to your list of fun; as long as your money holds out, we've got just about every enticement to keep you happy. The only disappointed customers are the ones who want to go up in a fighter jet. There are a few too many complicated issues to deal with there, issues we can't resolve at present. Generally speaking, the tourists we cater for are the new millionaires on the mainland, or young and middle-aged businessmen from Hong Kong and Taiwan. They're the type of people who've done it all; the only things they've never done are arson, murder, and abduction. They've never had a chance to be Rambo. If they've got the money, we can make their dreams come true.

For a while we were doing a roaring trade in providing these services. That was until about three years ago, when the Central Military Commission began pulling in the reins. They said we'd taken the live-ammunition theme a little too far, and we were ordered to stop advertising the guns and torpedoes and wind down operations. Still, if anyone really expresses an interest in playing with fire, they're welcome to come aboard. Once we're out on the high seas, we're not averse to negotiating a mutually satisfying arrangement.

What do I personally think about all of this? The way I see it, as long as we're not at war, our ordnance is sitting idle and just going to waste, and that goes for military personnel as well. I don't believe that there is anything wrong with what we're doing. We're simply making profitable use of a corps of qualified personnel. Of course, from a different perspective, you could say that we're cheating the state and exploiting national resources, or even squandering the military budget. Take, for instance, something as trivial as deploying naval vessels for fishing trips or to catch crabs. The state is picking up the tab for food and fuel costs, on top of footing the bill for the depreciation of equipment. As for what you catch, what you don't eat yourself you hand over to the government or sell off to a state-run fish company. You have to be able to see the potential in every little thing. Do I really need to spell it out for you?

What if we hadn't built this hotel? This would simply be an overgrown vacant lot. If we weren't involved in travel, transportation, fishing, and farming businesses, all of those resources would be sitting idle. There'd be zero profit, and if you factor in the cost incurred by depreciation, you'd actually be taking a loss. Even charging people to fire live ammunition—what we're doing is recycling material that would be useless otherwise. Now if it's okay to waste ammo by letting rookie sailors fire it all over the shop, what's so wrong with letting some tourist cough up some money to do the same? We're talking about conventional weapons, after all, not nuclear warheads. There's no particular expertise involved; anyone can do it. If you happen to save a couple of rounds of ammunition during training, you might as well let someone else play around with them; they make the same noise no matter who lets them off. Our comrades get their drill, and our compatriots get their thrills. Aside from the obvious financial gains, there's really little difference between the two. I say we've got absolutely nothing to feel guilty about.

Feel free to think whatever you like. If you believe I'm being straight with you, that's fine; if you prefer to think I'm just being sarcastic, that's okay, too. The words of the lowly carry little weight, right? I don't really care what you think.

My comrades and I have built up a multimillion-dollar business by working together, but I haven't earned anything myself. In the last eight years all I've gotten are two promotions, two more pips on my shoulders, so I'm now a colonel. As for all the things we've got in the hotel—hot water twenty-four hours a day, air-conditioning, satellite TV, international direct-dial phones, even the hookers outside the door—you sure as hell won't find any of that where I live. Come and have a look if you don't believe me. This is my last line of defense.

"I am a soldier, I come from among the masses," as the old song goes. To tell the truth, I'm the third generation in my family to have sung this tune. My grandfather joined the army in Hong'an, Hubei Province. In the history of our great ever-victorious army, the name Hong'an has a particular resonance. In the roll call of great generals who helped found the People's Republic, the name Hong'an features more frequently than any other. Over three hundred of the great founding generals of the PLA were born in our humble little district. It was these men who successfully completed the Long March, fought against the Japanese invaders, and dug the grave of Chiang Kai-shek and his Nationalist dynasty. These were the men who escorted our leaders, Mao Zedong, Liu Shaoqi, Zhou Enlai, and Zhu De, into Beijing, and their successors as well. When I have some time to spare—I'm sorry, I'm not really getting carried away—it's just sometimes I don't know if I'm really still a soldier or what. Sometimes, I feel I've been really successful, but then other times it seems like I'm a pathetic failure. Though I'm sure of one thing: if there is a day of reckoning and everything I've done is judged to be wrong, I'll still be confident that I've earned the right to face those great generals who went before me and say, "I may have disgraced the principles you stood for and I may be scum, but at least I was always honest."

[Later, he rang me in my room, out of the blue. There was something he wanted to add to everything he'd told me earlier.]

There was this soldier who worked at an intercontinental missile base for three years without one day's R&R. It was dangerous work, and casualties were high. His squad often went out on emergency calls, and before setting out the soldiers would always make out a will and leave it with their commanding officer. He'd give it back to them if they returned alive. In the unit there was a tradition that the soldiers would keep all the unused wills—those witnesses to the fact that they'd made it back alive again—in their pillowcases for good luck. When they left the army, they burned them.

Over three years, this guy wrote seventeen wills. Instead of burning them when he left, he took them off to university with him.

[Just in case I didn't get what he was telling me, he added softly:]

That guy was me. Goodnight.

19

Generating Income
The Reeducation of an English Professor

It was snowing that night. My tape recorder conked out halfway through.
"It really is terribly cold!" she said. "Even tape recorders are freezing up."
Of course, that was impossible. I'd been ripped off again, that was all: the
batteries were duds. But her apartment really was freezing. It turned out that
the provision of heating for public apartments had been outsourced, and sup-
ply was irregular. Everyone had been forced to buy their own heaters, but that
meant that now the demand for electricity was so great that there were frequent
power outages. "What can you do?" she asked.

Jilin Province

Before I retired, my monthly wage plus sundry allowances came to a little
over seven hundred yuan. My pension is 85 percent of my original wage.
Strictly speaking, people who joined the revolution after the founding of the
People's Republic are only eligible for 80 percent, but there's a local policy
that treats intellectuals employed by the Ministry of Education as a special
case, so they upped my pension by 5 percent.[1] Since I live by myself, it's adequate for my basic needs.

Even in my wildest dreams I would never have thought that one day I
would be earning seven to eight hundred yuan a month. Wages have really
shot up over the past few years. Even though there were salary increases
throughout the fifties, sixties, seventies, and in the first half of the eighties,

---

1. Those who "joined the revolution" before 1949 (the year the People's Republic of China
was founded) were given special privileges and perks as "old revolutionaries."

it was only ever a few yuan each time, ten yuan or so at most. I rose through the ranks that way: starting out as a teaching assistant I earned 48 yuan, and that was increased to 56 and then 72; as a lecturer, it was 89 yuan, then 105; and as an associate professor, I made 124 yuan. And then, right out of the blue, we were suddenly getting increases of tens and then hundreds of yuan. Suddenly you found yourself receiving a fat wad of banknotes each month, though the cost of basic necessities shot up so your wages could never keep up. Originally you could buy a kilo of belt fish for thirty *fen*. But just prior to my retirement, five hundred grams cost thirty yuan.

Professors dread retirement even more than government bureaucrats do. When we so-called mid- to high-level intellectuals retire, we can keep about 85 percent of our wages, but we lose all other subsidies and supplementary allowances. In real terms, that means your income is cut in half. If you have any financial burdens, dependents like children or elderly parents to care for, you can weep and wail as much as you like, but no one's going to lift a finger to help you. We've given our whole working lives to the university in good faith, but it's only when you're forced to step down from the lectern that you realize just how useless you are. Teaching is the only thing you can do. You don't have any other skills you can make a living with. "Professors, professors, profess yourself poor!"

Well, if I hadn't been a teacher, I'd have been even worse than poor.

There are two assistant professors in my department who retired at the same time as me. One of them has a son doing graduate studies; the other has an elderly mother. Both families are in really dire straits. They're much worse off than me. I should tell you about the one with the elderly mother. After retiring, he just disappeared. Even though we lived in the same building, I never caught sight of him. It was ages before I happened to bump into him one day, and I asked him what kind of mischief he was up to that kept him out all day. "Nothing," he said. "I sleep all day and go out for a bit of a stroll in the evenings. Come over during the day some time; I'll be there." Eventually, one of my students let the cat out of the bag. It turns out that my fellow professor really was at home asleep during the day. And at night he really did take a stroll—right off to a nightclub where he was working as a restroom attendant, opening doors and turning on taps and handing towels to rich entrepreneurs just to get a few tips.

Things are hard for everyone, not just us useless retired people. If the younger teachers in our department don't have a second job, they have a very hard time maintaining a decent standard of living. Their income is about the same as my pension, but they have the added burden of families to support. Fortunately, they are "new people."[2] Unlike us, some of them are really enterprising. They have their own ways and means of making extra money, translating novels and editing dictionaries and suchlike. But the capable ones are in the minority; the rest of them are a bunch of earnest bookworms who can't do anything except teach. The best they can hope for is to earn a little on the side by renting classrooms and running English classes after hours.

So that's how I came to organize this after-hours English class of ours. Sounds fairly simple and straightforward, but what a business it was to set the class up! Dear me, that's quite a story.

At first a group of teachers from the university tried to get things going by self-reliance. They managed to set up the basics, but no students turned up. No one could understand why. It wasn't until they hired this dreadful man as a manager that things got on track. This scoundrel introduced us all to the subtleties of the trade. For instance, the initial advertisement they had published hadn't said that the instructors would include professors; it only mentioned lecturers and tutors. It didn't have any appeal. People simply aren't interested in paying out good money for after-hours tuition if the standard isn't high enough. The students might not even know the alphabet, but they'll still only go for a class taught by a full professor. It's a buyer's market—just listen to me, I can use the fashionable vocabulary! What can the seller do? There are far too many foreign-language classes, and the competition is very stiff. What with four universities and over one hundred high schools in this city, there must be several hundred English teachers at the very least who are moonlighting as tutors.

Anyway, they put out the ads in a big rush—beginners, intermediate, and advanced, plus business English conversation, four classes in all. In two weeks they only got five takers. Five Gods of Wealth! But all at different levels. That was a real lesson for my dimwit colleagues. They had dived into the sea of commerce at the deep end, and now they were floundering around and couldn't get out again. But there was no turning back; they'd taken out a loan to set up the class and put out the ads. Naturally, they had a euphemism for the mess they'd gotten themselves into. To save a bit of face

2. *Xin renlei,* a term introduced from Japan, where it is pronounced *shinjinrui.* It signifies younger people who have not experienced the poverty of the past and who are not as fettered by traditional values as their elders.

they said that they had "sourced capital through interest-bearing loans." What that really meant was that they hadn't achieved anything at all but were several thousand yuan in the red, stuck between a rock and a hard place. A few thousand yuan is what rich people might pay for dinner—but that debt plunged my class of bookworms into profound despair. They went about cursing: "This society is so vicious, so terribly vicious!" They could fulminate all they wanted, but none of them had even the ghost of a plan.

They were so upset they couldn't think straight. Once they were done railing against the inequities of society, they turned on the university. "Even our school is taking advantage of our bad luck by making us pay rent for four classrooms." That was patently absurd. Obviously, they were the ones who'd wanted to rent four classrooms, but now they only wanted to pay for one. The rent was very low; the problem was that they didn't have any students! Eventually, a few of these clowns came to see me. They had once been my students, after all; I had picked them out to stay on at the school to teach, and I was the one who had got them through their graduate studies. I realized that despite my good intentions, I'd clearly taught them the wrong things. My advice was simple: the scheme was a failure, and they should close up shop. As for the debt, I said, I can help you; I'll lend you enough to pay it off. That got them really mad. "No way!" they declared. "This is our last chance. We're going to get these classes up and running no matter what." And they went off saying things like "Nothing on earth is impossible!" and "Anything can be achieved if you're determined!"

They turned up again just a couple of days later, all bright and cheerful. They said they'd be able to set up "our English classes" if I agreed to let them use my name. "What do you mean, *our* English classes?" I inquired. "They're your English classes." "Don't worry about it," my foolish colleagues said. "We've got everything under control. We've found this guy who's made a name for himself setting up classes like this. He's a real whiz. We'll bring him over tonight. He's our manager now, and he'll explain everything." So they had a manager now! I was absolutely dumbfounded.

Of course, their manager was a real scoundrel. I never realized that there could be such people in China. And he wasn't even breaking the law. He was completely frank about his skulduggery. "I used to be employed at the Workers' Cultural Palace," he told me straight out, "but after the reforms were introduced I decided to quit my job. Now I specialize in running tutorial classes. I set up over half the classes in this town and the surrounding counties. Look, I'm not going to play games with you. If you ask the people at the Cultural Palace about me, they'll say I'm bad news, just a big cheat. But don't worry, I'm a crook with a sense of honor and professional standards. Pay me a start-up fee and I won't lead you into any traps. In fact, I'll guarantee that I'll work my butt off to help you rip people off. I've already made a deal with your students. I'm offering you my services for three months, at three thousand yuan a month. I swear, after three months you'll have at least 150 students. That's number one.

"Second, as a demonstration of good faith, I'll present you with something you can't refuse: I pledge that you'll be able to start classes on the day that you originally advertised. This coming Monday, I'll bring you fifty students. They'll sign up for at least six months of two classes of English conversation a week. I know you intellectuals always talk big but are cheapskates when it comes to forking out, but in the business world you've got to make the investment. That's why I expect a token of your cooperation in return. The students I'm bringing in aren't free, but I'm giving you a discount: you have to pay me fifty yuan a head, goods on receipt.

"Third, once these students are on board, I'll lay on a First Day of School ceremony for you at no extra charge. I'll arrange for TV and newspaper coverage too, so that's free publicity. That's my offer; all I ask in return is your agreement to take personal charge of the operation. You can be school principal or head teacher, whatever you like. You'll be earning top dollar."

I said no. "You might think you've got it all worked out, but you're not going to talk me into it," I told him. "I'm retired; get the others to do it."

Guess what the blackguard said to that? "Actually, your colleagues have already agreed on your behalf. They only need you to get them started. That is to say, we don't need you to teach, but you're a full professor, and none of them are. A professor is a major draw. Look, we're begging you—can't we just put you in the ad?"

He had it all figured out. What could I do? If I refused, what would my foolish pack of colleagues do? Since he'd put it to me in this way, I knew I'd have to give in. If I didn't, my colleagues would think that the whole deal had fallen through because of me. They'd hate me for the rest of their lives.

You live and learn. It's only since I retired that I've realized that what good people can't accomplish, scoundrels can achieve with ease. In those three months, I suppose I saw him no more than ten times in all. And he made off with over ten thousand yuan of our money. But, scoundrel though he was, he was as good as his word. He left us with over 170 students; that's 20 more than he'd originally guaranteed. Our school was built on the foundations he laid, and we've been developing steadily for three years now, virtually without a hitch.

That rogue manager was a real operator, and he knew how to play both sides against each other. The fifty students that he initially sold to us weren't people who had responded to the ads at all. They were actually staff at the Lantian Hotel. He had heard that the hotel wanted to organize some on-the-job training for its service personnel, so he contrived a meeting with the management and told them he could liaise with the foreign-languages department of our university on their behalf and get the university teachers to set up special tutorial classes for them. And it wasn't just an empty offer. He'd been scanning the daily press carefully and spotted our little ad, so he knew we were setting up classes. He was savvy enough to know that we'd never attract enough students, because it's a buyer's market.

That's what information can do for you. Knowledge is power! He made 2,500 yuan out of us in one go. After that, it was an easy matter to get another 9,000 out of us. Having sold us our first fifty students, he set about organizing the inauguration ceremony. The rogue actually stage-managed a very impressive occasion and contrived to have some top local officials on hand to perform the ribbon cutting. His timing was impeccable. All of this was set up at the height of a government campaign to get universities to provide paid services for the public. So the deputy mayor accepted the invitation without hesitation and, once he had been dragged into it, all the old folks in the National People's Consultative Committee—people who are always desperate for some public exposure—got wind of it. They were eager anyway, and they heard that the ceremony would be followed by a free feed at this luxury hotel. Why, there was even a chance that they might get to be on TV. Nothing could keep them away. With so many senior government people in one place, the TV people sprang into action. Isn't this just the kind of item that they fill the evening news with every night?

After the ribbon had been cut, that rogue led the deputy mayor and the old fogies off to the Lantian Hotel for a banquet. The hotel management was ecstatic, too. Here they had all these VIP guests, and their manager got to be on TV into the bargain. That's how a commonplace event—language training for a few hotel employees—got blown up into a major news item. Heavens, but the manager was excited: "Come back any time for a few more meals on the hotel's tab."

During the meal, that scoundrel addressed the reporters himself.

"This kind of training is not the only thing we do. We are also accepting students from the broader community. The courses will be taught by professors, and we cater to all levels of proficiency, from learning the alphabet to taking the TOEFL to study in the United States. We would be grateful if you could spread the news and just put in a few good words for us."

The reporters all said they were happy to oblige. They included his whole spiel on the evening news. There were several shots of me, too; the voiceover said that this old professor was enthusiastically supporting the program and teaching some of the classes herself.

You could write a novel based on the scams that fellow has been involved in. Of course there'd be enough to write about! Where could you find a more shifty character?

I teach four classes a week spread over two evenings. Others have it much harder; they do four nights and half a day—or even a whole day—on Saturday. My silly gang is earning two to three hundred yuan extra every month on top of their salaries. It's not all that steady, though. Sometimes we have fewer students, or there's a bit of a slump and our takings fall sharply. For example, one of my former tutors only made eighty-six yuan last month. She was so upset she was almost in tears. Do you know what eighty-six yuan is worth nowadays? Six fake Big Macs.

Our busy season is from the winter vacation right up to the high school graduation exams in the summer. We get a lot of junior high school students preparing for the exams to get into senior high and a lot of senior high school students preparing for university entrance exams. Several hundred will all arrive at once, so at our busiest times we have to take on extra staff. Initially, we were kind-hearted, and we hired on fourth-year and postgraduate students from our own university, so they could make a little extra to help with their studies. But we soon discovered it wasn't going to work out. The students were really no good; they were always making trouble. They went prying into our secrets, checking up on the accounts to see whether we were exploiting them. When I was a research student, I worked for my supervisor for free. My group of dimwit colleagues had been like that, too; they'd worked for me for nothing as well. Young people today are simply too much. They haggle over every cent and are constantly suspicious that they are being cheated. So I decided to get rid of the whole insolent bunch.

Now we hire high-school teachers instead. Before taking anyone on, however, we tell them straight, "You're going to be paid less than us. If that's acceptable, come on board; if not, there's the door. We are university teachers, you are high-school teachers. Moreover, we got this school going in the first place, so it's only right and proper that we should be making a little more." High-school teachers are in even more dire straits than university lecturers. They are so happy to get a chance to make a bit of extra money that they don't dare haggle over their wages.

We've discussed it among ourselves, and we all agree on the basic principles for running this operation. We're selling education; it's a business. All of us—teachers and students—take what we need and then part company once the deal is done. At least I can say that we have a clear conscience about our business ethics; educational value and probity are another thing altogether. We haven't set up these classes as some educational enterprise; it's a business, pure and simple. If we got caught up in all that talk about social conscience, serving the people and suchlike, we'd have to close up shop right now. We'd be bankrupt. I know Confucius said that to die of starvation is a trifle compared to losing your integrity, but in my opinion we'd better try and avoid starving first.

Take the short course we ran for hotel service staff, for example. Those kids had all studied English before, and they'd only just left high school. There's no way they would have totally forgotten all of the vocabulary and grammar they'd learned. From a purely educational point of view, we should have concentrated on their conversational ability and consolidated their vocabulary and grammar at the same time. But if we'd done that, the results wouldn't have been evident immediately. The hotel manager would have been most annoyed: "Look, when I sent them to you they were all stuttering and stammering. Now they've gone through your course and nothing's changed! What a waste of money. You won't be getting any more business from me."

Our experience with the Lantian Hotel taught us how best to proceed. We abandoned all attempts at teaching vocab and grammar; we just got them to learn a few dozen sentences of basic hotel-related conversation by rote. If they could recite some hospitality-speak fluently, we'd achieved our purpose. It wasn't of the slightest concern to us that they forgot all their other vocabulary and basic grammar. We each take what we need and part company once the deal is done.

Competition? This is competition! As time's passed we've become a little smarter and added a few more strings to our bow. Now, apart from myself, we have an American professor on board as a consultant. So it's a joint venture! Prospective students are impressed by ads that feature cooperation between China and foreign countries. The dimmer ones actually think we're a joint-venture company. We haven't forgotten that we are intellectuals, though, and we aren't going to cheat people the way the louts in the broader community do. But the American professor takes no interest in our affairs at all; everything is up to me. That's because he's my son. You mustn't write this up in China, though. Let's just say it's our little trade secret.

"When you have the leisure to look back, the scenery of life is truly long." This sentence has become part of the repertoire in the Chinese-to-English translation exams for the advanced students. They find it extremely difficult to translate. It's one of those sentences that can be parsed in any number of ways but, at the end of the day, no one knows which one is best.

What is the scenery of life? And which is long, life or the scenery? Can you even describe scenery as being long or short? The sentence doesn't conform to the standard syntax of Chinese, and on the surface it is illogical. But the reason they find it hard to translate has nothing to do with grammatical inconsistencies.

20

To the New World

Passport Protection

A bottle of Rémy Martin, a carton of Marlboro cigarettes, and one unwelcome guest.

Beijing

You're right; I'm a bit slow off the mark. But if I don't go now, it'll be even harder to get out later. Anyway, at the moment I have to consider my personal situation as well.

I've just had my fortune told. Not by one of those sidewalk crooks, if you know what I mean, but a serious master who has a suite in a five-star hotel. He specializes in telling fortunes for famous people from Taiwan. Well, he told me that at the moment I'm in a neutral situation: great fortune awaits me, but it won't necessarily be realized unless I work at it. Everything depends on how I handle myself, so I'm not sure whether I'll make it or not. The crucial thing is to avoid taking any wrong steps. The master said the ideal route for my development lies in "breaking through heaven's gate and retreating to repair my fishing nets." He wouldn't be any more precise than that, but he's a master, after all. He can divine the subtle workings of heaven, and they're not something that can be revealed lightly. If he were too precise, then my fate would not unfold as he told me.

Anyway, since the master's message was so vague, I decided that I needed someone to explain it to me. I was told that it appeared to be imprecise only on the surface and that in fact the master had pointed me in the right direction. Heaven's gate is in the south, so I have to head south without hesitation, as far south as you can go, without stopping or giving up. It's obvious that if you go all the way south—and I don't mean Antarctica, of course—you get to where the penguins live: that's right, Australia. But going overseas is not my goal; it's only a means to an end. I'm supposed "to retreat to repair my fishing nets"; that means by going overseas I'll be in a position to strike when the moment is right. That's when I'll be able to make a big comeback and to scoop up all the big fish in my nets, the ones that are currently beyond my reach.

As the saying goes, "In poverty, move house; when wealthy, build a tomb; and if in distress, seek out soothsayers." Things haven't been going well for me these last couple of years. I never believed in fortune-telling before, but I've had so much bad luck that I've come to think that it might be worth trying. That's how I was thinking when I approached the master—and he took one look at me and said, "Your heart is not pure. If you do not believe, then nothing will come of my words. You had best go now." One look, that's all it took for him to see through me, before I'd even had a chance to say a word. How could I doubt his powers?

He really is a great master. He doesn't take money; that'd be too vulgar. He said that money is just an external thing, and if I really wanted to make a donation, I should give money to the Hope Foundation to help some children get an education.[1] See how pure he is? It wouldn't be right to accept his guidance and give money in return. Luckily the guy who took me to see him gave me an idea: I left a check at the hotel registration desk to cover a few days of the master's bill.

So now the basic direction and aims of my life are clear. I have to leave China, no matter how difficult that may be. I'd guess you're about forty, so we're the same generation. We belong to a group that is prepared to work without rest to improve ourselves. The reform policies have brought about radical changes in the society we live in. There's no hope for people who believe they can still rely on their old work organizations or their families, or even on the party. The most advanced members of our generation know that striving to better themselves is the only way.

Let me be frank, I am definitely one of those people. Don't forget, the Cultural Revolution left the majority of us undereducated and unemployed. No-hopers. But it also made us down-to-earth and practical. A lot of us might have been satisfied to become members of the common petty bourgeoisie, but I wasn't. We couldn't just fall by the wayside and let those assas-

1. The Hope Foundation is a government-sponsored charity that helps needy children.

sins look even better than they were. Although Bei Dao was only a poet, his writings gave me courage and strength.[2] I was able to get another chance to go to school because I worked hard and relied on myself. I am one of the small number of individuals who weren't destroyed by the Cultural Revolution.

I'm talking about 1981. I'd been working in a synthetic-fiber factory for five years when I finally passed the entrance exams for a part-time university course. After three years of hard study I ended up with a diploma. I'd started primary school the year the Cultural Revolution broke out, so I hardly learned anything useful in that whole ten years of chaos. Most people in my situation figured there was no hope and decided they just had to put up with being workers. But I wasn't prepared to do that. I had to fight my way out; I was determined to make up for lost time. Until then I'd been trying to get into a formal university course; I'd had a few tries at the entrance exam, but, for various reasons, things didn't turn out like I wanted them to. But even that couldn't keep me down. Even though I ended trying for a part-time place at a college, the competition was still fierce, and if I'd lost heart and given in to hopelessness I would have never gotten in.

Passing those entrance exams was the first time I'd ever achieved anything in my whole life. The experience taught me that I could be the master of my own fate. That's why, at a time when most people still thought that an iron rice bowl[3] was the key to a successful life, I decided to quit my job at the factory and look for other work. That was back in 1985, a time when people all over China were setting up their own companies and were on the lookout for employees. After quitting the factory I used my not-so-impressive diploma to find a job outside the state system. That's how I found this job with the ChiSci Huipu Company. The years have gone by in a flash.

Huipu specializes in electrical parts and equipment; its buyers are generally small- to mid-sized power stations and transformer substations. So, even though the company's headquarters are in Beijing, most of our business is elsewhere. When I first started working here, we still had formal links to the Chinese Academy of Sciences; that's why we're called ChiSci Huipu Company, that is, the Chinese Academy of Sciences Huipu Company. It had no fixed assets; it was a company on paper only. At first there were only five of us, and we did all the marketing ourselves. Though we all had dif-

2. Bei Dao (the pen name of Zhao Zhenkai) was a nonofficial writer popular in the late 1970s and 1980s.

3. That is, assured employment in a government or state enterprise.

ferent titles and job descriptions, we were all essentially doing the same thing: dealing. We ran all over the place. The first question we asked was: "What do you need to buy?" If they didn't need anything, we'd say, without missing a beat, "What do you have to sell?"

All true pioneers build up their enterprises from nothing. Back then most companies were in this initial stage. You couldn't expect too much; it wouldn't have been realistic. I was only earning a few dozen yuan a month; even back in 1985, that was pretty poor pay. My main source of income was commissions, but that wasn't much either. If I signed a deal for a hundred thousand yuan, for example, I'd get a commission of two to three thousand. For the time it wasn't too bad. At college I'd studied engineering, and my true talent lay in drawing machine plans, but my job at Huipu had nothing to do with that. I'd come from a family of people who worked in electricity. My father worked in the Ministry of Electrical Power, and though he wasn't very senior—after the Cultural Revolution he was still only at bureau level—he still had some connections, so he could give me a helping hand from time to time.

Our company's had a pretty good run, and it's doing all right. We started our first inland factory, a switch plant, in 1989. It was a joint venture with foreign capital that we set up in South China. Our company liaised with the foreign investors as a way of reducing tax overhead. So we didn't get the full amount of money, but we could spend a few hundred thousand on equipment; no actual cash was involved. After that initial success, we followed the same formula to build a few other factories. We also constructed an office building for ourselves here in Beijing and bought a dorm. We became a real industrial and trading corporation. Our BB guns turned into cannons.

I specialized in running the out-of-town factories. My title was manager of industrial development. Though I was as busy as ever, I was finally in a stable situation. Just think of it; until then I'd spent four years on the road as a salesman. I'd been everywhere, including Xinjiang and Tibet. I'll spare you the details of all the hardships, and I won't deny that I was involved in my fair share of illegal scams. After all, "if you often walk along the river's edge, you'll never keep your feet dry." But now we were running a proper enterprise, and I had security. Banqueting and the like, the odd bit of corruption, all that's par for the course. Isn't that what everyone's doing these days? But it's not the same thing as major criminal activities; it's only what they call "getting drunk daily on the wine of the revolution; drink till there's no more party and no stomach lining."

Overseas study was all the rage a few years ago, and everyone who was anyone was leaving. It was as though it'd be the last opportunity for people of my generation, but I never thought of leaving. I was the CEO of a joint venture. Okay, so it was an enterprise that could only boast of owning a number of small rural factories, but I wasn't prepared to go through it all again in some foreign country. Sure, I had many opportunities to go overseas. Let me be frank: I had more than enough personal wealth to pay for overseas study in 1989 or so. What would it have cost back then? About ten thousand U.S.? Hardly a problem. I lent that amount more than once to friends or relatives to go abroad. Sometimes they just needed a deposit in some bank account as surety for an application for a foreign visa, you know, to fool the foreigners. But there were also cases when people really took a loan from me, and I didn't hear a word for two, maybe three years. It was only when they'd established themselves overseas that they suddenly remembered that they owed me. What I'm saying is that I could easily have gone then, but I just didn't want to. My business was thriving, so I let all those opportunities pass me by.

But now, if I want to go, it's virtually impossible. Never mind Australia, these days you can't even get to fucking Russia if you're over thirty-five! They've got a nerve being so narrow-minded. Don't they get it? Anyone under thirty-five is going to be as poor as a pauper. They want to go to Russia to make money, not spend it! People of my age are the youngest with any disposable income in China. But Russia? Forget it! I don't even want to go to America. That's why I've gotten in touch with you; I want to go to Australia.

Of course it's not just because of what the fortune-teller told me! I went to have my fortune told because too much has gone wrong these last few years. Let me be frank. You've got a foreign passport, haven't you? Okay, then I can be honest. It hasn't been anything in particular, just that things haven't been going smoothly. I feel like I'm living under a cloud; like I'm in the middle of a sorghum field and I can't see my way out. Even if I hadn't gone to the fortune-teller, I would still want to leave. It's just that I wasn't sure which direction I should set my sights on, so it would just be blind chance which one I chose. I'd probably miss the good fortune on the way, and it would all be for nothing.

My income is falling. Even though I earn a pretty high salary, its value is constantly being eroded. No one can live on their actual wages nowadays; you survive on bonuses or commissions. Gray income is many times higher than official wages. The envelopes are stuck to the stamps now, not the other way around. That's why even in our company a clever operator might be my subordinate and on a lower wage, but if they're good at making deals they'll be running around in a sports car and living in a country villa. What I'm saying is that my present income is far less than it was in, say, 1992, let alone 1989.

A new generation has come onto the scene. Look, it's not a bad thing; it's normal to give young people in their early twenties a bit of responsibility and power. But it wasn't them that struggled all those years to create the excellent situation we're enjoying today; they've got no commitment or sense of responsibility toward the company. They've all been job-hopping, and that's how they've ended up here. All they're interested in is money, and to them the company is just a meal ticket, plain and simple. If you were willing to flash me a million U.S. right here and now, I'd tell you all the company secrets. Why should I care? I'd have made my million, so that'd be it. The pity of it is, you wouldn't have to spend a million to buy these people. They'd do it for ten grand. They'd torch the place for that. Just think about it! We're in trouble.

Then there's the pseudo–foreign devils. They spend a few years overseas, set themselves up with a green card, and then launch themselves on China with shock and awe. There's a kind of indecent haste about it all. Those little shits in the first wave of returnees think the sun shines out of them. Then there's the ones waiting in the wings and taking stock of the situation. They're sharpening up their assassins' knives overseas and are on the lookout for the right opportunity. At head office we don't have any pseuds yet, but there's one in one of our subsidiary factories. He's a manager hired by our foreign partners. He was just some drifter who'd never even seen a Beijing duck banquet before he went off to waste some time overseas, and now here he is back in China earning sixty thousand U.S. a year. Do you think he's worth it? They say he has a degree in enterprise management, but if you ask me he probably bought it, or maybe even drew it up himself. Fucking hell, you know as well as I do that Chinese will try any scam.

So there you have it. I've given you three good reasons for leaving, and I could easily give you another ten. Given this complex and vicious state of class struggle, it's no wonder things aren't going smoothly for me. Some people might think the new rich are secure in their prosperity, but they don't realize we're fighting an uphill battle; they don't understand that if you don't advance, you'll be forced to retreat. My position is increasingly uncertain; in fact, I'm stalled. During the past ten years or so, people were very envious of me, but in the last couple of years—just two short years—it's the other way around, and I can't not envy other people. I've got to take some drastic measures and turn things around.

There's an old saying that goes, "Some quit the office and return to their old homes; others are staying up at night to prepare for the official exams." This has been the situation since ancient times. If you put yourself in my position, you'll see that all these comings and goings are understandable enough. But if I were you, I'd feel compelled to help me out here. All I want from you is a surefire method for getting away. Don't worry, all I'm doing is following the master's advice and taking one step back, a strategic retreat. There's no way I'd stay in Australia and make trouble for you.

I'm not interested in getting an immigration agent. I wouldn't let myself be cheated by those rip-off merchants unless it was a matter of life and death. Those people are all "karate experts."[4] When we first started out, I had this business card that said I was the general representative for China's largest gas-turbine, electrical-generator, transformer, and switch-cubicle factories. It looked as though the whole country's electrical industries were locked up in my briefcase. . . . That's how I scammed myself into this business. So I know how it's done, but I also know that if you fall into the clutches of some agent or other to help you get overseas, then you're as good as dead. They won't even find your corpse in one piece.

Look, I know that where you come from—well, actually, it's the same here—everything comes at a price. But you can see for yourself that money isn't an issue. I'm not asking you to do this for nothing.

Now, that only shows you've misunderstood my intentions. I've no desire to keep anything hidden from you. But we've only just met, and I reckon saying too much would be, well, in bad taste. Since you obviously know the setup, I won't treat you as a stranger. This is the real problem—I don't give a damn about those bastards earning big bucks. What really gets to me is they have foreign passports as well. They're the returnees' brigade, and we're the local landlords.[5] They're capable of doing anything at all to rake in the money, but when the shit hits the fan, they can hide behind their passports. At worst they'll give us the finger and go overseas again. As for

4. Karate *(kongshou dao)* in Chinese literally means "bare-handed"; thus the expression refers to experts in "the way of the empty hand."

5. The returnees' brigade *(huanxiang tuan)* were landowners and local worthies displaced by the Sino-Japanese conflict who, on returning to their old homes, took over from the land-lords who had stayed.

me, well, I don't have the guts for that. Things aren't as completely out of control as they were a few years back. You can see the money lying around just asking to be taken, but you can't touch it. You have to get by on small deals. But if you're not moving up, you're falling behind. It's not that I can't play the game; the sad thing is that I just don't dare. I'm chicken! And there's a sword hanging over me, too. If the people's courts want to fuck over a pseud, then they've got international litigation on their hands; and then there's all that stuff about human rights. As long as you're not stupid enough to piss in the authorities' faces, they'll make like you're a fart and just let you out. But if a Chinese citizen without a foreign passport gets in trouble, the full weight of the law comes down on you. It's like a game for the courts; they can fuck you over any way they like, and the law is always on their side. That's why I have to take a step backward before I can make my next advance. If I can hack it in Australia for a couple of years, it'll be time well spent. I'll get myself a solid, bona fide ID, one of your passports, and I'll come back to China and play some more.

Since you can understand what I'm saying here, you really have to help me out. Think about it; all you have to do is tell me how much I need and where it needs to be spent. Just give me a figure, say twenty or thirty thousand U.S. dollars. You take it out of China for me. I don't care who you have to give it to, just do it. I'll owe you more than money, seriously. After I get out, we're brothers, and I'll settle my account with you fair and square. Deal? . . .

One false step, and you regret it forever. I've been very shortsighted about going overseas. But it's still not too late. The essential thing is to get a move on right now. The fortune-teller gave me the greatest encouragement; he told me my period of good fortune has not come to an end. It's still there.

Hey, how about I spend a few grand or more on a phony marriage thing? Look, every struggle requires some sacrifices. As long as I end up with a real foreign passport, my wife is sure to be supportive.

Mastering New China

A Capitalist with the Party's Characteristics

A commentary in the Beijing Daily *declared that the most effective means for preventing the so-called peaceful evolution of China into a bourgeois democracy was to "identify and reward model workers in every profession" and to encourage people throughout the country to emulate their progressive socialist thinking.*

One particular group that was identified during the 1990s for just such encouragement were company managers working in private and semiprivate industry. The authorities declared that they would strive to encourage a cadre of prosocialist "red capitalists" among the model managers, who would in turn give their political support to the new economic order.

Hebei Province. He was a member of the Private Industrialists' Association and a Model Private Enterprise Leader for his province.

He wanted the interview to be conducted only after I had inspected his whole operation, so as to help me gain some "perceptual knowledge of the enterprise." So he came to pick me up at my hotel in his VW, the kind of sedan, he announced, that was generally used by county-level party secretaries. My "tour of inspection" had nothing to do with visiting his company, however, because he took me back to his home, a prosperous-looking compound in what was otherwise impoverished and backward hill country.

One thing about me is that I'm not afraid of displaying my wealth. Just take a look at this house of mine. It's over three hundred square meters; all of that for just three of us. And we have two cars, a sedan as well as an SUV. We're the ones who got rich first—not just compared to other people in this area, but relative to the whole of China.[1] Apart from personal infrastructure projects like this, I've also spent money on travel. In the past people only really traveled on business, and they were always strapped for cash. Now the situation is quite different, and I haven't only traveled in China; I've been overseas, too. I wanted to see what the rest of the world is like, broaden my horizons, and give the foreigners a look at a Chinese person at the same time. Let them see that we aren't some Sick Man of Asia, as poor as hell. In the past they came to China and went around wherever they pleased, ransacking, stealing, and cheating. The reason they could get away with it was that they were strong and we were weak; they had money and we didn't. Now we can go and take a good look at them. We can tell them what civilization and equality are really all about. This fact alone attests to the greatness of our open-door and reform policies.

As for the scale of our operation at the moment, I've got less than one million yuan invested in the company, plus a few hundred thousand in liquid assets. We're small fry compared to the big operations that measure their capital investment in the millions or tens of millions. But people with money tend to pretend they don't have any in everyday life; they tend to hoard their wealth or move it offshore. They're scared of showing it off like I do. When they were poor they were timid, and now that they're rich they're even more scared. The reason for that is not what people usually say; their insecurity has nothing to do with policies changing all the time or the legal system being deficient. It's exactly the opposite: it's precisely because the state is strengthening the legal system and because policies are consistent and stable that these people are less willing to take risks. Take our county, for example. There are a few thousand private businesses here, but are any of them operating within the law and paying their taxes? If so, how many? They're on tenterhooks because they've made their money by cheating the state and the people. They're always worried that someone is going to catch them out and find evidence of their scams. That's why when they go out for a meal, they don't dare have a real banquet. They're afraid to show they've got money.

What do I have to be afraid of? I run an enterprise that combines forestry and agro-business. My company has done more than just make me rich; it is publicly recognized for having made a positive contribution to the soci-

1. "Let some people get rich first" was part of the economic reform strategy launched by Deng Xiaoping and the Communist Party following the Cultural Revolution.

ety, the environment, and the greening of the Motherland. We have generally benefited the broad masses. I've made my money honestly, and that's why I'm not afraid to spend it. I'm not afraid of anything; as long as our socialist Motherland stands firm, I have no reason to fear for the future of either my business or myself. I'll show off my wealth and spend big, not only here at home, but when I go overseas. It's all been earned legally, and it's my right to do whatever I want with it. Why should I worry?

Just seven years ago I started the company with a loan of thirty yuan. So apart from my own brains and hard work—that is to say, intangible investments—all I put in was just that thirty yuan seven years ago. The main reason for my success is that I worked out the proper balance between myself and the state; and I've been able to establish an equitable relationship between my private aspirations and the public good. Our country is a socialist nation under the leadership of the Chinese Communist Party. We are working towards the realization of communism, the ultimate ideal of all Chinese, by the creation and accumulation of communal wealth. It is a sublime ideal. The encouragement of private enterprise is an economic strategy formulated under the wise leadership of Comrade Xiaoping, whose proposal that some people should be allowed to get rich first has been pursued since the Third Plenary Session of the Eleventh Congress of the Communist Party [in 1978]. There would be no way we'd be sitting here today discussing private enterprise in China if the party hadn't formulated policy targets aimed at enriching the people, or if we lacked the correct leadership in the party and the government. That is why I am happy to declare that my business is working within legal parameters and for the benefit of the state. Even though it's a private enterprise, it works under the aegis of the public and is incorporated into the public realm. I have always been absolutely clear about this. It would be nothing less than suicidal for small bosses like me, or even the directors of big companies, to try and undermine the state, set ourselves up in direct opposition to it, or even overthrow the public good and engage in bourgeois liberalization. That would be a dead end. If you don't negotiate a correct relationship between your operation and the state, and you try to cheat the state and the people, you might profit illegally as a result of the confusion, but only for a while. Your business won't be able to go any further; you'll be ruined in the end, and the state won't do you any favors.

Of course, tree seeds are pretty profitable. However, all the other seed companies that were established around the time I started up my business have gone bankrupt for one reason or another. Mine is the only private company of its type in the whole of North China, and it's the most profitable venture of its kind in China. I think that is proof enough that my approach of putting the public good above all else and sharing the benefits with others has been absolutely correct. That's how I've achieved my unassailable position.

I started the company in 1987. I'd really wanted to quit my state job back in 1983, when private enterprise first became an option, but I was working at the Education Bureau then, and they absolutely refused to let me go. I was in charge of doing the mimeographs for teaching materials. I have very good handwriting, as well as a high level of education, so I was able to detect and correct errors that the teachers made in compiling their materials for math, physics, chemistry, or whatever. I was a real asset to the bureau. But by late '85 or early '86 I was determined to get out of there, so I stopped going to work. They finally had to agree to release me.

I didn't get into this business right away. I ran another company for a year, doing whatever deals I could in and around the Chengde district.[2] I didn't make a cent, but at least that year taught me that I wasn't cut out for that kind of trade. You see, I'm disgusted by the general practice in business these days of lying to get things done, especially when it's private entrepreneurs cheating the state and the people. Even though I was psychologically unsuited to this, I couldn't avoid having to do it in the course of my business. I spent that year in a state of deep ambivalence, so it's no wonder I didn't make any money.

There wasn't any future for me in business, so I went to the provincial forest company and helped them gather tree seeds. That's how I became involved in this aspect of the forestry industry. I learned a great deal and got some ideas about how I could start up a tree-seed business of my own. At the same time I learned that there was no private dealership in tree seed in the whole North China region. The reasons for this were threefold: technical ability, capital, and outlets. In macroeconomic terms, the whole business cycle involved only one party. The state, or rather the local forestry commission, was both seller and buyer. If some individual could utilize his

2. Chengde, also known in English by its old name of Jehol (Rehe in Chinese), is northeast of Beijing in Hebei province. Located in the heavily wooded (although increasingly depleted) environs of the Yan Mountains, it was a summer resort and hunting ground used by the Manchu-Qing rulers until 1861.

own capital and know how to turn this into a proper business, there was money to be made. But it wasn't going to be easy. Luckily, I'm one of those people who likes trying their hand at doing things that other people won't do or can't do well.

My first deal was a big order of tree seed from the Chengde tree-seed storehouse.

Up to then things hadn't gone smoothly for me. The first half of my life was a disaster. Going to university, working for the government, and those useless years spent in the army—none of it came to anything. "Thirty years of vainglorious life!"[3] But in my thirtieth year I responded to the party's policy that was aimed at enriching the people, and I threw myself into private enterprise. And that's the secret of my success. I've done well because I've always been willing to give others the benefit of the profit. I've worked unstintingly for the public good and put the needs of the majority before my own personal interests. Step by step I have found the correct path. Now, I'm not saying that going to university or being in the army or working in the government are not also the correct path; they are all correct paths opened up for us by the party. Sometimes one particular path might not open up for you because of subjective limitations or objective conditions; but in the end all roads lead to Rome. As long as you follow the party, any one of them will get you to your destination.

Before I turned thirty? Didn't I just say that nothing I turned my hand to worked out for me? Okay, if you want the details I can tell you that when I graduated from high school in 1973, I was one of the best students in my year, and there was no doubt I could make it to university. But in those days you could only go to university with a recommendation from your school, and in my case my family background was not good enough,[4] so I had to give up on that. I went to work in the countryside instead and that's where I . . .

What? Are you telling me that back then I couldn't have gone directly to university even if I'd wanted to? Really? How come I remember that in the Cultural Revolution, if you didn't go to the countryside after high school,

3. *Sanshi gongming chen yu tu,* a line from the Song-dynasty general Yue Fei's song/lyric poem sung to the tune *Man jiang hong.*

4. Being from a bad class background meant that as members of former exploitative classes (landlords, bourgeoisie, rich peasants, and capitalists), people were penalized and did not enjoy the privileges of the proletariat (the workers, peasants, and soldiers) favored by the Communist Party.

you could go directly to university? Oh well, forget it. Anyway, it was over twenty years ago, and we shouldn't get mired in petty historical detail. The upshot of it all was that I didn't get to university. I turned out to be a good worker in the countryside, though. After starting out as a point scorer, marking everyone's work points in a production team, over the next five years I moved on to become a militia-company leader, a storeman, deputy brigade leader, brigade leader, assistant team leader, assistant party branch secretary, and right on up to party branch secretary for the whole production brigade. We spent our time doing just what city cadres did: mobilizing people to participate in political movements. Things like the Anti–Lin Biao Anti-Confucius Movement and the Counterattack on the Rightist Attempt to Reverse Verdicts.[5] Although I hated political purges like this, as a leader and party member in the commune I had no choice but to lead the peasants in the denunciations. I was frustrated and resented the fact that I had to spend most of my time involved with such things. I decided there was no future in any of it, so in 1978 I applied to join the army, the artillery in fact.

My time in the army was the all-time low point of my life. A month after joining up I got appendicitis, but the medics in our company were inexperienced, and they misdiagnosed it as a stomachache. Then regimental doctors said it was gastric perforation. By the time they decided to send me to the divisional hospital I was in such agony that I was sure I was going to die. I went into shock, and although I was saved by emergency treatment, I still spent four months in hospital. Then when I finally got out I discovered I was suffering from intestinal adhesion. I couldn't do any heavy physical work and was now completely unsuited to life as a soldier. I was discharged in 1982.

That's when I went to work for the Education Bureau and was put to work making mimeographs. The average monthly wage for the job was thirty to forty yuan, but because I worked hard and the person who gave

5. The Anti–Lin Biao Anti-Confucius Campaign (*pi Lin pi Kong yundong*) was launched in early 1974. The Counterattack on the Rightist Attempt to Reverse Verdicts (*fanji youqing fan'an feng*) was sparked by attempts within the educational establishment and Beijing universities in 1975 to change the selection criteria for high-school-graduate entrants to university from purely political to academic. During the early months of 1976 the rhetoric surrounding this issue escalated, and eventually Deng Xiaoping, "the unrepentant capitalist-roader within the party," was publicly attacked as the advocate of policies that were aimed at "reversing the verdicts" of the Cultural Revolution.

me the job was my old high-school teacher, and he knew I was pretty good, I earned over sixty yuan. That was the same wage as teachers got, so it really was pretty good treatment. Even so, my girlfriend was convinced I had no future, so she ended our relationship. So my mother decided to find me another girl who was a couple of years older than me, and she rushed us into getting married. I didn't have any money, so I couldn't buy anything except a few new clothes for her. So there I was, stuck in an unsatisfactory job and a hasty marriage. Even my wife wasn't happy with the way we'd been rail-roaded into matrimony. She thought I was pretty good-looking and a decent person, but she resented the fact that I earned so little and that we were so poor. Soon we had a baby, and the three of us had a very hard time surviving on such a limited income. My wife often sat at home moping and crying, and she ended up giving herself a stomach illness. Given the situation, I felt it was impossible to stay with the Education Bureau and so, after three years, I demanded that they let me go. I left home in the hope of making a go at business. I did it all to provide my family with a better lifestyle. But after a year of running around I still ended up nowhere.

When I started working with tree seed, I didn't have a cent to my name, so I approached a bank for a loan. They wouldn't even give me the few hundred yuan I needed, so I ended up borrowing thirty yuan from relatives. That was my sole investment in the new company, if you could call it that; it was really just start-up capital for a tree-seed supplier who was new to the game. I spent it all to get to Chengde, where I bought tree seed on consignment from the local state forestry office. It was only a small deal: half a ton of locust-tree seeds and another three hundred kilos or so of larch seeds. The going rate for that lot was about twenty thousand yuan. I signed a promissory note offering my good character as sole collateral. So I took on a huge debt, and they agreed to let me pay them once I'd sold the seed.

This was the private sector, and there's no way you could compare my operation with a state enterprise. They could get a government loan when they ran into money troubles, or they could just stop trading and wait until business picked up; the state would continue to pay their wages regardless. That wasn't the case for me. I had to keep going regardless of whether there was any money coming in. Even now I make other people's money work for me. In some cases I still operate like I did in the early days, taking a shipment of seed on consignment and paying for it once I've sold it. Other times the buyer pays up front, and I can use the money to buy the seed.

Maybe other people couldn't get away with doing business like this, but

I can. And that's because both my buyers and suppliers have confidence in me. They know I'm reliable and a man of my word; they also know that I have a professional knowledge of the goods I'm dealing in, and they can rely on the quality of my merchandise. In short, my way of doing business is built on the solid foundation of my personal probity and the excellence of my product. It's proved to be a highly successful combination.

Before I started trading in tree seed, I studied the industry and worked out that the central problem was that people couldn't get enough capital and couldn't get access to sales outlets. But I had both of these things sorted out, as I've just outlined—or I wouldn't have gone into business in the first place. Most private entrepreneurs can get a profiteering business up and running with virtually no money at all. They borrow ten to twenty thousand yuan and they're away, and they make a return in no time. But tree seed isn't like that. For example, it costs at least sixty thousand yuan for a ton of Chinese pine seed; a ton of larch seed is twenty thousand; the more expensive seeds are not sold by the ton but individually, for as much as two to three hundred yuan apiece. To run a viable business you have to be able to supply at least ten different varieties of seed, and at any one time you have to be prepared to buy a few tons of a particular seed. The capital outlay involved runs into the hundreds of thousands, if not millions. Add to that the fact that tree seed can only be harvested and planted once a year. That means that your capital expenditure can only turn over after a year. So, from a purely economic point of view, most companies don't have what it takes to deal in tree seed.

Connections, or rather one's business network, are also most important. Apart from a tiny number of private enterprises, the vast majority of customers for tree seed are publicly owned organizations, or, to be more specific, they operate with state-allocated budgets under the aegis of the national forestry ministry or local forestry bureaus. So if you don't have the proper connections, or a network, you can forget about trading in tree seed; you won't be able to buy it, and you won't be able to sell it, either. Tree seeds are living things, and according to the law you can only keep them in storage for a fixed period, about three years. Every year in storage reduces the sprouting ratio of the seed; by the third year you're left with third-grade material or worse, and all you can do with it is throw it away. Even if you only keep it in stock for a year—say we're talking about a ton of larch seeds—you'll take a loss of over sixty thousand yuan. Who can cope with that? You simply can't afford to overstock tree seed. You have to be able to get rid of it, and if you don't have the right business connections you'd be insane even to try.

In my efforts to establish a viable network and build a market for my product, I've been traveling all over China from the very outset. Over the past few years I've been everywhere, from the forestry ministry in Beijing to the small co-op stations in country towns. I've focused on cultivating as wide a circle of friends as possible. And it hasn't been easy. I was something of a late starter in this business. I was getting in at a time when people were already very wary of private companies; they didn't trust them. To convince people that I was a viable businessman, I've had to live in big hotels, eat at good restaurants, and always get about in taxis, even if I lost money that way. You've got to win people's respect, convince them that you've got the money behind you to run a serious operation. Since the advent of the open-door policies, too many private entrepreneurs have been pushing fake, shoddy, and inferior goods. The negative impact on the state has been enormous, not to mention the near-universal public distrust of private businessmen. At the same time, this kind of thing threatens honest businessmen like me who operate according to the law. That's why I've had to emphasize providing top-quality goods and being absolutely trustworthy. My product has to be first-rate, and that's not all; my customers must have absolute confidence in me as well. They must be assured that they are giving their money to a reliable and honest man. The success or otherwise of a deal often depends on first impressions. I have to be adaptable; I have to be able to take things in my stride. No matter what, I can't afford to let people have any doubts about me, or speak ill of me behind my back if a deal falls through.

I don't have any dealings with other private businesspeople as such. People in today's marketplace are incredibly calculating and fiercely competitive and, personally speaking, I don't think I'm made for dealing with such individuals. I stick to dealing with state enterprises. They're run by government officials who don't have much of an idea about business. My prices are good, the quality is excellent, and I deliver right to the doorstep, so they'll buy from me. We deal strictly in cash, and the money comes directly from state allocations. There are no IOUs or deferred payments, and certainly no debt chain. It's just one transaction after another, steady and reliable. Naturally, I'm prepared to take a loss on their behalf when necessary, if they are in difficulties or strapped for cash. I'll even provide goods free of charge if the buyer really needs them. You have to keep your eye on the big picture; you can't afford to be shortsighted. You have to understand that in dealing with the state, you might take a loss in the short run, but in the long run they'll see you right.

On the eve of the 1990 Asian Games in Beijing, the authorities realized that they had underbudgeted for planting trees and the greening of the area around the car-racing circuit. To remedy the situation was going to require an operation that would not be just unprofitable for the company that won the contract—they'd actually end up taking a loss. Despite this, I took up the contract, and I donated trees worth some forty thousand yuan into the bargain. All those businessmen who can only think in terms of immediate profit thought I was a complete idiot, but I was willing to take it on because I had my own agenda: the racetrack was in Changping County, home to the world-famous Ming Tombs. Visitors to Beijing—both Chinese and foreign—all want to visit the tombs. I had my eye on replanting the area around the tombs, so when I took up the contract for the racing circuit I also put in a bid to plant trees along the whole length of the Spirit Path leading to the tombs. My proposal was to transplant seven-meter-high, fully grown Chinese pines. A successfully transplanted tree of that size is worth over thirteen thousand yuan, and even the most shortsighted businessman knows that's good money. Why did I win that contract? Because the state had confidence in me. They knew that I put the public good first and didn't bicker over petty profit-making during the Asian Games. I completed the second contract on time, providing the required number of trees in top condition, as I had promised. In fact, 99.8 percent of the trees survived, a new record for the transplantation of Chinese pines in Beijing.

Leaving profit aside, successfully fulfilling these two major contracts was proof positive of what our company can achieve. Just think of it:

"Have you been to Beijing?"

"Yes."

"Did you know that the pines along the Spirit Path on the way to the Thirteen Ming Tombs were planted by our company? And, by the way, we also did a major contract for the Asian Games."

That's far more convincing than any advertisements. The administrators of the most important tourist destination in China, as well as the organizers of the Asian Games, trusted me. How can you beat that?

We didn't submit a bid in either case. Superficially speaking, going through a bidding process might seem reliable and fair, but in reality the situation is quite different. Calling for bids puts you in a straitjacket from the get-go; it means that neither you nor the contractor has much room to move. The company that wins the contract is not necessarily going to give the contractor a good deal, and is not necessarily to be trusted. So, in cases like the one I've just described, competing companies are asked to submit a price, and the contractor makes a decision on the basis of various factors and considerations. It's not necessarily the lowest bidder that wins the contract.

Being willing to give your fellow businessmen an advantage, turning adversaries into friends; letting your opposite number make money before you do, or letting him gain the advantage—that is my unique contribution to doing business. People said no one does business like that and I was bound to fail, but I actually succeeded. And in fact it's the people who prattle on about business being like warfare and winner-takes-all who are the losers. Warfare? I'm doing business with the state; do you think I'm stupid enough to treat the state like the enemy? Business is business; and I have taken the initiative to pass on the benefit to the state—that is, the public. When it comes to profits, you shouldn't demarcate so sharply. And there is no need to do so. So whenever I start working with a new partner I concede the initial advantage to them. I don't even have to get an equal share; in fact I'm happy to let them get most of the profits. I've always done this, because next time around they'll let me take the major share of the profit. Whether you're dealing with the state or with an individual, it's the same thing. After all, state companies are not some abstraction; they're run by individuals. Furthermore, their immediate colleagues and business acquaintances will hear about how I do things, and they'll know that I am a very loyal person, I don't set much store by money, and I'm good at what I do—so there will be more people wanting to deal with me. Sometimes they even come and seek me out. But if you try to get the advantage over a new business associate, or cheat them outright, they certainly won't come back for more. And you'll end up getting a reputation as a crook, and that'll do you more harm than good.

A perfect example is those people who started out in private business around the time I did. Initially, they did much better than me, but gradually they found themselves being locked out of many deals and opportunities. They got a bad reputation. They hadn't had a particularly good social position to start with, and it got worse as they went on. They ended up completely broke. And they were always on edge because they were obsessed with making a short-term profit. Ask yourself: why have the landlords, rich peasants, reactionaries, and bad elements always been attacked in every political movement?[6] Because when they were on top, they behaved self-ishly. They cared about profits, not justice, and people were outraged by that. But enlightened men could always see the bigger picture; they saw making money for themselves as something intimately connected with the fortunes of China at a time of crisis. They cooperated closely with our party and have advanced hand in hand with us.

Businesspeople like me must on no account repeat the mistakes of the old landlords and moneyed classes of China, who pitted themselves against the nation, bringing the private and public into conflict, and inciting the opposition of the party and the people. There will be a cry for revenge. Public outrage is one of those things that you can't see or hear, but it is an objective reality nonetheless, and when the time comes it will find expression. The reason why most private businessmen don't dare let people see their wealth, apart from the reasons I gave earlier, is that they're scared, even if they're operating legally and above board. They're afraid that the state will treat them like pigs that it has been fattening up for slaughter. So we have more reason than ever to let the state profit from us, and it is on this basis that people like me can afford to get as fat as we want. We can get so fat that we'll be the fattest hogs of all, fat and sturdy like cows. Let's not forget that cows can be used for farming, and they can be milked. They're useful in a whole lot of other ways, so you can afford to look after them well. There's no need to slaughter them.

My slogan is "Put the public first, and allow others to profit." That's how our company has managed to keep in step with the needs of the state. That's how I got to where I am today and how I've been able to expand my influence. I've been advancing from one victory to the next, and when the crucial moment comes, my position will be unassailable.

In 1991, the Hebei provincial authorities banned all private trade in tree seed and revoked the licenses of all individual business operators. They did this for two obvious reasons. In the first place, the monopoly trade in tree seed is tax-exempt, and it was deemed inappropriate for individuals to be in competition with the state. Secondly, there were problems with the quality of the seed being traded by private concerns. Strictly speaking, of course, my company should have lost its license too, but the county government and local business bureau both argued that we were an exception.

6. *Di fu fan huai,* categories of "bad elements" under Maoism.

We were not just a model county business, but a provincial-level model private enterprise too, a true banner of the achievements of the reform policies. They couldn't ban us; on the contrary, they gave us further support. So there you have it; my obsession with promoting the public interest stood me in good stead at the crucial moment, and effectively protected me. And it's true that our company had contributed to the welfare of the county. We had provided seed for aerial planting at a 30 percent discount, in some cases 40 percent. The going rate for a ton of Chinese pine in Beijing is 78,000 yuan, and I sold it to the county for 52,000. Over the years I'd given up tens of thousands of yuan in profits. They knew I had sincerely put the public good ahead of my own profits. And so in that crisis they gave me their full support, and granted us official status as a forestry business enterprise. The people who had just been out for a profit and who had been fattening themselves at the expense of the state for years were all closed down. Why should the state make any effort to protect them? Ban them all and be done with it!

From that time on, I've had the only private company in the seven provinces of North China, including Beijing, that trades in tree seed.

Of course, I didn't purposely go out to buy myself political insurance. I've always had a market for my product, but on account of my approach there have been some pretty lean times. But I've never forgotten the fact that I'm just an insignificant individual, an entrepreneur who has been nurtured and protected by the public sector. I may have money now, but that's no excuse to abandon my philosophy or attempt to break free from the state sector that has supported me all along. I've always been mindful of the public good, and I've tailored my actions accordingly. Since our county government has limited funds, isn't it only right that I should curtail my own profits when dealing with it?

With regard to my future plans, let me first reiterate a point I made earlier: ours is a socialist country, and although a lid has been put on nitpicking debates about whether we remain socialist or are going capitalist since Comrade Xiaoping's Progress through the South, China is still a socialist nation. Thus individual enterprises cannot be seen in isolation from the public sphere. Without the support of the party and the people's government, my company, like all legally run private enterprises in China, couldn't survive for a moment, let alone have any hope of a future. Seen in this larger context, my own hopes for my company can be summed up in the following way:

One, we will contribute to the greening of the Motherland by transforming denuded mountains into wooded mountains. I want to change the backward state of affairs in which we have only 12 percent forest cover throughout China. Through the hard work of both this and the next generation, I hope that we will soon be able to overtake the greenest nation on earth, Canada, and achieve forest cover of over 60 percent.

Two, citizens have the right and the duty to participate in public affairs. We need to take practical steps to create a public image of socialist private business that reflects our sense of self-worth and independence, and to be active in the construction of the socialist legal system and spiritual civilization. Although we might not have the official position or rank enjoyed by state cadres, we must do our best to gain social recognition for our efforts and win the trust of the party and the people. We must not betray the faith that the party and the people have placed in us.

My family? They're all very supportive of my work. In the past my mother often used to say I was a complete no-hoper. But now she has no complaints. My father has always been encouraging and has given me great support in my efforts to engage in the greening of China for the benefit of the people. Okay, to be precise, my father is also involved in the forestry business. He has given me mainly practical and technical support, nothing else. All right, to be frank, my father is a state cadre; but he has never inquired about the details of my business, let alone allowed me to take advantage of his connections or position. Most of his support—no, all of it—has been purely moral support.

Why are you so fixated on my family connections? Have you been listening to what other people say behind my back? My father has absolutely nothing to do with my company. He is him, and I am me. So what if you want me to be more precise—even if I give you all the details, so what? All right then, my father also works with tree seed. Yes, what you heard is true: he's in charge of the state-run forests of the province.

22

Down to Earth

Reflections of a Former Red Guard

At the height of the Cultural Revolution in the late 1960s, in response to Chairman Mao's call, nearly twenty million "educated urban youths" were settled in villages and on farms throughout China.

When Deng Xiaoping returned to the political stage ten years later, the majority of these no-longer-young people returned to the cities. It was a prelude to an era of economic reform.

By the 1990s, some of the former educated urban youths had become generals, government ministers, professors, deputies in the National People's Congress, even millionaires. Various products, restaurants, books, films, and music productions now catered to the nostalgia of the rusticated urban youths. Organizations such as the Armed Services League, the Great Northern Wilderness Urban Youth Club, and the Bittersweet Memory Foundation were established. Even words and expressions related to that age of Maoism became trademarks.

He left Beijing more than three decades ago to settle in the Shanxi countryside. Of the millions of young people who were sent to this area of China, he is one of a handful who decided to stay on.

What do you want me to say? It's not like I'm a radio, where you turn it on and it'll never stop talking. You've come all this way because of some bullshit story. The scenery isn't even any good around here. You're wasting your time.

I'm the only one in my whole class who stayed on. Back then, they shipped us down here by the truckload. The trains were packed to the brim as well. Must have been two to three thousand of us in this county alone.

Eventually, the others all left. Some got promoted out of the countryside and became officials; the ones who didn't ended up getting back to the cities one way or another too.

We arrived in 1969. A whole generation has grown up since then. Last year I told my son, "You're the age your dad was when he first came here." He doesn't get that part of my history at all. He asked me whether I had come drifting in with the tides of itinerant workers you see everywhere these days. Our county produces coal, and the smaller coal mines have become ghettos for drifting workers.

My former classmates think I'm an oddball. They think the reason I refuse to go back to the city is that I'm against the reforms and I disagree with the new policies. But I'm a peasant. What right do I have to disagree with anything? They think things are far more complicated than they really are. Even now they're still trying to help me escape from the countryside. They say that urban household registration isn't as strict as it used to be and that it won't be hard to find me a job. But I don't need their help. If I'd really wanted to go, I'd have left years ago.

When we first came, they were just like me. We all vowed that the heavens could rend and the earth split open, but we'd stay settled in the countryside for the rest of our lives. But vows are only words; what you say is one thing, but what you do is another matter altogether. You can't shackle people to their vows. Okay, I might have stayed on here, but that's not because I'd vowed to do so. I don't have any grand justification really. It's just that I love the mountains here, and I find Beijing too noisy. It's not worth going back. I never argue with my old classmates. The sight of them is enough to irritate the hell out of me; do I have to fight with them as well? Don't people say that reform is about pluralism? Doesn't that mean I can be disgusted by their lifestyle if I want to?

They don't agree with me. "Our troubles ended long ago. How can we relax while you're still suffering here?" Sounds ridiculous, doesn't it? But that's exactly what they say.

I remember how, soon after we first got here, everyone planted a "taking-root tree." We all thought we'd be just like those trees and take root here in the countryside forever. Except for the ones that were eaten by the sheep or trampled by horses, they grew into good timber. Some years back when the commune was dissolved, people cut down all those long-neglected trees on the sly for building materials. The one I planted isn't there anymore, either. I cut it down myself to repair my courtyard gate. All that talk back then about "sharing suffering" and "heroic intentions" was a pile of shameless garbage.

I come from an old academic family, teachers for three generations. We were important people once. My mom was the principal of my primary school. I scored 199.5 in the high-school entrance exams. A score of 196 or above was enough to get you into a key school, so I was doing pretty well. In the normal course of things I would have followed in my father's footsteps and gone on to university. He was a famous professor. But events didn't follow the normal course; we had the Cultural Revolution instead. It didn't have much of an effect on me. On reflection, I guess I was quite happy; I was okay about the whole thing. I was sick and tired of school, so when the revolution came along I thought at least it meant I didn't have to worry about exams anymore. Life was hard after I came here to Shanxi, but I was psychologically prepared for everything that happened. During the Great Link-Ups in the early winter of 1966, a group of us trekked from Beijing to Yan'an, lodging with peasants on the way.[1] We learned a lot about what was going on. We came to realize that life in the countryside was incredibly harsh, very different from the cities. It was as though there were two countries in China. You could say it was one system, two countries; and it's much worse now than it was back then.[2]

Once we'd moved here, we set up a collective household. We shared everything, all the food as well as all of the misery. If someone got a parcel from home, they would divide the goodies up with everyone else. It was primitive communism. But that was only in the beginning. Gradually things changed, and everyone began setting aside small stashes of private property. They hid the good food and stuff away so they could enjoy it alone. We kept it up for quite a few years, until things just fell apart. We eventually split up and lived separately. It's like deaf people setting off fire-

1. *Da chuanlian.* The link-ups dated from mid-1966, when Red Guards started traveling around China on foot, by train and by bus, to exchange experiences with other Red Guard groups and carry the message of the Cultural Revolution to outlying cities and the countryside. As they were allowed to travel free of charge, these journeys were the first taste of freedom for many. Some Red Guard groups walked to the wartime Communist base of Yan'an in Shaanxi Province, in western China, in emulation of the heroes who took part in the Long March of the mid-1930s.

2. "One system, two countries" *(yizhi liangguo)* is a satirical reprise of the official Deng Xiaoping line on the mainland takeover of Hong Kong in 1997, after which he declared China would be "one country, two systems" *(yiguo liangzhi),* that is, a socialist mainland and a capitalist Hong Kong.

crackers—they give up and leave because nothing seems to be happening. The head of our household was a former classmate of mine, a model student of Mao Zedong Thought and a total hypocrite. He didn't stay in the countryside for long, but he didn't go back to Beijing. He's ended up as a bureaucrat in Taiyuan;[3] he always was a member of the conniving local gentry. A few years back, Beijing gave out awards to the Far-Flung Sons and Daughters, you know, the people who'd stayed on in the countryside. They actually gave him a medal as a representative of the urban youths who hadn't returned to the capital! We were represented by ten delegates in that particular farce. The joke was that not one of them was actually engaged in agricultural work in the countryside any more.

Before they let everyone go back to the cities in 1979, I never had a chance. All the opportunities, job allocations, and university admissions passed me by because my family had been something in the past, and so I had a bad class background. The only way someone like me could expect to get back home in those days was on account of special circumstances, for example, if my parents had no other children to take care of them. Trouble was, my elder sister was in Beijing. On top of that, I was as strong as an ox, so I couldn't apply for leave to return on the grounds of ill health. When the chance to go back finally came around in 1979, I didn't give it much thought. By that time I'd been here for ten years, and I'd come to love this part of the world. So I decided not to bother.

You probably don't believe me when I say that I just didn't want to make the effort to go back. By staying here I didn't have to get into all of that business of wanting things. My life here was okay, but if I returned to Beijing I'd have to look for a house, a job, a network of relationships, and I'd have to suck up to people all over the place. It would all be too much trouble. Besides, once I'd finally settled in, I'd have to try and arrange for my wife and son to relocate as well, and that would mean more bootlicking. What was so great about Beijing? It wasn't worth it. My wife was a high-school student in the city of Datong before being sent here in the Cultural Revolution. She was a farmer for a few years before she became a King of the Children,[4] a teacher in the local primary school. The rules about relo-

3. The capital of Shanxi Province.

4. *Haizi wang,* a term for teacher, is also the title of a famous story by Ah Cheng about a rusticated youth turned teacher that was subsequently made into a film by Chen Kaige in 1987.

cating urban youth meant that she wouldn't have been allowed to go to Beijing with me; our son wouldn't have been eligible to go either, as the policy says that children's registration follows their mothers. It's not easy to establish a home in the first place, and to break it all up just so I could get back to Beijing was never really an option. After all, Beijing's not heaven.

I was a tractor driver when the party document about splitting up the communes was issued. I got a piece of land when the contract system was introduced because the people in the village didn't think of me as an urban youth any more. They felt I was one of them, so they gave me some land as well. The year before last, I took out a loan to buy a big East Wind truck and started transporting coal out from the mines. I'm not all that well-off, but it's not too bad, either. I'd say I'm somewhere in the middle. But then again, everyone says that these days. From scrap collectors to millionaires, they all say they're just doing okay. There's always someone better off and someone who's worse off. So I suppose it's true. Like they say, Deng Xiaoping is at the top, and the army recruits are at the bottom. Everyone else is in the middle.

My parents have no say in what I do. I'm not going back, and they can't do anything about it. They care more about me than I do about them. After all, even vicious tigers don't eat their own cubs. I'm just not all that keen on them—they've always been scared of getting into trouble on one hand and concerned to make their mark on the other. They've spent their lives working on their little schemes. All they've succeeded in doing is showing me how not to live. Whenever I think about them, I know I don't want to go back. So what if I achieved something back there? At best I'd end up being just like them.

In 1990, they introduced a new policy that said urban youths who'd stayed in the countryside were allowed to send one child back to their home city. My boy could have got a Beijing residency permit. My old classmates got all worked up about it. They told me I should really send my son to Beijing to get a proper education, otherwise I'd ruin his future. What rubbish! What were they on about? Did they really want me to break up my own family? It's not that I'm ungrateful, but there isn't anything for him in the city. What difference does it make whether my son is educated or not? He'll be doing just fine if he can recognize a few written characters so he doesn't get lost. Anyway, if my boy wants to go to Beijing, he doesn't need me to send him. Don't they say things are different nowadays? He can buy himself a train ticket and go to Beijing as an itinerant worker if he wants to.

I still get back to Beijing once in a while. That's where my parents live, after all. Besides, I have business around there sometimes. When I go on a long haul in that direction, I'll stop over in Beijing; there's nothing wrong with going and having a look at the place. But I'm not a native any more. I feel more like an out-of-towner. When I'm driving around on those over-passes, I never know how to get off; I don't know which exit to take, and I'm afraid to stop. Even so, when I do go back, I don't mind scoring stuff from my parents and sisters. They're rich enough. If they want to give me an old TV set or something else that they don't need anymore, I'll take it because I'm poor. But I never let them help me out with my finances. If I'm short of cash I'd rather get a loan from a bank or the credit union. I'd never ask them for a handout. I don't want anything to do with their money. I'm the unfilial son in our family; always have been. If I did accept money from them, things would get all complicated sooner or later.

I really don't have any particular views or complaints. Making speeches about politics or the economy is something for people who are keen on that sort of thing. They have the time and the inclination for it. Most people are like me, pretty far removed from all that useless business. It's a merciless world, as vicious as a fire or flood. The further you keep away from all that, the better.

"At sunrise I work, at sunset I rest. What does the emperor have do with me?" Even Confucius couldn't dispute the truth of that.

"Avoid the countryside during minor unrest, avoid the city during major upheavals. Maintain a steady heart, and you'll be at ease."

23

Just One Party

A Challenge from the Grass Roots

The friend who introduced me to him said: "He may not want to talk to you, but it's worth having a chat with him, even if he won't go on the record. He really is an incredible character."

Shanxi Province

I graduated from Taiyuan Agricultural College in 1982. I was one of the few students who actually went there in order to study agriculture, not just to escape the countryside by getting a college education. I didn't have any particular ambitions; I just loved the land and wanted to be able to work in agriculture. It's not as dirty as working in industry. And my family have been farmers for generations, so we didn't think there was anything wrong with my coming back to work on the land after I finished college.

I was given a state-allocated job on Red Star Farm, a subsidiary business run under the auspices of the State Farm Bureau. I started out as an apprentice accountant in the office. We weren't far from the place Zheng Yi wrote about in his story *Old Well*.[1] The film based on the novel was very realistic. Water's always been scarce in the limestone mountain regions of Shanxi. It's as precious as oil. In the film, they finally overcome the lack of water by successfully sinking a well; in reality, though, that hardly ever happens. But films are idealized views of life, after all. To work a farm with no water means

1. The nationally popular novel *Old Well* depicted the scramble for water among Chinese farmers in the northwest. It was made into a film by Wu Tianming of the Xi'an Film Studio in 1987.

you're confronted with serious poverty, poverty so grinding that most people can't even imagine it. The National Agricultural Policy Research Center conducted a survey in which they found that some peasant households have less than ten yuan worth of possessions: you can have a family of five that only has two bed quilts, one wok, and three bowls. There are even girls in their early teens who don't have pants to wear, and that's not uncommon. But there's actually an even more typical thing that they didn't notice. Even the way poor people speak is different. The most common greeting you find among farmers in North China is "Have you eaten?" It's the equivalent of saying "How are you?" in the city. But people around here don't say "eat"; they ask, "Have you drunk?" That's because the relationship people have with food here is one of drinking, not of eating. All they have is a watery gruel made out of corn or millet that they drink. When they want to praise you, the peasants around here say, "This guy's okay. He eats dry food, and his shit's solid." To be able to eat real rice and not just gruel means that you're someone important.

The papers criticized the director of the film of *Old Well* for deliberately seeking out a backwater in the mountains so he could make a film that would ridicule China and curry favor with foreigners. I thought that was ridiculous, so I wrote to the *People's Daily* and said that where I live, you don't have to go searching for poverty because it's there wherever you look. Though the director *was* prejudicial in the location he chose: you could say he searched out a relatively prosperous place; remember, the peasants in the movie are rich enough to donate furniture and TVs to cover the costs of sinking the well. In most of the impoverished districts, like the places around our state farm, you could line up the peasants and threaten to shoot them, and they still wouldn't be able to hand over any furniture, or even a length of electrical wire, let alone a TV set.

Okay, so I knew they'd never publish my letter. Anyway, the people who read the party press don't want to know about things like that. But I wrote to them anyway. I like stirring up trouble.

There's been constant armed conflict between villages and clans in this area for over a century, and it's all been over water. The clashes have been vicious and bloody, and neither the Communists nor the Nationalists before them have ever been able to put a stop to them. The only way you'll stop the violence is if you can find enough water for everyone. It's ridiculous for the authorities to think they can prevent it by posting official announcements or sending in work teams to talk to people. Ideological propaganda isn't going to do anything; even if you rounded up all the ring-leaders and punished all the murderers, you still wouldn't solve anything. It's not about clan tensions or a clash of belief systems, let alone family disputes or factional feuds. This is the most primitive kind of warfare, a life-and-death struggle for survival, a battle for basic resources.

I suppose I should give you a short history of the Red Star Farm. It's actually the product of policy makers getting it wrong again and again. It is the perfect counterexample to Mao Zedong's dictum that "under the leadership of the Communist Party, any and all human miracles are possible." This area was originally called the Great Desolate Slopes, and people have been living here for generations, although no one was ever able to do much with the land. Basically, it's always been a wasteland. Why? It's obvious. If the authorities had any sense at all, they would have realized there was a reason for the desolation: there's no water. However, in its wisdom, the party declared that the absence of water wasn't a problem. As Chairman Mao said, "Human beings can conquer nature!"[2] So back in the 1950s, before I was even born, the air force fenced off the area and decided to build a combat-ready airfield. They sank dozens of wells until finally they hit a bit of water. The well was 280 meters deep and could only pump a few liters per hour. It provided just enough drinking water, but the soldiers had to wait their turn to get water for washing. They called it the August First Well,[3] and it's still the only viable source on this farm.

For every meter of cement they laid for the airport, they needed dozens of liters of water. Since the well water wasn't enough, they had to build a road through the mountains and bring water in by truck from forty kilometers away. The runway was built in the shape of a huge X. Originally it was supposed to be four thousand meters long, but they ran out of money after the first thousand meters. Everyone was penniless then, not just the army. It was during the Three Years of Natural Disasters.[4] There wasn't even enough food to drink.

The air force must have been going crazy with hunger because the bas-

2. *Ren ding sheng tian,* originally a line in a Song-dynasty poem used by Mao to extol the power of human volition.

3. 1 August 1927 marked the official founding of the military arm of the Communist Party, later the People's Liberation Army.

4. The years 1959 to 1961, during which the failures of the radical Communist policies of the Great Leap Forward combined with bad weather to result in mass famine in the countryside.

tards gave up on the airport and tried to turn the place into a grain-producing farm. They stuck it out for the first winter and managed to clear about two square kilometers of ground that they planted with dwarf corn. At least they chose the right variety; it's drought-resistant and can survive on rainfall alone. Dwarf corn's very low-maintenance as well; it'll give you the same yield whether you look after it or not. There is one problem, though: it's a low-yield crop, and it's not particularly resistant to disease and pests. It's hard to harvest and especially hard to husk, and when you grind it you end up with a lot of husk along with the grain. If you don't remove the husks, it's horrible to eat, but it takes a lot of winnowing to get rid of them. Originally, none of this should have been a problem; it was never meant for human consumption. The low yield and the husking problem didn't matter because it was only used for fodder. Normally you'd just cut the whole lot down before it was ripe, leaf and stalk and all, and feed it to the animals.

But there was the air force, marooned on the Great Desolate Slopes with no food to drink, or water for that matter. All they had was this inedible dwarf corn. When the economy finally began to pick up in the early 1960s, they decided to abandon the airfield. Now they were faced with a couple of choices. They could have given up on farming altogether, or "let things lie fallow," as the euphemism has it. In other words, they could have dumped the place and moved on. Alternatively, they could make an effort to divert water and develop the area. Instead of taking the logical course of action and abandoning the whole project, those idiots decided to divert water and build a farm. They were going to "establish a huge granary in preparation for war and want." Remember the slogans back then? "Be self-reliant, struggle hard amid difficulties, turn heaven and earth on their heads"; "The army must also operate factories, farms, and schools, and must also persist in denouncing the bourgeoisie." Mao Zedong gave the party an ideological weapon all right. Without it, how could they have been stupid enough to try something like that?

They decided they'd use the water from a new dam that was being built up in the mountains. But it was only after the dam was finished and slowly filling up that they woke up to the fact that this is Shanxi. It's not Jiangxi or Guangxi, where you have a high annual rainfall. Here we only get a little over two hundred millimeters a year. That wasn't going to be nearly enough for their farm. So now they were forced to build a series of pumping stations that would get the water up here into the new dam and then out of the dam onto the farmland over ten kilometers away. Of course, to get the water here they had to build a canal, actually more like a river suspended in the sky.

To construct the canal, they had to dig channels through the hills and construct an aqueduct over the valleys, in some places dozens of meters high. It crossed the road at two points, and instead of building culverts, they decided to use two inverted siphons. Now, I don't know much about moving water, but specialists tell me that they could tell at a glance that the canal was designed by air-force engineers because they applied the same principles that you'd use for constructing an airfield. Who knows how much money they wasted on that? They were insane. But the most ridiculous thing of all was that they didn't build a reservoir here at the farm. If the water wasn't being released from the big dam, they had to rely on the August First Well. They reckon that this tactic was in keeping with the principle of "pursuing frugality for the sake of the revolution."[5] But if you ask me, I'd say they had spent all their budget on the siphons. It took them five years to build the Good Fortune Canal that would supposedly bring us the water of prosperity. Once that was finished, they had to keep the farm going no matter what.

That's the first half of the story about this place. So why did I take on farming here? The answer lies in the next installment in the history of the Red Star Farm.

The Red Star could never be classified as a model production unit. It wasn't even an "advanced work unit." Mao Zedong selected a model farm at Shashi Gully in Hebei, about one hundred kilometers east of Beijing, and called on all five hundred million Chinese peasants to emulate it. Back here, meanwhile, once the army had its "Good Fortune water" on tap, they planted wheat and White Horse corn. They tell me that the wheat crop did okay, but the corn was wiped out by pests. Long-stalked crops always suffer badly from pests here at Red Star, and they infect the neighboring villages as well. We seem to be something of a local source of pestilence. Anyway, they planted dwarf corn seven years running. They were shortsighted all the way. Despite all the cross-fertilization between crops, they kept harvesting and sowing straight away, keeping some of the better stuff for seed for the next season. Of course the quality of the crops deteriorated rapidly; yields and resistance to pests also fell off dramatically. They didn't even burn

5. *Jieyue nao geming.*

the stalks or let them ferment. Apart from taking some home to be used as fuel for cooking fires, they left the rest in the fields. It was the same old method they've been using since the days of Emperor Qin Shihuang.[6] It's amazing that the place didn't end up completely infested!

During the Cultural Revolution the army had to go off to participate in the Three Supports and Two Militaries,[7] so they handed Red Star over to the State Council in Beijing, and it was designated a May Seventh Cadre School.[8] Subsequently, the State Council bundled off a whole ministry's worth of cadres to the place for reeducation, or rather for labor reform. The cadre school lasted for seven years, and then two momentous things occurred. First, to increase the area of arable land on the farm, the cadres managed to break up that thousand-meter-long cement runway without any tools to speak of. Those Foolish Old Men at the cadre school actually moved a whole airfield![9] The second momentous thing was that they also managed to plant a season's worth of rice! Of course, no one had calculated how much it would cost to produce rice using water from the Good Fortune Dam. Just counting the money spent on maintenance and repairs on the dam water, it ended up costing at least ten times more than it cost in the city. And they thought they could turn the place into paddy fields!

As the cadre schools were wound down and more and more people were sent back to the cities [in the early to mid-1970s], large tracts of land that they'd put under cultivation were abandoned. By the time the cadre school itself was closed, over half the fields were lying fallow. This was another

6. From the second century B.C.E.

7. *Sanzhi liangjun.* The army was deployed to support the groups in favor of the Cultural Revolution, known as the "revolutionary left," while helping to maintain agricultural and industrial production. This practice was the result of a number of directives from Mao Zedong in 1967, when the army was used to reestablish order in the country following the chaos of 1966 and early 1967.

8. Cadre schools were set up in agricultural communes and state farms during the Cultural Revolution, ostensibly for the labor reeducation of government-employed white-collar workers. Mao Zedong's directive on the need for cadres to engage in manual labor was taken from a letter addressed to Lin Biao and dated 7 May 1966, hence the name. The first cadre school was established in 1968.

9. The Foolish Old Man was a legendary figure who, by dint of his own effort and with the help of his descendants, achieved the seemingly impossible task of removing two mountains that stood in front of his house. Mao Zedong acclaimed the determination of the Foolish Old Man in an address to party members on 11 June 1945. People memorized Mao's essay about this story as a model work during the Cultural Revolution.

opportunity for a clear-thinking leader to make the decision to give up on the place. For all those years it had only ever been a farm in name anyway, and closing it down wouldn't have created any problems at all. More to the point, no one would have cared less if it was abandoned. Aren't the Communists particularly scared of throwing people out of work? Well, no one would have lost a job, either. But those dim-witted bureaucrats in the agricultural bureau didn't think that way. They thought to themselves, look, we've got the Good Fortune Dam and all the buildings constructed by the cadre school, not to mention acres of arable land that we've been given for free. It's a bargain. What possible reason could there be to give up on the place?

So they sent in three regiments of workers plus logistical support, that's well over five hundred agricultural workers, and set up the Red Star State Farm.

When I arrived here the place had been limping along for over six years, losing money from the start. The authorities were determined to keep the show on the road, so in the seventh year they decided they could save the place by introducing a wage system that linked farmers' income to their actual agricultural output. They were busy implementing this new scheme when I was allocated a job here after graduation; it was my job to tally up all the accounts and assign work hours. The system they had put in place was the exact opposite of everything I had learned about agricultural management. I knew full well that in a large state farm like Red Flag, only complete bastards or halfwits would try to use that kind of model.

And this is where water comes back into the picture again. Since the moment the Good Fortune water appeared on the scene, the authorities have been engaged in an endless struggle to keep the local peasants from stealing it. All along the new canal, the old rivalries and feuds between families and villages over water all but came to an end. Now they had Good Fortune water, they realized that all those other piddling little sources of water just weren't worth fighting over. Now they were after the big one, and neither the army nor the cadre school could keep them at bay. That was back in the days when the peasants were still scared of the state, so all they were doing was stealing water. They made holes in the aqueducts or added their own runoff canals. Whenever water was released from the big dam, patrols had to be sent out to keep an eye on them and repair holes they had made. The guerrilla warfare continued for over a decade. Over time the peasants became more daring, especially when the place was taken over by the agricultural bureau. The peasants despised the agricultural workers employed on the land. They'd been afraid of the soldiers and cadres, but that was because they were the government, the rulers; but they thought of the agricultural workers as just another bunch of stinking farm laborers, and they weren't afraid of them at all. They started stealing water right out in the open, and they were prepared to fight to the death if you attempted to seal the holes they made. When agricultural land was parceled out into private lots, they went absolutely crazy, blatantly making big holes in the canal. Pretty soon, the water flow was cut off and not a drop was reaching us here. We'd only get water once they'd taken as much as they wanted.

The agricultural workers were afraid of the peasants, though, and they didn't dare get into conflict with them because they knew that they had nothing to fear, nothing to lose. When everything you own in the world isn't worth much more than ten yuan, when you get involved in a fight over property you take it very seriously. Agricultural workers, on the other hand, are state employees with wages. No matter how poor they may be they've still got some property, and they really care for their own skins. For the peasants, stealing water is a matter of survival; why should the agricultural workers bother risking their lives to fight them off? To the state farmers it was all the same whether there was water for the state farm or not, because they'd get paid even if they didn't harvest a single grain.

All of that changed when they introduced the new wage regime in 1983. If the workers didn't produce their quotas of grain, their point average would be low, and they wouldn't get paid enough. So I told them that unless they started making some serious efforts to protect the canal and prevent the peasants from stealing water, we'd all be bankrupt by the fall.

I believed that the only way we'd achieve a sustainable peace was to have an all-out battle with the peasants and decide the issue once and for all. So I organized the workers into a brigade and then, just before the water was released, we moved along the length of the canal fighting off every group of peasants we came across. At first they thought we'd only try to block the holes, and the minute we encountered resistance we'd be scared off. It came as a complete surprise to them when we stood our ground and fought back. Not that we gave them much time to wake up to what was happening; we simply charged right in swinging pickaxes and left a trail of wounded and bleeding peasants in our wake. Although there were a lot of bones broken, it did give us about three years of peace.

Because of our blitzkrieg style, the peasants could only ever muster a few dozen people in a confrontation, and it didn't occur to them that they should all join forces. From their point of view, a gang of agricultural workers had decided to attack the Zhang family village one day and the Li family village the next. It didn't occur to them that the agricultural workers had launched a campaign against the peasants in general. We'd beaten the crap out of them before they ever got around to thinking about an organized opposition. All their old family and village rivalries continued to fester away; they were like a plate of loose sand,[10] a complete mess. They lacked leadership; they needed a Mao Zedong.

But they did know how to complain to the officials. They tried to make a bit of money by claiming compensation for the people who had been injured. Since the farm leadership was afraid of being forced to take responsibility, they hung me out to dry. The court found me guilty of hooligan activities and gang warfare. I was sentenced to eighteen months' labor reform, though in fact I only served a year.

Arresting me was not the way to stop the peasants from pilfering water, though my campaign gave us a few years' respite. After that, things started getting out of hand again, and eventually, in 1988, the peasants decided to blow up the aqueduct. That put an end to the water supply for everyone. This is all hearsay, but they tell me that Red Star Farm is still operating, though most of the land has been abandoned. A few plots have been divvied up among the farmers, and the rest is planted with dwarf corn that is used as malted feed for pigs. You can imagine how many pigs five hundred farming families would need to keep from going broke.

That's all I can tell you about the history of Red Star and my involvement with the place. During that year I spent in the labor-reform team, I had lots of time to think through my experiences at Red Star. I came to the conclusion that this was the problem: despite the introduction of the reform policies, no fundamental changes had been made to the governing structure of the place. Once I had realized this, I was even more determined than ever to set up and run my own operation.

Confidence can only come from two things: either from your own abilities or from the sheer incompetence of your opponent. Although I wasn't particularly strong, I did take the measure of my opponents, and I knew they were no match for me. So, as soon as I got out of jail in 1984, I put my

10. *Yi pan sansha*, an expression used by Sun Yat-sen to describe the supposed inability of Chinese people to unite and fight for a cause.

plan into operation. Instead of hanging around looking for work in the city, I came straight back to the countryside, and over a six-month period I organized a group of about twenty peasant families. Some were related to each other, and some weren't. Anyway, our plan was to start up our own cooperative farm, with shares allocated on the basis both of the size of the land each family committed to the project and on the amount of labor people were willing to contribute.

This was just about the time that the old village structure was splitting apart. Some people simply gave up the land they'd been allotted under the contract system, when the communes had been dissolved, and were getting into things like local transportation, starting up small businesses, becoming itinerant laborers, whatever. Anyway, they'd stopped working on the land. So I suggested they invest in our farm by giving us their land not as part of a rental agreement but as their share in a co-op. The peasants who'd decided to leave the land anyway were happy to do this. Not only would they get a small dividend every year, but—more important—they would still have a connection to the village, even though they'd left the land. They felt that they still had a base in their home soil. That took care of the problem of land. As for the production materials, the equipment that we needed, well, you'll recall that when land was allocated to families after the breaking up of the communes, all capital goods and workshops, like farm machinery, mills and so on, were also contracted out to individuals. Most of the people who got these contracts had special connections: they were people who didn't have to "drink their food." They didn't necessarily care about making a go of it, and by the mid-1980s many of them were so deeply in debt that they didn't know what to do with the equipment on their hands. Okay, I said, hand everything over to us, and we'll give you a share in our co-op. You'll get an annual dividend without having had anything to do with the actual running of the business. The only other things we needed were farmhands. I told people that if they contributed their land and labor they'd have plenty to do. Their labor would be equivalent to a share in the co-op, too, but once they became shareholders, the land they were working would be part of our co-op. They'd be wrong if they thought the land was theirs under state contract.

That's right, I was purposely vague about the ownership of capital goods right from the start. I don't think we have to get into all of that here, do we?

The peasants whose primary investment was labor felt that the setup worked pretty much in their favor. They figured that anyone who was going to get rich out of the reforms had already done so. They themselves couldn't, so they felt very vulnerable. No matter what happened, they'd come to realize that they'd be better off in some kind of collective in which they shared the good—and the bad—times with other people. The people who'd been renting out their land also thought our co-op was a good deal. It was better than letting the land lie fallow, and they were getting a share and a split of the dividends without having to work for it. As for the party authorities, they knew exactly what was going on, and they were very wary of what I was up to. They had done it themselves, after all—they had gone through the process of integrating government administration and economic management in an earlier era,[11] and they had their suspicions that this was not a simple and unambiguous economic cooperative, so they refused to let us register. At least the party didn't accuse me of breaking the law, though; they simply turned a blind eye. They took the view that we were all individual farmers who were free to collaborate if we wanted to. They called our operation a mutual-aid group and washed their hands of us.

I've just worked through the final accounts for our grain crops this fall, and I can tell you that the basic laborers are earning an average of around one thousand yuan. That's not a bad average, mind you, as farmers all heave a sigh of relief once the autumn harvest is in, knowing that there will be food to drink in the coming year. The superiority of a co-op farm like this is particularly evident during the harvest. We harvest collectively, then transport and husk the grain using our own machinery. Or, as the peasants put it, "We're using the old communal methods to farm for ourselves. This is the way to do it!"

After we brought in the first crop, the farmers were wary. "Do we have to repair the water system now?" they said. They were worried because in the days of the communes, everyone was forced to do maintenance work on the water system during the winter months. People were still haunted by the memory of all the work they put into collective projects back then. I told them we could get by without any repairs for a few years yet, though that didn't mean they could afford to hibernate like they have over the past few winters. I set things up so we could all go into town to earn some money stoking furnaces. None of these people had ever got anywhere in the

11. The integration of government administration and economic management, or *zheng-she heyi,* was a policy used to create party-dominated agricultural co-ops that were eventually converted into people's communes in the late 1950s.

past because they were scared, but now they were in a collective and felt brave enough to go to Taiyuan, the provincial capital. People in the city welcome laborers like us, and there's no lack of seasonal jobs. Every winter the bigger work units had to hire a dozen men to stoke the boilers for heating, but they generally avoided itinerant workers because they tend to be unreliable; there was no telling when they might just pack up and leave. Around the Spring Festival holiday season, smack in the middle of winter, they'd all disappear to be with their families. But as we were seasonal laborers, people were happy to hire us. They didn't have to keep an eye on us, either, because I was the foreman and there was nothing for them to worry about.

This past year I've kept back a little over half of the money we've made. It's the most we've earned so far—thirty thousand yuan, in fact. That's not bad, is it? It's enough to buy seventy tons of dwarf-corn seed. But I've used it to set up a winery.

Yes, the farmers were happy with the decision. The more we hold back for reinvestment, the more their shares are worth, and the more we can invest in expansion. As they say, it's no use letting meat rot in the wok. What would they do with the money if I gave it all out? Probably just hide it somewhere at home and worry about thieves stealing it all the time.

The general political situation in China in the fall of 1986 was pretty good, and I finally worked out how we should be going about things. It turned out to be relatively easy to get our co-op registered with the authorities as a private company, and that's how we turned ourselves into an agroindustrial business conglomerate, with me acting as the legal representative. Although on paper we are using an industrial business to support our agricultural work, the real aim is to give our private farm some legal status.

We're in our tenth year of operation now, and we've got 256 families working the land. The area under cultivation is larger than Red Star Farm at its height, and that's not counting over ten square kilometers of forest, three factories, two shops, a hospital, an old people's home—oh, and that's right . . . a party branch. I look after that as well.

Yes, sure, if that's the way you want to put it: the farmers are actually farmhands who are paid a wage by the farm. They've got a small share in the place, but they're not actually in partnership with me.

The only real pressure I've felt over the past decade was back in 1991, though it all ended up as a bit of a joke and we all had a good laugh about it. That was the year in which the leftists had their best chance to launch a counterattack on the reforms and implement their own agendas.[12] There was even talk about "carrying out the struggle against peaceful evolution from the economic front first" in Beijing. Just the hint of a change at the top was enough to set off a chain reaction in the lower echelons. There were people in our district government who had always resented me because they felt I'd usurped their power, but up until then they'd only muttered under their breath. Now they openly announced that it was time to settle the score. They said I was involved in illegal activities and that I was an old-style landlord in a Western suit. They even said I wanted to take revenge on the Communist Party for the murder of my father. It was just at this critical juncture that a few academics and bureaucrats were sent down from Beijing to "evaluate" the farm. Although they said they were here to investigate and study the general situation, I knew they were up to no good and were out to make trouble for me.

But I was so naive! I still hadn't seen through the Communist Party. I'd overlooked one crucial fact: the people sent from the big central yamen were even more moronic than our local bureaucrats! Dealing with them was like being caught in some kind of time warp; they analyzed everything according to their own logic, and they'd lost the ability to think for themselves. You see, being good socialists, they reasoned that anything that was "an organization engaged in collective activities," like our farm, was by definition superior to an individual enterprise. They reckoned that collectives were "the one and only way to develop a healthy socialist rural economy." So their official evaluation of my farm was that an economic conglomerate such as this "provides an efficacious model for discouraging unemployed agricultural producers from leaving the land, as well as being an efficacious means for the resolution of certain issues concerning the reinforcement and strengthening of grassroots-level political stability in the countryside during the present phase of deepening the reform and open-door process"!

I could have died laughing! Now suddenly the landlord in Western dress was "an efficacious model" of socialist enterprise. Those people in the district government just had to shut up. For decades now they had made one mistake after another. They'd virtually never got it right. It wasn't a matter

12. Following the Beijing Massacre of 4 June 1989, the political struggles in the Chinese government led for a time to antireformist leaders' regaining some of the ground they had lost during the late 1980s. Supporting Maoist-style socialist policies, these leftists *(zuopai)*, as they were dubbed, attempted to overturn, or at least hinder, many of the economic reforms.

of individual aberrations, it was the product of the system itself. The system simply has to be reformed.

I've always been of the opinion that revolution is not the best method for carrying out a systemic change in a country in which over 80 percent of the population works on the land. Sure, it's easy to overthrow an emperor, but what's really hard is keeping another idiot from trying to take the throne. If you really want to carry out systemic change in China, you must be able to build up a base in the countryside as well as take charge of the economic levers. According to Archimedean mathematics, there's no way you can find a fulcrum from which a lever can move the whole planet, but here in the countryside we have just such a fulcrum. We can use the leverage of our economic system to move the whole of China.

I can say things now that I would never have admitted back in 1991. What my farm is really doing is creating bankrupt peasants, or what the big boys from Beijing would call "unemployed agricultural producers." I encourage peasants to give their contracted land to work on our farm, and in our factories and shops. They come to me as landowners but end up as mere laborers, new members of the proletariat. At the same time I am undermining the old grassroots political setup, or rather I have already undermined it. I've altered its organizational structure, especially insofar as it used to function from top to bottom, with party and county bosses appointing their political representatives at the lower levels.

Intensive farm management is the only way you can run an operation like this. I'm confident that in this regard at least I'm in an unassailable position. As for my real aims, that's simple: gradually, I want to see the type of farm that I'm running at the moment expanding to become a mini-society, and that will be a transitional stage on the way to creating an autonomous village, which will be ruled and owned by the people, and which will also profit the people. I want to see the Communist Party end up being just one party.

China is a huge country. From what I know, there are countless people who are far smarter and more efficient than I am in transforming the places where they live and work. That's why I'm confident that, even if this farm fails, within my lifetime the Chinese Communist Party will become like all the other Communist parties: one party among many.

No, no, they got that wrong. My father's still alive. I don't have to avenge myself on the party for his death. The old landlord they killed during the land reforms was my grandfather.

Parting Shot

24

Beam Me Up

The UFOlogist

Born in Shanghai in 1937, he received a degree in international trade from a university in Beijing in 1962. He had been president of the Chinese UFO Research Organization since 1986 and would, in accordance with a 1995 decision of the Preparatory Committee for Human Contact with Extraterrestrials, be number five in a lineup of dignitaries ready to make the first contact. The list was headed by Boutros Boutros-Ghali, the former secretary-general of the United Nations, and former U.S. president Jimmy Carter. Apart from his work as founder of China's National Federation of UFO Organizations, according to his name card he was also a university professor, a consultant to the Executive Board of the National Association of Qigong Science, a superior assessor of the Institute of Paranormal Studies, a member of the executive board of the Investigation Association on the Hong Kong and Macao Economies, a permanent member of the executive council of the International Association of Cultural and Commercial Development (United States), etcetera, etcetera. Over the past thirty years he had had various careers as a diplomat, interpreter, research scholar, and government bureaucrat.

Many people in China have been fortunate enough to see UFOs, myself included. My own sighting was during the darkest age of Chinese history. It was 1970, and I was at a May Seventh Cadre School in the countryside. Only one year earlier I had been in the stratosphere myself, when I acted as Chairman Mao's Spanish interpreter. I was one of the lucky few who spent some time in the presence of our own Red Sun. In 1970, however, I had very much returned to terra firma. I was undergoing self-renewal through labor and thought reform.

Of course I didn't think that extraterrestrials would be our salvation. It never occurred to me; no one would think that. Anyway, there's no such thing as a savior.[1] The only person qualified to save us was Chairman Mao. He'd already liberated us, and now we were working to save others, to liberate all of humanity. At the time we were incessantly warned that we were surrounded by enemies: American imperialism on the one hand and Soviet revisionism on the other. We faced the ever-present threat of a new world war. The Soviets encroached on our borders, so they were the more dangerous foe; they might launch an invasion at any moment. That's why, when I saw my UFO, the last thing I thought of was extraterrestrials. I was convinced it was the Russians.

It was dark, and the UFO was as bright as a full moon, though smaller. It was turning over and over in the sky; maybe that's how it generated power. There are many ways of generating power, after all. For example, you can wind an automatic watch just by moving your hand.

I don't know if that's how this particular UFO worked, but I believe we should be prepared to entertain such hypotheses. Our race, the human race in the twentieth century, may be relatively familiar with our own immediate physical environment, which we can access through our own senses and artificial extensions of them—various tools and instruments—but there is no conclusive proof to suggest that the universe conforms with our narrow perceptions of it. After all, it's only in the last three decades, with the development of space technology, that we've been able to search for extraterrestrial civilizations. Of course, up to now these efforts have proved fruitless, but we must be willing to admit that we are hardly in an ideal position to explore the universe yet. Our efforts to learn the truth are frustrated by the limitations of modern science, and it may take several generations before we get results.

Telescopes extend our range of vision, just as spacecraft act as new means for physical movement. Humankind may have taken one giant step on the moon, but it was still just one step. We are still a long way from understanding the world, let alone the universe. I attended a UFO conference in Brisbane not too long ago. I was there for a few days and saw a number of places, but on that basis alone I could hardly claim to know Australia.

1. This is a reference to the refrain of the "Internationale."

Every year we hear of numerous eyewitness reports of sightings. There's been an increased frequency of sightings and also of the discovery of physical evidence of visitations, particularly in the last few years. People have taken pictures of UFOs, and some have actually been on board them. People have even found the remains of spacecraft. However, scientists remain skeptical, even when presented with the actual pieces. All they can tell us is that some of the metal shards are special alloys. Although they maintain they're not from UFOs, they can't really say for sure. The point is that the facts behind all of this evidence are far beyond the realm of general human experience. People's minds are closed to other possibilities, and when they are confronted with something that's outside the bounds of the conventional, they feel threatened. Apart from that, a UFO experience cannot be repeated on demand; we can't replay it at will—so all of the evidence remains inconclusive. Life is short, and opportunities are limited. If you say that the only way you'll be convinced about the existence of UFOs is if you can see one, get on board, and bring back some concrete evidence, then, given the present situation, we have a problem. UFOs aren't at your beck and call.

Our organization has numerous contacts with scientists, and a number of our members are top-ranking scientists. Take Xue Chengwei, for example, the present head of our Beijing branch. He's a noted rocket scientist. And Shen Shituan, our honorary chairperson, is the president of the Chinese Aeronautical University. We also welcome the most hardened skeptics who are convinced that there's no such thing as extraterrestrial life. Zhou Yousuo, for instance, insists that UFOs are nothing more than atmospheric phenomena or balls of plasma. He claims that he can reproduce these so-called UFO phenomena in his laboratory on request.

That's to say, even top scientists have blind spots. We are all limited by our contingent framework of knowledge. Our thinking is bound by objective conditions; our views and methodologies are similarly constrained. I am convinced by facts, not by the reproduction of plasma effects in a laboratory. Zhou may well argue that the UFO I witnessed was nothing more than a ball of plasma, but that doesn't deter me. He can keep on saying that. What I find convincing is something like the map of Piri Re'is.[2] Once upon

2. Maps by Piri Re'is (Piri ibn Haji Memmed) were discovered in Constantinople (now Istanbul) in 1929 and date from 1513 C.E. They are said to depict the ancient world from long before the mapmaker's time.

a time people treated that old parchment document as though it was little more than a joke, a wildly inaccurate fantasy. But as human knowledge has advanced, it's proved to be extraordinarily accurate. Although Antarctica looks a bit misshapen to us, it just happened to be marked in the correct position on the map eight thousand years ago. Today we have to rely on satellites and spaceships to get such accurate pictures of the Earth. I believe people eight thousand years ago must have needed them as well.

We have a membership of over five thousand, most of whom have had a university education. Our funding comes from a range of sources: membership fees, financial support from local government technical and scientific associations, and grants that we've gone out and applied for ourselves. The central government has never given us a cent.

No, we don't get any help from extraterrestrials either! Though, to be more precise, I should say that we have no evidence that we've received support from extraterrestrials. Again, because of our limited perceptions it is impossible to say categorically whether we've been getting covert aid or not. Naturally, that brings us to the question of "men in black." MIBs are extraterrestrials who live among us disguised as human beings. They're more than just observers, as they also take part in human affairs. They have great power, and they play an important role in fostering—and actively discouraging and preventing—certain developments on Earth.

As superior life forms they are a force for good. They constantly inspire humanity and contribute to our collective wisdom, helping us move on to ever higher planes of civilization. Statistical studies done overseas have shown that some 80 percent of all important discoveries throughout history were made semiconsciously or by people in a state of hypnotic suggestion. It's more than likely that these discoveries were actually inspired by aliens transmitting information through extrasensory perception. It's also possible that they've employed other media to relay messages. For example, some scientists admit they've received documents containing data that's a little more advanced than contemporary scientific research—more advanced, but not so far ahead of our own science that it's beyond our comprehension. They've never been able to discover the genius behind it.

As to the question of how aliens have hindered certain developments on Earth, we are convinced that MIBs have prevented us from pursuing in-depth research into certain mysterious phenomena. In some cases, they actively discourage people from their investigations. That's why, on one level, UFOs remain just that: unidentified flying objects. The mystery may itself be the result of direct intervention by MIBs. Manipulating politicians and scientific authorities to launch attacks on so-called pseudoscience is one of their most common tactics.

During his presidential campaign Jimmy Carter announced his commitment to making public all government information related to UFOs, but when he got into office he reneged on that pledge. Making these things public could have been the single most important political decision in the history of the human race. By revealing those secrets he could have sparked widespread social chaos, as well as creating a major threat to established religions and belief systems. But that was only one reason for his decision. There may well have been another: the aliens themselves decided they didn't want to reveal themselves. Perhaps everything that has happened is part of an elaborate extraterrestrial ruse.

The time isn't yet ripe for aliens to establish open and sociable communications with humanity. Although we've been in contact now for at least ten thousand years, the gap between our civilizations is still far too great. If relations were established today that led to people-to-alien exchanges and visits, I fear they would be counterproductive for both sides. It's like a relay race. We want to take the baton from those running ahead of us, but we're too slow. We have to put on a spurt to get up to speed. The baton cannot be handed over until we are running fast enough.

As for the origins of our species, people in China generally accept the Darwinian-Marxist theory that we have evolved from apes through manual work. But if you look at it from another angle, you could just as well argue that the human race is part of an alien experiment. This is not unreasonable. After all, modern science has proved that it must have taken longer than the known life span of the Earth—calculated to be forty-six billion years—for humans to have evolved from the simplest organism. Thus, it is quite likely that aliens developed our human stock elsewhere and then transferred it to the Earth, where we have gradually evolved to the stage at which we find ourselves today.

But I don't believe that aliens observe us in the same way, say, that we watch ants fighting with each other. Certainly the earth has been supervised and controlled by extraterrestrials throughout human history and will continue to be in the future, but that knowledge doesn't change my view of life itself. It hasn't made me particularly fatalistic or pessimistic.

Jesus Christ could have been an extraterrestrial. After all, he cured diseases and averted disasters by telekinesis. He even modified the spiritual makeup of humankind. There are many accounts of his powers. As for other gods, spirits, and the bodhisattvas, so-called idols, there is nothing mysterious about them at all. They are all agents of alien intelligence.

Chairman Mao? Chairman Mao was Chairman Mao, plain and simple.

As for other mystical phenomena like astrology, fortune-telling, the belief in superior civilizations that existed before recorded history, and so on, I'm interested in them all, especially extrasensory perception and *qigong*.[3] UFO research is a vast field that inevitably leads to an investigation of all of these things. But, take my word for it, I'm not gullible; I don't believe everything. The deceptions of fake *qigong* masters and the like have negative effects on our work, though they're not all that damaging. After all, our organization pursues aims that are closely related to the work of modern science. Ours is a serious enterprise that has nothing to do with the gamut of superstitious *qigong* beliefs or all that talk about adepts who have trained secretly in the mountains for five hundred years or inherited a tradition handed down by masters over several generations.

False UFO sightings are reported for any number of reasons. Some are honest errors of judgment by people who have mistaken natural phenomena for UFOs. Some are hoaxes concocted by individuals who have nothing better to do with their lives than make up wild stories for their own amusement. The perpetrators are usually crooks who are trying to work some swindle. They act in a secretive and covert fashion but, despite their best efforts to fabricate fake aliens, alien medicines, alien agents, intergalactic linguistics, and so on, their scams are easily exposed.

Just because you come across a few fakes is no reason to think that the real thing doesn't exist. There've been cases of itinerant workers in China pretending to be the children of high-level cadres. But they've only been able to get away with it because there really *are* high-level cadres.

In general, the state maintains a hands-off attitude toward the issue of UFOs. This allows us to pursue our activities in an environment that's so relaxed that even our overseas colleagues are quite surprised. Despite this, however, our legitimacy is still questioned: conventional science does not recognize the validity of our inquiries.

"You're just like a small group of religious fanatics. How can you be sure your beliefs aren't just another heresy?" Journalists asked me questions like that when members of the Heaven's Gate cult in America committed sui-

3. Traditional Chinese yogic practices involving breath control, exercise, and meditation.

cide in the belief they'd be taken to heaven by an alien mother ship hidden in the tail of the Hale-Bopp comet.[4] I said it was an excellent question, but no, we can't find anyone qualified to act as a guarantor of our beliefs. However, the cult members who committed suicide do not represent us or our beliefs. Indeed there may have been a quirky extraterrestrial among them with strong nonscientific fixations. Their leader may have been such a being, and that would explain how he attracted all those aberrant followers.

I told that reporter just to forget all about it. But enough of that, let's get back to what we were talking about.

I don't want to get involved in discussing the policies of the past. For the moment, at least, the government is concentrating its efforts on building up China's market economy. People fortunate enough to be living in this transitional age are easily overwhelmed by materialism; they lose sight of the important things in life. That's why I believe that our mission to explore a phenomenon that many people believe doesn't even exist, that is to say alien civilization, is of value in and of itself. We can claim that we have already achieved something: we are doing our best to provide some spiritual nourishment for a pragmatic society.

I'm in a minority even at home. My sons don't believe in aliens, and their mother is even more skeptical. They're extremely critical of my views. That makes it three against one, and one of them is a high-level cadre into the bargain: my wife is a bureau chief. If we were all on an American-style jury, they'd have to work very hard to get me to agree with their verdict. In China that's not necessary; the minority has to defer to the will of the majority.

The thing is that there's no jury to adjudicate on these issues. If you don't agree, that's your tough luck; there's no place for you to make your case. As for being allowed to arbitrate the question yourself, you couldn't imagine it even in your wildest dreams. The truth will never be put in the dock and tried. People who take it upon themselves to judge the truth will be struck down to the sound of God's laughter.

Human knowledge can no longer be simplistically categorized into opposing schools of materialism and idealism.[5] We have to contemplate the problems facing humanity from a higher level. If you insist on labeling my

4. The Heaven's Gate cult, also known as the Total Overcomers Anonymous Monastery, was led by Marshall Herff Applewhite. In March 1997 Applewhite and his followers committed mass suicide at Rancho Santa Fe in San Diego County, California.

5. The basic epistemological categories of Marxist-Leninist ideology.

approach in terms of some "ism" or other, I suppose you could say it's a superior form of materialism. But even that's an artificial category. Trying to draw a distinction between science and pseudoscience is always a subjective exercise. If you are confronted by something that can't be found in any of your weighty tomes, then you shouldn't presume that you're in a position to judge its validity impartially.

History has proved that most of the predictions that Nostradamus made three centuries ago were accurate, including the timing of the explosion of China's first hydrogen bomb. The new millennium is upon us. Whether or not the Armageddon he foresaw will come to pass is a pressing issue. But to obsess about such things only serves to undermine our commitment to life in the here and now. Our very existence on this planet is precarious, and perhaps one day humanity will be confronted with a holocaust of its own making. That's when I believe aliens will come to our aid. And when they do appear on earth, our small group—the Preparatory Committee for Human Contact with Extraterrestrials—will be ready to carry out the task for which it was set up.

Yes, of course I'm a member of the Chinese Communist Party.

[I subsequently chanced again upon the president of the Chinese UFO Research Organization at the time of the Falun Gong protests in 1999. The Chinese Communist Party was attempting to suppress the nationwide cult, which boasted sixty million adherents on the mainland and had staged a surprise protest outside the party headquarters, Zhongnan Hai. Meanwhile, there was more stirring news for UFO activists. The president told me that a higher form of intelligence, formerly covertly active in northeast China, was preparing to move on Beijing. This being had already revealed that many Chinese politicians and social leaders were actually aliens.

Despite this confirmation that perhaps even Chairman Mao had been an extraterrestrial in disguise, the visitors to earth were experiencing financial difficulties. Increased economic pressures meant that finding new sources of funding had become a key issue for further UFO research; more important, the aliens active in human guise—the MIBs—needed more money to deal with the inflationary pressures that they were experiencing both in reformist China and elsewhere. Despite these problems, the most startling news was that researchers in China had uncovered the secret of propulsion used by alien spacecraft, as well as having discovered an alien-sourced cure for cancer, among other diseases. "As a by-product of our investigations into UFO phenomena," the president remarked to me, "these discoveries will not only have a profound impact on the economic well-being of China but will have long-term payoffs for our nation in terms of energy resources, transportation, and medicine. This will put China at the forefront of the advanced nations in the new millennium."

In parting, he reminded me that their activities were sanctioned by no less an authority than Vladimir Ilyich Lenin, for did not that great Russian revolutionary say, "Contact with extraterrestrials will force mankind to radically revise all preexisting philosophical and moral tenets"?]

25

Parting Shot
A Beijing Executioner

Remember, you might be publishing a sanitized record of this conversation. And it is only a conversation, not an interview. Therefore I don't want you adding any extraneous details apart from the three basics: time, place, subject—August 1996, China, a man who issues travel permits to hell.

There are four schools of thought regarding the death penalty in China: the proexecution faction, abolitionists, a group that wants to keep it on the books but not use it, and another group that thinks it should be used only rarely.

To date the proexecution lobby has held the day, and it is only in recent years that they have been challenged by abolitionists. It's a challenge that has consisted of little more than a few academic articles. As for those in favor of retaining the death penalty but not applying it, they exist only in the space created between the fantasies of the abolitionists and the pro–death penalty group. On the surface they emphasize the practical value of the death penalty, and they talk of the need for a transitional period—like the idea of gradual abolition that is common in the West, especially as recognized by international law—so that we will eventually be in step with Poland, a country held up as an exemplary model. In actual fact their rationale is based on Confucian philosophy—and not even the part that speaks of the Middle Way. Their political reasoning favors a due process that covers all contingencies. As for the fourth school of thought, those in favor of the occasional use of the death penalty, they appear mild and reasonable but offer no great challenge to the status quo and to those in favor of the death penalty. In reality theirs may well be the most extreme and the most Confucian form of politics. In many respects it seems that the differences between East and West are shrinking, but many things are mutually exclusive; you're growing melons and I'm growing beans, and it's only in the early days that the two crops look similar. Since the debate in favor of the occasional application of the death penalty is still only an academic question, we have to ask whose head that "occasional use" will fall upon? If we enact such a policy, won't you have the whole range of options to choose from, each suited to a different contingency? I'm only asking, since I've also learnt from Confucius, who said that out of every three people you meet, one can teach you something.

You know about the regulation that states that "foreign journalists shall not interview people without official permission," don't you? Then you'll appreciate how difficult it is for both sides to abide by it. Relatively speaking, you are fairly free; generally no one will interfere with you; you can hardly be expected to go and get official permission for every interview you want to conduct. That is, of course, unless you try and search out people involved with the democracy movement. Then the authorities will get involved. It's not that the activists don't enjoy personal freedom as such; the problem lies with you for conducting interviews illegally.

So I hope you don't think I belong to any particular school. I'm a very practical person. My job is to carry out executions. Now, I don't want to get into a discussion of whether one person has the right to deprive another of their life, or whether one group of people or even humanity itself has the right to kill someone. Because I wouldn't like you to give me a "parting shot."

What are we doing talking about this again? Okay, I suppose you could say there is a fifth school. You can say whatever you like, but you only have a sense that there is such a fifth option; it's not been part of the debates I've just described. That's because it doesn't function on an academic level at all. You can judge it on the basis of your subjective assumptions and claim there is an excessive faction that promotes broadening the use of the death penalty. One could claim that this approach is sanctioned by a traditional belief that "in an age of chaos it is necessary to apply severe punishments." You can think what you like; it's not my responsibility to reform the way you think. But we require a line of demarcation between us. You shouldn't force me to comment on your subjective assumptions. As everyone knows, there is a "strike-hard" campaign under way in China at the moment. But that's enough on that subject. Let me say once more, the very fact that I'm talking to you is quite improper. Don't try and use this conversational style of exchange to do me in. Let's move on and discuss the actual process involved.

Execution orders are signed by the court president of the Supreme People's Court and then issued to the criminal division of the higher or intermediate-level court, generally the latter. Upon receiving such an order, the court must immediately report to the court president—from now on I will only refer to what happens at midlevel courts—who will then set a date of execution and notify the judicial police.

We call the period from that time, until the order has been carried out and we quit the execution ground, one "police action." In private we generally call it a "red errand." Prisoners refer to it as "setting out," while prison guards call it "casting off the leg irons." Most people use terms like "execute by firing squad," "put to death," or just "kill." They are all related to the concept of departure, and people like to use more worldly and light-hearted expressions to talk about such serious matters. Some terms are really rather offensive; for example, when prisoners fight among themselves, they might say "Don't worry, you'll be frothing soon enough." It's interesting that even in those aggravated circumstances, they still use metaphorical expressions, choosing to employ such a revolting term as *froth* instead of *shot*. By the same token they use the word *pen* instead of *jail*, although there is a difference in the selection of such a term in this particular discursive environment: the former term *froth* is a metaphor, while *pen* is actually synecdoche.

Another point I should make here is that throughout the performance of an execution, the bailiffs of the basic-level court are put under the jurisdiction of the bailiffs of the midlevel court. This temporary arrangement alters the usual relationship of responsibility between them and the judge of the basic-level court. In normal times the midlevel court has no direct authority over the bailiffs of a basic-level court, merely a supervisory role. At the execution ground, however, that relationship undergoes a transformation, and the middle-level court exercises direct control. Why is this so? There are many possible explanations, but I'm sure you have already realized that in reality it is due to exceptional circumstances.

Preparations start the day before the actual execution. In the first place, depending on the number of prisoners, an execution squad of appropriate size is assembled. Regardless of how many criminals are to be executed, there are always three commanders, as well as various technical personnel, including a court doctor and a photographer. The ratio of bailiffs to prisoners is generally four to one. Of course, if a large number of prisoners is to be dealt with and has to be executed in batches, the ratio is smaller. For the parting shot, however, it is always four to one. Technical personnel also include traffic police, who are under the command of the bailiffs from the time that our vehicles enter the execution ground.

The place of execution is determined at the time that the execution squad is assembled. It also depends on the number of people to be executed. Here we have a choice, but in small cities that have only one execution ground, this issue doesn't arise. Once the place is fixed, the Public-Security Bureau [PSB] is notified, and they organize the police to clear the area and maintain security. They have it pretty tough as well, as they have to go on duty the day before the executions. The PSB is in charge of the ground from the time that the site is cleared the day prior to an execution until the executions are completed.

Individual jobs are allocated when the squad is set up, and, as I said earlier, the ratio that applies is four to one. That is, one of us is to fire the shot, and one of us is backup. Then there are two more to support the prisoner. *Support* is a rather particular technical term, since it is their job to support the prisoner right up to the spot where the execution is performed. After the duties are assigned, everyone has to go to the execution ground for a rehearsal. No matter how many times you've done the shooting, you have to attend this practice session.

After that, a complete inspection of the guns, ammunition, execution vehicles, and mobile radio equipment is carried out. Then we take a break and have a meal. The regulations forbid any of us to return home that night, although if someone has an urgent matter to deal with, they can absent themselves for a short time. Before lights-out we all get together, mostly to chat and watch TV, though sometimes we might play cards. Strictly speaking we're on duty all night and shouldn't really play cards, but I'm telling you what really goes on here. You grow your melons; I grow my beans. I suppose nobody would think about what the people in charge of the police and the prisoners do on the eve of an execution.

On the execution day itself, apart from the commander, we all arrive at the execution ground an hour ahead of time dressed in fatigues, with face masks over our mouths, sunglasses, and caps with visors. We check the safety precautions at the grounds, a fairly routine job that everyone can repeat like a catechism: "Present?" "Present and accounted for!" "All in order?" "All in order."

After the vehicles arrive, the prisoners are "supported" to the place of execution. The prisoner who is to be executed is then ordered to kneel. Generally, at this point, one of three things will occur. One is that the prisoner might have already fainted from fright, and if the escort relaxes their grip, the prisoner just crumples in a heap. Another possibility is that when you order the prisoner to kneel, they just comply without a fuss. The third possibility, however, is that the prisoner might put up a fight and refuse to kneel. If this occurs, the two escorts will kick the prisoner behind the knees when the escort orders the prisoner to kneel a second time—and they will be forced to do it whether they like it or not. Now, what I mean by the spot of execution is merely a shallow pit that has been dug especially for the occasion. The prisoner will be required to kneel about half a meter from the pit. When they're shot they'll fall forward so that the head lands right in the hole, so the blood flows into it rather than splattering all over the place. Colloquially we call the process of escorting the prisoner to the execution spot "finding the pit."

Once the prisoners have knelt down, the field commander will report to the commander-in-chief, and he will issue an order: "Preparations complete; stand ready." This is followed by the words "You may proceed." Although all of this has been completely routinized, it is a very practical process that signifies that the authority to carry out the execution is thereby transferred from the commander-in-chief to the field commander. This means that if any development should interfere with the proper implementation of the execution, the field commander is empowered to order the executioners and the other police who are present to shoot, and that means first and foremost to execute all of the prisoners. Of course, if only one prisoner is being executed, or just a few, then this right of command is just a formality, but it is a procedure put in place to deal with situations in which a large number of prisoners are to be executed, as a result of which they have to be divided into groups and shot in batches. After the shooting of the first lot, it is time for the second group to find a pit. When you're on a red errand like that, if something out of the ordinary occurs, you really need a practiced and professional commander to take immediate and decisive action by shooting all of the prisoners at the execution ground at once, regardless of whether they have found their pit or are still waiting. Of course, emergency situations include things like sudden floods and earthquakes, or say a satellite happens to come crashing to earth on the execution ground; although in reality what we are talking about is a sudden attack on the execution ground or a disturbance among the prisoners. Such occurrences are rare, but the People's Republic has been in existence for half a century now, and so, not surprisingly, you get every type of situation. There have been a number of instances, both successful and unsuccessful. Successful breakouts have usually occurred when the prisoners are on the way to the execution ground. But enough said about that; let us proceed.

The field commander then leads the chief and backup executioners to their positions, that is to say a position behind the prisoner. Then the field commander gives the order "Ready!" following which the main executioner takes one step forward and aims his gun directly at the back of the subject's neck, releasing the safety catch. The two escorts step away from the prisoner, and when the field commander orders "Fire!" the executioner shoots.

Thereupon the adjunct commander leads the executioner out of the execution ground, and the court doctor examines the prisoners to certify that they are dead. If the doctor is of the opinion that another bullet is required, then the field commander will order one or more backup executioners to deliver another round. Following this, the photographic record of the execution will be placed on file, and the field commander will lead the backup executioners from the ground.

We use rifles and aim at the head at short range, a few dozen centimeters. After the bullet enters the base of the occipital bone, it will travel through the basis cranii and come out through the forehead or some part of the face. In the vernacular this is called "lifting up the crown" or "blossoms on the face." Goddammit, language like that is disgusting! Theoretically, this leads to instant death. Just how "instant" death is, however, only the one who dies knows for sure.

Yes, of course it's a bullet in the back of the head.

Starting in the 1990s, the work of executing prisoners has been placed under the jurisdiction of midlevel court bailiffs whenever conditions permit, resulting in the regularized process that I have just described. However, discrepancies continue to exist. For example, in some places the escorting officers do not wear fatigues, or there might still be some spectators, and so on and so forth. Although the process of carrying out an execution is basically the same wherever you go, local conditions lead to variations and irregularities when it comes to the finer points. For example, although some execution grounds can be cleared of spectators, you can't entirely prevent people from looking on. There might be residential buildings only a few dozen or a hundred meters away, so if people want to watch, they can do so from their homes. Furthermore, the level of development in places varies. Where the conditions are poor and there are limited numbers of police, then things are carried out fairly much as they were in the past, and the armed militia has to be called in to assist in the operation. China is a land of 9.6 million square kilometers, so it's understandable that in many respects we are still in a transitional situation.

It is our practice to notify the crematorium in advance so that their vehicle will be on the spot outside the execution ground. When it's all over, family members place the body in a bag and put it in the vehicle, and off it goes; if there is no family to claim the body, we put it in a bag and have it removed. We act to remove the corpses with all possible speed; we don't let the bodies lie around out there. If people want to start crying and wailing, they just have to move on and do it at the crematorium.

Anyway, by this stage the prisoner is dead, so in some places they don't allow families to go anywhere near the execution ground. They are told they can identify the corpse at the crematorium. Of course, this obviously puts a lot of pressure on the crematorium. Therefore I'm particularly interested in how overseas scholars look at the evolution of Chinese legal practices in terms of institutionalization. I plant my melons; you plant your beans. If you've got chickens and rabbits in the same cage, you know it is impossible to calculate how many legs they have in total. In reality, the people at the crematoriums are pretty hardheaded too. If no one claims the body and some scientific organization wants it, then the crematorium acts as legal custodian, and they charge various fees before releasing it. That is to say, if no one claims the body, then it belongs to the government by default, so the crematorium believes they have a right to recoup their costs before cremating it.

In biological terms, the best method is to shoot them in the head. It results in instant death. There's a saying that when you slaughter a pig you should kill it from the butt. But that's only making trouble for yourself. A modern execution has the purely technical aim of depriving the guilty party of life in accordance with the law. Thus speed and efficiency are of the essence, for this reduces or at least limits their suffering. Modern executioners eschew traditional methods such as death by a thousand cuts, using horses to pull the body apart, and crucifixion. This not only signifies a rejection of such barbaric acts but also is evidence that the modern executioner rejects the view that a condemned person has to suffer both physical and psychological torture when being executed, extending thereby the agony experienced prior to death. This is a sign that humanity has made progress. Yet, while bearing all of this in mind, we cannot ignore the fact that China is a multiethnic nation with many different belief systems. We have to respect the customs and beliefs of ethnic minorities. Some minority customs are determined by habitual but not codified practice. They are not opposed to executions as such but disallow shooting people in the head. Thus we do not forbid executioners to shoot the prisoner in the heart. An execution is an execution; there is no use getting caught up in excessive discussions about methodologies.

I've been expecting that you'd try and fire one from behind at this very juncture. The Liu Qingshan–Zhang Zishan case is a historical anomaly.[1] The provincial government produced a document that was authorized by Party Central that the two prisoners were shown prior to their execution. The document clearly stated that they were "not to be shot in the head but in the back, near the heart. The children are not to be classified as the family members of counterrevolutionaries, and they will be wards of the state up to the time of their majority." I'm just as perplexed by this as you are. I believe that this de facto "guarantee" was the outcome of a unique historical moment. Yet no matter how you look at it, I think it was disgraceful. Shooting one's own cadres in the heart rather than the head obviously raises the question of whether it was to cause undue suffering, or to signify that their ideology was sound but their hearts were corrupt?

Generally speaking, an officer who hasn't done escort duty will not be given the job of main executioner unless there are exceptional circumstances. A person who has not previously acted as a main executioner will not be sent in as a backup, either. The process that is carried out at the execution ground is an extremely solemn one, and those involved need time to familiarize themselves with the environment as well as time to prepare themselves psychologically and practice their technique. You can only be the backup when you've already served as main shot. It's not a question of the system, and there's no subtle logic behind it. This is the way we generally arrange things here; perhaps it's the exact opposite elsewhere. From our experience, we have come to the conclusion that the psychological as well as technical demands placed on a backup executioner sent on a red errand are extreme and exacting—even more so than for the main executioner. Even if the prisoner is killed straight out, human beings aren't just lumps of wood. After the first shot, the corpse will invariably go into spasm and start kicking around. Brain matter will come spurting out of the head, and

1. Liu Qingshan and Zhang Zishan were executed for graft in 1952, during the first major political campaign of the People's Republic, which saw both party members and many others summarily dealt with. Liu was the former secretary of the party's Tianjin Prefectural Committee, and Zhang was in the city commissioner's office.

there will be blood; it's all pretty revolting. Even more so when the backup executioner has to deal with a prisoner who hasn't been killed by the first shot and is still struggling. Not that it really matters; for a bailiff this is far from an unusual situation. Especially during a period like the present strike-hard campaign, bailiffs have more than ample opportunity to practice all of the necessary skills.

As for the main executioner, unless you are determined to see what happens after you've shot the prisoner, you are free to leave the scene and will be escorted from the spot immediately. When a backup is called in, it is not necessarily a one-on-one situation—for obvious reasons. The field commander may well send in a few executioners to finish the job together. It's like "the moon in the middle of the month."[2] Would foreigners understand what I'm saying here? You get it, so you can explain it to them.

Yes, it's happened. If you often walk on a riverbank, you can't help getting your feet wet. Anyway, if I denied it had ever happened, no one would believe me. Fortunately, such occurrences are few and far between. I say fortunately because if something like this does happen, it's a mess. Once there was this prisoner who didn't die with the first shot, and the doctor called for a backup. Thereupon the doctor gave the okay; they took the picture and removed the corpse. It was ten in the morning, and the whole process had gone according to routine. But what happened then was anything but routine. The family had claimed the body, but on the way to the crematorium he came around. He wasn't just breathing or anything like that; he could actually talk! That's when things started falling apart. The family demanded that he should be taken to the hospital instead of the crematorium. When the bailiffs heard this, they called their superiors for advice; they took the precaution of blocking the road to prevent the family from taking the body away and forced the vehicle to go to the crematorium.

The family made an incredible fuss. They felt he'd only been condemned to death once; since he had survived he deserved to live. Representatives of the PSB, the procuracy, and the courts rushed to the crematorium and tried to reason with the family. The general principle is that you should speak with the family before shooting the condemned person again; but, regardless of how that goes, we still have to shoot them. There is no way a prisoner would be released. A death sentence means that the prisoner is to be

2. A reference to a song that talks about how hard it is to determine ultimate responsibility.

deprived of his or her right to life. For the family to argue that he was only under one death penalty is a modern-day version of the feudal concept that a crime is only "worthy of one blow of the executioner's blade." It has no basis whatsoever in law. Moreover, the fact was that the death penalty had not been successfully carried out; it wasn't a matter of carrying out a second execution. The standoff continued until after one o'clock in the afternoon. The death penalty is just that; to carry it out does not, nor can it, require the agreement of the family of the prisoner or of the prisoner himself. The prisoner was forcibly removed from the family, and those who had gathered around to watch the altercation, and shot again. Not surprisingly, in such circumstances it was hardly possible to take the prisoner back to the execution ground, so he was taken outside the crematorium and shot. Three shots were fired. If you add that to the two earlier attempts, that left him with ten holes in his body.

The main—no, the only—reason this occurred was that the medical officer was incompetent. He couldn't tell the difference between life and death, and his pronouncement on the condition of the prisoner was incorrect. A subsequent analysis of what went wrong indicated that since so many prisoners had to be shot that day, the executioner's first shot was late by a half to a whole second. When he heard the other shots go off, the officer himself moved slightly, and his shot went through the side of the prisoner's neck as a result. Blood spurted out of the mouth and nose, but the bullet had actually passed between the medulla oblongata and the artery in the neck. On the surface of things it seemed like a fatal shot, though in reality, apart from flesh and teeth, nothing else had been hit. Now, when it came to the backup shot, another coincidence occurred. The bullet entered the body slightly to the right of the *jizhong* acupuncture channel and exited from the left breast. On the surface it looked like there was a large wound where the heart is, as though the heart had been hit, but neither the heart nor the main artery had actually been touched. It was a completely freak occurrence. Add to all of this a sloppy doctor, and you have a prisoner who had a difficult passage to his death.

The most common situation is where we execute a large number of prisoners together. Although there are times when only one prisoner is executed, that is a very inefficient way of working. To shoot one or many is pretty much the same thing; it entails exactly the same process, although the number of bailiffs is different. But there are limits to everything, and we certainly don't want to go to extremes—nor do we wish to execute several batches of prisoners at a time. By overdoing the numbers, you can create problems of scale for yourself. If you're shooting batch after batch, you don't leave the execution ground after each shot; at most you move from your original position to stand in front of another hole and shoot again. Not only is there more work required for the executioner, but there is a considerable increase in both the psychological and physiological pressure on you. Executioners are people too; and what they're shooting at is not just skittles. And of course the prisoners have never seen anything like it either: after the first round of shots, the bodies fall right in front of the next line of people to be executed. Even if they are kneeling by then and can't see the extent of the mess, just the sound of the shooting is enough to paralyze a few of them. But actually this is better than if, after the first round of executions, the escorts have to go over to the vehicles and get the next group out and line them up at the holes. In that case the prisoners would be standing and would see exactly what had been happening.

All in all, executing prisoners in batches is a method that has evolved out of necessity. Just think of the figures: four people for every criminal. If you have ten criminals, that makes forty people. If you can only get an execution squad of forty and you have thirteen prisoners to execute, then you have to divide them into two groups. In these circumstances you require twenty-six men to escort the criminals and prepare two rows of holes, seven in front and six behind. The escorts lead all of the prisoners to their holes, and after they've got them to kneel down the fourteen executioners, main and backup, shoot the first lot and then the second. That works fairly well. Now, if you're dispatching twenty people, then you need two rows of ten holes; you shoot the first lot and then escort the second batch. If you're shooting thirty, then the same applies, you just increase the number of holes accordingly. What do you mean, how could there ever be that many? A strike-hard campaign, that's how.

Of course, for both technical and humanitarian reasons you want to do your best to ensure that the prisoners don't see the disgusting scene left by those who have been shot. But you can only do your best; either way, the prisoners know they are going to die. So for even more important technical and humanitarian reasons we can't shoot the back row first and move forward. It would be too easy for a shot to go astray, or a ricocheting bullet might accidentally hit one of the escorts in the front line. It's the same routine as target practice: once the safety catch of your gun has been released, there should never be anything in front of you except a target, or a prisoner.

Good guess! You're right, when we shoot a group of thirty we usually divide them into four batches: eight, ten, six, and six, or eight, eight, eight, and six. No matter how extraordinary the circumstances may be, it's an execution ground—not a battleground. Anyone who has experienced a battle situation will tell you that soldiers tend to become more and more hyper when they are fighting. On an execution ground, however, it's not a struggle between two opposing sides. It cannot be. It's not a situation that could elicit a sense that "I'm fighting you to the death," that is to say a situation in which the executioners get carried away on a wave of bloodlust. People can only maintain a state of high tension for a limited period of time. When directing the execution squads the commander has to take all of this into consideration and must remain fully mindful that, as his orders are being carried out, various contingencies may occur. Therefore he will be careful to make sure that the main executioners and the backups take turns. On any given occasion, some of them will not have to shoot as many as the others. This is part of the normal course of events. We are not living in the days of the Gang of Four. There's none of that nonsense about "if you don't kill this class enemy you will be letting down the party and Chairman Mao."

There's no doubt that there were cases in which prisoners had their vocal cords cut before being executed. That was under the Gang of Four. Zhang Zhixin's vocal cords were cut before her trial, and after that she was shot. The aim was to prevent the prisoner from shouting out slogans in public before dying. But the *People's Daily* story got it wrong. They reported that she had her throat cut just before being executed. Why would they have bothered cutting her throat? Nonetheless, it was that line about her throat having been cut that outraged the whole nation and concentrated people's fury on the Gang of Four and the whole judicial and public-security network that operated under them. People don't generally have much of an opportunity to kill anything or anybody themselves. At most they know about using a cleaver to kill a chicken. Everyone knows that when you cut a chicken's throat, you end up with blood and feathers all over the place. It leaves a deep impression.

Nowadays, for mass sentencing rallies, or when we take prisoners to the execution ground, we always tie a rope around their necks so they can be silenced if they decide to play up and shout out bad things to the masses. All the bailiff has to do is pull on the rope, and the prisoner shuts up. We call the rope "a voice lock." But that's the formal appellation. Prisoners in jail call it a "neck-warmer," and when it's tied on they call it "dragging the dead dog." When you pull on it, they shut up all right—a live dog couldn't bark, let alone a dead one.

Most places have seen mass parades of convicted prisoners at one time or another. It's often been a feature of traveling exhibitions about criminal activities. In some places they've even been known to parade the defendant with a placard around the neck before the trial. Sometimes prostitutes and their tricks are put on display at some very public place, like the entrance to a cinema or a theater. The authorities claim that this is one of the most effective ways to propagate the rule of law, inspiring awe in felons and educating the masses at the same time. But following the repeated orders issued by the Supreme People's Court and the public-security bureau, I'm sure that such things have basically disappeared, even in mid-sized and small cities. No matter what you say about how bad other people are, in the past, during the strike-hard campaign of 1983, for example, we employed a variation of the street parade ourselves—prisoners were sent off to the execution grounds through the streets in an open lorry, with their crimes and names written on "death placards" on their backs, like they used to have when they beheaded criminals in the feudal past. But that's over and done with now. We don't do that kind of thing here any more; as for what the situation is like elsewhere, you can go and find out for yourself. But I can tell you they still do it. There were news reports on mass public-sentencing rallies on TV a few days back—they seemed to be on every night for a while—and sometimes there was a fleeting camera shot of a prisoner listening to their sentence. An insider like me could tell immediately exactly how they'd be taken to the execution ground after the mass trial was over.

I can give you an obvious example: You can still come across places that hang death placards on prisoners during public sentencing rallies.[3] The average height of a male prisoner is 1.7 meters, and if you put a death placard on their back, that makes it about three meters. There's no other way to send them to the execution ground except in an open lorry. Take my word for it, I'm not exaggerating. I picked up a magazine at a street stall a few days ago, and there was a picture of a prisoner being taken down from a lorry by two bailiffs. The authorities keep on issuing orders prohibiting it, but they can't prevent it happening. What the hell do they think they're up to? It's worse than killing pigs from the butt!

---

3. A death placard *(wangming biao)* is a large placard bearing the name of the criminal and a description of his or her crime.

Speaking of the bailiffs who oversee the transporting of prisoners to the execution ground, that's a whole other area of specialization. It's another process. Let me give you a simple overview—I've done it myself, of course I have, so I know. When the order comes for an execution, you're either put on execution detail or made a bailiff. Given the present situation, it's not practical to demand too much specialization. When they're not on call in court, some bailiffs even double as drivers or office staff, especially if they're women. They don't have many chances to appear in court. But they've got to do something with themselves.

Now I should explain here that after a person has been condemned to death, they are generally not kept in solitary confinement. In the first place, the conditions in most detention centers simply don't permit such a luxury; but, more important, it is neither convenient nor safe to isolate a prisoner on death row. After the trial, they return to their cell in heavy shackles, and their handcuffs are replaced with chains and manacles so as to limit their movements as much as possible, that is to say to prevent them from making any trouble or committing suicide. Of course, there is a downside to all of this, since it means that the prisoners can't take care of themselves; other people have to help them with everything. So the condemned man is generally put into a cell with four or more other prisoners. The others are called "company"; sometimes they're assigned to that cell specifically, or they may have been there to start with. They'll be inside for various crimes, and often they haven't been tried yet, but we've estimated how long they'll probably be in for. They're assigned as company because they've shown themselves willing to cooperate with the warders; they're given a bit more authority than the average prisoner. So it's their task to help take care of the condemned man, chat with him and suchlike, as well as to assist the guards by keeping an eye on him. They take a measure of responsibility for the prisoner's safety and wellbeing.

To be quite honest, people are happy to be put on company duty. Everyone in the cell of a condemned prisoner gets to eat their fill, and the food is better than average, too. But the real benefit of the job is that you demonstrate a willingness to cooperate with the authorities, and you've got an opportunity to prove that you deserve lenient treatment in the future yourself. You probably can't appreciate the psychological state of these common prisoners. When they were on the outside they were terrified of being caught up in the strike-hard campaign, but after they're caught—and as long as they're not put on the execution list—they undergo a radical change of attitude. You see, prison is just like a bus. Before getting on, people are anxious that it'll stop long enough for them to get on board. But once they've got on, all of that changes and they're impatient for it to get going. So these prisoners think that the more severe and merciless the strike-hard campaign, the better; they hope it'll result in social stability as quickly as possible so that their sentences can be reduced.

As for the death-row prisoner, he has even less grounds for complaint about being in a big cell. Once he's physically restrained, it's hard for him to do things, and he needs people to help him when he has to eat and defecate. And there's someone for him to talk to as well.

Experience proves that this is more effective than confining the condemned man to solitary. If we did that, the guards would have to keep a constant eye on him. He's going to die anyway, so who knows what he might get up to? Now, if you want to make the case that we're using some prisoners to control others, then we've got a difference of opinion, and I think we should end our discussion right now. . . .

A death sentence isn't the final verdict. The prisoner might appeal, and then they have to see their legal counsel and family members. Some might even ask to see religious functionaries and suchlike. The night before the execution takes place, regardless of whether there is to be a public sentencing rally, the prisoner is woken after midnight. It is probably a bit of a shock for the prisoner, since they're not psychologically prepared for it, and their biological clock is running low. It's just when their powers of resistance are weak that their restraints are removed. You obviously can't wait until after they're shot for them to be taken off; you'd only be creating problems for yourself. The manacles and shackles are replaced with ropes, the so-called "five-knotted flower." Don't ask me where people get these god-awful expressions; how would I know what the five flowers are? People generally don't know either. Anyway, what we do is tie ropes around the ankles and knees, where the original shackles were. Thus the prisoners can only take small steps; they can't run away. Their wrists are tied behind their backs, and then a long rope is wound around their neck and twice around the shoulders to give us control over the arms. We also tie up the cuffs of their pants so that if they piss or shit themselves from fright at the public rally or on the way to the execution ground, the filth won't go all over the place. Actually that's not a big deal, as the other ropes would already keep anything from spilling out, but it's a matter of habit to add the extra ones. Last but not least, we drag the dead dog, that is, we put a rope around the neck to keep the prisoner from calling out.

Apart from all of this, there are a number of other standard procedures that we run through at this point: the prisoner is questioned prior to the execution; they are taken to a public rally; their identity is formally confirmed; and they are allowed to make final requests and to leave a will. You know the kind of thing. But rather than getting caught up in details, let's move straight on to the execution ground.

The will? Generally it's a verbal statement, and if there is any practical content to it, such as who owes what to whom, then it has to be passed on to the family. If it's in writing, it's usually passed on to the family in full. But not in all cases. If, say, it contains statements that vilify the party and the government, or if it has other unsuitable material, then it may be confiscated in accordance with the relevant regulations. In such cases, the family will only be given access to the pertinent portions of the will, and they are not permitted to make it public. When the sentence is formally announced, a statement is made to the effect that "the prisoner is sentenced to death. The sentence is to be carried out immediately and the prisoner is deprived of his political rights for the rest of his life." That means that the prisoner no longer has any right to express political views, and thus the contents of the will cannot be published.

Now that they're actually facing death, it's all but over. So when it comes to their last meal, the final breakfast in fact, they can usually eat it. Some of them even relish it. The food's not as good as it's rumored to be. There is no extravagant spread with lots of meat and seafood. It's just better than usual prison food. Generally speaking, it consists of bread and sausage purchased outside the jail. There are sometimes embarrassing misunderstandings when we go shopping for these meals. When the shop assistant sees that you're buying dozens of loaves and such a load of sausage, and that you want a receipt for it all, they might ask you: "Where are you going? On a spring outing?" All you can do is give a friendly smile and pass over it. Things like this happen. Take, for example, the popular belief that after an execution all the police get together for a big meal and booze-up. It's clear how such rumors got started, because a few years back we asked the militia to assist us with executions. People got it wrong, though, because we felt duty-bound to give these guys a meal after they'd helped us out; we couldn't very well let them go without even feeding them. After all, don't you offer cigarettes and tea to the telephone repairman who comes to your house?

After the prisoner has eaten his last meal, he'll ask for a smoke. They're not allowed cigarettes in jail; you can't let prisoners on death row have access to fire. After the trial we even take the buttons off their clothes; they can't be allowed to have anything in their possession that's hard, in case they try to use it to commit suicide. Some prisoners on death row are determined not to die on the execution ground, and they'll spend all their time thinking up ways to kill themselves. They come up with some pretty weird ideas, too, like sharpening toothbrushes to cut their arteries. Anyway, now that they're about to die, we let them have a smoke. Cigarettes and booze belong to all, as they say. I always take an extra pack so I don't run out. Some of them are pretty relaxed even though they're facing imminent death. "How come the government doesn't smoke foreign cigarettes?" they might ask. It'd never occur to them that locally made cigarettes are all I can afford on my salary.

The prison environment produces its own argot. The average reader might find the language of *The Gulag Archipelago* boring and repetitive, but we understand it completely. We may be vastly separated geographically, but we share a common language. There are many startling similarities, numerous familiar expressions. For example, our prisoners also call the guards "chief," regardless of whether they are chiefs. And when they address us, that is, people who work for the procuracy, judges and bailiffs, they call us simply "the government." They never address you as "you," just "the government."

Many people look on death as something that awaits us all, and so not such a fearful specter. What does scare people is the feeling of nostalgia that sweeps over them as they realize that the trivia of day-to-day life will be lost to them forever. So when the sentence is handed down, relatively few people get really upset. They generally only break down when they're on the way to the execution ground. It's not because they are afraid of the disgrace, but because they know they'll be seeing their city or village for the last time, and they'll be faced with all the people out there who are free. That's why suicide can be such an issue. You can look at it from two different angles. Some fight to the bitter end, while others simply feel too weak to go on; they can't face being taken to the execution ground. They just can't stand the thought of seeing the outside world that one last time.

That's why the ideal time for executing people is at night. The best place is a small execution ground with no other prisoners. As for the actual method of execution, whether it be by shooting, electrocution, or a needle, each has various things to recommend it. But to my mind these considerations are secondary to the questions of time and place. So much for the ideal. In purely technical terms there is inevitably a discrepancy between the ideal and reality.

At this point prisoners don't usually talk among themselves unless they are involved in the same case or happen to be friends or relatives. They have the opportunity all right, but they are simply unwilling to talk. They are facing death, and they feel that they share nothing in common with the other condemned men. If they do call out, it's usually some nonsense they've concocted well ahead of time, for the benefit of themselves or their friends.

But they generally do say a few words to us, unless they're so frightened they can't speak. They feel that there is some connection between us and them. Some of those clowns even say, "See you later!" or "Enjoy the rest of your life, government!" They're not making fun of you, not now. We have the simplest relationship that can exist between two people, one that's purely inimical—but it is still a kind of relationship. If you want to be upbeat you could say it isn't that negative, since we are all human beings—remember what I said at the beginning of our talk—and we share a common humanity, and that's the basis of our relationship. After the shot's been fired, my job is at an end, and their life is finished. Society has settled its score with them. But there is still a sense of leave-taking. According to the logic of the situation I'm probably the person they've felt the most hate for in their whole lives, for I'm the one who has sent them on their journey to the Yellow Springs.[4] So we are fated to hate each other. Superficially that might seem true, but it is only so if one ignores the complexities of life. That's not all there is to it.

No, I never respond. I act as though I haven't heard anything. I'm not that stupid. So what if a government pardon was to drop from the skies in the time it takes to say "Ready" and "Fire!" If he actually did live after having said "Enjoy the rest of your life, government," then things would be different, and that unique moment would be lost forever. That's why when they face death they remain aloof, and they face us impassively; there is no need for any exchange of pleasantries. For me they are criminals on the point of execution, and that's the only relationship I have with them. In reality, it's not just them, sorry, don't get me wrong, but it's a matter of us—people.

It sounds as though I'm trying to have it both ways. But that's the truth of the matter. You go figure it out for yourself.

The annual number of executions in China is a major state secret. I don't know what it is, though I don't think it would be greater than the number

4. The afterlife.

of suicides. Suicide is now a major social issue. There are over 2,500 urban suicides each year. The majority of suicides are to be found in small towns and cities just like in the West, so in some counties there are over 1,000 suicides a year; that's why I say the number of executions isn't greater than the number of suicides. There's no county in China that would execute 1,000 people in a year; even one hundred would be pushing it. Are figures like this useful? I can give you more. . . .

It's little wonder that I'm well-informed about death in China. It's inevitable that a person's professional activities will influence the way they look at things and the issues that they're interested in. Inevitably then I'm interested in questions of life and death. Common people may joke in their repugnant fashion that "executioners look at everyone's necks as though they're studying where the blade should fall." There's nothing funny about that at all. Petty people judge others according to their own crass standards. The reason I'm so interested in death is that I've seen more of it than you have. I'm more passionate in my hope that people will cherish their lives, live well, not break the law, and certainly not commit suicide. One should value both one's own life and the lives of others.

I'm a university graduate, although it goes without saying that my present work has nothing to do with what I studied.

We never discuss my work at home. Of course my wife is curious, and she's asked me about it—whether it scares me or not—but that's all. It's the same as in a doctor's family; they generally don't know what's actually involved in operating on someone. So what does your wife do? I suppose the most you ever ask is how many hours she's taught that day. Wouldn't she get fed up with you if you were always asking how she prepares for her classes, what she's been teaching, what her students are called, and all that? Even if I did want to tell her, she'd get bored. She's only interested in nagging me for always being too busy, even when I'm not. She complains that I don't take enough notice of things at home. But then I couldn't be bothered to talk about it. That's just how people are. Perhaps only actors are an exception to this rule. Everyone sees what they do, and they're always expected to talk about their work even when they're offstage. They're always explaining, and they carry their excitement about their work with them when they go home.

26

Days in the Life
of the People's Republic

THE QUICK . . .

Since 1 May 1995, an honor guard of thirty-six military policemen in dress uniform has been performing a daily flag-raising ceremony in Tiananmen Square. An honor guard of sixty conducts the ceremony on the first day of every month, accompanied by a band playing the national anthem.

Tiananmen Square, a twenty-year-old armed policeman.

We raise the Five-Star Red Flag every morning at sunrise, and take it down again at sunset, no matter what the season, even in rain or snow.

The time for the two ceremonies is adjusted daily, and the exact time of the following day's ceremonies is posted every afternoon on a blackboard back at our base. There's an electronic board next to the flagpole in Tiananmen Square that announces the time for the tourists. There are always a lot of people there to watch; sometimes people come hours before the ceremony. There are men and women of all ages, even lots of foreigners, and there are TV crews a lot of the time, not to mention all the people who want to take photographs.

The national anthem is played as we hoist the flag. Lately they've started playing a recording, so you've come on a bad day. On important occasions an army band plays it.

Lots of people think we're PLA soldiers, but in fact we belong to the People's Armed Police. Our force was established in 1983 according to Party Central's directive on "Building up a New Great Wall to Maintain Long-

Term Stability and Peace." We are an armed force directed by the party and the state, a pillar of the people's democratic dictatorship, and the sons of the people, just like the People's Liberation Army. And, like the soldiers, we're here on military service; most of us are conscripts.

Unlike the PLA, though, we're mostly deployed for domestic tasks: border patrol and firefighting. As I see it, we're not really like the army—you know, like the old saying goes, "trained for a thousand days to be used only on one."[1] We're trained for a thousand days and deployed every day, so we have a pretty tough time of it.

Our training consists of constant education in the party's political line, policies and directives, and ideological work, as well as cultural and technical training. They are all essential, and we have to put them all into practice constantly. Okay, to be precise, then, when a new man joins the force, one of our officers will moderate a major group discussion on issues related to the history of the party's enterprise, in particular the situation since the introduction of the open-door and reform policies and whether it's worth being a soldier in a market economy. We also talk about the kinds of values and aspirations that we should have. Through serious discussion and the example of older soldiers, new recruits are able to understand that the value of a revolutionary soldier lies in selfless service and sacrifice.

Through political study and an education in positive ideals, we've learned that Deng Xiaoping's theory about letting a few people become rich before the rest in no way denigrates or undermines the collectivist and sacrificial spirit expected of progressive elements in our society. We know that for a revolutionary fighter, self-realization is a matter of putting our revolutionary ideals into practice; to achieve such self-actualization requires strict organizational discipline and a heightened sense of social responsibility.

Military training is more than just training for battle and technical training. Training in discipline and the right attitude is even more important. Through rigorous training we can overcome delinquent and lax attitudes and wipe out any trace of the permissive, slipshod, and lazy approach we may have indulged in as common members of society, thereby enhancing our quality as individuals. This training instills in us the habit of adhering strictly to army discipline and speaking, moving, and acting in a precise and orderly fashion. It becomes automatic for us to demand the utmost of ourselves, as army men, at all times. To give an example, when we go to eat or

1. *Yang bing qian ri, yong bing yi shi.*

relieve ourselves, or go for a walk, we march with precise steps in a coordinated group, two abreast or three in a line.

Marching out from Tiananmen Gate to the flagpole and back again twice a day might seem to be just a few hundred meters' march, but the training you need before you can march those few hundred steps correctly is a Long March of a thousand miles.

We are expected to train until "each step kicks up a wind, each footfall makes a hole in the ground." And that's only the beginning of it. During intensive training sessions we have to march nonstop until we can't move another step—your legs swell up, your feet are covered in blisters, and your legs feel as though they're breaking. We are the honor guard that hoists the national flag in Tiananmen, and we must move and act as one. That's why we have long sessions of coordinated formation drilling. Every move—how high we lift our legs and arms, how far our feet can be apart—is measured to the nearest millimeter. The aim isn't just to get it right for a few steps or a few hundred steps; it's to be able to maintain exactly the same standard no matter how far you have to march. You won't find any of that civilian attitude of "getting it more or less right" among us. From the first step we take until the final stand-at-attention at the end of the drill, we won't be so much as a millimeter out. Every day we literally follow in the footsteps of the day before; there's an invisible path that we march along, one we always keep to.

We do our drill during the coldest days of the winter and at the height of the summer heat so we can get acclimatized to different weather conditions. Days when there is a strong wind, or a big rainstorm or snowstorm, are ideal for testing our mettle and strengthening our willpower. Only when you voluntarily take on the hardest and most difficult tasks can you possibly achieve the maximum in training. Apart from marching, we also have to practice standing at attention. It looks easy, but it requires rigorous training. Unless you've sweated yourself dry a few hundred times in training, you are simply not worthy of being in the Five-Star Red Flag honor guard; you're unworthy of being on duty in Tiananmen Square, a place that billions of Chinese hold dear to their hearts.

You want me to be more specific about myself? Well, I'm from Shandong Province. A lot of people from Shandong tend to do something of a duck walk—with their feet turned out—and I'm one of them. I had to correct my habitual walk, though we discovered that no amount of drilling would do the trick. My damned feet just wouldn't take orders! The second I let my attention wander, I'd be turning my feet outward. An older soldier taught me how to overcome the problem by tying my feet together really tight before going to sleep each night. A year of that finally corrected the problem. Every soldier has different problems. The ones who don't stand with their backs ramrod-straight have to spend all the time they can standing against the wall. People who are liable to suffer from heatstroke wear extra clothes and stand in the sun as often as possible. As long as you're willing to put up with hardship, you can change anything.

We are thoroughly educated in the need to enhance our revolutionary tradition and constantly aim for even greater glory. Thanks to the instruction and the help we have received from our leaders and the older soldiers, we are absolutely clear about the great honor and heavy responsibility we bear when we are on duty in Tiananmen Square. We are serving the Central Committee of the Chinese Communist Party and honoring the national flag and our socialist Motherland. We are special troops, and we have cultivated an attitude of purposeful action and achieved toughness through arduous training and a steadfast resolve in fighting for revolution.

In my spare time I watch TV, write letters home, play ball games, and clean up in the barracks. My colleagues and I exchange thoughts about the things we have learned in training and on duty. On holidays we share a big meal together and have a party with singing and dancing. We don't smoke, drink, go shopping, enter karaoke bars or dance clubs, gamble, or harass women. We may live in the dusty world, but not a speck of dirt falls on us.[2]

The sole guiding principle at the core of everything we think and do is to offer ourselves up to Tiananmen Square and work to bring greater glory to the Motherland. Through our wordless actions we strive to enhance the majesty of our army and our nation. This is the criterion of our every thought and action.

No, not yet. Through my best efforts I am working to prove myself worthy of being admitted to the party. No, I don't. We are not permitted to have a girlfriend in the city where we're stationed. We are under strict discipline that forbids us from engaging in such liberalization.

Most of us are from the countryside. Okay, to be more precise, my grades were pretty good, so I went on to do senior high school. The general rule is that if you go on to be a senior, then you'll continue on to uni-

---

2. An allusion to traditional Buddhist monastic precepts that talk of the enlightened individual as one who, like the lotus, is mired in filth but not polluted by it.

versity; otherwise you go back home after a few years of high school. My friends and family all think I'm stupid and a bit of a no-hoper for giving up my studies to become a soldier. But other people don't see it like that now. I'm the pride of my hometown, though they're always embellishing the story about me. They say I'm already wearing a general's uniform and that I have gold epaulets, as though I'm a member of the Imperial Guard or something. They think I get to see Jiang Zemin going to work every morning and knocking off at night. I don't; but I do get to see foreigners.

. . . AND THE DEAD

*A forty-seven-year-old undertaker at Babao Shan,
the main crematorium and cemetery in Beijing.*

The government started promoting cremation in the 1950s. Chairman Mao took the lead by signing a document requesting that his body be cremated when he died.

In practical terms, we here at the Babao Shan Public Cemetery were the first in the business in Beijing. That's why people still refer to us as the Babao Shan Crematorium.

None of the people who originally worked here are still alive. Some made it to retirement age; others died before they got there. After having burned people day in, day out all their professional lives, finally it was their turn. But that's the nature of the job: the more you burn, the fewer there are. To go up in flames in your own work unit, now, that's what I call a real convenience. But, in the end Chairman Mao wasn't cremated, even though the other leaders were. And they built a memorial hall for him as well. That was really going a bit too far.

A few years before Xiaoping died [in 1997], they instituted simplified funeral procedures for the leadership. No more big send-offs, no memorial meetings, just a standard leave-taking of the corpse. Even Xiaoping's funeral was pretty basic, so now no one can complain about discrimination. If you cut it back to a simple leave-taking, you make things easier all around. If you hold a memorial service, there's always going to be a big fuss about the wording of the official memorial speech. The corpse may be lying there stone-cold, but all the family members will be in a frenzy disputing with the deceased's work unit about what will be in the funeral oration. All anybody really cares about is how they can make the corpse work for the living. The negotiations go back and forth. Was the deceased's departure "an incalculable loss," "a severe loss," or just "a great loss"? For all they know, the work unit probably doesn't think it was a loss at all; since they don't have to pay the person wages any more, they haven't lost anything.

You shouldn't make too much of yourself, that's what I say. Don't think you're such a big deal when you're alive, and don't expect people to make a fuss over you when you're dead.

The living come in here to have a look around and then go home again; the dead come in and spend a bit of time, and then they take their leave, too. It's just that they exit as a wisp of smoke. For those of us working here, life and death are all much of a muchness, really. Although we actually do cremate people here, just about everything else we do here is similar to the kind of fakery you get in the society at large. There's nothing real; it's all ritual, procedure—it's all a show.

It's a good job, and I like working here. There's always plenty to do; the market's stable, supply steady, and we always show a profit. The wages, conditions of employment, and so on are not too bad either. Nowadays lots of work units are going bankrupt or being forced to retrench workers. But one thing's for sure: we're never going to go under. If we go belly-up, the streets'll be full of rotting corpses.

My general impression is that there are simply too many Chinese. Nowadays even cremations are divided up according to districts. If you die in the east of the city, that's where you'll be cremated; if it's in the west, you'll be sent over here. You might think you'd like to go up in smoke over in Babao Shan, but if you've died in the wrong part of town, you can forget about it. When all the fireworks are over, the family is allowed to leave the ashes here on deposit for two years. After that they either have to buy a plot here or, if they can't afford it, they have to remove the ashes.

In my line of work, the only thing you really have to be careful about is to never, ever show your anger. No matter what the sons-of-bitches do, you should never lose your temper. If they want to rent memorial wreaths, that's fine by me, we'll supply them. If they want the death march to be played, I'll play it. If they want to buy one of our urns for the ashes, I'll sell it to them. If it's too expensive, fine, I'll find a cheaper one. If they're grief-stricken, I'll console them; if they want to pick a fight with someone, I'll try and calm them down. I have it all down pat. I might be thinking to myself, "Fuck you, asshole!" but I'll jolly them along and keep things moving without a hitch.

When I returned to Beijing after having been in the countryside in 1977, I was an angry young man. But a job like this slowly wears you down; it leaches all the anger out of you. You learn that sooner or later we all go up in smoke, so why even bother saying "Fuck you, asshole!" out loud?

Just before they take receipt of the ashes, I have to ask the mourners whether the deceased was a Communist Party member or not. We have a regulation that says party members get a red flag on their urns, while non-party people get a piece of yellow cloth. If the family say the deceased was in the party, I'll take them at their word. By now they've gone up in smoke, after all, so who cares if they're only a pretend party member? The colors might be different, but they cost the same.

Take your pick; you can have whichever one you want.

TRANSLATORS

Chris Buckley: "The Union Rep"; "The People's Deputy"

Andrew Endrey: "Generating Income"

Jonathan Hutt (with Geremie R. Barmé): "An Army on the March"

Linda Jaivin: "Shine"; "Moonwalking"; "A Life of Sex"; "Time as Money"; "Little Sweetie"

Liu Guozhi (with Lisa Gay): "Down to Earth"

All other chapters were translated by Geremie R. Barmé.

INDEX

abandoned children, 100–101, 105

abortions, 199–200

"accommodation fees," 38

Accord between the General and Prime Minister, 67

advertising, 184, 237, 239

agricultural workers, 89. *See also* peasants

agriculture: collective, 42–43; cooperative farms, 3, 281–82, 283; in Shanxi, 272–73, 275–80. *See also* agricultural workers; agro-business; peasants

agro-business: ban on private trade in tree seed, 263–64; cooperative farm as, 283; dealing with state enterprises, 260–61, 262, 263–64; establishing a business, 258–60; public benefit of, 253–55

Ai Jing, 146–47, 147n1

AIDS, 198

air force, 225, 274–75

air-conditioning, 228

airports, 274

amateur overseas Chinese, 18, 18n4. *See also* pseudo-foreigners

American imperialism, 46, 290

Anshan Normal University, 129–31

Anti-American War in Support of Korea (Korean War), 56, 139, 213

Anti–Lin Biao Anti-Confucius Movement, 208, 208n3, 257, 257n5

antipornography campaigns, 192, 192n11

Antirightist Movement, 214, 214n3

anti–Zhou Enlai May Sixteenth Clique, 82, 82n4

aphrodisiacs, 178, 179, 189, 192

Applewhite, Herff, 295n4

Armed Services League, 266

art classes: for children, 97–99, 150; taken by Zhao Li, 125, 127, 131

art dealers, 155

art exhibitions, 59–60, 98–99, 152

artists: and foreigners, 147, 149–50, 151; livelihood of, 147, 149; trained in art school, 150; unofficial arts scene, 145–46, 148, 150–56. *See also* art exhibitions

Asian Games (1990), 51, 168, 261

astrology, 294

athletes: company sponsorship of, 175; donations requested from, 180; and drugs, 169, 170, 172, 177–79; education of, 168, 180; hired for sports meets, 178; ideological work, 172, 175; international travel, 167–68; interviews with, 166, 167; pressures on, 176–77; restrictions on, 175; training of, 168, 171–72, 173–75, 176. *See also* sports

Athletics Training Bureau, 167

August First Well, 274, 276

Australia, 245, 248, 250, 251

Babao Shan cemetery, 321

Bai Jianrong, 109

to, 62–63, 256; members of, 52, 296, 320, 323; mistakes of, 43; Ninth Congress, 74–75; as one party among many, 285; and the reforms, 44, 69, 254; and the Third Force, 6–7; and the writing of history, 5–6; underground work in the cities, 52, 55–56; and unions, 67; and the younger generation, 163. *See also* old cadres

Chinese Lives, 4, 5–6, 8

Chinese medicine, 172

ChiSci Huipu Company, 246–47

Chongqing, 207, 207n1

Christianity: and the Communist Party, 214–16, 218, 219–20; during the Cultural Revolution, 216–17, 220; denunciation of, 217–18; in Sayingpan, 212, 213; in Shimenkan, 215; Three-Self Movement, 213, 213n2, 214, 216, 217, 218, 219; underground, 216

cigarettes, 35

circulation of commodities, 21. *See also* profiteering

civil engineering, 76

class background, 187, 187n5, 256, 256n4, 269

clinics, sexual-health, 184–85

clothing trade: clothing stalls, 16–19, 22; factories, 20–21; foreign clothing, 18; secondhand, 17–19; sportswear, 168

coal mines, 267

collective agriculture, 42–43, 282n11

communism, 42–43, 44, 47, 254. *See also* Chinese Communist Party

company shells, 25–26

computers, 157, 158, 159

condoms, 200, 201

Confucianism, 9, 298–99

Confucius, 218, 242, 271; descendants of, 208, 208n2. *See also* Anti–Lin Biao Anti-Confucius Movement

connections, 247, 259, 265

construction companies, 35–36

Consumer Protection Association, 4, 137, 140, 141, 142–43

contract system, 270, 281

cooperative farms, 3, 281–82, 283

corn, 275, 276

corruption: in business, 141n5, 247; in the Chinese Communist party, 44, 45; of doctors, 193; of officials, 117, 125–26

Counterattack on the Rightist Attempt to Reverse Verdicts, 257, 257n5

counterfeit money, 139, 140

countryside. *See* rural China

courtyard houses, 77

cremation, 304, 321–23

Cultural Revolution: army deployed in, 277, 277n7; attacks on Christianity during, 216–17, 220; and delay in industrial development, 47; destruction of mosques during, 89; "educated urban youths" sent to countryside in, 266–69; excesses of, 51–52; in the factories, 64–66; and lack of education, 245, 246; negation of charges after, 90, 90n3; portrayed in film, 209n5; prelude to, 62n2, 88n2; purge of the "black line in the arts," 51n15; in the scheme of recent history, 62; and sports training, 173; struggle sessions, 1, 51, 74, 74n1; Three-Way Combinations, 65, 65n4; and the universities, 74, 82, 256–57. *See also* Red Guards

Darwinist-Marxist theory, 293

days off, 37, 37n10

death penalty, 115, 298–99, 307. *See also* executions

death placards, 310, 310n3

democracy movement, 299. *See also* June Fourth Incident

Democratic Reforms of 1956, 214–15

demonstrations, 44–45, 112–13, 296. *See also* June Fourth Incident

Deng Tuo, 88n2

Deng Xiaoping: and ceiling height, 83; economic reforms of, 47, 49, 54, 208n4; Four Cardinal Principles of, 59, 59n1; funeral of, 321; on intellectuals, 48; "let some people get rich first" policy, 252, 253n1, 254, 318; mentioned, 268n2, 270; Progress through the South, 54, 54n21, 264; and "reversing the verdicts," 257n5. *See also* reform policies

disabled people, 19, 27, 127–29, 131, 133,

Four Cardinal Principles, 59, 59n1, 79
Four Cleans, 62, 62n2, 215–18
Four Heavenly Kings, 157n1; of Pirating, 157, 162
Four Olds, 65, 65n3, 186, 186n4
"four simple dishes," 52, 52n18
Fragrant Buddha Pavilion, 76
fraud, 139–40. *See also* Consumer Protection Association; counterfeit money; pirated goods
freedom of expression, 48
Freud, Sigmund, 193
Fujian Province, 17, 18
funerals, 89, 321
Fuyuan Cun Village (Beijing), 145. *See also* Yuanming Yuan Artists' Village

gambling, 36
Gang of Four, 29n2, 51, 187, 309
Gao Xingjian, 151n5
garbage transportation business, 101
Garden of Eden (sex store), 179, 183, 190–91
gift giving, 35
Gongan County (Hubei Province), 89
Great Hall of the People, 73, 76, 82
Great Leap Forward: focus of, 56n23, 212n1; mentioned, 47n11, 56, 62; slogans of, 227, 227n2; Ten Great Buildings of, 76; Three Years of Natural Disasters, 274, 274n4; in Yunnan, 212, 215
Great Link-Ups, 268, 268n1
Great Northern Wilderness Urban Youth Club, 266
Guangdong Medical College, 187
Guangdong Province, 16–17, 31–32
Guangzhou (Guangdong Province), 16
Guizhou Province, 61, 64–65, 70, 110
Gulag Archipelago (Solzhenitsyn), 40, 314
Guo Fucheng (Aaron Kwok), 157n1
gymnastics, 168, 172

Hainan Island, 195, 223
Haizi wang (King of the Children), 269n4
Hale-Bopp comet, 295
handicrafts stalls, 26–27
He Yonggui, 100, 105
heating, 235

Heaven's Gate cult, 294–95, 295n4
heihua (black paintings), 152, 152n7
Heilongjiang Province, 110
helicopter rides, 232
Hengshan (Hunan Province), 203, 204, 204n1
Hengyang (Hunan Province), 197, 203
high-rise apartments, 76–77
History Museum, 76
homework, 122
homosexuality, 35, 189, 201
Hong Xiuquan, 46, 46n8
Hong'an (Hubei Province), 233
Honghu Red Defense Force, 29n1
Hong Kong: businessmen, 50, 203, 232; "one country two systems," 268n2; during the Cultural Revolution, 185
hooliganism, 15, 280
Hope Foundation, 245, 245n1
hospitality, 207
hospitals, run by the military, 226, 257
hotels: English training for employees, 240, 242; prostitutes and, 196, 203, 230–31; run by the military, 223, 225, 229, 230, 233
housing: apartments for mistresses, 211; in Beijing, 75–77; ceiling height, 83; of the new rich, 13, 252
Hu Yaobang, 30, 30n6
Hua Guofeng, 29, 29n3, 82–83
Hui nationality, 88, 89, 105
Hunan dialect, 139, 139n1
Hunan Province. *See* Changsha; Hengshan
Hundred-Day Armed Struggle, 185

ideological training, 172, 175, 318
immigration agents, 250
impotence, 189, 190
industrialization, 47, 62
industrial workers, 60–64, 66–68, 71, 72, 246. *See also* factories
inequality, 38
information fees, 35–36
Institute of Paranormal Studies, 289
insurance, 36, 66
intellectual property, 159–60, 189
intellectuals, 48. *See also* professors

Internationale, 52, 289n1
international capitalism, 49, 49n12, 50
International Women's Day, 112
interviews, official permission for, 299
iron rice bowl, 246
itinerant laborers: aspirations of, 39; and
  Beijing "people market," 28, 32–33, 35;
  days off, 37; exploitation of, 35, 36, 38;
  mentioned, 267, 270; posing as children of high-level cadres, 294; restaurant work, 33–34; travel by, 31–32; in
  trucking business, 34–35

Japan, war with, 50, 55, 57, 105, 207n1,
  250n5
Japanese goods, 143
Jesus Christ, 293–94
Jiang Chunyun, 83
Jiang Qing: and the Anti–Lin Biao
  Anti-Confucius campaign, 208, 208n3;
  and Christians, 218; mentioned, 29n2;
  purges of cultural figures, 51, 51n15
Jiang Wen, Days in the Radiant Sun
  directed by, 209, 209n5
Jiang Zemin, 54, 54n19, 193, 321
Jianli (Hubei Province), 29, 37–38
Jilin Province, 110
Jingsha (Hubei Province), 87
June Fourth Incident (1989), 44–45, 162,
  194, 284n12

kidnapping, 110–16. See also missing
  children
kindergartens, 97–98, 101
King of the Children (Haizi wang), 269n4
knights-errant, 26
Korean War, 56, 139, 213
Kwok, Aaron (Guo Fucheng), 157n1

labor reform: during the Cultural Revolution, 89–91, 277n8; difficulty finding
  employment after, 16, 91; for hooliganism, 15, 280; lessons learned from, 22;
  Red Guards sent for, 186; in Shanxi, 277
Lai, Leon (Li Ming), 157n1
Lai Zhichun, 105
landlords, 7–8, 41–42
land reform, 41–42, 213, 285

Lang Ping, 176
Lantern Festival, 87
Lantian Hotel (Jilin Province), 240, 242
Lau, Andy (Liu Dehua), 157n1
layoffs, 70–71
Le Songsheng, 45
leftists, 40, 283–84, 284n12. See also old
  cadres
legal system, 300, 310, 312. See also death
  penalty
Lei Feng, 138, 138n2
Lenin, Vladimir Ilyich, 79, 297
Li Jingzhi, 109
Li Maiqin, 109
Li Ming (Leon Lai), 157n1
Li Ning, 168
Li Yingru, 50–51
Li Zicheng, 30, 30n4
Liangshan, 42
Liao Mosha, 88n2
Liaoning University, 126
Liberation Daily, 46
Lin Biao: Anti–Lin Biao Anti-Confucius
  Movement, 208n3, 257, 257n5; death of,
  208n3; designated as successor to Mao,
  75; May 7 letter from Mao, 277n8;
  "touching the soul," 216–17, 216n4
little sweeties, 203, 204, 206, 209, 210–11
Liu Dehua (Andy Lau), 157n1
Liu Qing, Pioneering History by, 17, 17n3
Liu Qingshan, 305, 305n1
Liu Ren, 51–52
Liu Shaoqi, 41, 41n2, 52, 218, 233
Liu Wencai, 41, 41n3
Liu Wenjun, 147
lobbyists, 117
local protectionism, 24
Long March, 173, 233, 268n1
Luo Guanzhong, 42n4

Ma Desheng, 152, 152n8
Ma Junren, 171, 171n4, 172–73
Mandarin, pronunciation of, 138, 139
mangliu. See floating population
mansions, 13, 252
Mao Zedong: arrival in Beijing, 39; and
  Christianity, 214, 217–18; compared
  with Li Zicheng and Qin Shihuang,

private business: connections in, 247, 259–60, 265; inferior goods, 20, 141–42, 260; money to start, 20, 259; reputation in, 262; and the state, 253–54, 255, 260–61, 262, 263, 264. *See also* agro-business; businessmen; factories; pharmaceutical companies

Private Industrialists' Association, 253

privatization, 47, 54. *See also* private business; reform policies

professors. *See* teachers

profiteering, 21–27, 259; in Russia, 25

promotions, 63

prostitutes: and AIDS, 198; in brothels, 201; compared with little sweeties, 206; and drugs, 198; hierarchy of, 197, 203; and hotels, 196, 203, 230–31; and itinerant laborers, 36; laws against, 193; in movie theaters, 198–99, 200–201; parades of convicted, 310; in Shenzhen, 195–203; police and, 196, 204

pseudo-foreigners *(jia yangguizi)*, 151, 151n4, 159, 249. *See also* amateur overseas Chinese

Public Security Bureau. *See* police

public sentencing rallies, 309–10, 312, 313

qigong, 289, 294, 294n3

Qin Shihuang, 2, 30, 30n5, 277

Qingming Festival (1976), 45

radio, 186, 217, 220

real estate, 227, 230

"red capitalists," 252

Red Cross, 101

Red Defense Forces, 29, 29n1

Red Flag farm, 278

Red Guards: anti–Zhou Enlai clique, 82, 82n4; children of, 162; combat teams, 185, 185n1; destruction of mosques, 89; Great Link-Ups of, 268, 268n1; meeting with Zhou Enlai, 65; as predecessors of floating population, 28

Red Star Farm 273–75, 276–77, 280, 281–82

reform policies: and China's status in the world, 253; and consumers' rights, 142; and corruption, 141n5; as current buzz-word, 62; in the factory, 66–67, 68–69; "let some people get rich first," 252, 253n1, 254, 318; leftist attempt to overturn, 283–84, 284n12; mentioned, 208n4, 245; and the military, 229, 318; as revisionism, 43, 47, 48, 54, 69; and teachers, 208–9. *See also* Deng Xiaoping; privatization; private business

regional protectionism, 116

religion, 8, 89, 105, 218. *See also* Christianity

Rent Collection Courtyard, 41n3

residence permits: for children in orphanages, 96–99, 104, 106; for children of youths sent to countryside, 270; mentioned, 92, 96n5, 267; purchase of, 38

restaurant business, 33–34, 38, 204

retirement: of industrial workers, 61, 71; of old revolutionary cadres, 45, 51, 57, 235n1; pensions, 57, 235, 235n1; of professors, 235, 236

returnees' brigade, 250, 250n5

revisionism, 43, 48–49, 69

rice, 277

rich middle peasants, 41–42

Romance of the Three Kingdoms, 194

Rong Yiren, 45

running, 122, 126, 166

rural China: educated urban youths in, 266–69; marriage in, 203; not represented, 2–3; poverty of, 29–30, 31, 37, 273; return from, 323; Shanxi, 272, 273, 274–80. *See also* agriculture; peasants

Russia, 25, 248. *See also* Soviet Union

satellite launches, 47, 59

Sayingpan (Yunnan Province), 1, 212–20

scientists, and UFOs, 291, 292, 294, 296

seasonal laborers, 283

secondhand clothing, 17–19, 103

self-reliance *(zili geng sheng)*, 225, 225n1

sex: compared to politics, 188; during the Cultural Revolution, 186; homosexuality, 35, 189, 201; and marketing, 186. *See also* prostitutes

sex aids, 185, 190, 192

sex education, 190, 193–94

Third Force, 6–7
Third Front, 64, 65
Three-Family Village, 88, 88n2
Three-Nine Group, 230
Three Nots, 97, 98–99
Three Proceed-Froms and One Maximize, 174
Three-Self Movement, 213, 213n2, 214, 216, 217, 218, 219
Three Supports and Two Militaries, 277, 277n7
Three-Way Combinations, 65, 65n4
Three Years of Natural Disasters, 56, 274, 274n4
Tiananmen Square: demonstrations of 1989, 44–45, 162, 194, 284n12; flag-raising ceremony at, 317, 319; Mao Zedong Memorial Hall, 82, 321
Tianjin, 17
Tongxian County (Beijing), 145
torture, 304
"touching the soul" *(chuji linghun)*, 216–17, 216n4
tourism: new rich and, 232, 253; People's Liberation Army and, 231–33; and the restaurant business, 204; tourists from Taiwan and Hong Kong, 232
track and field, 171
train travel, 7, 31–32
translation, 243
trees, 261; "taking-root trees," 267; tree seed, 255–56, 259–60, 263–64, 265. *See also* forestry
triangular debt, 69
trucking, 34–35
Tsinghua University, 158, 162
Tu Xiaofeng, 107
turtle soup, 172–73
tutorial classes, 237–43
TV, 122, 129, 144, 240–41

UFO Research Organization, 2, 289, 291–92, 296
UFOs, 289–90, 291, 294, 296. *See also* extraterrestrials
unions, 36, 67–69, 71
universities: and class background, 187,

256; classes for the public, 237, 240, 241; during the Cultural Revolution, 74, 82; entrance exams, 127–28, 132, 164, 241, 246, 272; physical fitness requirement, 129; selection criteria for, 257n5; study by soldiers, 231, 234; study of agriculture, 272; tuition, 130–31
urban planning, 76

venereal disease. *See* sexually transmitted diseases
virginity, 204–5
volleyball, 168, 169, 170, 176

wages, 38, 48, 235–36, 248–49
Wang Hai, 143–44
Wang Hongwen, 29n2
Wang Shuo, 155n11, 188–89, 189n7; *Wild Beasts* by, 209n5
Wang Yongmin, 164
Wangcheng County (Hunan Province), 138
Water Margin (Shuihu zhuan), 42n4
water, in the Shanxi countryside, 272, 273, 274–76, 277, 278–80, 282
water-skiing, 231
weapons, 230, 231, 232, 233, 303
weightlifting, 172
West Willow Village, 130
wheat, 276
White-Haired Girl, 30, 30n7
Williams, John (Zhang Weilian), 8, 212–13, 214, 215
wills, of execution victims, 313
Windows software, 161
wineries, 283
Women's Federation, 101, 109, 112
women's rights, 194
wool mills, 70
"worker-peasant-soldier" students, 187
workers: agricultural, 89; industrial, 60–64, 66–68, 71, 72, 246; model, 63–64, 252
Workers' Cultural Palace, 238
work points, 213, 257
"work responsibility bond," 36
Wu Han, 88n2

Text:	11.25/13.5 Adobe Garamond
Display:	Adobe Garamond
Compositor:	Bookmatters, Berkeley
Indexer:	Susan Stone
Printer and binder	Maple-Vail Manufacturing Group